RAJPUT POLITY

RAJPUT POLITY

A Study of Politics and Administration of the State of Marwar, 1638-1749

G.D. SHARMA

MANOHAR
2025

First published 1977
POD reprint 2021, 2022, 2023
Reprinted 2025

ISBN 978-93-88540-73-5

Published by
Ajay Kumar Jain *for*
Manohar Publishers & Distributors
4753/23 Ansari Road, Daryaganj
New Delhi 110 002

Printed at
Replika Press Pvt. Ltd.

To

My Guru

Prof. Satish Chandra

PREFACE

The state of Marwar occupied a prominent place in Rajasthan during the period under study. It played an important role not only in the politics of this sprawling region but also of northern India in general. Although a number of monographs have been published on the history of the erstwhile states of Rajasthan, these have mainly been concerned with the political activities of the Rajput rulers, their relations with the Mughal Emperors, and with inter-state relations. No attempt has, however, been made to understand the evolution of the politico-administrative structure in Rajasthan—the changes that took place in it, and the social and economic forces that were responsible for these changes. The choice of Marwar for studying these aspects has been determined by the fact that, of all the Rajput States of Rajasthan, Marwar presents the best model for understanding the Rajput polity within the perspective of the rise and fall of the Mughal Empire.

With Mewar's decline after Rana Sangram Singh (A.D. 1509-28), the centre of political gravity in Rajasthan shifted from Chittor to Jodhpur. Before the rise of Rao Maldeo (A.D. 1532-62), the state of Marwar was a loose confederation presided over by the Rathor rulers. Rao Maldeo expanded his dominion and tried, though unsuccessfully, to forge a new relationship between the ruler and the nobles. However, it was only after his death that the internal political structure, the position of the ruling class, and the administrative pattern gradually began to assume a new form. An effort was made to restructure the Marwar polity by introducing in it some aspects of the *jagirdari* system of the Mughals. This was the basis of the *pattadari* system which was evolved by Maharaja Sur Singh (A.D. 1595-1619) and which later became crystallised during the time of Maharaja Jaswant Singh (A.D. 1638-78). This system began to crumble after the death of Maharaja Ajit Singh in 1724, and there emerged a different form of relationship between the rulers and the nobles, and a different system of government. These changes were overlooked by Colonel Tod and the historians following his line, who claimed that during the Mughal period the forms of government and land relations in Rajasthan were similar to the feudal system of Europe.

This study seeks to take a fresh look on the politico-administrative structure of the state of Marwar with the help of contemporary documents and records, tracing its historical evolution and the forces which helped to shape it. The development of institutions and the dynamics of change must, however, be related to the composition of the ruling class and to its political role. The political activities of the Rathor rulers and their relations with the Mughal Emperors and with the rulers of the neighbouring states have, therefore, been given with necessary details. These constituted a part of the milieu in which new institutional structure evolved and changes took place.

The first two chapters are introductory and they contain information that provides the background for understanding the institutional framework of Marwar under the Mughals as also the interplay of continuity and change in the Marwar polity. Greater space has been devoted to the discussion of the institutional structure on which the society and economy of Marwar rested during the reign of Maharaja Jaswant Singh. But in regard to the subsequent period only those details have been given which were relevant to the changes that occurred in the wave of the decline of the Mughal power. This has brought into sharp focus the circumstances in which the rulers of Marwar were forced to severe their ties with the Mughal court and to make necessary changes in the politico-administrative structure of the state.

An attempt has been made to retain, as far as possible, the social, economic and administrative terms in their original form. These terms and our discussion of them may further a broader understanding of the system under study. Deviating from the general practice among historians writing on Rajasthan, terms such as feudalism, feudal lords, fiefs, etc., have not been used. These terms may have a significance, particularly when we compare the medieval social structure of India with that of European countries. But the adoption of such terms in relation to the Rajput states during the Mughal period imposes upon the medieval Indian society images, some of which were perhaps alien to it.

In analysing the financial structure of Marwar state, technical terms and data have been used with all possible care. While finalizing the figures of land revenue demand and *hasil* a variety of sources have been used. The figures provided by these are at times discrepant. An attempt has been made in this study to work out a rational collation of these figures. But a margin of error is perhaps unavoidable.

The present approach towards the study of this subject and the treatment of source material would have not taken this shape without the keen interest of my teacher, Professor Satish Chandra. I express my profound sense of gratitude to him for suggesting me the importance of this topic and giving me the opportunity of working under him. At all stages of my work his constant encouragement, active guidance and valuable suggestions enabled me to complete this work.

The present work is a revised version of my Ph.D. thesis, *Politics and Administration of the State of Marwar*—A.D. 1638-1749, approved by Jawaharlal Nehru University in November 1974. I am grateful to Professor B.P. Saksena of Allahabad and Professor S.C. Mishra of M.S. University, Baroda who were kind enough to have given useful suggestions for the improvement of this work. My thanks are due to Professor M.A. Ansari, Jamia Millia Islamia and Shri B.R. Grover, Director, Indian Council of Historical Research, who were kind enough to discuss various problems connected with the present study. My thanks are also due to my friends Dr. Dilbagh Singh, Centre for Historical Studies, J.N.U., Mr. Hasan Mahmud, Research Officer, Indian Council of Historical Research, New Delhi, Dr. A.R. Khan, Himachal Pradesh University, Simla, Dr. Devendra Kaushik, Dr. G.S.P. Mishra and Dr. Mukund Lath, University of Rajasthan, for helping me in preparing the text for the press. Dr. Anil

Kumar Mathur, Mathematics Department, Rajasthan University, Jaipur, helped me in finalizing the statistical work of this study and I am thankful to him.

The authorities and the staff of the Rajasthan State Archives, Bikaner, Shri Raghubir Library, Sitamau, Shodh Samsthan, Chaupasani—Jodhpur, Oriental Research Institute, Jodhpur, Anup Sanskrit Library, Bikaner, Raza Library, Rampur, J.N.U. Library, New Delhi and Central Library, University of Rajasthan, Jaipur, deserve special mention for the fullest cooperation they extended to me.

I am grateful to the Indian Council of Historical Research, New Delhi for giving financial support towards the publication of this work.

I am also thankful to Mr. R.C. Jain of Manohar Book Service for taking extra pains in the publication of the present work.

G. D. Sharma

Jaipur
27-3-77

ABBREVIATIONS

Ain.	Ain-i-Akbari.
A.S.L.B.	Anup Sanskrit Library, Bikaner.
Ashub	M. Baksh, Tarikh-i-Shahadat-i-Farrukh Siyar wa Jalus-i-M. Shahi.
Badayuni	Muntakhabu-t-Tawarikh by Abdu'l-Qadir Badayuni.
B.N.	Bahadurshah Nama.
Bikaner Rajya	Bikaner Rajya ka Itihas.
Bib. Ind.	Bibliotheca Indica.
E.I.	Epigraphia Indica.
Hukumat-bahi	Jodhpur Hukumat-ri-Bahi.
Jodhpur-Rajya	Jodhpur Rajya ka Itihas.
Kharitas & Parwanas	Draft Kharitas and Parwanas.
K.K.	Khafi Khan, Muntakhab-ul-Lubab.
Kamwar	Tazkirat-us-Salatin-i-Chaghtai by M. Hadi Kamwar Khan.
Khush-hal	Nadir-uz-Zamani.
Mazmun-i-Halat	Mazmun-i-Halat wa Intizam-i-Marwar.
Maasir	Maasir-i-Alamgiri.
Marwar Rajya	Marwar Rajya ka Itihas by Pt. B.N. Reu.
Mirat	Mirat-i-Ahmadi.
Mundiyar-Khyat	Mundiyara-Thikana-ri-Khyat.
Nainsi-Khyat	Muhnot Nainsi-ri-Khyat.
ORIJ	Oriental Research Institute, Jodhpur.
Vigat	Marwar-ra-Pargana-ri-Vigat.
Parties and Politics	Parties and Politics at the Mughal Court.

P.I.H.C.	Proceedings of Indian History Congress.
P.R.H.C.	Proceedings of Rajasthan History Congress.
R.S.A.B.	Rajasthan State Archives, Bikaner.
S.C.	Personal Collection of Professor Satish Chandra.
Samkshipt Itihas	Marwar-ka-Samkshipt Itihas.
S.S.	Shodha Samsthan, Chaupasni, Jodhpur.
Siyar	Siyar-ul-Mutaakhkhirin by Gulam Husain.
S.P.L.J.	Sumer Public Library, Jodhpur.
Waqai	Waqai Sarkar Ajmer wa Ranthambhor.
Warid	Mirat-i-Waridat or Tarikh-i-Muhammad Shahi.
Yahya	Tazkirat-ul-Muluk.

NOTE ON THE RAJASTHANI SOURCES

An introduction to the Rajasthani sources is necessary as they have been the basis of writing the present work. Although many of these sources were utilized by historians during the past few years, they were not used with the object of presenting a coherent picture of the institutional structure and its bearing on the politics of the Rajasthan during the Mughal period. The survey of the sources presented here is not an elaborate one, but an attempt has been made to bring out their important features which have served as the basis of this work.

Broadly speaking these sources can be studied under the following categories:

(a) *Rajasthani Literature*

1. *Khyats, Bats, Vamshavalis, Vachnika*, etc.
2. Poetical works
3. *Vigats*

(b) *Archival and Private Records*

(a) The source material discovered so far does not suggest that there was a well developed tradition of writing history before the 17th century in Rajasthan. The writings of Muhnot Nainsi, the *desh-diwan* of Maharaja Jaswant Singh are considered to be the first among the historical works of Rajasthan. His *Khyat* (known as *Nainsi-ri-Khyat*) and *Marwar-ra-Pargana-ri-Vigat* are unique, and although he followed the line of Abul Fazl, his treatment of the historical events and the policies of the rulers is more objective than that of Abul Fazl. Besides narrating the dynastic histories of all the ruling Rajput families of medieval Rajput States since their origin, his *khyat* contains valuable information about the social structure and politics of the 17th century Rujput states of Rajasthan. For the present study, this work has been very useful, as apart from providing information about the origin of the various *khamps* (branches of the ruling clans), it tells us about the state land revenue demand, nature of the *bhom* rights, practice of *bhai-bant* and *pattadari* system prevalent in these States. This information finds corroboration in the *Hukumat-ri-bahi,* a later 17th century work, which tells us a lot more about the problems dealt with in this study. The only work to provide adequate information on the *pattadari* system of Marwar, and the bearing necessitated many corrections in the *jama* figures of the *jagirs* granted to the Rathor rulers upto Jaswant Singh, given in Nainsi's *Khyat* and the *Vigat*. Among the other sources worth mentioning in this category are the *Ratan Singh-ri-Vachnika* and *Ajit Vilas*. The former contains the details of the Rathor *sardars* who participated in the battle of Dharmat (A.D. 1658) and the latter work (*Ajit Vilas*), which is a contemporary work for the history of Ajit Singh's period, enriches our knowledge on many of the controversial issues concerning the period of instability (1679-1707).

Besides these, the other available works were written either in the first half of the 18th century or afterwards. They are thus contemporary to the period following the death of Jaswant Singh (November 1678), and the reigns of Ajit Singh and Abhai Singh. Of these, *Ajit Singh-ri-Khyat* is the most reliable for information on Ajit Singh's period since it was written either during the last years of Ajit Singh's reign or soon after his death. Besides providing details on the socio-political structure of this period, it contains a valuable record of the period of instability and enables us to make a substantial advance in resolving the debatable political problems of this period.

All other *khyats, vamshavalis* and *bats* could be placed in the category of the near-contemporary accounts. The first among these works, which requires special mention is *Rathora-ri-Vamshavali* (written in the form of a *bahi*), which is supposed to be the earliest and the most authentic work amongst the *khyat* literature of the 18th and the 19th century Marwar. It contains detailed account of the reigns of Ajit Singh and Abhai Singh and its comparison with the *Jodhpur-Rajya-ki-Khyat* (*Marwar-ki-Khyat*) establishes the fact that the latter account was based mainly on the information given in the former. *Jodhpur-Rajya-ki-Khyat* and other *khyats*, including the *khyats* of some of the other *thikanas* of Marwar, are later accounts compiled during the 1st half of the 19th century. However, information contained in these *khyats* is useful in tracing the origin of the various branches (*khamps*) of the Rathor clan and their role in the state as well as in Mughal politics. *Servedesh-ma-rajvioni* is also worth mentioning. Although, the author of this work is unknown, it gives a useful account concerning Marwar and provides additional detail on Rathor-Mughal relations, *jagirdari* system, etc.

There was also a tradition of writing *vigat* (lit. account of the past, a kind of gazetteer) in Marwar. The first work of this nature written in the latter half of the 17th century by Muhnot Nainsi, *Marwar-ra-pargana-ri-vigat*, has already been mentioned. There is no doubt that this work was written on the pattern of the *Ain-i-Akbari*. The *Vigat* contains the detailed information on the various aspects of society and economy of Marwar during the reign of Maharaja Jaswant Singh. In this work the author has recorded a systematic *pargana*-wise account of Marwar giving details about the evolution of each and every *pargana* as well as the history of their ruling families. The account of *pargana* Jodhpur is, however, very comprehensive. It being the capital of Marwar, Nainsi here gives information about the relationship of the Rathor rulers of Jodhpur with the Mughals as well as with the neighbouring states. He also describes the various political, social and economic aspects of all the villages of each *pargana*. The *Vigat*, which provides most significant information on the state finances as well as on the social and political structure of this period, which has been used extensively in the present work. Another work written on the same pattern and used in the present study is the *Arya-Khyan-Kalpdrum* written by Dayaldas Sindhyach in the early 19th century. Although it does not contain the kind of details we get in the *Vigat*, the *khamp-wise* account of the *pattas* held by the Marwar *sardars*, as well as of the *rekh* of the villages which it gives, enables us to understand the changes which took place in the composition of the nobility and the nature of the land revenue assignments in Marwar torwards the end of the eighteenth century.

The poetical works in *Rajasthani* (some of them are in *Dingal*) have generally been neglected in writing the historical accounts of Rajasthan under the Mughals, but if used properly they are very valuable for writing the political and social history of this period. Though these works are full of exaggeration, a careful study of the account contained therein yields material which can fill in the gaps in the contemporary *khyat* writers. In the present study, the poetical works, particularly, the *Gajgunrupak granth*, *Ajitodaya*, *Surajprakash* and *Rajrupak* have proved very useful. The *Ajitodaya* and the *Rajrupak*, besides telling us about the deeds of Ajit Singh and Abhai Singh, they have been useful for studying the composition of the Rathor nobility and the relations between the Rathor rulers and the Mughal Emperors. In fact, much of the information given in the *Hukumat-bahi* and *Waqai-sarkar Ajmer-wa-Ranthambhor* could be substantiated by these to works.

(*b*) It is only during the last decade or so that the historians started utilizing the archival records preserved in the State Archives, Bikaner, and some other private collections in Rajasthan, for studying the social and economic history of Rajasthan. It has now been realised that the historians of Medieval India cannot present a coherent and comprehensive account regarding the social, political and economic history of India in the absence of these archival records. As the aim of this note is to introduce only those records which have been used in the present work, the account given here does not cover all the Archival records available in the Rajasthan state Archives and the private collections.

Among the records which need special mention are *Vakil-Reports*, *Khatut-i-Ahalkaran*, *Khatut-a-Maharajgan*, draft *Kharitas* and *Parwanas*, *Chitthiyats* and collection under the title of *Amber Records* of the erstwhile state of Amber; and *Rukka-Parwana Bahis*, *Bastas*, *Byav Bahis* and *Haqiqat-bahis* of the erstwhile state of Jodhpur. Although *Vakil-Reports* are not exclusively related to the historical aspects of Marwar, the stray references, and to some places detailed account also, provide useful information for understanding the Mughal-Rathor relations, inter-state relations, and the Mughal policy towards the Rajput rulers. The other records of Amber Historical section contain details on the inter-state and matrimonial relations of the nobles, role of the nobility in the state politics, and nature of the Maratha inroads in Rajasthan including Marwar.

The archival records of Jodhpur state are not so rich as of Amber. However, *Rukka-Parwana-Bahis* and *Byar Bahi's* contain many valuable letters giving information on the basis of which a definite pattern of administration and politics in Marwar could be traced. The *bastas* contain the attested copies of the original documents, mainly related with *pattadars* and their rights, and the nature of revenue grants since the latter half of the 17th century. They also record information on the evolution of the *thikanas* and the rights and privileges of the *thikanadars* and *bomias*. In fact the details available in these *bastas* are very useful for studying the *pattadari* system, social structure in Marwar and the composition of the Marwar nobility. The *Haqiqat-Bahis* and *Byav-Bahis* contain rich information concerning the various aspects of the social and economic history of the 18th century.

Besides, there are useful collections of the historical records in the possession of many of the *thikanadars* and some other individuals in and outside Rajasthan. The collection of the *thakurs* of Bilada (Jodhpur) and Diggi (Jaipur) are very significant for understanding the social and economic history of Rajasthan. The documents of Bilada collection throw considerable light on the rights and privileges of the *thikanadars* and their relations with the Rathors rulers. The Diggi House Collection centains some useful letters which tell us of the role of Durgadas Rathor after his return to Marwar in 1687 and the role of the Champawat *sardars* in the Marwar politics during the same years. The collection of Dr. Raghbir Singh (formerly Raghubir Library) of Sitamau (Malwa) needs no introduction since its value is well known among the historians.

CONTENTS

1

ESTABLISHMENT AND EXPANSION OF THE RATHOR DOMINION

At the beginning of the thirteenth century there were small principalities all over western Rajasthan whose boundaries were ill-defined and mostly ill-defended. These principalities had no regular machinery for administration and were known after their capital towns, such as Khed, Barmer, Mandor, Jalor-Bhinmal, Mahewa, Sojat, and Sirohi-Abu. They were ruled by Rajput princes belonging to the Guhila, Panwar, Chauhan, Sonagara, Solanki, Parmar, and Deora clans.[1] Their internal feuds, particularly among the clan leaders, weakened them which later encouraged external interference in their affairs. The Guhila Rajput ruler of Khed, Raja Partapsi, was not on good terms with his Dabhi *pradhan* (Chief Minister) and other Dabhi *sardars* (Chieftains) holding powerful positions in the administration.[2] In Mandor the members of the Parihar ruling family had assumed independent power.[3] The territory around Pali was dominated by the Brahmins but the overlordship (*thakurai*)[4] was enjoyed by Kanha Mer of the Mer tribe.[5] It may be noted that the Paliwal Brahmins held the land as the *gurus* of the ruler (*Rana*) of Mewar. Partly due to the grants received from the *Rana*, and partly through trade, they had become very rich.[6] It seems that as long as the rulers of Ranthambhor and Khed were strong, the Paliwal Brahmins could live peacefully with the Mers. But, with the decline of these Rajput rulers, the leaders of the Mer tribe started asserting more and more. In the villages around Pali, the Brahmins, who had held the land and were carrying on cultivation had to face stiff opposition from the Mer tribesmen. Such was the situation that no one dared to camp outside the city or outside the village even for a night due to the fear of the Mers.[7] Many Brahmins were on the verge of fleeing the villages.[8]

During this period, it seems, the ruling class largely consisted of the Rajput clan-members and blood-brothers of the ruler. Below them were the leaders of the aboriginal tribes and *chaudharis* who formed the class of intermediaries and village headmen. They were responsible for the collection of revenue from their respective territories.[9] However, in order to extend cultivation and to populate the area, the Jats, Rajputs, etc., were invited from the neighbouring territories to settle in the villages of Pali. This could be the immediate cause for the hostility of the Mers.

Paliwals (Brahmins of Pali) and the *chaudharis* (headmen) of the neighbouring villages found it difficult to cope with the Mers.[10] So, they solicited the help of Rao Asthan and his brothers, Sonag and Ajay, who had camped at Pali on their way to Gujarat,[11] where they were going to seek their fortune. The Paliwal Brahmins agreed to pay 45½ *taka* every day to Asthan and his brothers[12] for dealing with the Mers. A *haveli* (house) was constructed for them in the town (Pali) and their followers, the Rathor *sardars*, were given lands in the neighbouring areas. The Rathors were quite successful in maintaining order (*zabta*) in the territory of Pali. Therefore, the *chaudharis* (headmen) of the neighbouring villages met Asthan and requested him to look after their security.[13] They agreed to pay a cess (*gughari*)[14] for maintaining law and order in their territories. Thus, a Rathor *sardar*, it seems, was appointed for security and collection of protection money (*gughari*). We are told that Asthan was obeyed in all the villages around Pali but the protection money which Asthan and his brothers received was insufficient. The Rathors (followers of Asthan) were also unhappy and wanted cultivable lands for their maintenance.[15] Their decision to leave caused anxiety in Pali and the neighbouring villages. The *chaudharis* (headmen) were asked to persuade the Rathors to stay in Pali.[16] They agreed to settle in Pali after being given some concessions. They were given the right to collect five maunds of grain on each *hal* (plough). On the eve of festivals, such as *holi*, *diwali*, *dashera*, etc., the *chaudharis* were to offer presents to Asthan. Cultivable land of five *hals*[17] was given to each Rathor *sardar* in various villages. By virtue of these rights Asthan established his rule over 50 to 60 villages of Pali.[18] He employed 400 horsemen (*sawars*) to defend this territory. Nainsi mentions that after establishing his *thakurai* (overlordship) over Pali, Asthan took over the control of eighty-four villages of Bhadrajun,[19] an adjoining territory.

The next move of Asthan was to control Khed where Raja Partapsi of Guhila clan exercised his *thakurai*. Taking advantage of the rivalry between Raja Partapsi and his *pradhan* of Dabhi clan, Rao Asthan succeeded in winning over the latter to his side. An agreement was arrived at according to which the revenue of the territory was to be shared equally between the two after dislodging Raja Partapsi.[20] With the support of Dabhis, Asthan defeated Partapsi and annexed Khed. But he did not adhere to his promise to the *pradhan* and killed him[21] instead. After removing Dabhis from his way Asthan established his rule over 140 villages of Khed.[22] He further annexed 140 villages of Khodena from the Bhati ruler and 140 villages of Mahewa from the Sonagara Rajputs.[23] He appointed his *sardars* in each of the villages he had acquired to consolidate his power.

The quest for acquiring more and more areas was continued by the descendants of Rao Asthan. Thus, by the time Rao Chunda (c. 1383 to 1423 A.D.), the eleventh ruler in direct descent, ascended the throne, the Rathors ruled over Pali, Khed, Bhadrajun, Kodna, Mahewa (Mallani), Barmer and some area of Janglu (Bikaner). However, compared to the total area of Marwar, the area under Rathor rule was small. It seems that the Khalji annexation of Siwana, Sanchor, Jalor, Mandor,[24] etc., put a check on the expansionist activities of the Rathor rulers. They could achieve success in their expansionist designs only during the time of weak successors of Sultan Firoz Shah Tughlaq and Saiyid Sultans when Rao Chunda extended the territories of the Rathor kingdom.[25] He occupied Mandor after an alliance with the Inda (Parihar) Rajputs and made it the capital of the Rathor dominion.[26]

After the death of Rao Chunda, his successors, Rao Kanha (A.D. 1419), Rao Satta (c. 1419-28), and Rao Rinmal (A.D. 1428-1438) ruled over Mandor, while the leaders of Rathor subclans strengthened their position in their respective territories. Nainsi mentions that after securing Mandor, Rinmal proclaimed Jodha as his successor and gave it to him.[27] After the murder of Rinmal at Chittor,[28] Jodha (A.D. 1446-1453) lost practically all the territories to the Rana of Mewar. But, when Kumbha was busy defending against the rulers of Gujarat and Malwa, Jodha got the opportunity to reoccupy his ancestral territories and extend them up to Sojat and Jaitaran which had been included in Mewar.[29] On 12 May 1459 (*Jyestha sudi* 2, V.S. 1515) he laid the foundations of a new fort and a new city some six miles to the south of Mandor, naming it Jodhpur after his own name.[30] At the time of his death (A.D. 1487) Rao Jodha's rule extended over a larger domain than that of any of his predecessors.[31]

Thus, the genesis of Rathor kingdom reveals that the relations which started with mutual agreement between the Rathor princes and the local chiefs of the area around Pali got transformed into the relations between a sovereign and his subjects. Rao Asthan set the ball rolling by taking advantage of the weakness of the local chiefs and acquired the rights of *thakurai*. In this process the ruling chiefs were either killed or they migrated to the neighbouring areas. The rise of Rao Asthan only shows the condition of the ruling clans and not the general condition of the peasants. The fact that after ousting Dabhis and the Guhilas, Rao Asthan sent his own *sardars* to these areas shows that the change in the ruling class did not affect the position of the cultivators. After the death of Asthan, his successors adopted a more practical policy towards the dislodged ruling families. Thus, Rao Chunda, after conquering Mandor, recognised the leaders of the Parihar, Balisa, and the Manglia Rajputs as the *bhomias*[32] of their respective territories.[33] At the same time, they also established matrimonial relations with the dislodged Rajput families.

In the process of expansion of the territory, the sons and brothers of the ruler were allowed to occupy the various territories conquered by them. These holdings were recognised as their *thikanas*.[34] This practice was called *bhai-bant*, because, being members of the same clan, they believed that it was their share in a cooperative effort of the clan. Though accepting the sovereignty of the chief of the ruling clan the *sardars* treated him just as *primus-inter-pares*.

Under this practice the rulers of Khed, who were the direct descendants of Rao Siha, remained the leaders of the Rathor clan while their relatives and sons who had established their *thakurai* remained semi-independent. But soon the ambitious princes started challenging the authority of the Raja. This led to the emergence of independent principalities[35] and set in disintegration of the Rathor rule. Thus, when Rao Jodha was in exile, the Rathors of Malani, the Jaitmalots of Siwana, the Pokarana Rathors of Pokaran, the Deorajots of Setrava, Sankhala Harboo of Roon, the Indas of Indawati, the Gogade Chauhans of Sekhala (in *pargana* Shergarh), the Khichis of Gargon, the Bhatis of Veekpur, and Poongal Bhati, grandson of Rawal Kehariji of Jaisalmer, etc., did not support him in the beginning though they accepted him, being the direct descendant of Rao Siha, as their ruler. It shows that under the practice of *bhai-bant* the bonds of political and moral obligation to render military service to the Raja was very weak and largely depended on the strength of the Raja and the good sense of the chieftains.

Rao Jodha did not change his policy towards his family members when he was again in ascendence. Following *bhai-bant*, he assigned the conquered territories to his sons and brothers who had fought either on his behalf or independently.[36] The territories of Khinvsar, Asop, Bikaner, Kherwa, remained with his sons, Karamsi, Raipal, Bika and Samantsi, who had conquered these areas and had established their *thikanas* (hereditary holdings—residence) at these places respectively.[37] After establishing his rule in Jodhpur, Rao Jodha assigned *pargana* of Merta to his two sons, Bar Singh and Duda to keep control over the subdued territories. Accordingly, they established their sway over Merta. Later on, after the flight of Bar Singh, his brother Duda declared himself the ruler of Merta.[38] We come across references to appointments of *Pradhan* and other officers by Duda.[39] It seems that practice of *bhai-bant* was followed by the other family members also who had been put in charge of the various territories. Like the earlier Rathor rulers, the princes or *sardars* who conquered any fresh territories on their own initiative held *thakurai* over their respective territories. As a leader of the Rathor clan, Rao Jodha recognized their right and allowed them to rule over the territories they had conquered. In fact, these Rathor princes enjoyed their privileges and position more because of their being members of the clan than as a favour from the Raja. The following table shows the distribution of the territories:

Territories Assigned by Rao Jodha to his Brothers and Sons

Brothers of Rao Jodha		*Sons of Rao Jodha*	
Name	Territories granted	Name	Territories granted
Akheraj Rathor	Bagari	Rao Satal*	Phalodi Pokaran
Champa Rathor	Kapardobana	Bar Singh and Duda	Metra
Dungar Rathor	Bhadrajun	Bika and Bida	Bikaner and Chhapardronpur
Bela Rathor	Kelwo	Bharmal and Jago	Kondeno
Roopa Rathor	Chadi	Shivraj	Siwano
Manda Rathor	Sandulu of Bikaner	Karamsi	Naharsar
Karan Rathor	Lunawas	Raipal	Asop
Pata Rathor	Karnu		
Bera Rathor	Budhad		
Jagmal's son Khetsi Rathor	Netdia		

*It seems that during his life time Rao Jodha had declared him his successor who was looking after the administrative affairs of Jodhpur.

These Rathor *sardars* and princes not only conquered territories, but also settled in their respective *thikanas* the Rajputs and the Jats by inviting them from the neighbouring areas.[40] The motive behind inhabiting these new groups in the conquered area was perhaps to increase the number of people loyal to them and to extend the area under cultivation.

For want of information regarding their obligation towards the ruler of Jodhpur, it is difficult to know the exact relationship between the Rathor ruler, the Rathor princes and other *sardars*. But it may be safely stated that they were free as far as the internal administration was concerned. However, it was expected that they would help the Rathor ruler if he needed their help. This system was similar to the system which prevailed in the territories ruled by the various Rajput rulers. Under such a political organization each of the *sardars* could assume an independent status and it happened so in many cases. After the death of Rao Jodha each of them became either independent or supported the Rao of Jodhpur according to his own will. During his lifetime Rao Jodha had himself recognized Bika as an independent ruler,[41] thereby setting a precedent that any prince of the royal blood could establish an independent principality.

Struggle Against the Forces of Decentralization

Rao Jodha, who died in A.D. 1489[42], was succeeded by his sons, Rao Satal (A.D. 1489-1492),[43] Rao Suja (A.D. 1492-1515),[44] and Rao Ganga (A.D. 1515-1532), the second son of Rao Suja. During their reign, the forces of disintegration continued and the local clan leaders who had earlier been crushed by the Rathor army became active.

Before the rise of Jodha the territory of Jaitaran was ruled by the Sindhal Rathors.[45] Now, taking advantage of the weakness of the Rathor rulers of Jodhpur, they became defiant.[46] Rao Suja sent his army to suppress them and after crushing their power he granted the territory to his son, Udaji.[47] The rebellion of Sindhal Khangar was similarly crushed by prince Salkha, the son of Rao Suja.

Apart from conflicts with these local chiefs, the Rathor rulers had to fight against their own family members. Nara Sujawat[48] who was made to accept the district of Phalodi after his ouster from the Jodhpur throne was not satisfied with it and waited for an opportunity to seize Pokaran[49] then ruled by Khiva, a descendant of Rao Hamir.[50] The rulers of Pokaran were known as Pokarana Rathors.[51] In A.D. 1498 (V.S. 1555) Nara, in the absence of Khiva, suddenly pounced upon Pokaran and seized it. But Khiva continued to harass and later on, in a battle fought at Nadenwai, he killed Nara. When Rao Suja came to know of this tragedy, he personally marched against the Pokarana Rathors and ousted them from their territories. Thereafter he gave Pokaran to Jaitmal Govinddas Narawat, and Phalodi to Hamir Jaitmal Narawat.[52] Later, Suja pacified Loonka, son of Khiva, by granting him the village of Bhumiyano along with 30 other villages.[53]

The period of Rao Ganga, son of Suja, (A.D. 1515-1532) also witnessed a conflict with his elder brother Rao Vikram. The latter had been deprived of the *gaddi* and had been given the *pargana* of Sojat.[54] It is worthwhile to note that the succession of Rao Ganga was due to the support of the Rathor *sardars*. It created a rift among them besides challenging the right of the reigning ruler to nominate his successor. But this arrangement could not satisfy Rao Vikram, while Rao Ganga continued his efforts to regain Sojat. In a clash near village Dholerao, Muhta Raimal, the *Pradhan* of Rao Vikram, was killed and Sojat passed into the hands of Rao Ganga who granted Rao Vikram the village of Bala.[55] Rao Ganga also came into conflict with Viramdeo, son of Duda, of Merta. On the basis of *Nainsi-Khyat* and the *Jodhpur-Khyat* it is said that Maldeo, son of Rao Ganga, got annoyed with Rao Viramdeo on the question of an elephant which was in the latter's possession.[56] But from the account of the *Vigat*, it appears that Rao Maldeo had not approved the control of Viramdeo over Merta. The latter had usurped Merta from Siha, his elder brother, and exercised power as an independent ruler.[57] This was possibly the main cause of Rao Ganga's resentment. Rao Maldeo kept the question open by rendering help to the sons of Rao Siha.

The successors of Rao Jodha upheld the concept of *bhaibant*. Accordingly, the *parganas* of Merta, Jaitaran, Siwana, Phalodi and Satalmer remained with the descendants of Rao Duda, son of Rao Jodha; Rathor Uda, son of Rao Suja; Rathor Bijo, son of Mandal Rinmalot; and Nara, son of Rao Suja, respectively.[58] These *sardars* of various Rathor sub-clans

(*Khamp*) acquired their possessions by dislodging others who also belonged to the same clan. This was done either by sheer force or with the support of the rulers of Jodhpur. The Rathor rulers used their *sardars* as intermediaries between themselves and the peasants. But the evolution of this relationship did not benefit the subjugated chiefs. With the rise in the power of the Rathor rulers the position of the dislodged chieftains sank to a considerably lower level in the society—mainly because of the practice of *bhai-bant*. Thus, the defeated groups were losing their position in the social hierarchy while a new group of nobility was assuming the top position in it. There is no doubt that this practice caused, on the one hand, internal rivalry among the Rathor *sardars*, and on the other, promoted conflict between these *sardars* and the Rathor rulers.[59]

The concept of *bhai-bant* also weakened the central authority. The principle of primogeniture had been ignored by Rao Jodha himself. The acceptance of the headship of Rao Jodha by his elder brother, Akheraj, confirmed that the most successful member of the ruling family was to be accepted as the head of the clan. But the choice of the Rao had to be confirmed by the *sardars*. It was a proverb, '*Rinhmalan Thapia Tika Raja*', i.e., only he can become the ruler, whom the *sardars* and descendants of Rinmal place on the throne. By virtue of their being the descendants of either Rao Rinmal or Rao Jodha, and the manner in which they held the various territories, these Rathor *sardars* could proclaim themselves independent under a weak ruler. Such a situation arose in Marwar after the death of Rao Jodha. The hold of the Rathor ruler had been reduced to such an extent that when Rao Ganga died the Rathor ruler exercised his sway only over Jodhpur and Sojat.[60] Jaitaran was under the control of the Udawat Rathors but they owed allegiance to the ruler of Jodhpur.[61] At the same time the chiefs of Pokaran, Phalodi, Merta, etc., were independent.[62] In all these areas the Rathor *sardars*, Rao Govind, Rao Jaitmal and Rao Viramdeo, had acquired their position as descendants of such Rathor princes or *sardars* as had conquered those territories or as a result of the grants from the ruler of Jodhpur.[63] Apart from these clan leaders, Sindhal Veera of Bhadrajun and Rao Dungarsi of Siwana had begun to disassociate themselves from the state of Marwar.[64] Gradually the allegiance to the king became nominal and the central authority in the Rathor polity became powerless by the end of the reign of Rao Ganga.

Rao Maldeo and the Rathor Dominion

With the accession of Rao Maldeo in A.D. 1532, the political environment of Marwar changed considerably. He believed that by virtue of his being the successor of Rao Ganga and a direct descendant of the founder of Rathor rule in Marwar, he was the ruler of the territories which the members of his clan inhabited or controlled. In a message sent to Rao Viramdeo through his *pradhan*, Maldeo wrote: 'Merta is yours, but in the house I am the *tikayat*, you are my *bhai-bandh-chakar*.[65] From this it is clear that he could allow the Rathor *sardars* to hold the territories provided they accepted the suzerainty of the *tikayat*, i.e., the ruler of Jodhpur. Thus the position of the Rathor princes as well as the *sardars* was reduced to that of the subordinates of the Rathor ruler. But Rao Viramdeo resisted on the ground that he had been granted his principality by the same person who had granted him (Maldeo) Jodhpur.[66] It appears that other princes or *sardars* held the same view *vis-a-vis* their relations with the ruler of Jodhpur. But Maldeo was bent upon effecting a radical change in his power by every means.

Maldeo's expansion of power in and outside Marwar can be studied in two phases: one comprising the period from his succession (A.D. 1532) to his defeat by Sher Shah in A.D. 1543 and the other from his re-occupation of Jodhpur (A.D. 1545) till his death (A.D. 1562).

The independence of Rao Viramdeo was a challenge to Maldeo's suzerainty. It could encourage other Rathor *sardars* as well to be independent of him. So, he attacked and chased Viramdeo who later sought shelter with Sher Shah in A.D. 1542.[67] A study of the military campaigns against Rao Viramdeo shows that Rao Maldeo had secured Ajmer, Didwana, Sambhar, Chatsu, etc., while he was pursuing him.[68] Even after the expulsion of Rao Viramdeo from the Kachhawaha territory and other areas, Maldeo continued his occupation of those areas. And, the fact that he assigned Didwana to Rathor Kumpa suggests that he had annexed these areas to his dominion. Thus Maldeo's motive in sending his army against Viramdeo was not only to force him into submission but also to expand his territory.

While Marwar forces were pursuing Rao Viramdeo and subduing other territories dominated by Rathor *sardars*, Maldeo hardly missed an opportunity to conquer other areas as well. He captured Nagaur in A.D. 1535, Jalor in A.D. 1537 and Bhadrajun in A.D. 1539. After the flight of Rao Viramdeo, Maldeo turned towards Bikaner, a sovereign state headed by the Rathor ruler, Rao Jaitsi. In A.D. 1541 (V.S. 1598) he conquered Bikaner after a stiff fight and killed Rao Jaitsi. The fort passed into the hands of the Jodhpur army.[69] Rao Maldeo's sack of Bikaner was an important event in the history of Marwar. However, no contemporary writer has mentioned the causes of Maldeo's attack on Bikaner. Pandit Ojha considers it a part of his expansionist policy.[70] As already mentioned the purpose of Maldeo's attack over Merta was not only to crush the power of Viramdeo but to force him to accept the subordination (*chakari*) of the ruler of Jodhpur. Possibly, he wished to apply the same principle of *bhai-bandh-chakar* to the ruler of Bikaner also.

In the second phase Rao Maldeo's power was considerably reduced after his defeat at the hands of Sher Shah in A.D. 1543, though his attitude towards the rulers of Merta and Bikaner remained the same as ever. Historians mention the span of his dominion without taking these two phases of Maldeo's rule into consideration, i.e. before and after his defeat at the hands of Sher Shah.[71] This mistake is due to inadequacy of the accounts given in the *Jodhpur-Khyat* and *Rathora-ri-Vamshavali*, which list these territories as part of Maldeo's dominion without referring to the date of their occupation.[72] In fact, the territories held by Rao Maldeo in the latter part of his reign had been reduced considerably. Now the territories in the east of Marwar, i.e. Sambhar, Didwana, Lalsot, Chatsu, etc., were out of his control. He had regained Jodhpur, Sojat, Jaitaran, Phalodi, Siwana, Pokaran, Jalor, Sanchor, and Merta and had occupied Barmer, Kotada and some parts of the territory of Jaisalmer. In the latter part of his reign Maldeo concentrated on the

North-West of Marwar and due to the establishment of the Mughal authority over Mewat, he avoided conflict with the Mughals by not asserting himself in the east.

Rao Maldeo's policy was resented by almost all the rulers of the neighbouring states. Even at the time of Sher Shah's invasion (A.D. 1543) there was hardly a ruler who offered his support to Rao Maldeo. He had also to face the enmity of Rao Kalyanmal and Rao Viramdeo. The situation became more acute when Rao Maldeo advanced against Haji Khan Pathan in A.D. 1556. At that time a number of rulers including Rana Udai Singh of Mewar, Jaimal Viramdeot of Merta, Rawal Pratap of Banswara, Rawal Ramchandra Solanki of Todedi, Rawal Kalyanmal of Bikaner, Rawal Askaran of Dungarpur, Rao Surjan of Bundi, Rao Durgo of Rampura, Naraindas of Ider, Ram Khedro of Jaitpur and Rawal Tejo of Devalia came to the help of Haji Khan against Maldeo.[73] Yet, it would be wrong to say that these rulers were united in their opposition to Maldeo; they opposed him because their individual interest lay in his downfall.

Rao Maldeo made efforts to dislodge those Rathor *sardars* or princes who had refused to serve under him. To him, a *sardar* was dependent for his position on the good-will of the Raja rather than on his inherent rights. So, he started the practice of assigning *pattas* (land revenue grants) to his *sardars* who were serving in his army.[74] Significantly, these *pattas* were assigned for the territory of Marwar as well as outside Marwar where Maldeo held his control.[75] From the *pattas* granted to Jaita, Kumpa and other Rathor *sardars* it is evident that these assignments were made in lieu of their service.

Apart from these assignments, Maldeo granted the territories to his sons and the *sardars*. After the conquest of Merta, Maldeo restored half of its territory to Rathor Jagmal, the son of Rao Viramdeo.[76] He restored Jaitaran to Rathor Ratansi Khiwawat, Siwana to Rathor Rinmal and Phalodi to Prince Udai Singh.[77] Although these assignments were made after dislodging the earlier holders, the nature of the assignments was similar to that of the distribution of territory under the system of *bhai-bant*. However, these assignees were not free to exercise their power independently under the new system.

The practice of assignment of the *pattas* to the *sardars* was an important change that took place during Maldeo's reign. It is difficult to say, for lack of evidence, if Maldeo had formed any rules and regulations regarding the grants different from the old system of *bhai-bant*. However, it can be maintained that the very idea behind the assignment of the *pattas* was to make the Rathor *sardars* subservient to the ruler of Jodhpur and Rao Maldeo succeeded in implementing this idea at least during his lifetime. Now the *sardars* accepted Maldeo's suzerainty and agreed to render certain services in lieu of assignments of new lands to them.

The practice of granting *pattas* for territories made no real change in the composition of the nobility. The superimposed *pattadars* belonged to the same families to which the earlier grantees had belonged. These *sardars* still claimed their right over their ancestors' domains. That is why in the battle of Sumel in A.D. 1543 with Sher Shah even after the retreat of Rao Maldeo, the Rathor *sardars*, Jaita, Kumpa, etc., refused to withdraw from Girri, a village in the *pargana* of Jaitaran.[78] They asserted that the territory on the west of Girri had been conquered by their ancestors.[79] These *sardars* fought against Sher Shah in defence of the Rathor territory of Maldeo. Thus the principle of becoming servant to the ruler of Jodhpur was still not crystallized when the Rathor army was defeated by Sher Shah in December, 1543, at Sumel. The situation remained the same even after Maldeo reoccupied Jodhpur after Sher Shah's death. When Maldeo died, the Rathor princes and *sardars* were trying to assert more and more. The nature of assignment of the territories to his (Maldeo's) sons shows that Rao Maldeo could not discontinue the old practice of *bhai-bant*,[80] although he never allowed a *pattadar* to secure a status equal to that of a ruler.

Pattas granted to Rathor *sardars* show that the grantee was not only the commander of the military force of the territory but was also responsible for the collection of the revenue, civil and judicial administration as well as maintenance of proper communications. Hence though in functional aspects their position was similar to the *iqtadars* in the administration of the Delhi Sultanate, the nature of their holdings was more permanent than of the latter by virtue of their kinship ties and clan status in their respective territories.

Marwar After Maldeo

Rao Maldeo's death (7 November, 1562) caused political instability in Marwar. Chandra Sen, the third son of Rao Maldeo was installed upon the *gaddi* on 31 December, 1562[81] which caused resentment among his brothers, Rao Ram, Udai Singh and Raimal. As mentioned earlier, Rao Maldeo had continued the assignment of the *pattas* to his sons and nobles. He had granted Phalodi to Udai Singh and Siwana to Raimal.[82] Rao Ram had left Marwar and at the time of Maldeo's death he was staying at village Kelwa in Mewar.[83] Maldeo had failed to see that by assigning territories to his sons he was developing the same practice which had earlier caused him great trouble. After Maldeo's death each of his sons assumed independence and started strengthening his power. In spite of the opposition of his brothers, Rao Chandra Sen would have maintained his position had he succeeded in securing the support of the Rathor *sardars*. But he had to face their opposition too.

The Rathor *sardars*, who were dislodged by Rao Maldeo, could not tolerate any move which would further diminish their importance in the Rathor administration. At the same time a group of powerful Rathor *sardars* was annoyed with Chandra Sen because of his behaviour towards Jaimal Jaisawat.[84] Many other Rathor *sardars* who were already unhappy over the succession of Rao Chandra Sen[85] began to conspire with his three brothers. At their behest Chandra Sen's eldest brother, Ram, created trouble in Sojat, Raimal in the district of Dunara and Udai Singh attacked and took the two villages of Baodi and Gangani.[86] This changed the entire political environment of Marwar. While Rao Chandra Sen's brothers were busy conspiring against him, he himself failed to secure the support of the Rathor *sardars*.[87]

This was a favourable opportunity for the Mughal Emperor Akbar. By this time, the Mughals had established their hold on Jaitaran and Merta. The Mughal Emperor Akbar, after capturing Ajmer from Haji Khan Pathan in A.D. 1559 had sent his army against Jaitaran.[88] Rathor Ratansi, a grantee of Maldeo, was killed in the battle. His two sons, Kalyandas and Gopaldas entered the imperial service and were granted

Jaitaran in *jagir*.[89] Following the conquest of Jaitaran, Akbar despatched the Mughal forces to Merta. Maldeo had restored Merta to Jagmal, son of Viramdeo, after removing his brother Jaimal, who had taken shelter in Mewar where he was given Badnor in *jagir*. Jaimal, later on, sought the help of the Emperor,[90] who gave Merta to Jaimal and sent Sharfuddin Hussain Mirza and Lunkaran Shekawat to help him in taking its possession.[91] But, soon after that Jaimal was suspected of intriguing with Sharfuddin Hussain, who had turned against the Mughal Emperor. Consequently, Merta was given to his brother, Jagmal. Thus, in both places Akbar recognised the hereditary right of the Rathor *sardars*.

When Rao Ram approached the Emperor, the latter supported his claim for the *gaddi* of Jodhpur and ordered Hussain Quli Khan to march against Jodhpur along with Rao Ram, who, with the help of the Mughals, captured Sojat. Thereafter, the combined army under the command of Hussain Quli Khan seized Jodhpur. On 3 December, 1565 (*Margashirsha sudi* 11, V.S. 1622) the Mughal army occupied the fort.[92] Rao Chandra Sen was forced to retreat towards Bhadrajun and the Mughals entrenched in Jodhpur.[93] This changed the political configuration of Marwar. The establishment of Mughal control over Jodhpur, Jaitaran and Merta left no chance for the Rathor princes to regain their territory. For the time being Rao Ram had to be satisfied with Sojat and Udai Singh with Phalodi and continued their hostility towads Chandra Sen. Thus, Rao Chandra Sen, after his flight from Jodhpur, was not only facing the Mughal army but also the opposition of Rao Ram, Udai Singh and the leaders of the Kumpawat and the Udawat Rathor clans.[94] The ruler of Merta and other Merta *sardars* were already opposing Chandra Sen.[95] The Marwar nobility was thus, in a state of crisis when in A.D. 1570 (V.S. 1627) Akbar reached Nagaur via Ajmer.

Both the Rajasthani and Persian sources mention that while Akbar was staying at Nagaur, Chandra Sen met him on 24 November, 1570.[96] It appears that having failed to receive the Emperor's favour he left for Bhadrajun while his son Rai Singh remained at the Mughal court.[97] At the same time Udai Singh also arrived at the court and was sent to village Samavali on behalf of the Emperor.[98] Rao Ram already held the imperial *mansab*, and Sojat in *jagir*. His control over Sojat remained undisturbed. These events suggest that at that stage Akbar was not prepared to bestow Jodhpur on Chandra Sen or any of the sons of Maldeo. He even removed Udai Singh from Phalodi, which shows that at this time he wanted to keep Marwar under the *khalisa*. Akbar's army conquered Bhadrajun in A.D. 1571. It is clear that the Rathor nobility and even Udai Singh had finally recognized the sovereignty of the Mughal Emperor. This is evident from the mediation of Emperor Akbar on the issue of the succession of Rao Ram.[99] The decision of the Mughal Emperor was honoured by the Rathor *sardars*. Akbar, who had finally decided to crush the power of Chandra Sen or any other successor of Maldeo, granted Jodhpur to Raja Rai Singh of Bikaner in A.D. 1574 which remained with him till A.D. 1577.[100] Later, in the same year, Rai Singh was sent with the royal army against Siwana which was captured.

By granting Jodhpur to Rai Singh, Akbar succeeded in keeping the sons of Maldeo weak and divided. Perhaps, the motive behind the grant of Jodhpur to Rai Singh was to mark time for the establishment of the Mughal power in Marwar. As soon as the Mughal army had succeeded in ousting Rao Chandra Sen from Marwar in A.D. 1577 and had won over most of the *sardars* to its side, Rai Singh was removed from Jodhpur and it was brought under the *khalisa*.[101] By this, Akbar made it clear that as a sovereign ruler it was his prerogative to exercise the right of granting the *gaddi* of Jodhpur. It also made Rathor *sardars* realize that their recognition was at the discretion of the Emperor. And the hereditary claim of a ruling family over the *gaddi* of Jodhpur was discontinued by this act. After the death of Chandra Sen, his son, Rai Singh, though he was in the Mughal service, was not given the throne of Jodhpur and later on it was given to Udai Singh in A.D. 1583. Akbar's intervention not only deprived Rathor *sardars* of the right of choosing their own leader, but it also made a fundamental change in the nature of relationship between the Rathor nobility and the ruler of the Rathor clan.

The rulers of the neighbouring states played a vital role in the establishment of the Mughal hold over Marwar. Maldeo's policy towards the neighbouring states had left no sympathy for Marwar and the internal rivalry and conflict among the Rajput Rajas had weakened them politically. So, when the Mughal aggression started against Marwar no ruler of a neighbouring state came to the rescue of Chandra Sen. The alliance of the Mughals with Rao Kalyanmal of Bikaner and Rawal Harraj of Jaisalmer in A.D. 1570[102] further prepared the way for invading the Rathor territory in Marwar.

The ruler of Jaisalmer, Rawal Harraj, took advantage of the weak position of Rao Chandra Sen. In A.D. 1576 (V.S. 1633) finding Rao Chandra Sen engaged against Akbar, he attacked Pokaran. Nainsi records that Pokaran was granted to Bhakharsi, the son of Harraj of Jaisalmer, in *jagir* but he failed to take it from the followers of Chandra Sen. He requested Rawal Harraj (the ruler of Jaisalmer) to help him[103] which might have been the reason for his attack on Pokaran. However, later accounts show that when Rawal Harraj found it difficult to conquer Pokaran, he suggested to Rao Chandra Sen to hand over Pokaran to him in return for which he promised to advance a loan of one lac *prozis* to him. He also promised to return Pokaran to the Rao when the latter returned the loan to him.[104] Rao Chandra Sen at that time was engaged against Emperor Akbar and was badly in need of this money. Therefore, he accepted the proposal and a compromise was made. The Bhatis of Jaisalmer kept their control over Pokaran till it was given to Maharaja Jaswant Singh of Jodhpur in A.D. 1696, although on paper it was granted to Mota Raja Udai Singh by Akbar. As the Rawal had accepted the royal service, he continued to support the cause of the Mughal state.

Here it may be noted that after leaving Siwana, Rao Chandra Sen took shelter in the territory of Mewar. While staying there Rao Chandra Sen, in A.D. 1574 (V.S. 1631), married the daughter of Rana Udai Singh.[105] But he did not receive any military help from the Rana as he himself was facing a difficult situation.[106] As all the Rajput rulers with the exception of Rana Udai Singh had accepted the suzerainty of the Mughal Emperor, Akbar, no possible help could be expected from them.

Thus the success of the Mughal Emperor became easy due to the internal crisis in Marwar. But at the same time the internal crisis also took a different shape due to the Mughal interference. The Rathor princes would have been satisfied with their recognition as chieftains in their respective areas by Chandra Sen, but the presence of the Mughal Emperor encouraged them to secure his help.

REFERENCES

[1]*Vigat*, i, 12, 14, 342; *Nainsi Khyat*, i, 134, 202, 203, 229 and ii, 278-79; pt. G.H. Ojha, *Jodhpur Rajya*, i, 77-80, 168; *Bankidas ri Khyat*, *Bat* No. 1832.

[2]*Nainsi Khyat*, ii, 278; *Vigat*, i, 12; *Rajasthan through the Ages*, 676-77.

[3]The territory was devided among the members of the sub-clans of the Parihar Rajputs who were called Inda, Manglia and Kotcha (*Jodhpur-Khyat* i, 30-31).

[4]*Thakurai* is an abstract noun from *Thakur*. In Ancient India it was never used for the sovereign but only for the grantee who got the land from the king. Even *Kayasthas* and *Brahmins* were called *thakur* in the inscriptions of the Chandellas (*E. Ind.*, i, 333ff; N.S. Bose, *History of the Chandellas*, 126). Bose agrees with Dr. Kane (*History of the Dharma-sastras*, iii, 984) that *thakur* was merely a title and not an office whereby a holder was entitled to wield some power in the state. In some Chandella inscriptions the minister and other officers were given this title (*Archaeological Survey Reports*, 1935-36, 90, 92). The account of later inscriptions makes it clear that the term *thakur* was used for the holder of land. Thus, by the close of the 12th century the term *thakur* was applied for the chief of the land and did not remain a mere title. Nainsi has used *thakurai* in connection with Asthan and Partapsi, who were sovereigns of their respective territories. The same term has been used for intermediary chiefs also. But in the later accounts the same term has been used for a person who got the land from the ruler. Hence, we cannot always equate *thakurai* with sovereignty. It simply meant chiefship or overlordship of the land whether independent or under some ruler.

[5]*Nainsi Khyat*, ii, 227.

[6]*Vigat*, i, 9.

[7]*Vigat*, i, 9. When Asthan and his brothers camped outside Pali, on their way to Gujarat, the Paliwal Brahmins told them about the fear of the Mers and requested them to stay in the city. Also see, *Dayaldas Khyat*, i, 41.

[8]*Vigat*, i, 9.

[9]*Nainsi Khyat*, ii, 227.

[10]Apart from the political conflict, the behaviour of Kanha Mer, the leader of the Mer tribe, was becoming intolerable as he used to snatch the girls before their marriage (*Nainsi Khyat*, ii, 227). Such practice might have been common in the tribal society, but to the Brahmins it was totally unacceptable.

[11]There is a controversy over the conquest of Pali by Rao Asthan. For detail see, *Rajasthan through the Ages*, 690-1. Rao Siha, father of Rao Asthan, had three sons from his Solanki Rani. But due to the trouble on the issue of succession caused by Kharkshi, the son of Siha from his first Rani, Asthan, Sonag and Ajay (sons of Solanki Rani) had left Kannauj. (*Vigat*, i, 8) Abul Fazl confused Mers with the Minah tribe. (*Ain*, tr. II, 276).

[12]*Vigat*, i, 10; *Dayaldas Khyat*, i, 41; *Servdes-ma-Rajvioni*, 96.

[13]*Vigat*, i, 11.

[14]*Gughari* was a cess levied to maintain the army.

[15]Asthan complained that his followers (employees) were unable to maintain themselves without sufficient cultivable lands. His horses were also not getting sufficient fodder. (*Vigat*, i, 11).

[16]*Vigat*, i, 11.

[17]*Ibid.*, i, 12. *Hal*, i.e. per unit of area which requires one pair of bullock and one plough to cultivate it. Roughly fifty *bighas* of land.

[18]*Vigat*, i, 12; *Servdes-ma-Rajvioni*, 97-8. In the *Khyat* (*Nainsi Khyat*, ii, 278) Nainsi has mentioned 84 villages of Pali. He further mentions that after his control over these villages he establised his *thakurai* over 84 villages of Bhadrajun.

[19]*Vigat*, i, 13; *Servdes-ma-Rajvioni*, 98-9.

[20]*Vigat*, i, 13.

[21]*Ibid*, i, 14.

[22]*Ibid.*

[23]*Ibid.*

[24]*I.A.* VL. 301; cf. M.S. Ahluwalia, *Studies in Medieval Rajasthan History*, 32.

[25]It is said that Rao Chunda also conquered Nagaur, Khatu, Didwana and Sambhar which had earlier passed into the control of Muzaffar Shah, the ruler of Mandu. Almost all the *Rajasthani Khyats* record the occupation of Nagaur by Chunda but it is difficult to believe the account as we have sufficient evidence to show that during that period Nagaur remained under the Muslim control. cf, Ojha, *Jodhpur Rajya*, i, 210-11.

[26]It is narrated in the *Khyats* that in A.D. 1394 the Inda Rajputs with the help of Rao Chunda, took possession of Mandor after defeating the Muslim army. Also see *Vigat*, i, 24. From the epigraphic evidences it shows that the territory of Nagaur and Jalor was ruled by the Muslim governors (*Annual Report on Indian Epigraphy*, 1969-70, No. D, 167), who possibly held their influence over Mandor.

[27]*Nainsi Khyat*, ii, 337.

[28]In Mewar, Mera and Chacha, the sons of a *paswan* of the Rana,

had killed Maharana Mokal in A.D. 1433 and had captured the power. When Rao Rinmal came to know about it he left Marwar and came to Chittor. He killed the culprits and placed Kumbha, the son of the deceased Rana, on the throne of Chittor. Afterwards Rinmal stayed to manage the affairs of Mewar. Since the Rana was a minor, he assumed all the powers. This caused great concern to the Mewar nobles who succeeded in creating suspicion in the heart of Rana Kumbha. One day when Rinmal was asleep in a state of intoxication, he was killed in his chamber in the fort of Chittor. See, *Vir-Vinod*, i, 317-22.

[29]*Vigat*, i, 36 Q 493; *Jodhpur-Khyat*, i, 45.

[30]*Jodhpur-Khyat*, i, 45; *Rathora-ri-Vamshavali* (SC), ii, 120.

[31]At that time he held under him Mandor, Jodhpur, Merta, Phalodi, Pokaran, Sheo, Siwana, Sambhar, Ajmer and a large portion of the Nagaur district. (Reu, *Marwar Rajya*, i, 144). Nainsi mentions that Rao Jodha had extended his power over Jodhpur, Merta, Sojat, Jaitaran and Janglu-Bikaner. (*Vigat*, i, 38). It seems that the *parganas* mentioned by Nainsi were those which remained under the Rathor dominion. Jodha's control over Sambhar, Ajmer and Nagaur remained for a short time and he never incorporated them into the Rathor dominion.

[32]The leaders of the dislodged ruling families were recognized as *bhomias* of their respective land since they were the descendants of the early conquerors of the land or its first colonizers. The villages held by the *bhomias* were known as *bhomi-chara-ra-gaon*. These holdings were free of assessment (*Vigat*, i, 532-5). The *bhomias* had the right of collecting land revenue from the peasants and also the right of allotting the uncultivated area to the cultivators (*Enquiry Committee Reports*, 1913, Jodhpur Administration, R.S.A.B.). They were obliged to render state service and to pay the *nalbandi* (a tax paid for the expenses of the army) and *peshkash* (tribute). As such, they served as land intermediaries.

[33]*Jodhpur-Khyat*, i, 28-30. The territory under Mandor then comprised 342 villages, out of which 84 villages were under the Parihars, 84 under the Balisa, 55 under Manglias and 35 under Kotechas (Reu, *Marwar Rajya*, i, 60n.)

[34]Here the term *thakurai* has been used for the grant of territory conferred by the ruler.

[35]After the death of Lakha, chief of Mahewa and Badnor, his elder son, Malo, succeeded him but his other son, Vikram refused to accept his right and with the help of the Sankhala *sardars* established his independent principality in Janglu. (*Nainsi Khyat*, ii, 284-6 and 289-300).

[36]*Vigat*, i, 38-40; *Jodhpur-Khyat*, i, 48-52; Ojha, *Jodhpur Rajya*, i, 251-4.

[37]*Rathora-ri-Vamshavali* (SC), 121.

[38]*Vigat*, ii, 46-7; *Rathora-ri-Vamshavali* (ORIJ), 40.

[39]Similarly these Rathor princes granted the *sasan* lands to their favourites in their territories. In the *Vigat* (Vols. I-II) many instances are given of such grants. For specific reference, see, *Vigat*, i, 484, 550-1.

[40]Nainsi gives the name of villages from where the Jats migrated to Merta villages (*Vigat*, ii, 40-2).

[41]*Dayaldas Khyat* (MS), ii, f. 5; *Vigat*, i, 39; Munshi Devi Prasad, *Rao Bikaji-ka-Jiwan-Charitra*, 31-2.

[42]Nainsi places it in V.S. 1541 (*Vigat*, i, 38).

[43]Ojha, *Jodhpur-Rajya*, i, 262.

[44]Nainsi mentions his death in V.S. 1571/1514 A.D. (*Vigat*, i, 41).

[45]The territory of Jaitaran was held by Sindhal Rathors who were in the service of the Rana of Mewar. During the time of Rao Jodha, his son Duda conquered Jaitaran from the Sindhal Rathors (*Vigat* i, 495; *Nainsi Khyat*, iii, 38-40).

[46]Asopa, *Samshipt-Itihas*, 223; *Jodhpur Rajya*, i, 269.

[47]*Vigat*, i, 495; *Jodhpur-Khyat*, i, 59.

[48]*Jodhpur-Khyat* mentions that Rao Satal adopted Nara, son of Suja. After Satal's death, Nara was persuaded to give up his claim to the *gaddi* of Jodhpur in favour of his father, Rao Suja. In the same *Khyat* it is also mentioned that the Rathor *sardars* supported Rao Suja and placed him on the *gaddi* because Nara delayed his coronation ceremony, *vide*, i, 62-3.

[49]*Vigat*, ii, 292.

[50]According to Nainsi, Hamir was the son of Jagpal, son of Rao Mala or Rao Mallinath Rathor of Mahewa (*Vigat*, ii, 291). According to *Jodhpur-Khyat*, Jagpal was the second son of Mallinath, *vide*, i, 25. Also see, *Jodhpur Rajya-ka-Itihas*, i, 191.

[51]Asopa, *Samshipt-Itihas*, 215.

[52]*Nainsi Khyat* (Hindi), ii, 137-44; *Jodhpur-Khyat*, i, 62-3.

[53]*Vigat*, ii, 292.

[54]*Sarvdes-ma-Rajvioni*, 9; *Nainsi Khyat* reveals that at the time of the *tika* ceremony all the nobles assembled in the fort. At that time the children of the *sardars* who had gone to the fort to witness the coronation felt hungry and the *sardars*, therefore, requested the mother of Viramdeo to arrange for meal. The mother of Viramdeo refused to do so. However, as soon as the mother of Ganga came to know of it, she prepared fresh food and sent it to the children and the *sardars*. The *sardars*, therefore, pretending that the time of the coronation was not auspicious, put off Viramdeo's coronation. After calling Gangaji from Mewar, they installed him on the *gaddi* of Jodhpur. Viramdeo was given Sojat. *Vide* iii, 81-6, *Jodhpur-Khyat*, i, 62; and *Rathora-ri-Vamshavali* (ORIJ p. 89) narrate the same story.

[55]*Nainsi Khyat*, iii, 81-6; *Jodhpur-Khyat*, i, 65; Bankidas, *Bat*, 104.

[56]*Nainsi Khyat*, iii, 93-4; *Jodhpur Rajya*, i, 279-80.

[57]*Vigat*, ii, 47-8. The sons of Rao Siha, Rao Jaiso, Rao Gango and Rao Bhojo, were not happy with Rao Viram who had disposed their father from the *gaddi* of Merta. They approached Rao Maldeo and the latter agreed to help them against Rao Viramdeo, *vide*, ii, 47.

[58]*Ibid.*, ii, 2-3, 47-8 and i, 495, 387, 217-18.

[59]This can clearly be seen in the case of Sojat and Jaitaran.

[60]*Vigat*, i, 43; *Jodhpur-Khyat*, i, 68; *Jodhpur Rajya*, i, 284; *Samshipt-Itihas*, 245.

[61]*Rathora-ri-Vamshavali* (R.S.A.B.), 144; *Vigat*, i, 495.

[62]*Rathora-ri-Vamshavali* (*R.S.A.B.*), 144-5.

[63]*Vigat*, ii, 3-4, 51-2, 218, 293; *Servdes-ma-Rajvioni*, 60-1.

[64]*Vigat*, i, 44, ii, 218; *Jodhpur-Khyat*, i, 68.

[65]*Vigat*, ii, 51; *Jodhpur-Khyat* (i, 68) mentions that Maldeo took the territories of *bhai-bant* and included them into his *Padshahi. Rathora-ri-Vamshavali* (p. 143) confirms it.

[66]*Nainsi Khyat*, ii, 118.

[67]Nainsi mentions (*Nainsi Khyat*, iii, 99) that after his exit from Kachhawah's territory, Viramdeo went to Malarna where he met a Muslim *thanahdar*. Through him he was introduced to the *thanahdar* of Ranthambhor. Later on, the *thanahdar* of Ranthambhor accompanied him to meet Sher Shah who agreed to help him. The same author in the *Vigat* (i, 56) mentions that both Kalyanmal of Bikaner and Viramdeo of Merta met Sher Shah at Sahsram, but it cannot be accepted as in A.D. 1540 Sher Shah had left Sahsram. Kalyanmal arrived at Sher Shah's court only after his defeat in A.D. 1542 by Maldeo. Therefore, it is more convincing that they might have met at Delhi.

[68]*Vigat*, ii, 54 and i, 44-5.

[69]*Dalpat-Vilas*, 5; *Vigat*, i, 44; *Sarvdes-ma-Rajvioni*, 60; *Jodhpur-Khyat*, i, 69; *Jaisom*, 205-18; *Dayaldas Khyat*, ii. f. 15-16; *Rao Jaitsi-ka-Jiwan Charitra*, 85.

[70]*Jodhpur Rajya*, i, 292-3.

[71]Tod, *Annals and Antiquities*, ii, 19-20; Reu, *Marwar Rajya*, i, 142.

[72]*Jodhpur-Khyat*, i, 78; *Rathora-ri-Vamshavali* (Bahi, ORIJ), 108. Though Nainsi gives the list of these territories at one place like the two *Khyats* and Vamshavali but he has mentioned the dates of conquest against most of the places (*Vigat*, i, 43-4).

[73]*Vigat*, ii, 60.

[74]For example, Didwana was given to Rathor Kumpa. Later, village Madaria of *pargana* Gorhwar was also given to him (*Vigat*, ii, 61). Rathor Jaitsi Udawat was given the *Patta* of *pargana* Badhnor, and the Villages of Kesithal and Bisalpur of *pargana* Gorhwar (*Vigat*, i, 44).

[75]Rathor Kumpa and Jaita held *Pattas* outside Marwar. Rawal Meghraj and Pancholi Abaha held *Pattas* in the territory of Jodhpur (*Vigat*, i, 54).

[76]*Vigat*, ii, 61.

[77]*Ibid*, i, 494, 66.

[78]*Vigat*, i, 56-7; *Nainsi Khyat*, iii, 100-1.

[79]*Jodhpur-Khyat*, i, 69.

[80]A number of such grants are mentioned in *Basta* No. 60/12, *Jodhpur Records*, R.S.A.B.

[81]*Jodhpur-Khyat*, i, 85; *Kaviraj-Khyat*, 20; *Jodhpur Rajya*, i, 333.

[82]*Vigat*, ii, 5, 219; *Jodhpur-Khyat*, i, 332; *Rathora-ri-Vamshavali*, ii, 118/184 (R.S.A.B.)

[83]*Jodhpur-Khyat*, i, 80.

[84]*Jodhpur-Khyat*, i, 85; *Vigat*, i, 67, 71; ii, 5; *Servdes-ma-Rajvioni*, 108. Once an accused, who was a servant of Rao Chandra Sen, fled away

and took shelter with Jaitmal Jaisawat. Rao Chandra Sen sent his soldiers to get back the servant. Jaitmal thereupon sent a message that the servant may be given any punishment except the capital punishment. This interference enraged Rao Chandra Sen and he at once ordered the servant to be executed. Therefore, Jaitmal and some of his associate *sardars* were annoyed with him. Rathor Prithvi Raj Kumpawat, who later on became Akbar's adviser for Marwar affairs, and other Rathor *sardars* united to oppose Chandra Sen.

[85]*Rathora-ri-Vamshavali* (SC), ii, 118-184.

[86]*Ibid.*; *Jodhpur-Khyat*, i, 85.

[87]On receiving the report of the subversive activities of Rao Ram, Udai Singh and Raimal, Rao Chandra Sen marched against them. Both Raimal and Ram did not resist Chandra Sen and left Udai Singh alone to fight against the Jodhpur army. After some desultory fighting between Chandra Sen and Udai Singh at village Lohawat, peace was concluded through the mediation of Rathor *sardars*. Without any further delay Rao Chandra Sen pursued Rao Ram, who at first came to Nadol and offered resistance. Ultimately out of despair he went to the Mughal Emperor in A.D. 1562 on the instigation of the Rathor *sardars*. Udai Singh, even after he had come to terms with Rao Chandra Sen, continued to plunder the latter's territory, keeping his control over Phalodi. The leading clan members of the nobility, the Udawat and Kumpawat Rathors, deserted Chandra Sen due to internal rivalry and went over either to the Mughal Emperor to receive the *jagirs* or to Rao Ram and Udai Singh (*Jodhpur-Khyat* i, 85-6; *Vigat* i, 70-1). Among the Rathor *sardars* of Kumpawat clan, the name of Prithviraj Rathor is worth-mentioning. He became consultant to Akbar on Marwar affairs (*Vigat*, i, 70-1).

[88]*Akbarnama*, ii, 66; *Vigat*, ii, 495.

[89]*Vigat*, ii, 495.

[90]*Ibid.*, i, 60.

[91]*Vigat*, ii, 66-8; *Akbarnama*, ii, 160-62, 196.

[92]Pt. Ojha (*Jodhpur Rajya*, i, 335) refutes the account of the *Khyats* that Akbar had to send the Mughal army three times to secure control over Jodhpur. He accepts the account of *Akbarnama* (ii, 197) and suggests that the Mughal army advanced only once. This version can be supported by the account of Nainsi (*Vigat*, i, 67-8). On the basis of the account of *Akbarnama*, Akbar's control over Jodhpur had been mentioned in 1563 (*Akbar the Great*, i, 79; and *Marwar and the Mughals*, 46). It is difficult to find a definite date for the occupation of Jodhpur, although the date given by Abul Fazl has been accepted generally.

[93]After his defeat, Rao Chandra Sen started increasing his strength and occasionally attacked the imperial territory. But he could not win over the support of his brothers. They kept themselves busy strengthening their own power. Now they also employed the non-Rathor *sardars* in their army. Udai Singh, taking advantage of the intervention of the Mughal forces, continued his efforts to occupy more and more territories.

[94]Rao Chandra Sen had plundered the *basi* of Rathor Kalyan Das. This act annoyed the *sardars* of the Udawat clan. (*Vigat*, i, 70).

[95]*Vigat*, i, 71.

[96]*Vigat*, i, 69; *Jodhpur-Khyat*, i, 88; Badayuni, ii, 133.

[97]*Jodhpur-Khyat*, i, 88; *Vigat*, i, 69.

[98]*Jodhpur-Khyat*, i, 88.

[99]After the death of Rao Ram in A.D. 1572 a dispute arose between his two sons, Kala and Karan. Rathor Surajmal Prithvirajot supported the cause of Karan, the eldest son of Rao Ram, while Rathor Maheshdas Kumpawat favoured Kala, the younger son of Rao Ram. Both the brothers made a representation regarding their respective claims to the Emperor, who, on the advice of Rathor Prithviraj Kumpawat, an adviser to the Emperor, gave the decision in favour of Kala. Karan was granted village Suraito along with 60 other villages (*Vigat*, i, 71).

[100]*Vigat*, i, 68; *Jodhpur-Khyat*, i, 118.

[101]Besides, Akbar had removed Udai Singh from Phalodi in A.D. 1574 (V.S. 1631) and granted him the village Samavali in *Jagir*. After removing Chandra Sen from Siwana, Akbar continued his control over it for sometime and later on gave it to the sons of Raimal (*Vigat*, i, 6; ii, 219).

[102]Akbar had given Bundi to Bhoj, son of Surjan Hada. In Sirohi Akbar neglected the claim of Rao Surtan and granted it to his brother Jagmal (*Nainsi Khyat*, i, 112 and 150-1).

[103]*Vigat*, ii, 296-7; *Nainsi Khyat*, ii, 97.

[104]*Vigat*, ii, 297.

[105]*Vigat*, ii, 63-5; *Bankidas Khyat*. Bat 205

[106]cf., *Udaipur Rajya*, i.

2

MARWAR UNDER MUGHAL HEGEMONY (A.D. 1583-1638)

During the period A.D. 1565-1582 the suzerainty of the Mughal Emperor was accepted by the Rathor princes and the leading Rathor *sardars* who enrolled themselves into the imperial service. Although, after the death of Chandra Sen in A.D. 1582 Akbar had approved the succession of his son, Rai Singh, who enjoyed the support of the Rathor *sardars*, and granted him the *pargana* of Sojat in *jagir* and bestowed upon him the title of the Rao,[1] Jodhpur was retained in the *khalisa*. Rai Singh was in the imperial service and had a valid claim for the *gaddi* of Jodhpur. But the rejection of his claim signified prerogative of the Emperor to bestow the *gaddi* of Jodhpur to a person of his choice. While making such a decision, Akbar faced little opposition from the majority of Rathor *sardars* since Jodhpur and its territories were under the firm control of the Mughals.

During the period when Jodhpur remained in the *khalisa* (land reserved for the revenue of the state) the Rathor *sardars* played an important role in shaping the political developments in Marwar. Some of them had entered the Mughal service and had been given *mansabs* and *jagirs* in Marwar.[2] Therefore, the Rathor nobility, which had so far claimed the relation of *bhai-bant*, now accepted the suzerainty of a ruler who did not belong to their clan. Another important feature of the period was the changes in the position and power of the Rajput states of Rajasthan. All those rulers, whose power had weakened considerably, had accepted the suzerainty of the Mughal Emperor. Many of them became the *mansabdars* and the areas of their respective states were fixed by the Mughal court. Thus, when Raja Udai Singh ascended the throne in A.D. 1583 a new phase in the history of Marwar started.

Administration of the parganas in and outside Marwar and the Mughal Emperors

Consequent upon the enrolment of the Rathor rulers into the Mughal service their right over the *watan* (ancestral dominion) changed considerably. A study of the *mansabs* and the *jagirs* granted to Raja Udai Singh, Sur Singh and Gaj Singh, enables us to understand the nature of relationship between the Mughal Emperors and the Rathor rulers, as also the nature of the right exercised by the Rathor rulers in their *watan jagirs*.

Tables 1a, 1b, and 1c, given at the end of the chapter reveal that when Raja Udai Singh was recognised the Raja of Marwar, he was assigned only the *pargana* of Jodhpur. Other *parganas* of Marwar were assigned to him later on. At the time of his accession Sur Singh, the son of Udai Singh, was assigned three *parganas*, viz., Jodhpur, Sojat and Siwana. The remaining six *parganas* were assigned to him afterwards. Similarly, Gaj Singh (Sur Singh's son) was assigned four *parganas*, viz., Jodhpur, Sojat, Jaitaran and Siwana at the time of his succession. From this it can be seen that all the three successive rulers of Marwar held only Jodhpur, and the assignment of other *parganas* of Marwar remained at the discretion of the Mughal Emperors. Thus, after the occupation of Marwar by Akbar, the claim of the Rathor rulers of Jodhpur was considerably reduced in the Rathor dominion.

It has been noted that the *jama* (assessed revenue) of the *parganas* of Marwar, on the basis of which the assignments were made to the Rathor rulers, did not remain static. This can be shown by the following table:

TABLE 2:1

Account of the Jama assigned to Raja Udai Singh, Sur Singh and Gaj Singh in Marwar*

Parganas	Maharaja Udai Singh (*Dams*)	Maharaja Sur Singh (*Dams*)	Maharaja Gaj Singh (*Dams*)
Jodhpur	58,85,000	68,85,000	1,02,55,000
Siwana	15,00,000	15,00,000	25,00,000
Sojat	40,00,000	50,00,000	60,00,000
Satalmer (Pokaran)	5,60,000	5,00,000	5,00,000
Jaitaran	39,40,297	56,00,000	56,00,000
Phalodi	——	27,00,000	27,00,000
Jalor	——	1,15,10,827	1,15,10,827
Sanchor	——	25,66,673	25,66,673
Merta	——	80,00,000	80,00,000

**Hukumat-bahi*, ff, 15a-16b; *Vigat*, i, 105-6; *Servdes-ma-Rajvioni*, 136-7; *Jodhpur-Khyat*, i, 122-4; 153-5, 160. Since there is contradiction in *jama* figures in the *vigat* (cf. i, 105 and 163), I have relied on the figures given in the *hukumat bahi*.

From Table 2:1, given above, it appears that apart from the *parganas* of Satalmer, Sanchor, and Merta, the amount of the *jama* increased constantly from the time of Maharaja Udai Singh to Gaj Singh. The reason of this increase can be explained in relation to the fact that the Mughal Emperors did not assign all the *tappas* or villages of a *pargana* to the Rathor rulers. In other words even within a *watan* of a Rathor Raja a number of *tappas* or villages were either administered directly by the Mughal Emperors or assigned to *jagirdars*. However, it needs a careful study before any definite conclusions can be drawn and we would discuss it in detail later.

During this period the Rathor rulers were assigned the *jagirs* outside Marwar also. This was done primarily to cover the balance of their salary which was fixed according to their *mansab*. It has been noticed that the assignments of the *jagirs* outside Marwar were made in spite of the fact that the territories of Marwar were held by other *mansabdars* or retained in the *khalisa*. Thus the assignment of the *jagirs* outside Marwar was not necessarily made after granting all the *parganas* of Marwar.

With the establishment of the Mughal supremacy in Rajput states, the nature of the relations with the neighbouring states also changed considerably. Now, in the new set-up all the Rajput Rajas[3] were in the service of the Mughal Emperor and, thus held the imperial *mansab*. They were granted *jagirs* in lieu of their salary which was fixed according to the *mansab* they held. Except for the capital town and its adjacent territories, it was at the discretion of the Mughal Emperor to assign to them a part or the whole of their ancestors' land. It has been mentioned that they could be assigned the *jagirs* outside their native land. In this new situation no Raja could expand his territory or extend his control even over his ancestors' land as long as the Mughal Emperor was powerful enough to subdue him.

It has been said that Raja Rai Singh of Bikaner was granted Jodhpur in A.D. 1574 and his control remained on it till A.D. 1577. Later, he was given Phalodi in *jagir* which remained with him from A.D. 1578 to A.D. 1615.[4] Earlier it had been given to Bhakarsi, son of Harraj, of Jaisalmer. In A.D. 1620 Jalor and in A.D. 1622 Sanchor were given in *jagir* to Prince Khurram. In A.D. 1620 on the recommendation of Khurram, Jalor was granted to *Bhiv*, son of Rana Amar Singh, in *jagir*.[5] There is reference to the effect that at the time of the succession of Raja Udai Singh, Jaitaran was held by the Rawal of Jaisalmer in *jagir*. These references show that in Marwar various *parganas* were granted to the rulers of the neighbouring states. Similarly, the Rathor rulers of Jodhpur were also granted the territory of the neighbouring states in *jagir*. Such practice minimized the possibility of their occupying the areas of the neighbouring states as it would be open violation of the imperial authority.[6] Thus this pattern of relationship reduced the claim of the Rathor rulers over their ancestral territory (*watan jagir*) considerably.

Pay Schedules

Being the imperial *mansabdars*, the Rathor rulers claimed a definite amount of their salary which was calculated and fixed according to the rates of the *zat* and the *sawar* ranks.[6a] Due to lack of adequate data, it is difficult to examine the nature of the salary claims of Rajas Udai Singh and Sur Singh against their *mansabs*. There is only one schedule available from the time of Maharaja Gaj Singh which provides a detailed information about the salary fixed against the rank of 5000 *zat* and 5000 *sawar*.[7] Maharaja Gaj Singh was raised to the *mansab* of 5000 *zat* and 5000 *sawar* in A.D. 1637 (V.S. 1694).[8] The total pay demand against the *mansab* of 5000/5000 was fixed at Rs. 1,30,000 or 52,00,000 *dams* per month of which the amount of Rs. 30,000 or 12,00,000 *dams* is stated to be the dues on account of his *zat* rank. The balance, being the pay for *sawar* rank, thus amounted to Rs. 1,00,000 or 40,00,000 *dams* per month, and was manifestly calculated at the rate of 9,600 *dams* per annum. This goes to suggest that as far as the rate of *zat* and *sawar* ranks was concerned, even in A.D. 1637, the claim of salary was made on the basis of rates prevailing during the early years of Jahangir's reign. It is worth mentioning that pay claim of Kunwar Karan of Mewar who was granted the *mansab* of 5000/5000 in A.D. 1615 was the same as the pay claim of Maharaja Gaj Singh in A.D. 1637.[9] On the basis of the reports of Sir Thomas Roe and the statement of the *Tuzuk* it has been argued that the reduction in the rates of *sawar* rank from 9,600 *dams* per annum to 8,800 took place in A.D. 1615-16 during the reign of Jahangir and the reduction from 8,800 to 8,000 *dams* was promulgated by Shahjahan.[10] Apparently this formula is not applicable in the above-mentioned cases. If this reduction in the rate of pay of *sawar* rank is accepted, it remains to examine the criterion on the basis of which the salary of Kunwar Ram Singh and Maharaja Gaj Singh was determined. It may be suggested that perhaps in relation to the local chiefs the old rates remained intact.

For the *zat* rank the term *khasa* has been used which has its own significance. This implies that *zat* rank was chiefly meant to provide the recipient with emoluments to maintain himself and his family, and the cost of his personal establishment. An important point revealed here is the salary shown against the *zat* rank. While comparing the pay scale of the *zat* rank of the time of Akbar,[11] we find that even in A.D.

1637 the rate of Akbar's period was still applicable in the case of Maharaja Gaj Singh. Thus, for both the ranks the pay scale of the time of Akbar was applied in respect to Maharaja Gaj Singh.

Rathor nobility and the Mughal Emperors

Mughal influence over Marwar considerably changed the character of the Marwar nobility. During the period of instability that followed the death of Maldeo the question of the right of succession of *tikayat* depended on the will of the Mughal Emperor. It has been stated earlier that excepting Chandra Sen, his two brothers and some prominent *sardars* of the Jaitawat and the Kumpawat clans had entered the imperial service and they were enjoying the *mansabs.* They were granted the *tankhawah jagirs* in Marwar in lieu of their salary which was to be paid against their respective *mansabs.* Under these circumstances their liability was shifted from the Rathor ruler to the Mughal Emperor who was more powerful than the former. The Mughal Emperor continued assigning of the *jagirs* to the Rathor *mansabdars* in various *parganas* of Marwar during the reigns of Udai Singh, Sur Singh, and Gaj Singh. When Jodhpur was granted to Mota Raja Udai Singh he was given only 14 *tappas*[12] out of 18 *tappas.* Out of the remaining four, two *tappas*—Asop and Bilada—were granted to Rathor Dhan Kumpawat and Rathor Badh Prithivirajot respectively and the remaining two were incorporated in the *khalisa.*[13] During the same period, Sojat remained in the *jagir* of Rathor Surtan Jaimalot.[14] From the *pargana* of Jaitaran 72 villages were given in *jagir* to Rathor Gopal Das (son of Ratan Singh) and to one of the sons of Rathor Kalyandas. The remaining part was assigned to Raja Udai Singh. But after his death these villages were again distributed amongst the sons of Udai Singh which remained under their control till 1604[15] when the *pargana* was assigned to Raja Sur Singh in *jagir.* As already mentioned, during the reign of Mota Raja Udai Singh, Phalodi remained under the control of Bhakharsi, son of Rawal Harraj of Jaisalmer, and Raja Rai Singh of Bikaner. In the beginning, the Mughal state retained the *pargana* of Merta in *khalisa.* In A.D. 1585 half of Merta was assigned to Rathor Surtan and half of it to Rathor Keshodas, son of Jaimal.[16] After the death of Surtan in A.D. 1596 his *jagir* in Merta was given to his son Rathor Balbhadar. Later on, in A.D. 1604 half of Merta was granted to Raja Sur Singh and the other half remained with the descendant of Jaimal.[17] During the time of Sur Singh, Sojat was granted to Rathor Karamsen Ugrasenot (the grandson of Rao Chandra Sen) for a year (A.D. 1607-08).[18] Rathor Surtan Jaimalot was granted Merta in *jagir*[19] in A.D. 1582. Being dissatisfied on the question of distribution of the villages, Rathor Narhardas (a *sardar* of Jaimal) joined the camp of Rathor Keshodas (son of Jaimal) and took him to the Mughal court. The Emperor restored Keshodas half of the *pargana* of Merta.[20] During the time of Gaj Singh, Prince Khurram, while he held Merta in *jagir* in A.D. 1621 (V.S. 1678), distributed the villages of Merta among the Rathor *sardars*.[21]

Thus, it may be asserted that since the time of the Mughal occupation of Marwar, the Rathor *sardars* were freely enlisted in the imperial service and they were granted *jagirs* in Marwar. Though it is difficult to say whether these *sardars* enjoyed the same privileges as enjoyed by the Rathor rulers, it is definite that they were directly responsible to the Emperor and had formed the second category of the *zamindars*.[22] There is no doubt that by 'creating a new class of allies' the Mughal Emperors reduced the power of the Rathor rulers and also the possibilities of their opposition. The Rathor rulers themselves had to depend on the mercy of the Mughal Emperor.

Administrative Organization

Before the recognition of Udai Singh as a ruler of Jodhpur, Emperor Akbar, apart from the assignment of the *parganas* in *jagirs* to the Rathor princes and *sardars*, held Jodhpur, Merta and Nagaur under his direct control (*khalisa*). A study of the *Pargana-ri-Vigat* and the *khyats* reveals that although the motive of keeping *khalisa* was mainly political, some important administrative reforms were implemented. Although there is evidence to show the existence of some kind of territorial units even before the advent of the Mughals in Marwar, these territorial units were vague and flexible depending upon the power and position of the Rathor rulers. It was between A.D. 1573 and A.D. 1583 that Emperor Akbar formed definite territorial divisions which were named as *pargana*. Each *pargana* was a separate administrative unit and its assessed revenue was shown against it. The *pargana* was divided into sub-units called *tappas* or *patti*.[23] Thus *pargana* Jodhpur was divided into 18 *tappas*, Merta into 9 *tappas* or *pattis* and Nagaur into 6 *tappas* (*pattis*).[24] In the year A.D. 1573 the area of *pargana* Merta was measured and its boundary was demarcated. The total area falling in the *pargana* was 26,12,958 *bighas* and the cultivable land was 23,96,415.3 *bighas*.[25] In the *pargana* Merta, a *karori* and a *qanungo* were appointed.[26] The introduction of these measures was significant in the context of the land revenue reforms of Akbar. In the year A.D. 1570-71 (15th Regnal year) Muzaffar Khan Tarbati with the help of Todarmal prepared a revised assessment of the land revenue based on estimates framed by the local *qanungo*.[27] It seems that the appointment of the *karori* (*amil*) and *qanungo* and the measurement of the area under cultivation and non-cultivable land were the direct attempts to implement the *zabt* system. Thus, as early as A.D. 1573 when Todarmal experimented his method of *bandobast* (*dehsala* system) in Gujarat, the same method was introduced in Merta also which was under the direct control of the Mughals. However, it is not known to what extent these methods were adopted in other *parganas* of Marwar. The accounts available for the *parganas* of Jodhpur and Nagaur suggest that Akbar had divided the *parganas* in *tappas* or *pattis*. These changes were made to provide more effective revenue and civil administration in the *parganas*.

Thus by the time Udai Singh ascended the throne, a framework of the Mughal administration had already been introduced in Marwar. In the absence of detailed information it is difficult to draw any conclusion about the administrative organization under Raja Udai Singh. On the basis of the references relating to the appointments of *pradhan*, *hakim*, etc., it may be said that attempts had been made to reorganize the administrative machinery. The period following his death was, however, significant from the administrative and political points of view as Maharaja Sur Singh evolved a system which was, to some extent, similar to the Mughal administrative organization.

During the reign of Maharaja Sur Singh (A.D. 1594-1619) Bhati Govind Das was appointed as *pradhan*. He had served in the imperial Court and had gained the favour of Raja Udai Singh. Being conversant with the imperial administration he used his experience in implementing the administrative reforms. Thus *diwan*, *hakim*, *potdar*, *waqia-nawis*, *khansama*, *bakhshi*, etc., were appointed. The descendants of Rao Rinmal, Rao Jodha, Rao Suja, Rao Maldeo and Udai Singh who were kept on equal footing, now became the *umrah*.[28] Their right of *kurab*[29] was fixed. At the court they were divided into two wings, called *davi* (left) and *zimani* (right). In the right wing were placed the descendants of Rinmal and the headship of the wing was bestowed upon the Champawats of Auwa. In the left wing were placed the descendants of Jodha and the headship of the wing was bestowed upon the Mertia of Raiya. *Khawas* and *paswan* were also appointed.[30]

These changes redueed the position of the Rathor *sardars* at the court. Formerly, the basis of relationship between the Rathor rulers and the nobility by tradition was family kinship. But now it changed into that of a ruler and his servants. Accordingly, Rathor *sardars* became the employees of the state and against their services they were paid the salary either in cash or in the form of a *patta*. Broadly speaking, a *patta* conferred on the grantee the right of collection of land revenue of the area granted.[31]

Nainsi mentions the details of a *patta* granted to Rathor Askaran Devidasot by Raja Udai Singh. Apart from granting him a *siropao* (robe of honour) and an elephant, he was also granted *piroji* 10,000 as cash. The villages granted to him in *patta* are shown in Table given on the next page.

The figures show that Askaran was given 34 villages amounting to *rekh* (assessed land revenue) Rs. 59,000 from Jodhpur *pargana* and 31 villages amounting to *rekh* Rs. 55,000 from Sojat *pargana*. The Jodhpur villages included in the *patta* were scattered over different *tappas*. It was not necessary that the grantee should be given *patta* villages at one place only. In the present case the assignments were made in two *parganas*, while in a *pargana* itself he was not being given all the villages in one *tappa*. This practice was adopted to prevent the *sardars* from consolidating their power. Askaran, the grantee, is mentioned as warrior and as a defender of the *desh* and was

Villages	*Tappa/Pargana*	*Rekh*[32] (*Rs.*)
11	Kherva/Jodhpur	16,400
1	Lewara/ -do-	1,700
5	Haveli/ -do-	8,400
10	Pipad/ -do-	20,500
5	Bahala/ -do-	9,500
2	Bilada/ -do-	2,500
31	Sojat ,,	55,600
65		1,14,600

in the state service.[33] This suggests that the above-mentioned *patta* was granted to him in lieu of his services to the state. An important point which needs clarification is the mention of *rekh* shown against every village. The term *rekh* denotes the amount of assessed land revenue of the village, but it is doubtful that during the time of Raja Udai Singh such assessment had been made. The amount of the *rekh* shown against these villages is the same as shown during Jaswant Singh's reign.[34] It seems that Nainsi, being aware of the *rekh* of each village of Marwar, has written the same figures which were prevailing during Jaswant Singh's reign against the above-mentioned villages.

The practice of assignment of the *pattas* continued during the time of Sur Singh and Gaj Singh. But the *pattas* granted in lieu of their services to the state were not permanent in nature. Villages or *jagirs* granted to them were transferable and were known as *cheda-untra-ra-gaon* under.[35] However, it would be wrong to presume that under such practice the old Rathor families had lost their claim over the areas to which they belonged. A study of the account of the holdings of some of the important (Rathor) sub-clans,[36] such as Kumpawats, Jaitawats, Jodhas, Mertias, etc., reveals that the ruler of Jodhpur did not dislodge them from their *thikanas*, though the areas controlled by them earlier were reduced considerably. Now the successor of a deceased *sardar* could hold one or more villages subject to the recognition by the state. Other areas were granted to him in *jagir* against his services. This problem would be discussed in detail in chapter 5.

Apart from these holdings, the Raja used to grant the *thikana* to the nobles as a reward or favour. Such grants were not transferable and remained with the successors of the grantee.[37] It is noteworthy that while keeping their *thikanas*, the Rathor *sardars* maintained their *jagirs* in various parts of the state or even outside the state.

The contemporary records show that the Rathor and other *sardars* who served in the imperial army obtained *jagirs* in Marwar from the Mughal Emperor and they were treated favourably. Thakur Gopaldas Mertia who had been serving in the Mughal army held Rampura (of Chandrawat clan) with a revenue of rupees three lacs. When he joined the service of Gaj Singh, he was granted Raiya (of the *pargana* of Merta) amounting to Rs. 28,200 *rekh* in A.D. 1630.[38] The example of Bhati Govinddas shows that even though he belonged to a non-Rathor clan, he enjoyed the highest post in the state. Earlier he held the imperial *mansab*. The Rathor *sardars* were welcomed in Jodhpur state after they left the service of a neighbouring state. In A.D. 1593 (V.S. 1650), Rawal Pattaji was given the *thikana* of Malani in *Bhomi-chara*[39] and he was also exempted from the payment of *rekh*.[40]

The reforms promulgated during the time of Sur Singh had as their object not only the reorganization of the nobility but also involved fiscal and administrative considerations. In the absence of detailed information, it is difficult to indicate the changes introduced during the time of Sur Singh and his successor Raja Gaj Singh, but it is clear that till the death of the latter a perceptible pattern of land revenue administration had emerged in Marwar with certain variations.

It has been noticed that during the time of Raja Udai Singh and for some time even in Maharaja Sur Singh's reign, Merta remained either in *khalisa* or in the *jagirs* of Mertia princes, descendants of Jaimal, Prince Khurram, and Prince Perwez.[41] From the account given by Nainsi we gather that during the period *kirori* (*amil*) and *qanungo* were appointed in the *pargana* of Merta. After the assignment of Merta to Sur Singh in A.D. 1604, the office of *amil* of the *pargana* was changed into that of the *hakim*, who was in charge of both civil and revenue administration of the *pargana*. The office of the *qanungo* and others remained the same. No details are available about the taxes and the rates of the cesses levied over and above the *mal* during the period mentioned above. But from the accounts of the time of Maharaja Jaswant Singh (A.D. 1638-1678) it appears that when the *pargana* of Merta was assigned to him the rates of agricultural and non-agricultural cesses had already been fixed.

Muhnot Nainsi, who had spent some time in the service of Gaj Singh and had also served as a *desh-diwan* under Jaswant Singh, has recorded the *amal-dastur* of Merta of the time of Jaswant Singh.[42] This *dastur* refers to the rates of agricultural and non-agricultural cesses prevailing during Gaj Singh's reign:

1. Rates of *ghasmari* (Grazing Tax)

Item	*Dogani*[43] *charged on each item*
1. Cow	5
2. *Berath* (calf)	4
3. She-goat, sheep	1
4. Buffalo	10
5. *Jhoutha* (Male Buffalo)	8
6. Camel	15

2. On the sale of *Kadebi* (fodder) of Rs. 100/- the state charges were Rs. 1.50.

3. *Zabt* (rates of cash crops)

Item	*Charges per bigha (Rs.)*
1. *Piyal Vani* (cotton produced in irrigated area)	1.38
2. Tarkari (vegetables)	1.38
3. *Van* (produced in unirrigated area)	0.25
4. *Kachera* (cucumber)	0.25
5. Opium	2.50

4. At the time of *kharif* harvest when the grain was collected in the *khaliyans*, the cultivators were under obligation to pay the following cesses:

Name of the cesses	*Charges levied on every Khaliyan (in Dogani)*
1. *Dawat Pooja* (Inkpot ceremony)	5
2. *Kagal Patha* (paper)	5
3. *Sut Agodi* (cotton)	5
4. *Fad Uthawani*	1
5. *Potdari*	1
6. *Khareda*	2

5. A tax called *bal* was charged from the village as a whole at the following rates:

Item	*Charges Rs.*
Smaller villages	20
Large villages	25

6. At the time of transfer of the *jagir* a tax named *tagir atbal* was levied. From a large village Rs. 60 were charged as a tax on the basis of its financial resources.

7. From the cess, known as *khichedi* the income was Rs. 600 to Rs. 700 per annum from Merta *pargana*.

The above-mentioned rates of taxes or cesses do not furnish adequate information to study the state land revenue and the other taxes and cesses levied by the state, though a rough idea can be formed about the system of land revenue. The existence of the cash rates on the production of cotton, vegetables, opium, etc., suggests that the *zabt* method of assessment was adopted in Merta.[44] From this it can be argued that for the cereal crops, the *batai* (crop sharing) must have been a widely accepted method of assessment. But the rate of the land revenue demand for the cereal crops has not been mentioned. The cultivators paid a cess to the state officials also who attended the *khaliyan* to determine the state share of the produce. The rates of this cess is given under various heads which shows that the officials were not free to fix the rates at their own discretion.

A study of these cesses and taxes suggests that in the *pargana* of Merta a tangible system of agricultural cesses was prevailing during the time of Raja Gaj Singh. In the absence of contemporary records it is difficult to state whether these rates were levied by the Mughal officers before the *pargana* was granted to Gaj Singh or these were fixed during his time. To what extent Gaj Singh might have tried to fix these rates in other *parganas* is a question which would be discussed later when we take up the period of his successor, Jaswant Singh.

APPENDIX 2:1

TABLE 1(a)

Raja Udai Singh (A.D. 1583-1595)

	Zat/Sawar
1. *Mansab* at the time of succession (A.D. 1585)[45]	1000/800
2. *Mansab* at the time of death (A.D. 1595)[46]	2500/2500

Pargana	*Year A.D.*	*Tappa/ Villages*	*Dams*	*Rs.*
1. Jodhpur	1583	14 Tappa	58,85,000	1,47,000
2. Siwana	1589	...	15,00,000	...
3. Sojat	1592	...	40,00,000	1,00,000
4. Satalmer-Pokaran	...	...	5,60,000	14,000
5. Jaitaran	...	140 villages	39,44,287	89,508
6. Kota Hadwalo	...	...	...	...
7. Champa Panjari (in Punjab)	...	...	...	...

Appendix 2:1 (Contd.)

TABLE 1(b)

Raja Sur Singh (A.D. 1595-1619)

	Zat/Sawar
1. *Mansab* at the time of succession (A.D. 1595)[47]	2000/2000
2. *Mansab* at the time of death (A.D. 1619)[48]	5000/5000

Pargana	*Year*	*Tappa/ Villages*	*Dams*	*Rs.*
1. Jodhpur	1595	18/1016	68,85,000	1,72,000
2. Sojat	1595	0/239	15,00,000	37,500
3. Siwana	1595	0/140	50,00,000	1,25,000
4. Phalodi	1615	0/62	27,00,000	67,500
5. Jalor	1617	0/421	1,15,10,827	2,62,771
6. Sanchor	1617/18	0/119	25,66,673	64,166
7. Merta	1604	110/381	80,00,000	2,00,000
8. Jaitaran	1604	0/140	29,40,297	98,507.48
9. Pokaran[49] (Satalmer)	...	0/1	5,60,000	14,000
10. Pisagan (Ajmer)	...	0/9	8,00,000	20,000
11. Sumel (Ajmer)	...	0/1	1,20,000	3,000
12. Telwaro (Merwaro Gujarat)	...	...	...	63,000
13. Village Naad (Ajmer)	...	...	64,000	800
14. Kuiralu (Gujarat)	1615	0/110	45,26,540	1,22,912.50
15. Badnagar (Gujarat)	1615	0/12	27,66,000	59,150
16. Ratlam (Malwa)	...	...	40,00,000	1,00,000
17. Three villages of Deccan	...	0/3	19,38,000	48,450

Appendix 2:1 (Contd)

TABLE 1(c)

Raja Gaj Singh (A.D. 1619-1638)

	Zat/Sawar
1. *Mansab* at the time of succession (A.D. 1619)[50]	3000/200
2. *Mansab* at the time of death (A.D. 1638)[51]	5000/500

Pargana	*Year*	*Tappa/Village*	*Rs.*
1. Jodhpur	1619	19/1039	1,99,125
2. Sojat	1619	4/239	1,25,000
3. Jaitaran	1619	3/140	98,506
4. Siwana	1619	5/140	37,500
5. Pokaran (Satalmer)	1619	...	15,000
6. Telwaro (Gujarat)	1619	...	63,389
7. Jalor	1620	7/421	2,62,771
8. Sanchore	1622	6/119	64,166
9. Phalodi	1622	8/62	67,500
10. Merta	1623	11/381	2,00,000
11. Jalgao-barad	1624	...	1,78,000

APPENDIX 2:2

Schedule of the Mansab of 5000/5000[52]

Dam	*Rs.*	*Asami*
1,32,00,000	3,30,000	For 5,000 *zat* (*khasa*) Rs. 30,000/ 12,00,000 *dams* of a month. (Rs. 3,36,000/-, 1,44,000 *dams* of a year). In a year the amount of a month was deducted for the name of *Ajnas*.[53] The amount of 11 months was Rs. 3,30,000/ 1,32,00,000 *dams*.
4,40,00,000	11,00,000	For 5,000 *sawars*, Rs. 20/800 *dams* per month for a *sawar*. For 5,000 *sawars* it comes to Rs. 1,00,000/ 40,00,000 *dams* for a month (Rs. 12,00,000/4,80,000 *dams* of a year). Out of 12 months the amount of a month was deducted as *Ajnas*. The amount of 11 months

Appendix 2:2 (Contd.)

Dam	*Rs.*	*Asami*
		would be 4,40,00,000 *dams*, i.e., Rs. 11,00,000.
5,72,00,000	14,30,000	Amount of 11 months for 5,000/5,000 was five crores 72 lacs *dams*/Rs. 14,30,000.
99,00,000	2,47,500	The amount for 11 months of the five thousand *zat* is Rs. 3,30,000. After deducting ¼th[54] (Rs. 82,500) the *talab* remained Rs. 2,47,500/99,00,000 *dams*.
4,40,00,000	11,00,000	Amount of 11 months for the five thousand *sawars*. It was made through jagirs.
5,39,00,000	13,47,400	*Talab*

Jagirs granted in lieu of the Salary[55]

Dam	*Rs.*	*Parganas*
1,89,65,297	4,75,132.40	Jodhpur
50,00,000	1,25,000	Sojat
39,40,297	98,507.44	Jaitaran
1,15,10,872	2,87,771.80	Jalor
5,60,000	14,000	Satalmer-Pokaran
1,00,00,000	2,50,000	Merta
77,16,085	1,92,902.17	Amount at his succession
22,83,915	57,097.93	Increment given in A.D. 1625/V.S. 1683
27,10,000	67,500	Phalodi
25,31,550	63,288.75	Telwara-Marwar
21,81,800	54,525	Telwara
3,50,550	8,763.75	Marwara
46,25,653	1,25,641.30	Jagir in Deccan continued
10,00,000	25,000	Sanctioned but not granted

Appendix 2:2 (*Contd.*)

Dam	*Rs.*	*Parganas*
		With effect from the *kharif* crop Gaj Singh was given the following parganas in Gujarat:
29,38,820	73,470.75	Badnagar, transferred from the *jagir* of Saiyed Yakut.
15,93,444	39,836.06	Sarkar Patan, transferred from Aziz Khan.

REFERENCES

[1]*Vigat*, i, 389; *Jodhpur-Khyat*, i, 93.

[2]e.g., Rathor Badh, son of Prithviraj, Rathor Bhopat, son of Devidas, Rathor Ram and Rathor Askaran were granted the villages, Bagadi, Katalio, Pipal and Mangalio respectively. *Rathora-ri-Vamshavali* (SC), 197-8.

[3]Although the Rana of Mewar was not in the active service of the Mughal Emperor, he held the imperial *mansab* and the *parganas* he enjoyed were assigned to him against his *mansab*.

[4]*Vigat*, ii, 7.

[5]*Ibid.*, ii, 105-6.

[6]There is a reference that the Rathor rulers came into conflict with the rulers of Sirohi, Jaisalmer and Kisangarh. But such incidents occurred when the Rathor rulers were asked to implement the imperial orders.

[6a]The Mughal *mansab* was dual, represented by two numbers, one designate *zat* (personal) and the other *sawar* (cavalry). Also see, infra. p. 29. For details, see, M. Athar Ali, *Mughal Nobility under Aurangzeb*, chapt. II.

[7]For details of the pay claim of *mansabdar* 5000/5000, see, Appendix No. 2 listed at the end of the chapter.

[8]*Jodhpur-Khyat*, i, 152-5; *Rathora-ri-Khyat* (S.S.) 54-5; *Juni-Bahi*, 55.

[9]The total pay claim of the *mansab* of 5000/5000 of Kunwar Karan was 5,39,00,000 *dams* per year or 52,00,000 *dams* per month. The amount of Rs. 30,000/12,00,000 *dams* per month is stated to be due on his *zat* rank. The balance of 40,00,000 *dams* per month remains for the pay of *sawar* rank. This was calculated at the rate of 9,600 *dams* per

sawar per annum. *Vir Vinod*, ii, 241. Also see, Irfan, "Mansab System", *P.I.H.C.*, 1961, p. 228.

[10]cf. Irfan Habib, "Mansab System", *op. cit* 230-4.

[11]*Ain*, i, 124; Also see, Abdul Aziz, *Mansabdari System*, 50.

[12]*Tappa*, a small tract or division of *pargana*; smaller than a *pargana* and comprising one or more villages.

[13]*Vigat*, i, 77.

[14]*Ibid.*, i, 389.

[15]*Vigat* i, 496; *Jodhpur-Khyat*, i, 97.

[16]*Vigat*, ii, 72.

[17]*Vigat*, ii, 73.

[18]*Ibid.*, i, 96. It was withdrawn from Raja Sur Singh for a year but later on in A.D. 1608 (V.S. 1665) it was again granted to him.

[19]*Ibid.*, ii, 69. In the same year Sojat was resumed from his *jagir*.

[20]*Ibid.*, ii, 69-70. Earlier he was granted Sojat in *jagir*.

[21]*Ibid.*, ii, 73.

[22]Prof. S. Nurul Hasan refers to the existence of this class. (*Agrarian Relations in Mughal India*, 37). In the case of the Rajput states of Rajasthan such *mansabdars* maintained the clan base in the territory where they were assigned the *jagirs*. But such *jagirs* were not treated as *watan jagirs*.

[23]In case of *pargana* Merta and Nagaur the term *Patti* has been used which is a synonym of *tappa*.

[24]*Vigat*, i, 129; ii, 77-8.

[25]*Ibid.*, ii, 77. For the terms, *Karori*, *Qanungo* and *Amil*, see *infra*. . . .

[26]*Ibid.*

[27]Moreland, *Agrarian System*, 86-7; 245-7; Irfan, *Agrarian System*, 203-5.

[28]*Basta* No. 43, *Bahi* No. 5, p. 5. *Jodhpur Records*. G.D. Sharma, "Some Land Revenue Grants of the time of Maharaja Ajit Singh and Abhai Singh", *P.I.H.C.* 1969, 288.

[29]*Kurab*, see, Glossary listed at the end of the chapters.

[30]*Basta* No. 43, *Bahi* No. 5, p. 5. *Jodhpur Records*; *Jodhpur-Khyat*, i, 140. It has been a matter of dispute among the modern writers, whether the division of the *sardars* in the court was made during the time of Jodha or after his death. It is said that these changes were introduced by Rao Jodha (*Vigat*, ii, Appendix 5, 456). But this is not acceptable as the clans by wnich the divisions, *Davi* and *Zimani* were made emerged only after the death of Rao Jodha. The persons after whose names the clans were identified lived during the time of Rao Maldeo.

[31]The term *patta* signifies a written document through which a specific right of land revenue, etc., was given to the grantee.

[32]See, Glossary.

[33]*Vigat*, i, 90.

[34]Cf., *Ibid.*, i, 260-1.

[35]*Basta* No. 202, Register No. 15, *Jodhpur Records*.

[36]*Basta* No. 60, Register No. 14, 15, 16, 18, 19, *Jodhpur Records*.

[37]*Vigat*, i, 66, 73-6. The term *thikana* implied for the hereditary holding of a *pattadar*. For the *thikana*, the holder was not obliged to pay any amount to the state as long as he was serving the state. *Basta* No. 202, *Jodhpur Records*, R.S.A.B.

[38]*Basta* No. 60, Reg. No. 14, 18; *Jodhpur Records*.

[39]It is a tenure enjoyed by those Rajputs whose ancestors held the land prior to the Rathor conquest. They paid a small sum of money to the *Darbar* as *Faujbal* or *Khichri lag*. *The Western Rajputana Residency and the Bikaner Agency Gazetteers*, pp. 145-6; *Report on Jodhpur Constitutional Reforms* (A.D. 1945) p. 49.

[40]*Basta* No. 60, Reg. No. 15, *Jodhpur Records*, R.S.A.B.

[41]*Vigat*, ii, 73-5. In A.D. 1604 half of Merta was granted to Raja Sur Singh in *jagir*. But after his death in A.D. 1619 it was resumed to *Khalisa* and later on granted to prince Khurram in *jagir*. In A.D. 1620 it was granted to prince Perwez.

[42]*Vigat*, ii, 88. The term *amal-dastur* is explained in chapter IV.

[43]*Dogani* was equivalent to 1 rupee.

[44]*Supra*. . . .

[45]*Vigat*, i, 76-7; *Hukumat-Bahi*, f. 2a; *Basta* No. 43, Register No. 5, p. 50, R.S.A.B.; *Servdes-ma-Rajvioni*, 129.

[46]*Vigat*, i, 77, 83; *Jodhpur-Khyat*, i, 108; *Hukumat-Bahi*, 15a-16b.

[47]*Rathora-ri-Vamshavali*, 99 (ORIJ); *Vigat*, i, 93; *Jodhpur-Khyat*, i, 112.

[48]*Vigat*, i, 93-7 and 400; *Jodhpur-Khyat*, i, 122-3 *Hukumat-Bahi*, f. 16a; *Basta* No. 43, *Bahi* No. 5, 65, *Jodhpur Records* (R.S.A.B.); *Rathora-ri-Vamshavali* (ORIJ); *Marwar-ra-Rathora-ri-Khyat* (S.S.), 33.

[49]In the *Vigat* the amount shown as a *Jama* of Pokaran is Rs. 5,65,000 (Vide, i, 93).

[50]*Jodhpur-Khyat*, i, 122, 150; *Mundiyara Khyat* (SC), 12.

[51]*Vigat*, i, 105-6; *Jodhpur-Khyat*, i, 150-1; *Hukumat-Bahi*, ff. 15a-16a; *Servdes-ma-Rajvioni*, 136.

[52]*Juni Bahi*, *Jodhpur Records* (R.S.A.B.) 44; *Jodhpur-Khyat*, i, 154-6.

[53]The term *Ajnas* (*ijnas*) implied for a deduction against which the Emperor presented horses to the nobles. This payment in kind was valued and deducted from the salary. For detail, *see*, Athar Ali, *Mughal Nobility*, 51.

[54]This deduction was known as '*Waza-i-dam-i-chauthai*'. This was established in time of Shahjahan. *Selected documents of Shahjahan's Reign*, 2, 18. For details, *see*, Athar Ali, *Mughal Nobility*, 50-1.

[55]*Juni Bahi* (R.S.A.B.) 44; *Jodhpur-Khyat*, i, 154-6.

3

MAHARAJA JASWANT SINGH AND THE MUGHAL PARAMOUNTCY (A.D. 1638-78)

For the first time in the history of the Rathor rule in Marwar a ruler, Jaswant Singh, succeeded to the throne when he was only eleven years old. It is all the more significant as he succeeded to the *gaddi* superseding his elder brother, Amar Singh, who already held the *mansab* of 3000/2000 at the time of his father's death.[1] The latter had taken part in several expeditions with the Mughal army. When Amar Singh was at Kabul with Prince Shuja, his father Maharaja Gaj Singh died at Agra on 6 May 1638. Although dislodged from the right to the *tika* of Jodhpur, Amar Singh's *mansab* was raised to 3000/3000 and he was given the title of *Rao*.[2] He was assigned the *parganas* of Nagaur, Shrigod, Mahedar, Barod, Chitrodi worth 11,25,000 *dams* in *jagir*.[3] It may be noted that apart from Nagaur, all the other *parganas* granted to Amar Singh were outside Marwar. The *zamindari* of Nagaur after his death remained with his son Rai Singh and later with Indra Singh (son of Rai Singh). The grant of Nagaur to Amar Singh and the right of *zamindari* created a problem for the rulers of Jodhpur since Amar Singh and his descendants tended to treat it as an independent appendage.

In the *Khyats* of Jodhpur and some Persian works various

versions are given for the nomination of Jaswant Singh to the *gaddi* of Jodhpur. According to the *Jodhpur-Khyat* prince Amar Singh was on bad terms with a favourite *khawasin* of Maharaja Gaj Singh, named Anara, who poisoned the ears of Gaj Singh against him. It is said, on the adivce of *khawasin* Anara, Gaj Singh made his choice in favour of Jaswant Singh.[4] The Bikaner *Khyats* mention that Prince Amar Singh had killed his brother-in-law, the Rao of Riya, after a verbal dispute. This incident annoyed the Maharaja.[5] In another version, prince Amar Singh is stated to have established intimacy with a princess of the Mughal royal family, which caused annoyance to Maharaja Gaj Singh.[6] However, the *Badshahnama* mentions that Maharaja Gaj Singh nominated Jaswant Singh as his successor because he was pleased with his mother.[7] The Mughal Emperor's decision in favour of Jaswant Singh and at the same time his action of granting the *pargana* of Nagaur to Amar Singh could serve the interests of the Mughal court in Marwar. As the conflict between the two was inevitable, the Mughal Emperor could have a discretion to extend his support to a person of his choice. The negation of the claim of Amar Singh, and at the same time the assignment of a *jagir* to him in Marwar, was similar to the policy adopted by Akbar in case of Rao Ram, the brother of Mota Raja Udai Singh. Thus, in the beginning of 1638, when Emperor Shahjahan visited the camp of Maharaja Gaj Singh, who was ill at Agra, to inquire about his health, the later requested the Emperor for the grant of the *gaddi* of Jodhpur to Jaswant Singh. The Emperor agreed but the Maharaja was told to win over the Marwar nobles to his side so that they might not raise any objection to the nomination of Jaswant Singh after the Maharaja's death. Accordingly, Maharaja Gaj Singh asked the Marwar *sardars* to remain loyal to Jaswant Singh failing which they would be punished by the Mughal Emperor.[8] That the Rathor *sardars* consented to it is borne out by the fact that after Jaswant Singh's succession no opposition was formed against him. Such an attitude of the Maharaja towards the Rathor *sardars* was possible in the existing circumstances. They had played an important role in deciding the question of succession in the past. But now change in their status had made them weak, particularly because the Mughal army could intervene at any time. Thus the succession of Jaswant Singh could not be opposed because he had been nominated by the Maharaja and the Emperor had agreed to it. It appears that the attitude of the favourite Rani (*khawasin*) played an important part in the nomination of Jaswant Singh by the Maharaja. The argument that it was due to the excitable temperament of Amar Singh is not tenable, though the chronicles do hint in this direction.[9] The choice of Jaswant Singh once again made it quite clear that succession to the throne depended on the Mughal Emperor, though consideration was given to the recommendation of the ruler.

State under Regency

As Jaswant Singh was only eleven years old at the time of succession[10] the Emperor appointed Rathor Raj Singh Khivawat as the *pradhan* to look after the administration and to maintain law and order in the state. The regent designate was of Kumpawat clan and was given a *mansab* of 1000/400.[11] Along with Rathor Raj Singh, the *padshah* bestowed earlier *siropao*[12] on Rathor Gordhan, Rathor Vithaldas, Rathor Jagat Singh, etc., who enjoyed high reputation among the Rathor nobility.[13] Rathor Raj Singh had worked as a *pradhan* during the reign of Gaj Singh. After the death of Raj Singh in A.D. 1640 Rathor Maheshdas Surajmalot was appointed *pradhan*. The appointment of Rathor Maheshdas as *pradhan* was again made by the Emperor, who also conferred upon him the *mansab* of 800/300.[14] In July 1643 Rathor Maheshdas was removed from the office of *pradhan*.[15] However, even after his dismissal Rathor Maheshdas continued to be in service in the Mughal court till A.D. 1657. He was granted Jalor in *jagir* which remained with him till A.D. 1655.[16] In place of Rathor Maheshdas, Maharaja Jaswant Singh appointed Rathor Gopaldas Sunderdasot of Mertia clan as *pradhan*.[17] Unlike his predecessors, Gopaldas did not hold any imperial *mansab* or *jagir* in Marwar. The removal of Rathor Maheshdas marked a significant change in the politics of Marwar. Since his succession to the *gaddi* of Jodhpur, most of the time Jaswant Singh remained out of Marwar.[18] It was only after his arrival at Jodhpur in A.D. 1640 that Maharaja Jaswant Singh made the change in the office of the *pradhan*. There is no evidence to show that the consent of the Mughal Emperor had been sought at the time of the appointment of Rathor Gopaldas. In the case of the earlier appointments, the *pradhans* were nominated by the Mughal Emperor and both of the earlier *pradhans* held the imperial *mansabs* as well as *jagirs* in Marwar. Apparently, in the absence of the Maharaja from Marwar and as he was minor, the administration of Marwar was fully under their control. Both Raj Singh and Maheshdas, being imperial *mansabdars*, remained in the court and they administered Jodhpur from there. It seems that Maharaja Jaswant Singh had realised the necessity of the presence of the *pradhan* in Marwar. But since his holding of the imperial *mansab* required his presence in the imperial court, Jaswant Singh felt that it was not in the interest of the state to appoint a person as *pradhan* who was holding an imperial *mansab*; moreover, such a person naturally had divided loyalties. Therefore, Jaswant Singh discontinued the practice and appointed a person of his choice.

Parganas	*Jama* (*Rupees*)
Jodhpur	3,43,000
Siwana	75,000
Merta	3,50,000
Sojat	1,50,000
Phalodi	67,500
Satalmer	14,000
	9,99,500

Relations with the Imperial Court and the Jagirs granted to Jaswant Singh

As has been stated earlier, the *jagirs* held by the Rathor rulers were assigned by the Mughal Court against their salary which was calculated on the basis of the *mansab* they held. On the contrary, the Rathor rulers had to fulfil their obligation to the Mughal Court.

At the time of his succession (A.D. 1638) Jaswant Singh held the *mansab* of 4000/4000 and the *parganas* gisted (on page 48) were given to him in *jagir*.[19]

In January 1639 an increment of one thousand *zat* and one thousand *sawar* was made in the *mansab* of Jaswant Singh which now stood at 5000/5000. The increment in *mansab* was made at the time of Emperor's birth ceremony.[20] In lieu of the increment he was given the *pargana* of Jaitaran amounting to one crore *dams*, i.e., Rs. 2,50,000. With the assignment of Jaitaran to him the total amount of the *jagirs* he held in Marwar amounted to Rs. 12,49,500.[21]

In April 1641 one thousand *sawar* were confirmed as *du-aspa sih-aspa*.[22] Later on in A.D. 1645 (*Jyeshtha sudi* 13, V.S. 1702) an increment of one thousand *sawar* was made.[23]

In A.D. 1646 (*Magha vadi* 11, V.S. 1703) another increment of 500 *sawar*, *du-aspa sih-aspa* was granted to Jaswant Singh when he was in Kabul.[24] For this (500 *sawar*) he was given 40,00,000 *dams* which were paid to him in cash. Thus his claim on cash payment rose to 78,00,000 *dams*.[25] In A.D. 1647 (*Chaitra Sudi* 7, 1704) 500 *sawar* were again granted. He was also granted *pargana* of Hindon in *jagir* worth 1,48,00,000 *dams*.[26] His total *mansab* had now reached 5000 *zat* and 5000 *sawar* out of which 2000 *sawars* were *du-aspa sih-aspa*.[27] The amount of total salary was raised to 7,40,00,000 *dams*.

Nainsi informs that with the addition of 1000/2000 *sawars* *du-aspa sih-aspa* in 1648 A.D. (V.S. 1705) his *mansab* was raised to 5000 *zat* and 5000 *sawar* out of which 5000 *sawar* were *du-aspa sih-aspa*.[28] It seems that the first increment was made on the eve of Jaswant Singh's departure for Marwar and the second when he reached Jodhpur. The amount of 2000 *sawar* was paid in cash.

In A.D. 1652 (*Phalguna sudi* 12, V.S. 1709) Jaswant Singh was given an increment of 1000 *zat*. Now his *mansab* stood at 6000 *zat* and 5000 *sawar* out of which 5000 *sawar* were *du-aspa sih-aspa*. The same year he was granted *pargana* Malarna of the *suba* of Ajmer in *jagir* worth Rs. 2,50,000.[29]

In A.D. 1654 (V.S. 1711) one thousand *sawar* were increased and the *mansab* of the Maharaja was raised to 6000 *zat* and 6000 *sawar*, out of which 5000 were *du-aspa sih-aspa*. The amount of total salary was 10,00,00,000 *dams*. Jaswant Singh was granted Badnor in *jagir* worth 90,00,000 *dams*. It was one of the *parganas* which had been confiscated by Shahjahan from Rana Raj Singh.[30] In A.D. 1656, Malarna was taken back by the Emperor and in its place *pargana* Jalor was granted to Jaswant Singh.[31] At the time of Maharaja Jaswant Singh's march to Malwa from Agra against Prince Aurangzeb and Prince Murad on 18 December 1657[32] he was given an increment of 1000 *zat* and 1000 *sawar* as a result of which his *mansab* rose to 7000 *zat* and 7000 *sawar*, out of which 5000 were *du-aspa sih-aspa*.[33] The total amount of the salary against the *mansab* was 11,00,00,000 *dams*.[34]

The details of the *mansab* salary are given below:

TABLE 3:1

Dams	*Rupees*	*Asami*
1,40,00,000	3,50,000	*zat*, seven thousand
9,60,00,000	24,00,000	*sawar*, twelve thousand[35]
11,00,00,000	27,50,000	*Talab*

The account of the *jagir* held by Jaswant Singh at the time of his departure for Ujjain in December 1657 is as follows:[36]

Dams	*Parganas*
1,47,25,000	Jodhpur; fourteen *tappas*.
8,00,000	Pokaran (Satalmer)
1,40,00,000	Merta
80,00,000	Sojat
80,00,000	Jaitaran
30,00,000	Siwana
1,15,00,000	Jalor
27,00,000	Phalodi
5,00,000	Gajsinghpura
6,32,25,000	

Table 3:1 (Contd.)

Dams	*Parganas*
87,80,000	(*dams*) were granted in *pargana* Rohtak and Sanchor but the Maharaja did not accept it.
35,00,000	(*dams*) were deducted in cash for the feeding (*khurakh*) of the horses and elephants.
3,44,95,000	(*dams*) remained in *talab* which was ordered to be paid in cash with effect from the *shravana* crop of V.S. 1716.
11,00,00,000	

The *Hukumat-Bahi* mentions that Maharaja Jaswant Singh was given an *izafa* (increment) of one crore *dams* at the time of his departure to Ujjain.[37] From the account of Nainsi it appears that against the said increment, the Maharaja was assigned the *parganas* of Ujjain worth 2,49,914 *dams*, Badnor worth 2,50,000 *dams*, Depalpur worth 1,82,000 *dams* and Nagaur worth 2,34,400 *dams*.[38] It seems that these *parganas* were granted to Maharaja Jaswant Singh against the increment of one crore *dams*. But the Maharaja never gained control over them because these were granted while he was about to leave for a campaign against Aurangzeb, and after his defeat the possession over these *parganas* was out of question. Aurgangzeb took these *parganas* after Jaswant Singh's arrival at Marwar from Dharmat on 19 April 1658.[39]

From the above it emerges that at the time of his succession Jaswant Singh was granted the *mansab* of 4000/4000 by Emperor Shahjahan which was raised to 7000/7000, of which 5000 were *du-aspa sih-aspa*, till A.D. 1657. The grant of the *mansab* of 4000/4000 was significant in itself as no other Rathor ruler before him had been given that rank at the time of succession.

Emperor Shahjahan conferred upon Jaswant Singh the *tika* of Jodhpur at Agra. Later, he proceeded to Delhi along with the Emperor on 18-19 August 1638.[40] Jaswant Singh remained with the Emperor at Peshawar during the latter's campaign against Persia.[41] It was only on 18 February 1640 that Jaswant Singh was given leave to proceed for Marwar.[42] Jaswant Singh reached Jodhpur in the month of April. As has been stated above, he had hardly stayed in Marwar for a year when he was asked to appear before the Emperor. Jaswant Singh appeared at the court on 18 March 1641. He was included in the army sent on the expedition against Qandhar under the command of Prince Dara. But due to the death of Shah Safi of Persia on 2 May 1641, the imperial army was withdrawn. Jaswant Singh started for Jodhpur on 20 June 1643.[43] When the Emperor set out for Lahore on 14 January, 1645, Jaswant Singh presented himself before the Emperor at Roopwas. The Emperor ordered him to look after Agra till the arrival of Shaikh Farid, *subadar* of Akbarabad, and then join the imperial court. Accordingly, Jaswant Singh, instead of accompanying the Emperor, stayed at Agra.[44] Later, following the order of the Emperor, Jaswant Singh reached Lahore and registered his presence before him on 25 October 1645. While staying at Lahore, Jaswant Singh was included in the army sent under the command of Prince Aurangzeb to regain control over Qandhar in February 1649. The imperial army failed to gain control over Qandhar and, consequently, had to be withdrawn in the end of 1649. Maharaja Jaswant Singh left Jahanabad for Marwar on 23 April 1650.[45] It seems that Maharaja Jaswant Singh stayed at Jodhpur till the Rathor army had secured its control over Pokaran in October 1650 and later remained at the court. This is proved by the fact that Jaswant Singh was given an increment of 1000 *zat* in 1652 and 1000 *sawar* in 1654 while staying at the court.[46] It is mentioned that Maharaja Jaswant Singh was granted leave to proceed to Jodhpur in 1655.[47] Later, in 1657, Jaswant Singh was given the command of the army which was sent against Aurangzeb and Murad.

The above-mentioned account makes it clear that during the reign of Shahjahan, Maharaja Jaswant Singh remained outside Marwar for thirteen years out of his total reign of 20 years. During this period he participated in all the imperial campaigns undertaken against the Shah of Persia. It is significant to note that almost every second year Jaswant Singh was granted an increment in his *mansab*. By the end of the year A.D. 1657 he had been assigned all the *parganas* of Marwar in *jagir*. In the year 1654, he was assigned the *pargana* of Badnor which was one of the *parganas* taken back from Rana Raj Singh of Mewar. All these references clearly indicate that during the time of Shahjahan, Jaswant Singh enjoyed the favour of Mughal Emperor, which put him on the top among the Rajput Rajas at the Mughal court.

Maharaja Jaswant Singh and the War of Succession

In the war of succession Jaswant Singh fought against Aurangzeb at Dharmat on 16 April 1658, and then left the field for Jodhpur.[48] After the defeat of Dara Shikoh, Aurangzeb sent a *farman* to Jaswant Singh in which the former instructed him to stay at Jodhpur and wait for further instructions.[49] On 16 August 1658 (*Bhadra vadi* 13, 1715) Jaswant Singh tendered his submission to Aurangzeb on the bank of the Sutlej.[50] The Emperor granted him five *parganas*, Narnol, Mathal, Rohtak, Maham and Athegaro in lieu of the *parganas* of Nagaur, Ujjain, Dipalpur, Badnor, etc., worth rupees one crore.[51] It has already been mentioned that Jaswant Singh had not secured his control over the latter five *parganas* and later on these were taken back by Aurangzeb. The new assignment in lieu of these *parganas* suggests that at that time Aurangzeb made no changes in the *mansab* of Jaswant Singh. But Jaswant Singh's action at Khajwa on 3 January 1659 (*Magha vadi* 5, 1715) strained his relations with the Emperor.[52] After having won the battle against Shuja, Aurangzeb dislodged Jaswant Singh from the *gaddi* of Jodhpur and granted the title of the Raja to Rai Singh, son of Amar Singh, on January 5-6, 1659 (*Magh vadi* 7-8, 1715).[53] He was granted the *parganas* of Jodhpur, Merta, Jaitaran, Sojat, Siwana and Phalodi.[54] *Pargana* of Pokaran was granted to Rawal Sabal Singh of Jaisalmer. *Pargana* of Badnor, which had been in the *jagir* of Jaswant Singh, was taken back and later granted to Rana Raj Singh.[55] Rai Singh accompanied by Amin Khan marched towards Jodhpur with an army of 12,000 *sawars*. They reached Harsuri, near Merta, in the beginning of February 1659 (*Phalguna vadi* 3, 1715). When the news of the arrival of the royal army reached Merta, Rathor Vithaldas, the *hakim* of Merta, ran away with his 1200 (or 1300) soldiers.[56] This change in the Mughal policy towards Marwar, the planting of another ruler, though belonging to the same ruling family, was mainly the result of Jaswant Singh's behaviour in the war against Shuja. The grant of Jodhpur along with other *parganas* of Marwar to Rai Singh and the appointment of Amin Khan as a commander of the imperial army sent against Jodhpur shows that Aurangzeb wanted to punish Jaswant Singh. Although at this time Aurangzeb had not so far decided to take the command of the Mughal army which was sent against Marwar, the development in the politics of Marwar made it necessary for him to be present in person over there.

Maharaja Jaswant Singh, after his arrival at Jodhpur, started preparations to meet the danger from the side of Aurangzeb. He started employing the soldiers on daily wages (*rozina*) and made new assignments to those who wanted *pattas*.[56] He also sent Muhnot Nainsi to Merta along with a huge army.[57] Jaswant Singh appears to have reached some understanding with Dara Shikoh, who was then staying in Gujarat.[58] Much has been written about Jaswant Singh's contact with Dara Shikoh.[59] Nainsi does not mention anything about the dealings of Jaswant Singh with Dara Shikoh prior to latter's arrival in Marwar.[60] *Hukumat-Bahi* mentions that when Dara Shikoh heard about the act of Jaswant Singh at Khajwa and the latter's arrival at Jodhpur, he collected 20 to 25 thousand horses and reached Dandiwada.[61] Although the accounts of the *Pargana-ri-Vigat* and the *Bahi* do not provide any information about the early correspondence between the two, the *Bahi* records that Dara Shikoh decided to come to Jodhpur after the breach between Jaswant Singh and Aurangzeb. Maharaja Jaswant Singh might have planned a combined resistance against the Mughal army which had been dispatched towards Jodhpur under the command of Amin Khan. Any way, it is not of much relevance to decide whether Jaswant Singh invited Dara or the latter requested him for help. It is a fact that both of them were facing danger from the side of Aurangzeb. For Jaswant Singh, any help from Dara could be appreciated, while Dara who was still waiting for the opportunity to defeat Aurangzeb, saw in it a favourable chance of obtaining the support from the Rajput rulers. It seems that Aurangzeb decided to march in person to Ajmer only when he became aware of the move of Dara towards Marwar.

The arrival of Aurangzeb at Ajmer along with a huge army consisting of all the prominent Rajput rulers compelled Jaswant Singh to reassess his position. Obviously Jaswant Singh was not in a position to face such a great challenge for a long time. All the three leading Rajput rulers, Jai Singh, Rana Raj Singh and Rawal Sabal Singh had been won over by Aurangzeb. Except the *Hukumat-Bahi*, all other contemporary Rajasthani accounts are silent on the response of Maharaja Jaswant Singh after the arrival of Dara in Marwar. The *Hukumat-Bahi* mentions that when Dara reached Sirohi, Rao Akheraj received him warmly.[62] Later, when Dara proceeded to Sojat and Merta, Muhata Askaran and Nainsi, the *hakims* of the *parganas* of Sojat and Merta respectively, visited his camp and presented *nazar* to him. Aurangzeb also reached Merta following the arrival of Dara over there.[63] As has been stated above, Jaswant Singh had started reassessing his position after the arrival of Aurangzeb in Marwar. Thus we see that when Sipah Shikoh, son of Dara, arrived at Jodhpur, Jaswant Singh did not respond to him properly.[64] As in spite of the repeated summons from the side of Dara, Jaswant Singh delayed his march from Jodhpur,[65] the former left Merta for Ajmer without waiting for the latter's arrival. It may be stated that Maharaja Jaswant Singh delayed his march to support Dara knowing the fact that Aurangzeb could attack Dara any moment. The delay from the side of Jaswant Singh made it clear that he was no longer inclined to help him.[66] Thus Dāra left Merta only when he became certain about the motive of Jaswant Singh.

As the change in Jaswant Singh's attitude towards Dara became clear only after the arrival of Aurangzeb at Ajmer, it left no alternative for the latter but to march against Aurangzeb. In fact Jaswant Singh could realise his position *vis-a-vis* Aurangzeb, particularly when the former could hardly get any help from any other Rajput rulers of the neighbouring states. He was also doubtful whether he would be able to put up resistance against the right of Mughal Emperor to grant the *gaddi* of Marwar to any other family member of the ruling clan. Earlier, Emperor Akbar had already ignored the succession of prince Ugrasen, son of Chandrasen, and had granted the *gaddi* of Jodhpur to Udai Singh. Being aware of these facts it would not have been a wise step for him to go in favour of Dara Shikoh. Maharaja Jaswant Singh had sent a letter through Asa Andholia to Jai Singh offering to arrive at a settlement with the Emperor.[67] Jai Singh approached Aurangzeb. After consultation, a *farman* with the signature of the Emperor, was issued according to which Jaswant Singh was given consolation.[68] Jai Singh had also written a letter to Jaswant Singh and had sent his man, Chaudhri Dungarsi, with Asa. He had advised Jaswant Singh through the letter that he should not support Dara and that he would be pardoned and his *mansab* would be restored. He was also asked to proceed towards Jodhpur.[69] As soon as he received the royal *farman*, also containing an order to send his son for service in Deccan, the Maharaja accepted the advice of Mirza Raja Jai Singh and sent his reply through Latter's messenger.[70]

The above description shows that through the mediation of Jai Singh, cordiality was restored between Jaswant Singh and Aurangzeb. Jaswant Singh was restored his former *mansab*. He was assigned all those *parganas* of Marwar which he held earlier and was appointed *subadar* of *Gujarat*.[71] After his defeat at Deorai,[72] Dara again approached Jaswant Singh but he refused to help him and asked him not to come to Jodhpur.[73]

Although old *mansab* of Jaswant Singh was restored, it was made clear that the local ruler had no power to resist against a powerful Emperor. It would be wrong to presume that the combined forces of Jaswant Singh and Dara would have achieved success against Aurangzeb.[74] As already noted, Aurangzeb had not only won over the rulers of neighbouring states in his favour, but had also weakened Jaswant Singh's position internally by the bestowal of the *gaddi* of Jodhpur to Rai Singh and this had rendered his (Jaswant Singh's) position difficult. A defeated ruler of the Rathor clan could hardly have enjoyed any sympathy from the majority of the Rathor *sardars*,[75] while there could be no major objection against the appointment of Rai Singh, for it was not the first time when the *tika* of Jodhpur was being conferred upon a person of the same family dislodging the right of the earlier. Under such circumstances the request of Jaswant Singh for submission before Aurangzeb was quite apt and was a result of his foresightedness.

In A.D. 1660 (*Bhadra sudi* 4, 1717) an increment of one crore of *dams* was made in favour of Jaswant Singh while he was holding the *subadari* of Gujarat. After the increment, the account of salary stands as below:[76]

Dams	*Rupees*	*Asami*
1,40,00,000	3,50,000	*Zat*, seven thousand
9,60,00,000	24,00,000	*Sawar*, seven thousand out of which five thousand *du-aspa sih-aspa*.
1,00,00,000	2,50,000	Increment made in V.S. 1717, *Bhadra Sudi* 4.
12,00,00,000	30,00,000	Total

In A.D. 1661 (*Margasira vadi* 8, 1718) *suba* Gujarat was resumed from Jaswant Singh and it was given to Nawab Mahabat Khan. Jaswant Singh was asked to proceed to the Deccan.[77] After the removal of Jaswant Singh from Gujarat, his *jagir* from that *suba* was taken back and he was granted another *jagir* in the *parganas* of Bahalgaon, Babal and Hissar.[78] Apparently Maharaja Jaswant Singh was granted the *parganas* of Hansi and Hissar in *jagir* while he was posted in the Deccan. It is noteworthy that these two *parganas* were given to him in absentia.

In A.D. 1667 when Jaswant Singh was again sent to the Deccan with prince Muazzam, he was granted two *parganas*, Thirad and Radhanpur, from the *suba* of Gujarat.[79] Jaswant Singh sent Miyan Farasat to secure his control over these *parganas*, but due to the protest of the local officials their possession could not be secured. Later on, in A.D. 1670 for the second time Jaswant Singh was appointed the *subadar* of Gujarat. He was then given 28 *parganas* of Gujarat in *jagir* including Patan, Viramgaon, Patlad, etc.[80] However, no details are available about the *jagirs* he held in Gujarat during his second tenure.[81] Still the references available show that there was no change in his *mansab*.

While he was staying in Gujarat a *farman* dated September-October 1673 was issued to Jaswant Singh in which he was asked to proceed to Kabul, where he was to serve as *thanadar* at Jamrud.[82] He had to comply with the order promptly and while passing through Marwar he did not even visit Jodhpur. He was posted to Jamrud to check the aggressive activities of the Pathans. There he died on 28 November 1678 (*Pausha vadi* 10, V.S. 1735). At the time of his death he held the *mansab* of 7000/7000 out of which five thousand were *du-aspa sih-aspa*. His *talab* was of 13,00,00,000 *dams*, out of which one crore *dams* were given to him for the *rasad*.[83] This leads us to the conclusion that his *talab* against the *mansab* was 11,00,00,000 *dams*, while one crore *dams* were given to him as an increment at the time of departure to Jamrud. The account of his *jagir* has been given in Table 3:2 on page 59.[84]

After the resumption of his *jagir* in Gujarat, Jaswant Singh was granted *pargana* Moham, etc., in *jagir* in *suba* Jahanabad. He was also granted Sanchor for the first time in his *jagir* held in Marwar. It seems that Sanchor was granted to him when he was asked to go to Jamrud.

The details given above show that even after the accession of Aurangzeb, Jaswant Singh continued enjoying a respectable *mansab* till his death. When Maharaja Jaswant Singh was sent to the Deccan to help Shaista Khan, he was given an increment of one crore of *dams*. Although Jaswant Singh failed to achieve success against Shivaji and was consequently removed from the Deccan,[87] his *mansab* remained the same. Even the amount of one crore *dams* which was given to him as an increment continued to be paid afterwards. After his arrival from Deccan,[88] Jaswant Singh was deputed in the army sent against Shah Abbas under the command of Muhammad Muazzam.[89] Maharaja Jaswant Singh returned to the court in March 1667.[90] In the same month Jaswant Singh was again sent to the Deccan along with prince Muazzam.[91] Later, in 1670 he was appointed *subadar* of Gujarat where he remained till 1673. While serving in Gujarat, Jaswant Singh was appointed to Jamrud in 1673.[92] As has been said, following the order he left Ahmedabad and reached Jamrud without any delay.

While serving at Jamrud as noted earlier, Jaswant Singh died on 28 November 1678 at Peshawar.[93]

A study of the appointments of Jaswant Singh would show that during the reign of Aurangzeb, he remained out of Marwar. But this was nothing new as far as the Rajput rulers were concerned.[94] The only significant fact is his appointment to Jamrud as a *thanadar*. It is generally argued that the motive behind this assignment was to keep him out of the court politics. Even if this point is conceded, no conclusion can be drawn which can prove that Aurangzeb wanted to take revenge on Jaswant Singh. In fact the appointment to the *thana* of Jamrud was very significant as it carried the responsibility of defending the territory against the invasion from Iran.

TABLE 3:2

Jagirs held by Jaswant Singh at the time of his death

1,55,25,000	Jodhpur, etc. (*Mahal*) (*dams*)	Jodhpur *Sarkar*.
	60,00,000	Haveli
	25,00,000	Peepad
	15,00,000	Asop
	12,00,000	Mahewa
	10,00,000	Bhadrajun
	8,00,000	Satalmer
	6,00,000	Welado (Balado)
	4,00,000	Pali, etc.
	3,00,000	Kheevser
	3,00,000	Dunado
	2,00,000	Gudoch
	75,000	Kodeno
	50,000	Idawati
	1,55,25,000	

3,56,80,000	*Pargana* Jalor, etc.	Jodhpur *Sarkar*.[85]
	1,15,00,000	Jalor
	80,00,000	Jaitaran
	80,00,000	Sojat
	30,00,000	Siwano
	27,00,000	Phalodi
	24,00,000	Sanchor
	3,56,80,000	

Table 3:2 (Contd.)

2,05,47,731	*Pargana* Merta, etc. *dams*	Nagaur *Sarkar*.
	1,40,00,000	Merta
	60,47,731	Amarsar
	5,00,000	Gajsinghpura
	2,05,47,731	
64,06,683	*Pargana* Parbatsar, etc.	Ajmer *Sarkar*.
	20,56,200	Parbatsar
	16,14,131	Banbal
	15,36,352	Tosino
	12,00,000	Balalo Jawala[86]
	64,06,683	
24,70,000	*Pargana* Poolio	Chittor *Sarkar*.
7,20,000		
8,13,49,414		
3,24,76,065	*Pargana* Moham etc.	*Suba* Jahanabad
11,38,25,478		
61,74,522	*Talab* remained	
12,00,00,000		

From the above it is apparent that at the time of his succession, Jaswant Singh was granted six *parganas* out of eight *parganas* of Marwar. Remaining two *parganas*, namely, Jalor and Sanchor, were taken back by the Emperor. These two *parganas* were granted to the Rathor *sardars*, Maheshdas and Rathor Bala respectively, who held the imperial *mansab*.[95] It may be observed that Jaswant Singh was not given any *jagir* outside Marwar either. It seems that the only reason behind the assignment of the *jagir* in Marwar was the minority of Jaswant Singh. As we have seen, the Mughal Emperor never assigned all the *parganas* of Marwar to any of the Rathor rulers at the time of succession. Therefore, the taking back of the *parganas* in Marwar after the death of Gaj Singh may be said to be a continuation of the old policy towards the ruler of Jodhpur.

As mentioned earlier, the assignment of the *jagir* within and outside Marwar was determined on the basis of *mansab*, as per rule obtaining at the Mughal court. Obviously, under that rule only that amount was given through the assignment of *jagir* to which the Raja had due claim against his salary which was determined against the *mansab* he held. The *jagir* given to the succeeding ruler shows that being recognised as a successor to the *gaddi* of Jodhpur by the Mughal Emperor, the right to maintain his control over the throne (*takhat*) of Jodhpur[96] as well as the area which had been under the Rathor rule was accepted in principle. Here some points deserve consideration. Being recognised for the *tikayat* by the Emperor, Jodhpur always remained in *jagir* of the Rathor ruler, but in general practice the ruler was never granted all the *tappas* of the *pargana* of Jodhpur.[97] Secondly, it was not obligatory on the part of the Mughal Emperor to assign all the *parganas* of Marwar to the ruler of Jodhpur. Any *pargana* excepting Jodhpur could be granted to any *mansabdar* whether Rajput or Muslim. While doing so a favourable attitude was adopted towards the ruler of Jodhpur. But, once a territory within Jadhpur state was granted to another Rajput ruler, the claim of the Rathor ruler over that area would diminish.[98] At the same time no protest was made when a *pargana* of Marwar was taken in the *khalisa*.[99] The assignment of *jagir* in Marwar to the ruler of Jodhpur was for the benefit of both the parties. For a *mansabdar* who was an outsider it was difficult to maintain law and order, because, generally, the local ruler would seldom support such an assignment. At the same time it was very difficult to change the attitude of the local clan leaders who mostly remained loyal towards their clan ruler.[100] For the Rathor ruler to maintain law and order in his *jagir* within Marwar was no problem as he was the hereditary ruler. The Mughal Emperor continued his influence in deciding the territory to be held by the Rathor king in Marwar. Thus even after the assignment of a *pargana* to the Rathor ruler it was not necessary that he would be assigned all the villages of that *pargana*. It has been observed that the Emperor used to assign the villages (or *tappas*) to the Rathor *mansabdars*, according to his will. Thus it can be said that although the Mughal Emperor was considerate in granting the *parganas* of Marwar on which the Rathor ruler held his hereditary claim, it was at his discretion

TABLE 3:3

Details of Mansab, Salary and Jagir etc. granted to Maharaja Jaswant Singh[101]

Year	*Mansab*	*Salary (dams)*	*Jagir in Marwar*	*Jagir outside Marwar*	*Talab*
1638	4000/4000	4,00,00,000	3,99,80,000	—	
1640	5000/5000	5,00,00,000	4,99,80,000	—	
1645	5000/6000 (1000 × 2-3) or 5000/5000	6,60,00,000	5,05,00,000	1,17,00,000	38,00,000
1646	5000/5000 (2500 × 2-3)	7,00,00,000	5,05,00,000	1,17,00,000	78,00,000
1647	5000/5000 (3000 × 2-3)	7,40,00,000	5,05,00,000	2,65,00,000	30,00,000
1648	5000/5000 (5000 × 2-3)	9,00,00,000	5,05,00,000	2,23,00,000	1,72,00,000
1652	6000/5000 (5000 × 2-3)	9,20,00,000	5,05,00,000	2,33,00,000	1,82,00,000
1654	6000/6000 (5000 × 2-3)	10,00,00,000	5,05,00,000	4,12,00,000	82,00,000
1655	-do-	10,00,00,000	6,20,00,000	3,23,00,000	57,00,000
1657	7000/7000 (5000 × 2-3)	11,00,00,000	6,32,25,000	1,22,80,000	3,44,95,000
1659	-do-	11,00,00,000	6,32,25,000	4,33,35,000	34,40,000
1660	-do-	11,00,00,000 + 1,00,00,000	6,32,25,000 (*Izafa*)	5,34,09,000	33,66,000

Table 3:3 (Contd.)

Year	*Mansab*	*Salary (dams)*	*Jagir in Marwar*	*Jagir outside Marwar*	*Talab*
1663	-do-	12,00,00,000	6,32,25,000	5,39,82,573	28,35,427
1674	-do-	13,00,00,000	7,17,52,731	4,20,72,747	61,74,522

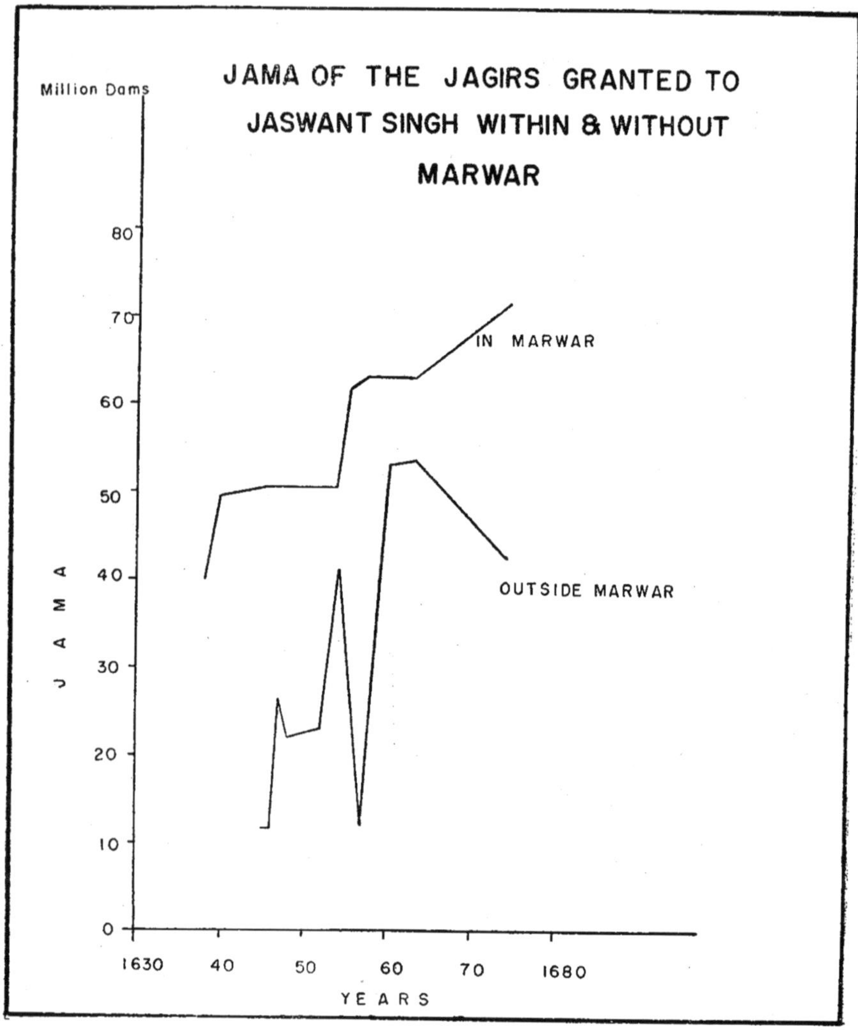
JAMA OF THE JAGIRS GRANTED TO JASWANT SINGH WITHIN & WITHOUT MARWAR
Million Dams
JAMA
80
70
60
50
40
30
20
10
0
IN MARWAR
OUTSIDE MARWAR
1630
40
50
60
70
1680
YEARS

to take the decision in this regard. It is difficult to assess the criteria on the basis of which the Rathor ruler could claim his hereditary rights over the various *parganas* of Marwar. It may be noted that Nainsi has recorded the account of seven *parganas* of Marwar, where Maharaja Jaswant Singh enjoyed the right of independent assessment of the land revenue. A study of these seven *parganas*, Jodhpur, Sojat, Jaitaran, Phalodi, Merta, Siwana and Pokaran, reveals that these areas were conquered by Rao Jodha. Later, Rao Maldeo proclaimed his right over them.

To understand the ratio of the amount of salary and the payment made through the assignment of *jagirs*, it would be necessary to show the amount granted to Jaswant Singh in and outside Marwar from the time of his succession to his death. The details are given in table 3.3 on page 62-63.

The figures of the amount of *jagirs* are shown in the graph appended after table 3.3.

A study of the table and the curves shown on the graph indicates that the amount of the *jagirs* granted in Marwar increased from about 3.99 to 5.05 crore *dams* between 1638 and A.D. 1645. The amount increased from 5.05 to 6.2 crore *dams* in A.D. 1655 whereas in 1657 the amount increased from 6.2 to 6.32 crore *dams* which later remained static between 1657 and 1663. In 1674 the amount rose from 6.32 crore to 7.17 crore *dams* . In relation to the amount granted outside Marwar, it is seen that the amount was increased from 1.17 to 4.12 crore *dams* between 1645 and 1654. The period ranging from 1655 to 1678 indicates that there was a continuous fluctuation in the amount granted to Jaswant Singh outside Marwar (the amount figured between 1.17 to 5.39 crore *dams*). This account clearly indicates that while the amount of *jagirs* granted in Marwar was never lowered, the amount granted outside Marwar fluctuated between 1.17 crores and 5.39 crores of *dams*. A study of the table will further reveal that the ratio of the *jagirs* granted within and outside Marwar was varying from year to year. In 1657 this ratio was approximately 6:1 while in the year 1660 and 1663 this was of the order of 6:5. The reason is quite apparent as we find that due to the war of succession, the *jagir* granted to Jaswant Singh remained out of his control. In 1659, when Jaswant Singh was assigned *jagirs* in Gujarat, the amount of the *jagir* granted outside Marwar was raised from 1.2 to 4.3 crores. Later, the amount granted outside Marwar remained between 4.2 and 5.39 crores. This was a significant increase as we find that this amount was higher than the amount granted to Jaswant Singh during the time of Shahjahan. Similarly, there was an increase from 6.32 to 7.17 crores in the amount granted in Marwar. This indicates that Aurangzeb did not adopt any rigid attitude towards Jaswant Singh as far as the assignment of the *jagirs* was concerned.

From the above it is quite clear that the amount of the *jagirs* granted outside Marwar always remained lower in comparison to the amount granted within Marwar, though the policy was not to hold back the assignment of the *jagirs* outside Marwar till the assignment of all the *parganas* of Marwar was complete. It seems that by adopting such a practice, the Mughal Emperors wanted to keep the rulers of Marwar aware of their subordinate position. This also limited the claim of the *watan* rights of the Rathor rulers in Marwar.

It seems that the logic behind granting *jagirs* to the Jodhpur rulers outside Marwar was to keep them in the rank of the other Mughal *mansabdars* whose *jagirs* were transferred after three to five years or even earlier or later, and who had no claim of *watan jagir*. For them these *jagirs* were transferable. As soon as the official assignment of *subadari*, etc., was withdrawn the *jagirs* of a *mansabdar* were also taken back and granted to some one else. But it is to be noted that when Jaswant Singh was posted at Jamrud he was granted *jagirs* in Shahjahanabad, Ajmer, and Hissar. On the other hand, while making all these changes in the *jagirs* granted outside Marwar, the assignments of the Maharaja within Marwar were hardly affected.

The withdrawal and the assignment of the new *jagirs* outside Marwar had hardly affected the claim of salary by the Raja. As soon as the order of the grant of a *jagir* outside Marwar was received, the Raja sent a *hakim* who took over the charge and looked after the administration of the area on behalf of the Raja. No evidence is available which could show that apart from *hakim* any other official was appointed by the Raja in his *jagirs* granted to him outside Marwar. The *Hukumat-Bahi* mentions that the *pattas* were granted to the Marwar *sardars* by the Raja in his *jagir* held outside Marwar.[102] This suggests that these *sardars* were appointed there to serve under the *hakim* and each of them maintained his own contingent. They were granted the *pattas* in lieu of their salary,[103] but as soon as the *jagir* of the Raja was transferred their *pattas* were withdrawn simultaneously. As these assignments were purely temporary, the local administration of such *patta* villages or *parganas* or *jagirs* were not affected by such changes. It seems that the functions of the local official and other agents remained the same, and only the *jagirdar* was changed. Thus the *jagirs* granted outside Marwar were purely of a temporary nature. But the *jagirs* granted to the Raja in Marwar remained with him till his death. Once the *jagirs* were granted to the Raja, the withdrawal of any of them was treated as a punishment by the Mughal Emperor, while, at the same time, continuous efforts were made by the Raja to regain his control over all the *parganas* of Marwar. Within Marwar the Mughal Emperor enjoyed the right to reduce the sanctioned revenue of a *jagir* without taking back the full *pargana* and the balance could be granted in different *parganas*.

In the pay schedules of Jaswant Singh no reference is available about any deduction out of the salary of the Raja in the name of *khurakh-i-dawwab* (fodder for animals) though the reference to such a deduction is made in relation to Maharaja Gaj Singh. This suggests that during the time of Jaswant Singh, particularly during the latter half of his reign, such practice might have been given up. This can be supported by the fact that in the 46th Regnal year of Aurangzeb's reign, the Emperor consented to the abolition of this system in respect of the *khurakh* for elephants.[104]

The service obligations of the Rathor ruler towards the Mughal Emperor seem to be similar to that of other imperial *mansabdars*. As the Appendix attached at the end of the chapter shows, Jaswant Singh maintained 3,000 *sawar* at the time of his campaign against Aurangzeb. Being the holder of the rank of 7000/7000, out of which 5000 were *du-aspa sih-aspa* (12000 *sawar*), according to the rule of one-fourth, he was obliged to keep the same number of *sawar* as he brought along with him in the field.[105] The same rule was also applied

TABLE 3:4

Increase in the Jagirs of the Marwar rulers (Mota Raja Udai Singh to Jaswant Singh)[106]

Parganas	Udai Singh (*dams*)	Sur Singh (*dams*)	Gaj Singh (*dams*)	JASWANT SINGH (*dams*)		
				(*dams*)	*Asal* (*dams*)	*Izafa* (*dams*)
Jodhpur	58,85,000	58,85,000	1,02,55,000	1,47,25,000	58,85,000	88,40,000
Sojat	40,00,000	40,00,000	60,00,000	80,00,000	40,00,000	40,00,000
Jaitaran	39,40,297	39,40,297	50,00,000	80,00,000	39,40,297	50,59,703
Siwana	15,00,000	15,00,000	25,00,000	30,00,000	15,00,000	15,00,000
Pokaran	5,60,000	5,60,000	5,60,000	8,00,000	5,60,000	2,40,000
Jalor	—	1,15,10,827	1,15,10,827	1,15,00,000	1,15,10,827	10,827
Sanchor	—	25,66,673	25,66,673	24,80,000	25,66,673	86,673
Merta	—	80,00,000	1,20,00,000	1,40,00,000	1,20,00,000	20,00,000
Phalodi	—	27,00,000	27,00,000	27,00,000	27,00,000	—

to other *mansabdars*. Thus it may be inferred that for all practical purposes there was no difference in relation to service obligations of a Rajput ruler.

Working of the Jagir Assignments against the Salary of the Raja

The above-mentioned account enables us to explain the nature of the *jagirs* granted to Jaswant Singh against his salary calculated according to the *mansab* he held. It has also been noticed that the *mansab* of Jaswant Singh was increased 14 times since he succeeded to the *gaddi* of Marwar. The statistics given in the tables 3:4 and 3:5 enable us to examine the nature of the increases of the amount in all the *parganas* of Marwar.

Table 3:4 gives the details of the assignments with subsequent increments from A.D. 1583 to A.D. 1678. Table 3.5 giving the revenue index calculated with base year A.D. 1583 as Rs. 100 shows an increase in the *jama* figures in all the *parganas* with the maximum rise in Jodhpur and minimum in Pokaran (excluding Jalor, Sonchor, Merta and Phalodi which were not held by Udai Singh).

TABLE 3:5

Index of the Jama on A.D. 1678 (with base year A.D. 1583 as Rs. 100)

Parganas	Revenue index year A.D. 1678
Jodhpur	250.21
Sojat	200.00
Jaitaran	203.03
Siwana	200.00
Pokaran	142.85
Jalor	99.90
Sonchor	96.62
Merta	116.66
Phalodi	100.00

The above tables (Nos. 3:4, 3:5) show an increase in the *jama* figures in all the *parganas* with maximum rise in Jodhpur and minimum in Pokaran. However no contemporary record gives a definite reason for the increase in the *jama* figures in Marwar, although on the basis of stray references some possible reasons can be put forward. It may be noted that the Mughal Emperors never assigned all the villages of a *pargana* to the Rathor rulers. They kept some villages or *tappas* either in *Khalisa* or granted them to the Marwar *sardars* who held an imperial *mansab*. Thus, Maharaja Udai Singh was granted only 14 out of 20 *tappas* of the *parganas* of Jodhpur and Maharaja Jaswant Singh 19 out of 20 *tappas*. In relation to the *pargana* of Jaitaran, Udai Singh was granted 65 villages while the remaining 82 villages were assigned to Udawat Gopaldas. Under this practice, whenever there was an addition in the number of villages granted to the Raja, *jama* figures increased automatically. The assignment of the villages in a *pargana* was considered in relation to the salary of the Maharaja. Thus the apparent reason of the increase in the *jama* was the assignment of the additional villages to the Rathor rulers.

Besides the assignment of the additional villages, fell out of the control of the Raja, which raised the *jama* of the *pargana*, the increase in the revenue was also responsible to fix the high *jama* figures. In reference to *pargana* Jaitaran, Nainsi records that the said *pargana* was granted to Maharaja Gaj Singh for Rs. 1,25,000. Later, during the time of Jaswant Singh, the Rawal of Jaisalmer requested the Emperor that he could accept Jaitaran in *jagir* at Rs. 2,50,000 (*jama*). Maharaja Jaswant Singh pleaded that Jaitaran should be assigned to him in *jagir* because it had been in the *jagir* of Maharaja Gaj Singh earlier. Consequently, Jaitaran was assigned to Jaswant Singh in *jagir* for Rs. 2,50,000 or 1,00,00,000 *dams*. In A.D. 1654 (V.S. 1711) Rs. 50,000 were reduced and Jaitaran remained with Jaswant Singh for Rs. 2,00,000 or 80,00,000 *dams*.[107]

In relation to *pargana* Merta, Nainsi gives a similar account. Merta was granted to Maharaja Sur Singh for Rs. 2,00,000. When *pargana* Merta was granted to Maharaja Gaj Singh its *jama* was raised to Rs. 3,00,000,[108] although it was made clear that the revenue of *pargana* Merta was Rs. 4,00,000.[109] Later, Merta was granted to Maharaja Jaswant Singh for Rs. 3,50,000.[110] A study of these two *parganas* makes it clear that the amount of these *parganas* was raised with the consideration that the *hasil* was higher than *jama*. Apart from these two factors, i.e., assignment of additional villages and higher realizations to *jama*, there were others, *viz.*, the extension of the area under cultivation, enhancement in the price of commodities due to expanding trade and commerce, the increase in the number of *mansabs* as well as *mansabdars* resulting in fictitious increase in the *jama* figures, could have influenced the increase in *jama*.

APPENDIX 3:1

Pancholi Manohardas, who was staying in the court, sent the following details of the *tankhwah* (salary) and the *jagir* of Jaswant Singh in the month of *phalgun* V.S. 1720 (A.D. 1663) of the revenue commencing with *rabi* crop of V.S. 1720.*

Tankhwah (Salary)

Dams	*Rs.*	*Asami*
11,00,00,000	27,50,000	Seven thousand *zat* and seven thousand *sawar* out of which five thousand were *du-aspa sih-aspa* and 2,000 *barawurdi, ek-aspii.*@ 1,40,00,000 seven thousand *zat* 9,60,00,000 *Tawindar.*** The payment was made 8,00,000 *dams* on 1,000 *sawar.*
1,00,00,0000	2,50,000	*Inam*
12,00,00,000	30,00,000	

Account of the Jagir

Dams	*Rs.*	*Asami*
6,32,25,000	*pargana* Jodhpur, etc., *suba* Ajmer	
	4,87,25,000	*Sarkar* Jodhpur, 16 *tappas* including Jodhpur.
	60,00,000	Haweli
	25,00,000	Pipad
	15,00,000	Asop

**Vigat*, i, 153. In *Jodhpur-Khyat* the assignment of the jagir of Hansi is mentioned (i, 231).

@The term *barawurdi* has been used for *ek-aspa* which implied that these terms were interchangeable.

***Tabinan-i-barawurdi*—contingent or troopers.

Appendix 3:1 (Contd.)

Dams	*Rs.*	*Asami*
	10,00,000	Bhadrajun
	12,00,000	Mahewa
	8,00,000	Satalmer
	6,00,000	Bilada
	4,00,000	Pali, Rohat
	3,00,000	Bahal
	13,00,000	Khevsar
	3,00,000	Kherwa
	13,00,000	Dunada
	2,00,000	Gudwach
	75,000	Koten
	50,000	Idawati
	1,55,25,000	
	1,15,00,000	Jalor
	80,00,000	Jaitaran
	80,00,000	Sojat
	30,00,000	Siwana
	27,00,000	Phalodi
	4,87,25,000	
	1,45,00,000	*Sarkar* Nagaur
	1,40,00,000	Merta
	5,00,000	Gajsinghpura
	6,32,25,000	Total
4,61,20,942		From Hisar *Pargana*
47,77,500		From Rohtak, Sarkar Jahanabad
12,00,000		*Pargana* Bahal, Suba Ajmer.
8,84,131		*Pargana* Bahal, Suba Ajmer.
11,71,64,573		Total [111]
28,35,427		*Talab* paid in cash

In this account Pancholi Manohardas also mentions the amount increased in *pargana* Hissar. The increment gives an impression that in these areas the *jama* figures were purposely inflated.

REFERENCES

[1]*Badshahnama*, i, 248; *Jodhpur-Khyat*, i, 178-88. Amar Singh held five *parganas* outside Marwar in *Jagir*, 1,50,000/- Barod, 3,75,000/- Bhilai, 20,000/- Waluwo, 70,000/- Sangod, 1,60,000/- Anterode (*Jodhpur-Khyat*, i, 178).

[2]*Badshahnama*, ii, 97. *Rathora-ri-Vamshavali* (ORIJ), 48 and *Jodhpur-Khyat*, i, 178, mention 4000/3500 and 2500/1500 respectively. But both the accounts are incorrect. The *mansab* of 2500/1500 was held in A.D. 1634 and not in A.D. 1638 as mentioned in the *Khyat*. Also *see*, *Vir Vinod*, 322.

[3]*Ibid*.

[4]*Jodhpur-Khyat*, i, 177; *Vir Vinod*, 821.

[5]See, *Vir Vinod*, 821; also see, Asopa, *Samshipt Itihas*, 373.

[6]*Vir Vinod*, 821.

[7]*Badshahnama*, i, 96-7.

[8]*Jodhpur-Khyat*, i, 186-7; *Mundiyara-ri-Khyat* (ORIJ), ii, 115-19.

[9]*Badshahnama*, ii, 97-9; *Samshipt Itihas*, 373. Rao Amar Singh was by nature an independent, reckless, and unyielding prince. Once a dialogue with his brother-in-law provoked this short tempered person so much that he killed the latter. (*Vir Vinod*, ii, 821). The *Khyats* of Marwar record that Rao Amar Singh ignoring the etiquette of the imperial court as well as the presence of the Emperor, murdered Bakhshi Salabat Khan in the court because the latter called him *ganvar* (rude) (*Jodhpur-Khyat*, i, 264).

[10]Born in *V.S.* 1683 and succeeded in *V.S.* 1694.

[11]*Basta* No. 43, Reg. No. 5, 135. *Jodhpur Records*, (R.S.A.B.) He held the *jagir* worth rupees one crore.

[12]*Siropao* stands for presentation of a turban and other cloths by the Raja to his noble. It was an honour for a noble.

[13]*Jodhpur-Khyat*, i, 194.

[14]*Jodhpur-Khyat*, 252-3. *Shahjahannama* (tr. Hindi), ii, 53; *Vigat*, i, 125; *Shahjahannama* (Munshi Devi Prasad, ii, 53) mentions that at the succession of Jaswant Singh he held the *mansab* of 800/300. *Rathora-ri-Pidia-ri-Khyat*, (ORIJ), 100.

[15]*Jodhpur-Khyat*, i, 252; *Vigat*, ii, 415. *Basta* No. 43/5, 135, *Jodhpur Records* (R.S.A.B.).

[16]*Vigat*, ii, 415; *Basta* No. 43/5, 135, *Jodhpur Records* (R.S.A.B.).

[17]*Jodhpur-Khyat*, i, 252-3.

[18]*Shahjahannama*, ii, 61-8; *Jodhpur-Khyat*, i, 195. He arrived at Jodhpur in April 1640 where his coronation ceremony took place. But hecould not stay there for a long time and appeared at the court on 18 March 1640. From there Jaswant Singh was sent with the imperial army under the command of Dara Shikoh against Shah Safi of Iran. Due to the death of Shah Safi on 2 May 1641, the imperial army was withdrawn

and Jaswant Singh was given leave for his *desh*, and he reached there on 19 June 1643.

[19]*Vigat*, i, 124; *Jodhpur-Khyat*, i, 200; *Kaviraj Khyat*, ii, 97; *Padshahnama*, ii, 97; *Maasir*, i, 754; *Basta* No. 75/28, *Jodhpur Records* (R.S.A.B.); *Munadiyara-ri-Khyat* (ORIJ), ii, 122.

[20]*Jodhpur-Khyat* mentions that the increment of 1000/1000 was given to Jaswant Singh at the time of Emperor's birth ceremony. Later he proceeded to Marwar (i, 195). According to Nainsi the increment was given when Jaswant Singh proceeded to his *desh*.

[21]*Vigat*, i, 124 & 496.

[22]*Jodhpur-Rajya*, *i* 416.

[23]*Vigat*, i, 125; Pandit Asopa (*Samshipt Itihas*, i, 139) asserts that the increment was made in A.D. 1645 (V.S. 1702, *Jyeshtha Sudi* 10) when the Maharaja stayed in Peshawar with the Mughal army.

The details of the account of the *mansab* are given below:

Salary claim (*talab*)

Dams	*Mansab*
5,80,00,000	*Asal* 5000/5000, out of which one thousand was *du-aspa sih-aspa*.
80,00,000	One thousand *sawars* as an increment.
6,60,00,000	Total

Jagir granted in lieu of salary (*Vigat*, i, 124-5).

Dams	*Jagirs in Marwar* (*Jodhpur*)
1,43,00,000	Jodhpur
1,45,00,000	Merta, Gajsinghpura
60,00,000	Sojat
1,00,00,000	Jaitaran
30,00,000	Siwana
27,00,000	Phalodi
5,05,00,000	
1,17,00,000	Rewari (outside Marwar)
6,22,00,000	Total
38,00,000	In Cash
6,60,00,000	Grand Total

[24]*Vigat*, i, 125; *Sankshipt Itihas*, 321; *Umara-i-hunud*, 155.

[25]The *talab* can be explained as follows:

Dams		*Mansab*
40,00,000		500 *sawars*
	38,00,000	Earlier *talab*
	40,00,000	*talab* of 500 *sawar*
	78,00,000	Total *talab*

[26]*Samshipt Itihas*, 391.

[27]*Vigat*, i, 126.

[28]*Ibid.*, i, 126-7.

[29]*Vigat*, i, 127; *Basta* No. 59/4, *Jodhpur Records* R.S.A.B.

[30]*Vigat*, i, 128. In 1654 Emperor Shahjahan had resumed the *parganas* of Pur, Mandor, Kherabad, Mandal, Jash, Jahajpur, Banera, Hurda, Badnor, etc. from Maharana Raj Singh as a punishment for his disobedience towards the Mughal Court. *See*, *Vir Vinod*, 413-14; *Udaipur Rajya*, i, 845.

In A.D. 1654 (V.S. 1711) Bahroda worth 6,00,000 *dams* was granted in *jagir*. Later in A.D. 1655 (V.S. 1712) Rohtak worth 50,00,000 *dams* was also granted in *jagir*.

[31]*Vigat*, i, 129.

[32]*Hukumat-Bahi*, f. 24b; *Vigat*, i, 130; *Vachanika* 7-8; *Maasir-i-Alamgiri*, 2; *Maasir-ul-Umara*, i, 754-6.

[33]*Vigat*, i, 130-1 *Jodhpur-Khyat*, i, 107; *Maasir-ul-Umara*, i, 754-6.

[34]The table is based on the descriptions given in the *Vigat* (i, 131, 133, 145); *Hukumat-Bahi*, f. 61ab, 62a, *Jodhpur-Khyat*, i, 107 and *Jodhpur Records* (*Basta* No. 90, Reg. 11, R.S.A.B.). The details of the *jagir* were written by Maharaja's *vakil* Manohardas who was posted at the Mughal court (f. 61ab).

[35]Nainsi mentions that at the court the account of twelve thousand *sawars* has been given as 5000 *du-aspa* and 2000 *ek-aspa*. These figures of Nainsi stand for 7000 *sawars* out of which 5000 were *du-aspa sih-aspa* which was prevalent at the Mughal court. It is significant that instead of 5000/5000 out of which 5000 were *du-aspa sih-aspa*, Nainsi mentions it as 12,000 *sawars ek-aspa* which would amount to the same number as obtained from the formula prevalent at the Mughal court.

[36]In *Hukumat-Bahi* (f. 61a) the *pargana* of Satalmer has been included in the *pargana* of Jodhpur which is not correct. It was a separate *pargana* and is known as Pokaran, but in the court it was registered under the name of Satalmer.

The *Jama* figures of some of the *tappas* of Jodhpur and other *parganas* in Marwar have been corrected after the comparison of the figures in *Hukumat-Bahi*, *Jodhpur-Khyat* and *Vigat*.

[37]*Hukumat-Bahi*, f. 71a.

[38]*Vigat*, i, 131, 133.

[39]*Ibid*, i, 131, 133.

[40]*Badshahnama*, ii, 52; *Jodhpur Rajya*, i, 414

[41]*Badshahnama*, ii, 59-61; *Vigat*, i, 125-6.

[42]*Badshahnama*, ii, 68.

[43]*Shahjahannama* (ii, 246) records August 18, as the date of Jaswant Singh's arrival at Jodhpur.

[44]*Padshahnama*, ii, 407.

[45]*Jodhpur-Khyat*, i, 207.

[46]*Maasir-ul-Umara*, iii, 600; *Jodhpur-Khyat*, i, 212; *Vigat*, i, 127.

[47]*Jodhpur-Rajya*, i, 424.

[48]*Hukumat-Bahi*, ff. 34b, 35a; *Jodhpur-Khyat*, i, 207; *Tarikh-i-Dilkusha*; *Maasir-i-Alamgiri*, 6.

[49]*Jodhpur-Khyat*, i, 228; *Hukumat-Bahi*, f, 40a. The *farman* was dispatched on May 31, 1658.

[50]*Vigat*, i, 132-3; *Jodhpur-Khyat*, i, 228. According to *Hukumat Bahi* (f. 42b) Jaswant Singh submitted on 19 August 1658, *Bhadra Sudi* 2.

[51]*Hukumat-Bahi*, f, 41b; *Vigat*, i, 133-4. *Jodhpur-Khyat* (i, 228) records that at this time Aurangzeb sanctioned Rs. 5,00,000/- from the treasury of Sambhar and sent a *hundi* worth Rs. 5,00,000/- to Jaswant Singh. The amount referred in the *Jodhpur-Khyat* has not been mentioned in the *Hukumat-Bahi* or the *Vigat*. On the other hand, both these accounts mention that the amount worth Rs. 5,00,000/- was sanctioned by Shahjahan to Jaswant Singh at the time of his departure to Ujjain (*Hukumat-Bhai*, f, 37b; *Vigat*, i, 157).

[52]Aurangzeb defeated Shah Shuja in the battle of Khajwa. Maharaja Jaswant commanded the right wing of Aurangzeb's army. It is said that Jaswant Singh informed Shuja for the combined attack on Aurangzeb's army in the night. However, since Shuja could not join the Maharaja in time, the latter, after sacking the imperial camp, took the route to Agra a day before the battle. This act of treachery annoyed Aurangzeb. For details, see, Sarkar, Vol. I & II, 298-302.

[53]*Hukumat-Bahi*, f, 46b; *Jodhpur-Khyat*, i, 230.

[54]*Ibid.*

[55]*Mundiyara-ri-Khyat* (ORIJ), 149. Aurangzeb was happy with the Rana and therefore he granted even Dungarpur, Banswara. Deolia along with Badnor. This shows the Rana's role in the war of succession was appreciated by Aurangzeb. For details, see, Satish Chandra, 'A Re-examination of the Factors Leading to the Breach Between Aurangzeb and Rana Raj Singh,' P.I.H.C. 1965, pp. 169-74.

[56]*Hukumat-Bahi*, f, 47b.

[56]*Pargana-ri-Vigat*, i, 136; *Jodhpur-Khyat*, i, 229-30.

[57]*Ibid.*

[58]*Hukumat-Bahi*, 58-60; *Jodhpur-Khyat*, i, 230. There has been a great deal of discussion whether Dara was invited by Jaswant Singh or not. It is said that Maharaja Jaswant Singh had sent one of his high officers to Dara with a letter professing his devotion to Shahjahan and asking Dara to reach Ajmer quickly, where Rathors and other Rajputs were ready to join a leader who would rescue their captive sovereign (Sarkar, ii, 167). It may be argued that Jaswant Singh, being aware about the possible move of Aurangzeb, would have invited Dara, but it is doubtful whether in anticipation of Dara's possible adventure Aurangzeb had moved towards Marwar. In other words Aurangzeb probably would not have personally marched against Marwar but for the fear of Dara's possible collusion with Jaswant Singh and other Rajput rulers. Jaswant Singh obviously over-estimated the strength of a joint action with Dara Shikoh. Even their combined force was no match for the imperial strength. In the absence of any definite date for the

despatch of Jaswant Singh's messenger to Dara it is quite likely that Jaswant Singh sent his man before the news of the result of war against Shuja reached Dara.

59*Jodhpur-Rajya*, i, 445-8; *Marwar-Rajya*, ii, 307.

60*Vigat*, i, 138.

61*Hukumat-Bahi*, f. 48a.

62*Ibid.*

63*Ibid.*, f. 48b, 49b.

64When Dara was passing through Bilada on his way to Merta from Sojat, he sent his son to meet Jaswant Singh at Jodhpur.

65Sipah Shikoh arrived at Jodhpur on about *Phalguna Sudi* 5. But Maharaja left Jodhpur only on Phalguna Sudi 11. For three days Dara waited for Jaswant Singh and even before his departure from Jodhpur, the former left Merta on *Phalguna Sudi* 10. (*Hukumat-Bahi*, ff. 48b-49b). Also see, Sarkar, (longman), ii, 313.

66According to Travenier, Maharaja Jaswant Singh delayed his arrival because he had negotiated with Aurangzeb. His aim was to deceive Dara at the last moment (*Travels in India*, i, 278). According to *Maasir-i-Alamgiri* (tr. 10) Maharaja Jai Singh started negotiations with Jaswant Singh when Dara arrived near Ajmer. This account does not throw light on the attitude of Jaswant Singh before the arrival of Dara near Ajmer.

67*Hukumat-Bahi*, f. 49b; *Vigat*, i, 136. According to Manucci, Aurangzeb asked Jai Singh to write to Jaswant Singh that he should not participate in favour of Dara (*Storia de Mogor*, i, 339). This statement of Manucci is not verifiable from the contemporary Rajasthani sources which are more reliable.

68*Vigat*, i, 136; *Hukumat-Bahi*, ff, 49b-50a. *Mirat*, i, 244.

69*Hukumat-Bahi*, ff. 49b-50b. At this time Jaswant Singh was staying at Rabdiak (*Vigat*, i, 136).

70*Hukumat-Bahi*. ff. 49b-50a.

71The details of his *mansab* and jagirs are given below (*Pargana-ri-Vigat*, i, 145-46):

Dams	*Rupees*	*Asami*
1,40,00,000	3,50,000	*Zat*, seven thousand.
9,60,00,000	24,00,000	*Sawar*, twelve thousand, i.e. five thousand *du-aspa* and two thousand *ek-aspa*.
11,00,00,000	27,50,000	Total :

Jagir given in lieu of *Tankhwah* (salary) :

Dams	*Parganas*
6,32,25,000	Nine *Parganas* of Marwar including Jodhpur.
4,33,35,000	Nine *Parganas* of Gujarat.
10,65,60,000	Total (Amount granted in *jagir*)
34,40,000	*Talab*
11,00,00,000	

Hukumat-Bahi, f. 50a; *Maasir-ul-Umara*, iii, 600; *Alamgirnama*, 55-72, 319-20; *Futuhat-i-Alamgiri*, 44b; Khafi-Khan, ii 64.

[72]The unsuccessful negotiations with Jaswant Singh left no strength with Dara, and the latter was defeated on 14 March, 1659 (*Chaitra Sudi* 1, 1716 V.S.) in the battle fought at Deorai near Ajmer. (*Hukumat-Bahi*, f. 50a.)

[73]*Hukumat-Bahi*, f. 50a; *Jadhpur-Khyat*, i. 231.

[74]Many writers hold the opinion that to avoid the danger from combined forces of Dara and Jaswant Singh, Aurangzeb sent Jai Singh to pacify the former and brought his submission before the combat. See, Sarkar (Longman), ii, 312-13.

[75]After his arrival from Dharmat Jaswant Singh had expressed his sorrow at his defeat. (*Jodhpur-Khyat*, i, 225).

[76]*Vigat*, i, 147. Details of the *jagir* are as follows:

Dams	*Rupees*	*Asami*		
6,32,25,000	15,80,000	Nine *parganas* of Marwar including Jodhpur.		
4,33,35,000	10,83,375	Nine *parganas* of Gujarat granted in A.D. 1659 (V.S. 1716).		
1,00,74,000	2,51,000	Later on 4 *parganas* were granted in lieu of *izafa*:		
		79,74,000	1,99,350	Bijapur
		12,00,000	30,000	Telwaro
		3,00,000	7,500	Merwaro
		6,00,000	15,000	Kakricho
		1,00,74,000	2,51,850	
		33,66,000	84,000	*Talab*

[77]*Jodhpur-Khyat*, i, 231; *Vigat*, i, 149;

[78]*Mundiyara-ri-Khyat*, (S.C.), 56; *Vigat*, i, 152-3. According to *Jodhpur-Khyat*, Jaswant Singh held the *parganas* of Hansi and Hissar. (*Vide* i, 231).

The *talab* was made out of the following assignments:

Dams	*Rupees*	*Asami*		
6,32,25,000	15,80,625	*Parganas* of Marwar continued in his *Jagir*.		
5,18,97,442	12,97,436	In Hissar—		
		60,63,640	15,591	Tobena
		81,29,544	22,02,228½	Sirsa
		32,00,000	80,000	Sahabad
		62,74,400	1,56,860	Jeed
		24,00,000	60,000	Veheinwal
		20,00,000	5,00,000	Athekhedo
		11,20,000	28,000	Khaudo
		50,19,732	1,25,493	Jamalpur
		15,65,000	39,125	Soran
		80,15,626	2,00,390	Muheem
		12,50,000	31,350	Ahrooi
		10,82,000	27,050	Ghatrath
		57,77,500	1,44,437	Rohtak
		5,18,97,422	12,97,434½	
12,00,000	30,000	*Pargana* Bahalgao, with effect from *Barsali* Rabi crop of A.D. 1662 (V.S. 1719.)		
8,84,131	22,103	*Pargana* Babal, with effect from *Unhalu* crop A.D. 1662 (V.S. 1719).		
27,93,427	69,835.75	*Talab* remained.		
12,00,00,000	30,00,000			

[79]*Mundiyara-ri-Khyat* (S.C.), 80; *Jodhpur-Khyat*, i, 242; *Mirat*, i, 276.

[80]*Jodhpur-Khyat*, i, 242-3.

[81]*Mirat-i-Ahmadi* records that the *parganas* of Gujarat were granted to Jaswant Singh in place of the *parganas* of Hissar. As the revenue of the *parganas* of Gujarat was less in comparison to the *jagir* he held in Hissar, he was sanctioned rupees one lac annually. *Vide*, (tr.) 247.

[82]*Jodhpur-Khyat*, i, 143, *Mundiyara-ri-Khyat* (SC) 84-5.

[83]*Jodhpur-Khyat*, i, 197.

[84]*Ibid.*, 197-8.

[85]The figures given in the *Jodhpur-Khyat* (i, 197-8) are not correct. They are rather accurate in *Hukumat-Bahi*. The total of the revenue of various *parganas* is mentioned correctly in the text of the *Bahi*.

[86]The revenue granted from Balalo was 12,00,000 *dams* as mentioned in *Vigat* (I, 156). 12,50,000 *dams* as the *Jodhpur-Khyat* mentions is wrong.

[87]There had been a controversy over the role of Jaswant Singh in the Deccan. Also see, *Jodhpur-Rajya*, i, 452-6.

[88]Jaswant Singh left Poona in March 1665.

[89]*Alamgirnama*, 975; *Jodhpur-Khyat*, i, 237-8.

[90]When the imperial army reached Lahore, Shah Abbas had died. (22 August, 1666). Therefore, Aurangzeb asked them to return.

[91]*Jodhpur-Khyat*, i, 239-40; *Tarikh-i-Dilkusha*, 31b.

[92]*Aurangzebnama*, ii, 31; *Vir Vinod*, ii, 827.

[93]*Hukumat-Bahi* f. 154a; *Jodhpur-Khyat*, i, 256.

[94]Being *mansabdars*, the Rajput rulers were obliged to perform the imperial service as desired by the Emperor.

[95]*Vigat*, i, 234.

[96]The reference '*Pai Takht Jodhpur*' denotes the right over the *gaddi* and area formed under the direct control of Jodhpur. The area was called *Haweli*, which consisted of 505 villages. (*Vigat*, i, 163).

[97]When Jaswant Singh ascended the throne he was granted 14 *tappas* out of 19.

[98]Making objection against the assignment of Jaitaran to Rawal Bhim of Jaisalmer, Jaswant Singh pleaded that if it was granted to Rawal Bhim his right of rulership over Jaitaran would end (*Vigat*, i, 124).

[99]After the death of Gaj Singh *pargana* Jaitaran was taken in *Khalisa*. In A.D. 1639 (V.S. 1696) when Rathor Bhiv, son of Rawal Kalyanmal of Jaisalmer requested the Emperor for the grant of Jaitaran in his favour, Maharaja Jaswant Singh protested (*Vigat*, i, 124, 196). But such objection was not made when Jaitaran was in *khalisa*. During the time of Gaj Singh, Merta was given to Shahzada Parwez in *jagir*. Maharaja Gaj Singh did not object as long as it remained with Parwez. When he came to know that Prince Parwez was giving Merta to some Rathor *sardars*, Maharaja Gaj Singh requested Emperor Jahangir to change this decision (*Vigat*, ii, 74-5).

[100]For example, Rathor Maheshdas and his son Ratan Singh, who were *mansabdars* and were granted Jalor in *jagir* failed to keep their control successfully. Therefore, later on, it had to be granted to Jaswant Singh. Jalor remained under their control from A.D. 1652 to A.D. 1655. (*Vigat*, ii, 415).

[101]The table has been prepared on the basis of the statistics available in the *Hukumat-ri-Bahi* (f- 15a-b, 16a), and *Pargana-ri-Vigat* (i, 124-34, 145-58).

[102]The *Hukumat-Bahi* contains a full account of the *pattas* granted to the Rathor *sardars* outside Marwar during Jaswant Singh's reign.

[103]The nature of the grant and the obligations of these grantees would be discussed in the next chapter.

[104]cf. Athar Ali, *Nobility under Aurangzeb*, 50-1.

[105]*Mansabdars* who held *jagirs* in any of the provinces of Hindustan and who were posted in the same province in which their *jagirs* lay, were to bring horsemen equal to one-third of their *sawar* rank. But if posted outside the province of their jagirs, they were only to bring one-fourth, if posted to Bulkh and Badakhashan, they were required to muster only one-fifth. (*Badshahnama*, ii, 506.)

[106]The table is prepared on the basis of the figures available in *Hukumat-Bahi*, ff. 15a-16a; *Pargana-ri-Vigat*, i, 124, 163-4 and ii, 7, 75-7, 109.

[107]*Vigat*, i, 124.

[108]*Ibid.*, i, 163.

[109]*Ibid.*, i, 109; ii, 75-7.

[110]*Ibid.*, i, 163.

[112]In the *Hukumat-Bahi*, the total amount of the *jagirs* is given as 11, 71, 86, 578 *dams* which is not correct.

4

STATE FINANCE

It has been stated that although *jagir* granted to Maharaja Jaswant Singh in Marwar was *tankhwah jagir*, yet due consideration was given to his claim over the *parganas* held by his ancestors. In principle, the Mughal Emperor continued to be the sovereign, but internally, the Rathor ruler was given almost a free hand in administering the areas granted to him in Marwar. From the figures given in the previous chapter it is obvious that the *jagirs* were assigned to Jaswant Singh in lieu of his salary in accordance with his *mansab*. In all the tables relating to the *jagirs* of Jaswant Singh the figures are given in *dams*. These figures represented the *jama* and were termed as *jama-i-dami*. All the nine *parganas* of Marwar were granted to Jaswant Singh on the calculation of his salary.

Rekh and Jama

A study of the accounts of the seventeenth century reveals that these *jama* figures did not form the basis for the assignment of the *pattas* to the Marwar *sardars* by the Rathor rulers. The *pattas* granted during Jaswant Singh's reign indicate the *rekh* figures against the villages.[1] It is worth noting that the *pattas* granted before the reign of Maharaja Sur Singh (A.D. 1596-1619) do not mention *rekh* figures against the grant of the village. *Rekh* figures began to be mentioned in *Pattas* against the names of the villages from the time of Maharaja Sur Singh when Govindas Bhati, the *pradhan* of the Maharaja reformed the administration of Marwar on the Mughal pattern.[2] But it is difficult to ascertain whether during the time of Sur Singh all the villages were included in *rekh* or not.

The term *rekh* is defined as a yearly military cess paid by the *jagirdars* to the Raja.[3] It has also been interpreted as a tribute fixed by a Raja on *jagirdars*.[4] On the basis of the statements in these reports, some writers have asserted that the term *rekh* was applied only in relation to the *jagir* land.[5] But this is not a correct view as the 17th century records use the term for both the *khalisa* and the *jagir* villages.[6] This can be proved from the text of the *pattas* included in the *Hukumat-Bahi* which indicates that whenever villages from the *khalisa* land were given in *jagir* the amount of *rekh* remained the same; and so also even after confiscation, when it was granted to another *pattadar*.

A study of the early administrative reports of Marwar shows that the various definitions of *rekh* were the result of the misunderstanding due to the changes introduced in the structure of the nobility during the later half of the 18th century. Owing to the decline of the power of the Mughal Emperor, the *Padshahi Chakri* (The imperial service) was no longer required in the reign of Maharaja Bijay Singh (A.D. 1752-1793). At this time Marwar was faced with the Maratha menace. Money was needed to fight or to purchase peace from the Marathas. Apart from imposing extra *bab* or *abwab* (cesses) on the *raiyats* (cultivators) the *pattadars* were called upon to pay cash dues (*mutalba*) to the *darbar* (Raja's court) in lieu of the military service (*chakri*) they used to render to the Maharaja. The dues (*mutalba*) were assessed for every *jagirdar* (*pattadar*). Thus Rs. 300 were fixed against Rs. 1000 of *rekh* as an extra amount for payment. As it was fixed in relation to the *rekh* it also began to be known by the name of *rekh*.[7] It was only from A.D. 1755 that this extra amount of *rekh* (*mutalba*) began to be realized from the *jagirdars*. It was recorded time and again during the reign of Maharaja Bijay Singh; but this *rekh* (*mutalba*) never remained static. It seems that writers have confused the *rekh* with tribute paid by the *jagirdars* to the Raja.

The following table showing the figures of *jama*, *rekh* and *hasil* from the *jagirs* granted to Jaswant Singh by the Mughal Emperors enables us to explain the difference between *jama* and *rekh*.[8]

TABLE 4:1

Jaswant Singh's Jagir in Marwar

Pargana	*Jama*	*Rekh*	Average *hasil* from the *Jagir* (for five years—1658-62)
	Rs.	Rs.	Rs.
Jodhpur	3,68,125	7,50,350	3,99,125
Merta	3,50,000	6,80,001	4,64,543
Jaitaran	2,00,000	2,07,200	1,63,089
Sojat	2,00,000	3,02,500	1,88,365
Satalmer	20,000	40,460	15,000
Siwana	75,000	89,660	40,313
Phalodi	67,500	1,23,800	36,640
Jalor	2,87,500	3,87,770	2,51,000
Gajsinghpura	12,500	15,200	12,000
Total	15,80,625	25,86,941	15,70,575

The *jama* and *rekh* figures shown in the above table clearly indicate the difference between the two in the *parganas* of Marwar. The proportion between *jama* and *rekh* was roughly 3:7 in *pargana* Jodhpur, 2:2.07 in *pargana* Jaitaran, 3:6 in *pargana* Merta and 2:3 in *pargana* Sojat. The *pargana* of Jodhpur (as shown in table No. 4:1) representing *jama* and *rekh* of 14 *tappas* shows the clear discrepancy between the two. In all the *tappas* the figures clearly show that the proportion of *rekh* was much higher than that of the *jama*. At the same time it has been noticed that *rekh* figures are given in rupees while the figures of *jama* are given in *dams*.

It is worth mentioning that *rekh* cannot be defined as

the revenue of a village (*jama*). The *jama* includes the revenue from land as well as from *lag-bag* (cesses, i.e., *Mal-o-jihat* and *Sairjihat*). The figures available in the *Vigat*, as mentioned in tables (Nos. 4:3-6) show that the income from the cesses was mentioned separately; on the other hand in the *pattas* themselves it was mentioned clearly that the grantee would not have the right of *lag-bag*.[9] In some cases the Raja could confer the right of realizing some of the agricultural or any other cesses.[10] Nainsi has used the term *rekh* for the figures which represented the assessed land revenue of the *khalisa* and *jagir* villages on the basis of which the *pattas* were granted to the *jagirdars* by the Raja.[11] This can be corroborated by the fact that each village had its *rekh* figures against the *hasil* derived as land revenue.[12] The *pattas* listed in the *Hukumat-Bahi* indicate the same *rekh* figures against the villages granted in *pattas*.[13]

From the references in the *pattas* mentioned in *Hukumat-Bahi*, *Vigat* and some other land revenue documents, it is revealed that while granting the *patta* to the *jagirdars*, the *pattadars* or the grantees were conferred only the right of realizing land revenue.[14] This makes two things clear: (1) that the *rekh* figures do not include the assessed income of the cesses other than land revenue, and (b) that the *jagirdar* or the grantee had no right to realize the tax other than land revenue without the permission of the state. There are instances relating to the assignment of *ghasmari* and other agricultural cesses to the grantee by the *Raja*.[15] Thus the *rekh* figures represent only the assessed land revenue (*mal*) of a village or villages, on the other hand *jama* figures represent the total revenue from villages or *pargana*. Thus it can be said that both *jama* and *rekh* were different from each other.

The introduction of a separate assessment in the Rathor territory (*watan*) of Marwar was not a new phenomenon. Other Rajput states also adopted the same practice in their respective *watan* territories.[16] The institution of *rekh* might have been necessitated due to the lower realization from *jagirs* against the *jama*. The fixation of a higher assessed amount as *rekh* raised the revenue figures. This enabled the Rathor rulers to increase the number of *pattadars* and thus maintain the army as required by the Mughal court. Thus *rekh* was fixed separately by the Raja or autonomous chief of the area. It is difficult to say as to how it could have been fixed directly with the peasants. Alternatively, it could have been fixed with the help of *zamindar* or the clan dominating the area or with their combined assistance.

Fiscal Revenues

The state finance was dependent on the revenue derived from the agricultural and non-agricultural taxes or cesses. The agricultural revenue comprised the land revenue, i.e., *bhog* (*mal*), *Kharach-bhog* (*malo-Jihat*), and other cesses which were levied over and above the *bhog*. Among the non-agricultural taxes and cesses, the income derived out of the *Rahdari*, *Mapa-dan* (transit and import duties) and other miscellaneous cesses are worth mentioning.

Land Revenue Demand

The land revenue realized on behalf of the state is termed as *bhog* in the land revenue records of the 17th century Marwar.[17] The term *bhog* is synonymous with the *mal* as used in the Mughal land revenue documents.[18] In his account of *pargana* Merta, Nainsi has given the *amal-dastur*[19] which contains information on the rates of the agricultural and non-agricultural taxes.[20] According to it, under crop-sharing (*batai*), the cultivators paid 50 per cent of their gross produce of cereal crops from the *kharif* (*siyalu*) crop.[21] For the *rabi* (*unhalu*) the rate was 40 per cent on the land where water was stored during rainy season and 33 per cent on irrigated land of the cereal crops.[22] The state also derived the *kharach-bhog* (*jihat*), i.e., the expenses incurred during the collection of *bhog*, at the rate of 4 per cent of the *bhog*.[23] It is noteworthy that the rate of *kharach-bhog* was 15 per cent of the *bhog* till A.D. 1650 (V.S. 1707).[24] But in that year, the rate was reduced to 5.5 per cent of the *bhog*. In A.D. 1657 (V.S. 1714) it was further reduced to 4 per cent of the *bhog*.[25]

In the areas where *zabt* was prevalent the state demand per *bigha* was fixed according to the nature of crops. Thus on cotton, opium, vegetables and *kharbuza* (musk-melon) the rate was Rs. 1.50, 2.50, 1.37 and Re. 1 per *bigha*, respectively.[26]

A study of the *amal-dastur*[27] of *pargana* Pokaran reveals that the state land revenue demand was fixed on the basis of castes. Thus the *Banias* and the *Mahajans* paid at the rate of 20 per cent to 22.5 per cent of the produce. For other cultivators, other than the Rajputs, the rate was 22.5 per cent to 25 per cent of the produce. On the Rajput cultivators, a separate assessment was made according to which they paid Rs. 3 and Rs.3.50 on each *hal* (plough).[28] The *dastur* contains separate rates of *kharach-bhog* for the *Banias* and other cultivators. The *Banias* and the *Mahajan* cultivators paid 15.62 per cent while other cultivators paid Rs. 18.75 per cent of *bhog* as *kharach-bhog*. The amount paid by the Rajput cultivators as *kharach-bhog* has not been mentioned which suggests that they were exempted from any extra taxes levied over and above the *bhog*.

In the account of *pargana* Sojat, as mentioned earlier, Nainsi does not give *amal-dastur*. But the account of the figures of *hasil* of *kharif* and the *rabi* crops shows the rates of the *zabt* (cash) crops. It is mentioned that Rs. 1.25 and 1.50 per *bigha* were charged on cotton and wheat respectively.[29] For the other *kharif* crops, except cash crops, the state levied 50 per cent of the produce.[30] The rate of the *kharach-bhog* of *pargana* Sojat has not been mentioned.

An examination of the accounts mentioned above reveals that the standard land revenue demand in Marwar varied from 1:4 (25 per cent) to 1:2 (50 per cent) of the produce and that no uniform rate specifying the share of the state was fixed.[31] This was slightly different from the general formula according to which the land revenue demand varied from 33 per cent to 40 per cent.[32] As regards the state share on *rabi* crops, the cultivators were required to pay 40 per cent and 35 per cent of the produce. The rates of land revenue for *Mahajan, Bania* and Rajput cultivators were concessional. Although the difference of rates for the *Mahajan* and the rest of cultivators was between 2.5 per cent to 5 per cent which was almost negligible, the separate rates for the Rajput cultivators were considerably low. They had to pay only Rs. 3 to Rs. 3.50 per *hal*—a *hal* comprising fifty *bighas* of land.[33] Thus the amount to be paid by the Rajput cultivators was a token payment.

The rate of the *kharach-bhog* (*mal-o-jihat*) was also not uniform and it varied between 4 per cent to 18.75 per cent of the *bhog* (*mal*). A significant feature noted in respect of *pargana* Merta was the reduction in the rate of *kharach-bhog* from 15 per cent to 4 per cent during the time of Jaswant Singh. Such reduction was not made in *pargana* Pokaran where the land revenue demand was comparatively low. Perhaps the new rate of *kharach-bhog* was implemented only in those areas where the state land revenue demand was 50 per cent of the gross produce.

It is apparent from the above account that in Marwar the methods adopted for the assessment of land revenue were both *batai* and *zabt*. A study of the accounts of *parganas* Merta, Jaitaran and Sojat reveals that the *zabt* system was adopted only for cash crops. Perhabs, the same practice was adopted in other *parganas* also. The *zabt* system for the first time was adopted by the Mughals when Akbar incorporated Merta in the *khalisa*. In the years A.D. 1573 (V.S. 1630) the territory of *pargana* Merta was measured and the land was divided into various categories.[34] The measurement effected in Merta was a part of the land revenue reforms introduced under Akbar. The existence of the *zabt* and *batai* during the time of Jaswant Singh makes it clear that the *zabt* was not fully adopted even till the latter half of the 17th century. Obviously the area of the *zabt* was extended and apart from the cash crops it was enforced for wheat also in some of the places. In general the *batai* remained in practice for cereal crops.

A study of the *hasil* figures of various *parganas* of Marwar makes it clear that generally the realization was made in cash. The account of the *pargana* Sojat indicates that even in areas where *batai* was prevalent the share of the state calculated in grain was commuted into cash.[35] This was similar to the mode of payment in the other parts of the country where *batai* was prevalent. In the *patta* villages, the rates of *bhog* and *kharach-bhog* were the same as prevailed in the *khalisa* land. The *pattadars* in theory, were not entitled to increase the amount of the *bhog* or *kharach-bhog*, upon the peasants. This was possible because of the fact that in both categories, *khalisa* and *patta* villages, the assessment was made by the state revenue officers or the hereditary officers recognized by the state.

On the basis of the above observations, it can be maintained that in Marwar the rates of the land revenue, realised on behalf of the state or *pattadar*, were not uniform and varied from *pargana* to *pargana*. Different rates were fixed for the *kharif* and the *rabi* crops which varied from 50 per cent to 33 per cent of the produce. As the *zabt* was adopted mostly in case of cash crops, in some areas for wheat also, the *batai* system was the widely accepted mode of assessment for cereal crops. In the areas where the state share was 50 per cent of the produce the amount of *kharach-bhog* was reduced considerably; but in the areas where the state demand was 25 per cent, the amount of *kharach-bhog* remained the same as prevailed during the time of Maharaja Gaj Singh (A.D. 1619-1638) and Sur Singh (A.D.1593-1619). It is understandable that in those areas where the state demand was 50 per cent of the gross produce, it weighed heavily upon the *raiyat*. Therefore, the reduction in the rate of *kharach-bhog* was made to extend some relief to cultivators.

Hasil in relation to Rekh and Jama

A detailed account of the *hasil* of all the villages of the *parganas* of Jodhpur, Jaitaran, Merta, Sojat, Phalodi, Siwana and Pokaran, from 1658 to 1662, provides us information about the exact realization made through land revenue. A close study of the tables (Nos. 4:3-6) shows that the *hasil* from the land revenue (of the *khalisa*, *jagir* and *sasan* land) was 53.19 per cent to *rekh* and 108.42 per cent to *jama* of *pargana* Jodhpur; 68.3 per cent to *rekh* and 132.72 per cent to *jama* of *pargana* Merta; 78.71 per cent to *rekh* and 81.71 per cent to *jama* of *pargana* Jaitaran; and, 68.30 per cent to *rekh* and 94.18 per cent to *jama* of *pargana* Sojat. The proportion of the realization shows that in general the percentage of the *hasil* in relation to *jama* is much higher than that of *rekh*.

The figures given in table 4:2 would clarify it further.[36] The figures reveal that in seven *parganas* the *hasil* was lower than *jama*, i.e., 82.93 per cent, but in two *parganas*, Jodhpur and Merta, it was substantially higher than the *jama*, i.e., 121.65 per cent. While on the other hand the relationship of *hasil* to *rekh* does not show such a marked variation, being 59.94 per cent in the seven *parganas* and 61.09 per cent in other two *parganas*, *hasil* was 99 per cent of the *jama* and 60.71 per cent of the *rekh.*

TABLE 4:2

Jama, Rekh, and Hasil of some Parganas of Marwar

Pargana	*jama*	*rekh*	*hasil*	Percentage of the *hasil* to the *jama*	Percentage of the *hasil* to the *rekh*
7 *parganas* (excluding Jodhpur & Merta)	8,52,500	11,79,320	7,06,907	82.93	59.94
2 *parganas* (Jodhpur & Merta)	7,19,125	14,30,351	8,63,668	121.65	60.00
Total	15,71,625	25,19,671	15,70,575	99.00	60.71

This tends to suggest that *jama* signified the actual capacity of the peasant to pay, while the *rekh* figures were the maximum assessed revenue of the area, which could have been hardly paid to the Raja even if demanded. It seems that the demand for increasing the amount of *jama* in the Mughal Empire could have been considered in the light of these *rekh* figures. Another factor in the increase of *jama* figures was the demand of those *jagirs* on the higher *jama* by some other *jagirdars.*

A study of the following tables (4:3-6) and the graphs prepared on the basis of these tables further provides us few important information on the nature of the relationship among the *jama*, *rekh* and *hasil*.

A study of the curves indicating the *hasil* in relation to the state land revenue demand of the *parganas* of Jodhpur, Jaitaran, Sojat and Merta shows that the former tended to fluctuate. Thus we find that in the *parganas* of Jodhpur, Jaitaran, Sojat and Merta, the state revenue derived from land never remained static. In the year A.D. 1658, it was lower in all

TABLE 4:3

Pargana Jodhpur

Jama of the *Jagir*	Year A.D.	Total revenue realized from Land and Cesses	*Rekh* of the *Jagir*, *Khalisa* and *Sasan* Land	*Hasil* from *Khalisa*, *Jagir* and *Sasan* Land	*Hasil* from *Khalisa* Land	*Hasil* from *Jagir* Land	*Hasil* from *Sasan* Land	Realization from Cesses	*Rekh* of the *Sasan*
3,68,125	1658	1,55,869	7,50,350	1,28,248 17.09% of the *rekh*	72,271 9.63% of the *rekh*	51,566 6.87% of the *rekh*	4,409 0.58% of the *rekh*	27,721	26,290
	1659	6,81,949		5,30,743 70.73% of the *rekh*	1,27,434 16.98% of the *rekh*	3,87,634 51.66% of the *rekh*	95,675 2.09% of the *rekh*	1,51,206	
	1660	4,78,634		4,54,919 60.63% of the *rekh*	1,78,084 23.73% of the *rekh*	2,58,808 34.49% of the *rekh*	18,027 2.40% of the *rekh*	23,715	
	1661	6,96,518		5,47,192 72.93% of the *rekh*	1,98,143 26.40% of the *rekh*	3,48,949 46.50% of the *rekh*	23,240 3.09% of the *rekh*	1,49,326	
	1662	4,67,772		3,34,490 44.58% of the *rekh*				1,33,282	

Table 4:3 (Contd.)

Jama of the *Jagir*	Year A.D.	Total revenue realized from Land and Cesses	*Rekh* of the *Jagir*, *Khalisa* and *Sasan* Land	*Hasil* from *Khalisa*, *Jagir* and *Sasan* Land	*Hasil* from *Khalisa* Land	*Hasil* from *Jagir* Land	*Hasil* from *Sasan* Land	Realization from Cesses	*Rekh* of the *Sasan*
Average *hasil* of a year		58,00,816 136.04% of the *jama* 66.74% of the *rekh*		3,99,125 53.19% of the *rekh* 79.69% of the total revenue 108.42% of the *jama*	1,43,983 19.19% of the *rekh*	2,61,739 34.88% of the *rekh*	18,901 2.52% of the *rekh*	1,01,691 23% of the total realization	

Note:—The total number of *tappas* were 20 and their *jama* was Rs. 3,88,125.

TABLE 4:4
Pargana Jaitaran

Jama of the *Jagir*	Year	Total revenue realized from Land and Cesses	*Rekh* of the *Jagir*, *Khalisa* and *Sasan* Land	*Hasil* from *Khalisa*, *Jagir* and *Sasan* Land	*Hasil* from *Khalisa* Land	*Hasil* from *Jagir* Land	*Hasil* from *Sasan* Land	*Realization* from Cesses	*Rekh* of the *Sasan*
2,00,000	1658	96,626	2,07,200	94,168 45.45% of the *rekh*	59,354 28.64% of the *rekh*	32,644 15.75% of the *rekh*	2,170 1.04% of the *rekh*	1.518	10,200
	1659	1,69,611		1,67,517 80.85% of the *rekh*	68,529 32.08% of the *rekh*	1,13,076 54.57% of the *rekh*	5,920 2.86% of the *rekh*	2,094	
	1660	2,28,371		2,26,306 109.22% of the *rekh*	1,19,381 57.62% of the *rekh*	99,875 48.02% of the *rekh*	7,050 3.04% of the *rekh*	2,065	
	1661	1,95,992		1,93,978 93.62% of the *rekh*			6,276 3.02% of the *rekh*	2,014	
	1662	1,35,473		1,33,476 64.42% of the *rekh*			8,100 3.09% of the *rekh*	1,997	
Average *hasil* of a year		1,65,018 82.69% of the *jama* 79.64% of the *rekh*		1,63,089 78.71% of the *rekh* 81.54% of the *jama*	75,543 36.46% of the *rekh*	81,865 39.51% of the *rekh*	5,882 2.83% of the *rekh*	9,688 4.67% of the total revenue	

Source.—*Pargana-ri-Vigat*, i, 508.

TABLE 4:5
Pargana Merta

Jama of the *Jagir*	Year	Total revenue realized from Land and Cesses	*Rekh* of the *Jagir*, *Khalisa* and *Sasan* Land	*Hasil* from *Khalisa*, *Jagir* and *Sasan* Land	*Hasil* from *Khalisa* Land	*Hasil* from *Jagir* Land	*Hasil* from *Sasan* Land	Realization from Cesses	*Rekh* of the *Sasan*
3,50,000	1658		6,80,001	1,87,019 27.50% of the *rekh*	1,81,466 26.68% of the *rekh*	5,553 0.81% of the *rekh*			21,840
	1659			5,26,335 77.40% of the *rekh*	5,10,772 75.11% of the *rekh*	15,563 2.28% of the *rekh*			
	1660			6,19,370 91.08% of the *rekh*	6,02,081 88.54% of the *rekh*	17,289 2.54% of the *rekh*			
	1661			6,52,539 95.96% of the *rekh*	6,26,974 92.20% of the *rekh*	24,565 3.61% of the *rekh*			
	1662			3,37,456 49.62% of the *rekh*	3,23,162 47.52% of the *rekh*	14,354 2.10% of the *rekh*			
Average *hasil* of a year				4,64,543 68.30% of the *rekh* 132.72% of the *jama*	4,48,891 66.01% of the *rekh*	15,425 2.26% of the *rekh*			

TABLE 4:6

Pargana Sojat

Jama of the *Jagir*	Year	Total revenue realized from Land and Cesses	*Rekh* of the *Jagir*, *Khalisa* and *Sasan* Land	*Hasil* from *Khalisa*, *Jagir* and *Sasan* Land	*Hasil* from *Khalisa* Land	*Hasil* from *Jagir* Land	*Hasil* from *Sasan* Land	Realization from Cesses	*Rekh* of the *Sasan*
2,00,000	1658	1,28,187	3,02,500	1,24,261 41.08% of the *rekh*	30,093 9.90% of the *rekh*	89,850 29.61% of the *rekh*	4,318 1.106% of the *rekh*	3,926 (4,056)	2,23,000
	1659	1,95,422		1,91,937 63.45% of the *rekh*	45,527 15.05% of the *rekh*	1,39,786 46.01% of the *rekh*	6,624 2.15% of the *rekh*	3,485	
	1660	2,24,348		2,20,292 72.82% of the *rekh*	50,868 16.75% of the *rekh*	1,60,266 52.31% of the *rekh*	1,958 3.01% of the *rekh*	4,056	
	1661	2,23,734		2,20,302 72.82% of the *rekh*	34,752 11.81% of the *rekh*	1,77,219 58.51% of the *rekh*	8,331 2.09% of the *rekh*	3,432	
	1662	1,89,463		1,84,935 61.14% of the *rekh*	28,125 9.30% of the *rekh*	1,49,601 40.95% of the *rekh*	7,209 1.05% of the *rekh*	4,528	
Average *hasil* of a year		1,92,230 96.13% of the *jama* 63.54% of the *rekh*		1,88,365 62.26% of the *rekh* 94.18% of the *jama* 97.99% of the total revenue	37,873 1.89% of the *rekh*	1,43,544 47.45% of the *rekh*	7,128 2.36% of the *rekh*	3,885 1.94 % of the total revenue	

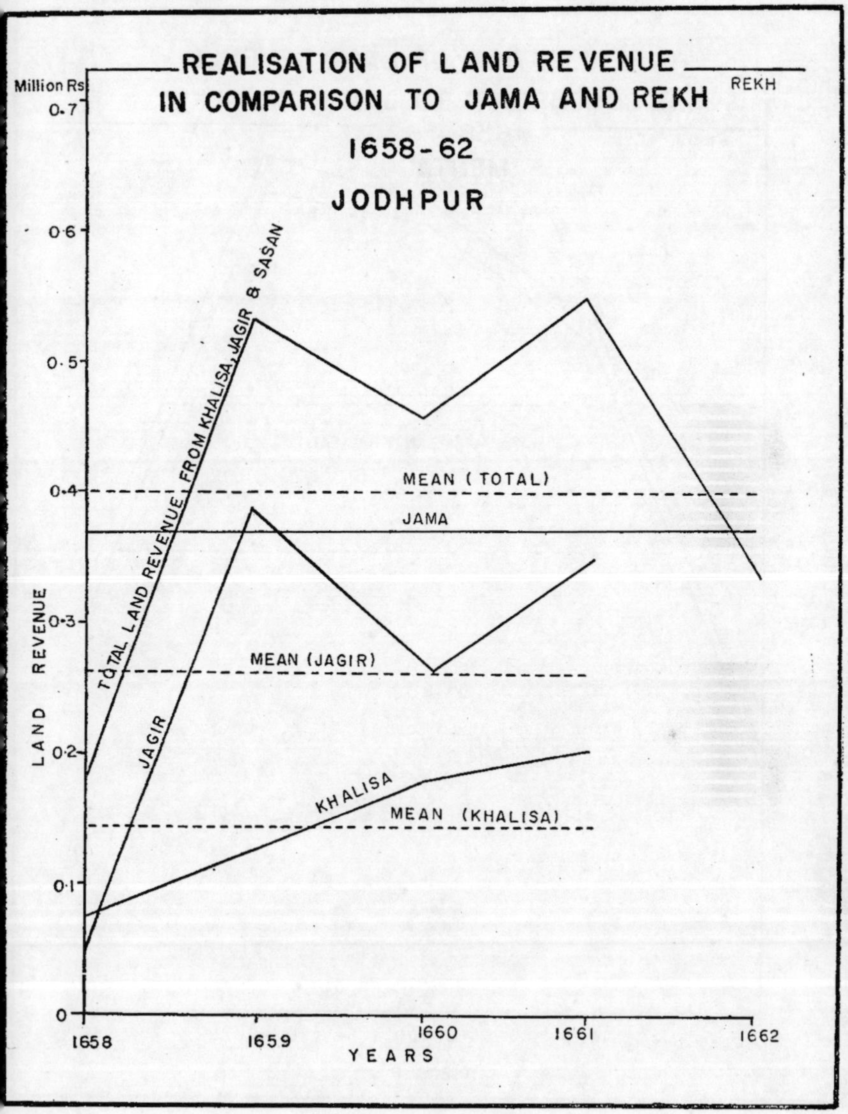
REALISATION OF LAND REVENUE
IN COMPARISON TO JAMA AND REKH
1658-62
JODHPUR
Million Rs
REKH
TOTAL LAND REVENUE FROM KHALISA, JAGIR & SASAN
MEAN (TOTAL)
JAMA
MEAN (JAGIR)
JAGIR
KHALISA
MEAN (KHALISA)
LAND REVENUE
YEARS
0
0·1
0·2
0·3
0·4
0·5
0·6
0·7
1658
1659
1660
1661
1662

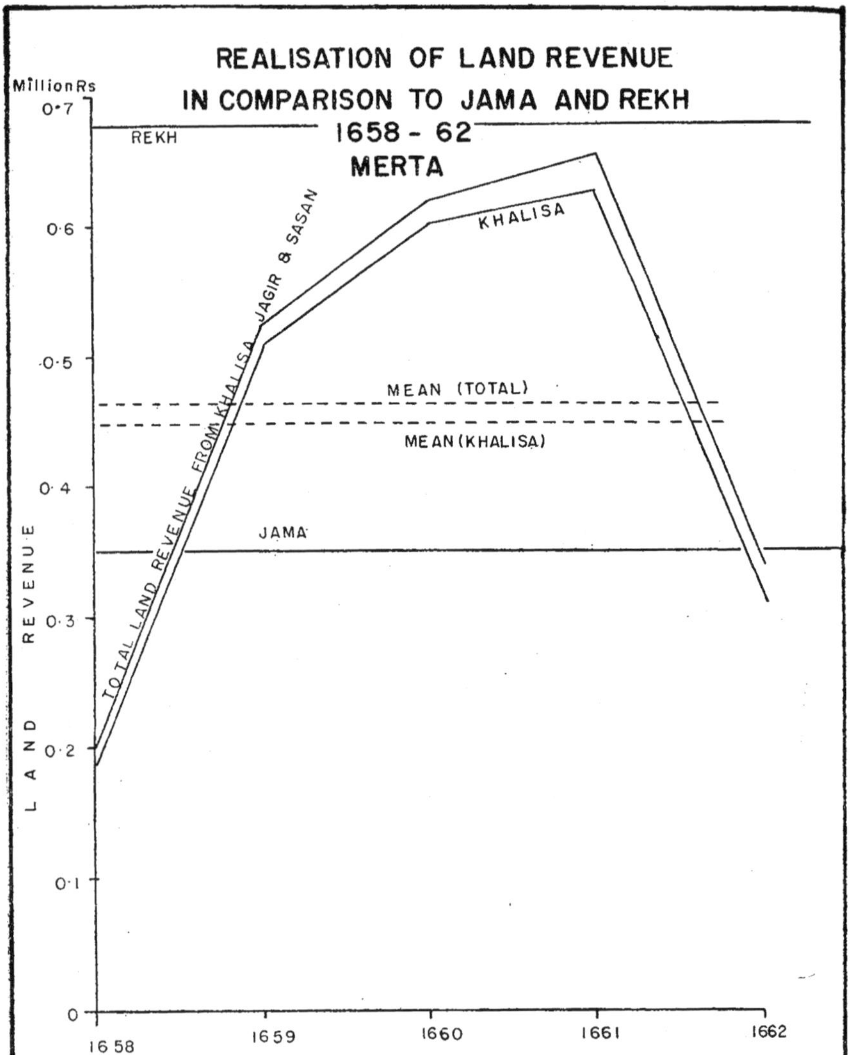
REALISATION OF LAND REVENUE
IN COMPARISON TO JAMA AND REKH
1658 - 62
MERTA
Million Rs
REKH
TOTAL LAND REVENUE FROM KHALISA, JAGIR & SASAN
KHALISA
MEAN (TOTAL)
MEAN (KHALISA)
JAMA
LAND REVENUE
0·7
0·6
0·5
0·4
0·3
0·2
0·1
0
1658
1659
1660
1661
1662
YEARS

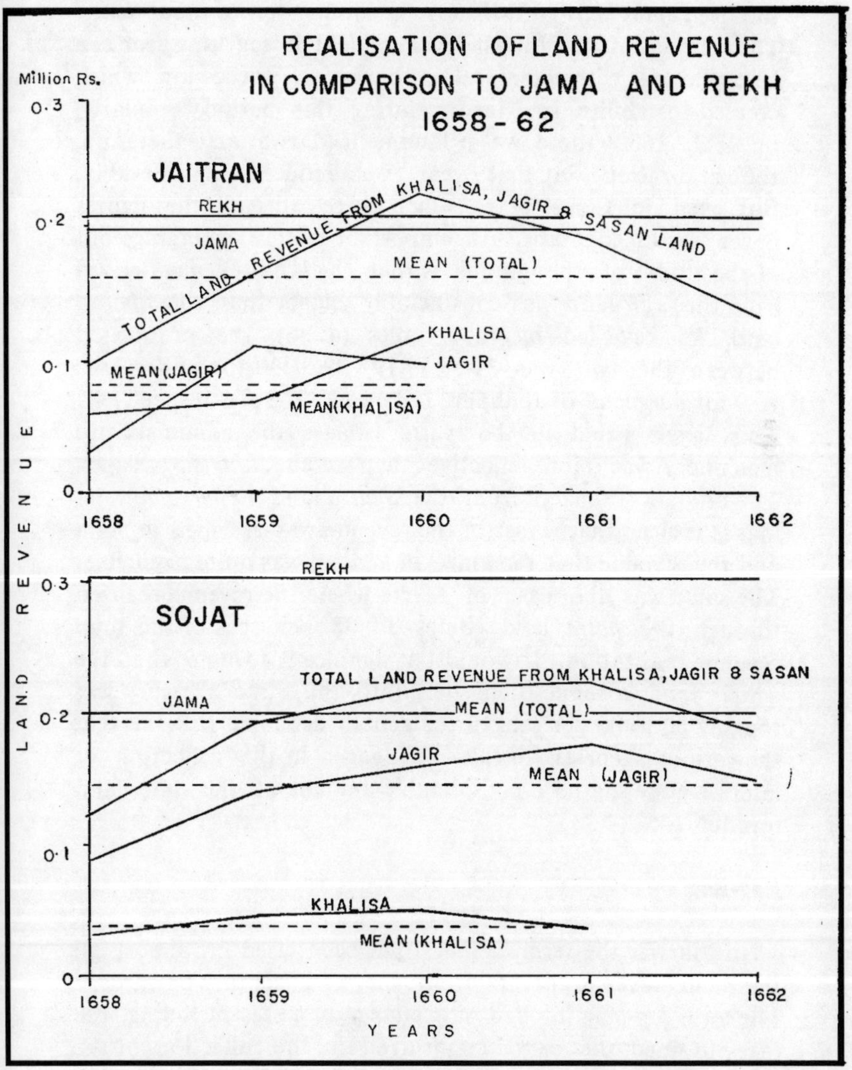
REALISATION OF LAND REVENUE
IN COMPARISON TO JAMA AND REKH
1658 - 62
Million Rs.
JAITRAN
REKH
JAMA
TOTAL LAND REVENUE FROM KHALISA, JAGIR & SASAN LAND
MEAN (TOTAL)
KHALISA
JAGIR
MEAN (JAGIR)
MEAN (KHALISA)
SOJAT
REKH
TOTAL LAND REVENUE FROM KHALISA, JAGIR & SASAN
JAMA
MEAN (TOTAL)
JAGIR
MEAN (JAGIR)
KHALISA
MEAN (KHALISA)
LAND REVENUE
YEARS
0
0·1
0·2
0·3
1658
1659
1660
1661
1662

the four *parganas* of Marwar in comparison to other years. The reason of the lowest revenue yield during this year can be explained with reference to the war of succession, which created instability in Marwar during this period. Similarly, in A.D. 1662 there was a famine in Marwar and therefore, the realization in that year was reduced considerably. But even in those years which were normal, the figures never remained static. An important feature emerging out of the study of the graphs is that the land revenue derived from the *jagir* land was considerably higher than the *khalisa* land. As revealed by the tables (4:3-6), the proportion between the two was 34.88:19.19, 39.51:36.46, and 47.45: 1.89 for *parganas* of Jodhpur, Jaitaran and Sojat respectively. This suggests that in the *patta* villages the administrative machinery was more effective than in the *khalisa* villages. The amount realized from the *khalisa* land in *pargana* Sojat makes it clear that most of the revenue was assigned in *patta* and the revenue that remained in *khalisa* was quite negligible. The same was the case of Merta where the revenue realized through the *patta* land comes to 88 per cent of the total revenue realization. It would be significant to note that the actual land revenue deposited into the state treasury was roughly 50 to 80 per cent of the actual demand. It seems that the various agencies which were engaged in the collection of land revenue shared a considerable amount of the state land revenue.

Lag-Bag

In Marwar the term *lag-bag*[37] has been used in almost all the land revenue grants from the 17th century onwards.[38] The term *lag-bag* implied miscellaneous cesses including the taxes to meet the expenses incurred in the collection of the land revenue and the tax levied on pasture land.[39] According to a recent enquiry it seems that the term *lag-bag* was used in a wider sense which generally meant both regular and irregular cesses levied on agricultural produce.[40] Thus the cesses collected under *kharach-bhog* were also included in *lag-bag*.[41] As has been mentioned, the term *kharach-bhog* was used in a specific reference which is synonymous with *mal-o-jihat*. It is noteworthy that in the list of the cesses, other than *bhog*, Nainsi has included the income of those cesses which comprise *kharach-bhog* as well as other agricultural cesses. Therefore, the term *lag-bag* is more suitable for the cesses mentioned in the tables.

The account of the realization from various items is given in the *Pargana-ri-Vigat* which enables us to study the nature of the taxes and cesses levied over and above the *bhog* (*mal*) and *kharach-bhog*. The lists contain the *hasil* for the years A.D. 1658 to 1662 (V.S. 1715 to 1719) realized under the various heads.

TABLE 4:7

Pargana Jodhpur—Hasil for five years A.D. 1658 to 1662 (V.S. 1715-1719)

Items	*Jama* Asal Rs.	1715	1716	1717	1718	1719	Total average *hasil* of a year Rs.
Sereno	6,563	4,775	5,715	5,666	5,176	1,552	4,577
Bal	1,114	750	932	942	808	860	585
Karab-ghas	560	243	552	564	588	718	533
Rasat	1,998	1,325	0	1,525	0	1,608	1,446
Dumalo	571	488	491	194	494	500	414
Pancharai	0	2,105	1,852	2,186	2,675	2,517	2,227
						Total	9,781

TABLE 4:8

Pargana Sojat—Hasil for five years A.D. 1658 to 1662 (V.S. 1715-1719)

Items	*Jama* *Asal* Rs.	1715	1716	1717	1718	1719	Total average *hasil* of a year Rs.
Sereno	2,391	2,102	2,241	2,068	2,194	2,161	2,153
Gughari	693	541	600	530	593	573	567
Bal	397	247	234	226	273	248	255
Arhat-Mandli	164	71	114	91	93	93	92
Mukati	0	56	63	45	47	61	54
Pancharai	0	245	50	90	98	154	107
Rasat	1,333	872	0	872	0	888	860
						Total	4,088

TABLE 4:9

Pargana Jaitaran—Hasil for five years A.D. 1658 to 1662 (V.S. 1715-1719)

Items	*Jama Asal* Rs.	1715	1716	1717	1718	1719	Total average *hasil* of a year Rs.
Sereno	1,781	945	1,540	1,104	919	1,024	1,106
Shikdari	1,397	996	1,295	930	838	925	996
Bal	194	169	169	159	155	140	158
Milno	59	38	51	49	40	67	48
Rasat	579	536	0	538	0	536	536
Pancharai	0	0	0	0	0	67	67
						Total	2,911

A study of the tables (4:7-9) would show that among the cesses mentioned by Nainsi, *sereno*, *bal*, *rasat* and *pancharai* were commonly levied in all the three *parganas* of Marwar.

The remaining seven cesses, *karab-ghas*, *dumalo*, *gughari*, *shikdari*, *arhat-mandli*, *mukati*, *milano* were levied only in some *parganas*.

From the statistics given in the tables, it is quite obvious that *sereno* was an important cess and in comparison to other cesses the revenue from that cess was considerably higher. It was a regular cess levied in all the *parganas* of Marwar. A later manual of the year A.D. 1863 describes it as a cess levied on the *hasil* which the *jagirdars* realized from the cultivators. The manual further mentions that the *jagirdars* realized *sereno* from the cultivators at the rate of one-sixth of every maund of produce whereas the *jagirdars* paid to the state only at the rate of one maund on every hundred maund.[42] From the term used in reference to *pargana* Pokaran it appears that it applied to the demand of a *seer* on a maund.[43] As the figures of the cess are given in rupees, it appears that the *jagirdars* collected it in kind from the cultivators and used to pay the cess in cash to the state.

Another important cess levied in all the *parganas* of Marwar was *bal*. This was also known as *hujdar-ri-bal*.[44] The term *bal* signifies the force, and *hujdar* stands for the *Raj*, i.e., the cess levied to meet the expenses of the state army. It was collected from the *kharif* crop and was charged at the rate of Rs. 20 from small villages and Rs. 25 from big villages.[45] Later in A.D. 1657 the amount was reduced to Rs. 5 and Rs. 10 respectively.[46]

Other cesses mentioned in the tables are *pancharai* and *ghasmari*. In the tables Nainsi shows the income from these cesses under the heading *pancharai*, but while mentioning the rates he has included them under the term *ghasmari*.[47] A study of the various items included in *ghasmari* and *pancharai* would show that it included both types of animals: those who eat grass and those who eat leaves. Thus it seems that Nainsi has used them interchangeably at different places.

Apart from these, following cesses were levied in different *parganas* of Marwar:

For *pargana* Siwana *dumalo* is noted in the table of cesses. It was collected in cash from each house of the village on the basis of the economic resources of the family.[48] Another cess *milano* my be defined as present or *nazr* offered to the *hakim* at the rate of Re. 1 per house. It was charged alongwith other *kharif* cesses.[49]

Besides the above there were many other cesses which were levied to meet the expenses of the officials who visited the area to collect the land revenue. These officials—*amil*, *kamdar*, etc., were paid their daily expenses by the cultivators which was known as *gughari*.[50] The peasant also paid a cess to the *karwaries* or guardsman who watched and protected their crops.[51] It was known as *firohi*.[52] The cultivators also paid a cess to the officials at the time of collection of grain in *khaliyan*. It was known as *rasad*[53] and charged at the following rate:[54]

Item	Charges made on every khaliyan in *dogani*
1. *Dawat Puja*	5
2. *Kagal-patha*	5
3. *Sutgodi*	5
4. *Faduthawani*	1
5. *Potdari*	1
6. *Kharreda*	2
Total	19

From the above figures it is obvious that in all the cesses were paid in cash.

The state levied an extra cess on the fields where facilities of irrigation were available. It was known as *arhat-mandli*. *Shiqdari* cess was levied on the *kharif* crop and it was collected in favour of the *shiqdar*. In *pargana* Siwana a cess was levied on the trade of *ghee*. It was known as *gheeai*.[55] In *pargana* Siwana a cess was levied on milch cow, she-buffalo, she-goat, etc. It was known as *sadi*[56] or *saudeni-ri-gineti*.

In reference to *pargana* Pokaran, the term *Mukata* or *Mukati* has been mentioned as a tax levied on *hal* at the rate of Rs. 3 or Rs. 3.50 per *hal*. It was charged only from the Rajputs.[56]

The examination of the nature of the above taxes and cesses shows that all these were not agricultural. The cesses, *bal, rasad, dumalo, gughari, arhat-mandli, shiqdari* could be included in the category of *kharach-bhog* or agricultural cesses collected over and above land revenue (*mal* or *bhog*). The available data of the actual realization made through these cesses present the following picture:

Pargana	*Hasil* from agricultural cesses (Rs.)	*Hasil* from land revenue (Rs.)	Column 2 as percentage of Column 3
1	2	3	4
Jodhpur	7,022	4,05,722	1.58
Sojat	3,981	1,71,417	2.19
Jaitaran	2,911	1,37,398	2.00
Total	13,914	7,24,537	1.70

The figures mentioned above show that the revenue from these cesses was considerably lower in comparison to the state demand of *kharach-bhog*.[57] The examination of revenue derived from the agricultural taxes in various years shows that Nainsi did not include the revenue of all the cesses falling in this category.[58] At the same time it may also be noted that under the category of *kharach-bhog*, the peasants had to pay many cesses to the local officers of which no records are available.

Non-Agricultural Taxes

The items given in the lists of taxes and cesses also contain the revenue of those taxes which cannot be included among the cesses falling under *kharach-bhog*. They are mentioned as *pancharai* and *ghasmari*. It has been discussed that in reference to the total revenue, the revenue from these two items has been given under the title '*ghasmari*'. The rates were fixed according to the category of the animals. In the year A.D. 1662 the rates of *ghasmari* were fixed for *pargana* Merta, which are given below:[59]

Items	Charges in Dogani[60]
1. Cow	5
2. *Berath* (calf)	4
3. She-goat, Sheep	1
4. Buffalo	10
5. *Jhoutha* (Male buffalo)	8
6. Camel	15

The rates mentioned above were the same as those prevailing during the time of Maharaja Gaj Singh.[61] The revision of these rates in A.D. 1662 indicates that after the death of Maharaja Gaj Singh, the rates on various animals must have been raised. This may be supported by the fact that in the same year rates on other items were also reduced.[62]

It is doubtful if the same rates were prevailing in other *parganas* of Marwar. In the *Pargana-ri-Vigat* there is hardly any reference to these rates. In the *amal-dastur* of *pargana* Pokaran, where the state land revenue has been mentioned, no mention has been made of the rates of *ghasmari*.

The state derived considerable revenue from *ghasmari*. The statistics given in the *Vigat* regarding *pargana* Jodhpur reveal that the *hasil* from this tax alone was Rs. 26,328 while the *hasil* from the land revenue (*bhog*) was Rs. 26,22,800 on an average from the year A.D. 1654 to 1662.[63] This shows that the realization from *ghasmari* was 7.7 per cent of the land revenue (*bhog*). If the amount of *ghasmari* is added to the amount of *kharach-bhog* it would come roughly to 12 per cent of the land revenue in the *pargana* of Jodhpur and about 22 to 25 per cent in the *pargana* of Pokaran. But such a conclusion would be misleading because the peasant derived extra income from cattle in various ways of which the principal was the sale of *ghee* and stock of young cows and buffaloes, the sale of sheep wool, and hire charges from camels. Thus the taxes paid under the *ghasmari* were separate from the *kharach-bhog.*

Among the non-agricultural taxes, the revenue from *mapa-dan* and *margvahin* constituted a considerable portion of the revenue of the state. A tax levied in *thikanas* on goods imported and exported was called *mapa.* The term *mapa* was often employed as a generic term for various taxes imposed on sales. The *dan* was in fact the same as *mapa* but was calculated *ad valorem.*[64] The term *margvahin* is synonymous with *rahdari* used in the Mughal documents.[65] During the reign of Jaswant Singh the rules relating to the internal and external trade, and the taxes on the sale of various commodities were in prevalence. In reference to *pargana* Pokaran, Nainsi mentioned the duties imposed on the sale of various articles.[66] The state made the distinction between local traders (*mahajans*) and the traders from outside of Marwar. The outsiders paid *dan* and in addition to it they had to pay *biswa,* i.e., 5 per cent of the total value of the goods. The local traders were exempted from *biswa* but they paid *dan.*[67]

On the sale of silk and cotton cloth the charges were made at the rate of 8 *dogani* per maund.[68] The *biswa* was also levied on it. Similarly, the same rates prevailed on the sale of copper, *kansi* (bell metal), brass (*peetal*), zinc, lead, *kathar gesi,* coconut, *meerach* (chillies) and *pipal.*[69] On sugar, *sut* (thread) *sodha* and ghee, 6½ *dogani* were charged as sales tax. The rate on the sale of *jeera* (stamen), *ajwain, sowa, ghana, bilali* and *haldi* was 3.5 *dogani,* and on *gur,* oil, cotton, iron and *lakh* was 5.5 *dogani.*[70] On *methi, rai, sarso, alsi, til, munj* and *saji,* 5.6 *dogani* were charged as sales tax.[71]

It is noteworthy that on the above-mentioned articles the traders had to pay both *biswa* as well as sales tax. This suggests that the trade of these articles was in the hands of outsiders. The local traders were mainly engaged in the internal trade and they paid the tax in kind at the rate of one seer on each maund.[72] The difference in the mode of payment indicates the difficulty of the local traders in making cash payment as they would not have sufficient cash in hand. But on the other hand the traders who came from outside had sufficient money to invest. The articles brought for sale by the traders were not only for Jaitaran but covered the whole of Marwar. The reference made by Nainsi in his account of *pargana* Pokaran should be considered along with the fact that Jaitaran was situated on the imperial trade route and, therefore, the external trade was possible from there only. The reference of *mapa*, is thus understandable as the charge from the import and export of articles made in that *pargana*. For the internal trade no account is given by any contemporary source. But the trend suggests that the state earned a large part of its revenue from these tariffs.

The state also received considerable revenue from the fairs (*melas*). The term used for this tax was *mela-mapa*, i.e., state duty on the sale of the articles in the fairs and other taxes of similar nature. The revenue from this source also contributed a notable amount to the state exchequer. This statistics available on *pargana* Jodhpur show that the revenue from the fairs was 2.7 per cent of the total revenue in 1662.[73]

Another important source of state revenue was *margvahin* (*rahdari*). It was a tax levied on the traders passing through the routes connected with the boundary of Marwar. From *pargana* Pokaran the revenue received from *rahdari* was Rs. 5,000 in the year A.D. 1659.[74]

The above-mentioned details reveal that the rates of the *bhog* varied from *pargana* to *pargana* in Marwar. These variations were due to various reasons such as productivity of land, irrigation facilities, caste structure, and the general condition of the peasants. The magnitude of the *lag-bag*, similarly, varied from *pargana* to *pargana*, though any increase in the rates could be challenged by the preasants. In the context of *pargana* Merta it has been stated that the incidence of these cesses bore heavily upon the cultivators. During the reign of Maharaja Gaj Singh the hardship of these taxes was realized though little was done to reduce the burden.[75] It seems that after the death of Maharaja Gaj Singh and during the period of the regency of Jaswant Singh some new cesses had been imposed and rates of some taxes were also increased.[76] Consequently, in the beginning of A.D. 1643 (V.S. 1700) Miyan Khoja Farasat, *desh-diwan* of Jaswant Singh, made some concessions reducing the rate of some taxes and cesses.[77] But it is not known what he did in this regard. It was only after the post of *desh-diwan* was given to Muhnot Nainsi that some important measures were adopted to reform the system. In the year A.D. 1657 (V.S. 1714) with the efforts of Nainsi some of these cesses were removed which were imposed during the regency and he tried to fix the old rates prevailing during the time of Maharaja Gaj Singh.[78] It seems that these efforts could hardly decrease the amount of the heavy cesses. Thus again in the year A.D. 1661 more concessions were made. In the same year a delegation from Merta went to the Mughal court and protested against the excessive burden of the taxes.[79] As a result of this two cesses, *kanwaria* and *tagirat-bal* were removed.[80] Apart from these some other cesses, which were levied on *khaliyan* known as *khet-kharach*, etc., were also discontinued.[81]

Again in A.D. 1662 (V.S. 1719) some *jat zamindars* of the *tappas* of Lawera and Rahin of *pargana* Jodhpur protested against the heavy burden of taxation to the Mughal Emperor and requested him to abolish those cesses which were levied as additional cesses during Jaswant Singh's reign.[82] With the consent of Bhati Raghunath, the then *vakil* in the Mughal court, the Emperor issued an order to Muhnot Nainsi to continue only those cesses which were levied during Gaj Singh's reign. Accordingly some additional cesses were withdrawn and the taxes which were dropped in the year A.D. 1661 (V.S. 1718) were reimposed, though Nainsi reduced the rate of some cesses.[83] These instances show that whenever a complaint was lodged against the local Raja or his administrative measures to the Emperor by the local people, the Emperor was not slow to intervene in the internal administration of the state and his decision was respected, though generally, the Emperor did not interfere. The contents of *Pargana-ri-Vigat* give an impression that Nainsi also tried to stop the illegal practices adopted by the *amins*.[84] We have already mentioned that he fixed the mode of payment made to the *kamdars* and *kanvaris* in cash. Thus during the time of

Jaswant Singh attempts were made to reduce the burden of cesses on the cultivators.

Fiscal Administration

During the reign of Maharaja Jaswant Singh a definite pattern of the fiscal administration was evolved. Although the *pradhan*, being the chief of the administration of the state, enjoyed supreme power in the state, the *desh-diwan* and *tan-diwan* were responsible for financial matters.

The offices of the *desh-diwan* and the *tan-diwan* were considered second and third in the rank of the administrative machinery. It is noted that prior to Jaswant Singh's reign the office of *tan-diwan* was not in existence. It seems that the additional post of the *tan-diwan* was created to limit the powers of the *diwan*, although the necessity to create a separate office to keep the balance between the claim of the *pattadars* and the *jagir* granted to them in lieu of their salary cannot be overlooked. The *tan-diwan* was to assist the work of *desh-diwan*. As the main function of *tan-diwan* was to keep the account of the salary of the *pattadars* and other accounts related to the same subject, his work was inter-connected with the function of the *desh-diwan*. The charges made against Muhnot Nainsi and Muhnot Sunderdas, who were *desh-diwan* and *tan-diwan* respectively, show that both were jointly responsible for the wrong practices in the office. From a letter addressed to Nainsi by Raja Jaswant Singh it is revealed that the *desh-diwan* was not only incharge of the management of the state finances, but also shouldered the responsibility of the assignment of the *pattas* to the nobles against their salary on behalf of the Maharaja and the general administration of the state.[85] Whenever needed he also discharged the duties as a military commander.[86] Thus the inner working and the details of the procedure followed reveal that the position of *desh-diwan* was higher than that of the *tan-diwan*, but the latter cannot be considered his subordinate.

In the court of the Maharaja both of them had the right to appear and put matters relating to their duties before the Maharaja, but the *desh-diwan* enjoyed the position of placing his suggestions on political and financial matters. He had the privilege of putting the seal upon *farmans* and other documents issued from his office. The office of *desh-diwan* maintained all the revenue records of the income and expenditure of the *parganas*.[87] He was also responsible for looking after the interest of the cultivators and kept check on the officials engaged in the collection of revenue.[88] He issued instructions to the *hakims* of the *parganas* on all the financial matters.[89]

The *hakim*, apart from his civil and military duties, was also responsible for the revenue administration of the *pargana*. It may be noted that in the *pargana* where a *hakim* was appointed, the posts of *amil* and *faujdar* did not exist. This suggests that as long as the *pargana* remained in imperial territory, the *amil* remained incharge of the state land revenue but when the appointment of *hakim* was made the former ceased to function. Thus the *hakim* combined the functions of *faujdar* and *amil* in the *pargana*. The Rathor ruler entrusted the same responsibilities to the *hakim* when he was appointed in the *jagir* granted to him outside Marwar.[90]

The appointment of the *hakim* was made on merits. Consequently, the most experienced persons who possessed both administrative and military qualities were appointed on that post. The consideration of the clan and the preference on the basis of the hereditary claim were not given much weight.

The *hakims* of Merta and Jodhpur were paid Rs. 200 per annum in addition to the *patta* they held for their *military* services. The *hakims* appointed at Sojat, Phalodi Siwana, Jaitaran, etc., were paid @ Rs. 100 per annum.[91] Apart from that fixed amount which was paid in cash, the *hakims* held *pattas* for military service they had to perform. The worth of the *patta* was determined on the basis of the position and the strength of the contingents of the *hakims*. The same consideration was made when the assignment of a higher office was made to a *hakim*.

As the *hakim* had to look after the general administration, the over-all responsibility to collect the land revenue was entrusted to the *amin*. It was he who was directly concerned with the payment made by the peasants as state dues. He implemented the orders of the *desh-diwan* and fixed the rates of *bhog* and *lag-bag* as formulated by the state.[92] It may be noted that the appointment of the *amin* was made directly by the *desh-diwan*. The *hakim*, though superior in power to *amin*, had no right to remove him without the consent of the *desh-diwan*. It is difficult to say to what extent the removal of *amil* influenced the power and position of the *amin* in Marwar.[93] The references in the *Pargana-ri-Vigat* regarding the status of the *amin* show that the position remained the same in the *pargana* ruled by the Rathor ruler. But in comparison to his position under imperial *khalisa*, a definite change was inevitable as we find that, earlier he (the *amin*) had to work under *karori*.[94] But at the same time the position of *amin* was hardly changed. This further suggests that he was the local person and thus remained on that post without any change, although his appointment had to be confirmed by the *desh-diwan*.

Under the Rathor rule the *amin* not only assessed the land revenue but was also responsible for the collection of the share of the state from the cultivators. He was assisted by another officer known as *qanungo*. During the time of Akbar when Merta was incorporated into the *khalisa*, the *qanungo* was referred to as an accountant who maintained and preserved the land revenue records.[95] The post remained unchanged even after *pargana* Merta had been granted to the Rathor ruler. The post of *qanungo* existed in other *parganas* also.[96] He kept the information concerning the revenue receipts, area statistics, local revenue rates, and practices and customs of the *pargana*. He provided the administration the revenue and area figures of *patta* assignments.[97] Thus his functions were very much similar to the functions of the imperial *qanungo*.

Apart from these officials there were others who formed an important part of their revenue administration, but because of local variations they had different designations. Generally, they belonged to the same area where they had to serve. The *chaudharis*, besides being cultivators and thus possessing the right of a self-cultivator (*khud kashtkar*), enjoyed the special power and position in the village.

They enjoyed many illegal perquisites over and above the legal cesses incorporated in their *sanad*.[98] As there were a number of *chaudharis* within a specified area paying *nazarana* to the Maharaja, they divided the amount of contribution among themselves. On the death of a *chaudhari* his post along with its emoluments passed on to his heir by the rule of primogeniture, who became *chaudhari* in name, but frequently shared the emoluments with all of his brothers or such of them as were strong enough to insist on having a share. The post itself, in addition to and distinct from the emoluments was often partitioned, on succession by inheritance, following the death of a *chaudhari*. As regards the removal of *chaudharis*, there were three contingencies in which it occurred: (1) in case of inefficiency, the incumbent was obliged to make over the whole or part of his office to a more capable man in lieu of some consideration; (2) a superior officer might order transfer of *chaudhariship* because of inefficiency; and (3) a stranger from outside the village might make a bid for the post. The *chaudhari*, if he wanted to keep his post and emoluments intact, would have to bid higher and a sort of auction would ensue in which the outsider frequently won. Having thus obtained a share in the *chaudharai* he would get a portion of the village area separated for himself in which to found a new village. This frequently happened in villages where the cultivated area was unusually small, and the transfer was generally sanctioned by the state on the pretext of developing the country. The partition of the original area was not meant to confer any land claim on the new *chaudhari*, its object was to provide an area in which he could establish a new village and increase the state revenue.[99]

Thus in the *khalisa* land the major responsibility of the collection of land revenue and general administration fell on the officers appointed by the state. In all *patta* villages, the work was done by the *pargana* and village officials in accordance with the state regulations. Although the assignee had to employ his own officials and soldiers for the collection of land revenue, it was done in collaboration with the village and *tappa* officials, the *muqaddam*, *patwari*, *chaudhari*, and the *qanungo*.

In the *Pargana-ri-Vigat* we come across references of *Kanwaria* and *Kamdar* who as the state's or the *pattadar's* representative collected the land revenue from the *khaliyan* (threshing field).[100] They were not paid their salary directly by the state treasury but as a custom they had the right to claim their share out of the produce.[101] More often than not these officials got their daily expenses met by the village peasants, from whom it was realized as gifts in kind.[102] Thus the peasants ultimately had to accept an extra burden on their shoulders. To make the things simple Nainsi stopped the practice of payment in kind. But it made no change, as the officials continued exacting these presents in kind in addition to payments in cash.[103] Naturally, the burden increased doubly, though it was designed to bring relief to the peasants. Hence the administration again reverted to the old system.

REFERENCES

[1]*Hukumat-Bahi*, ff. 104a-152b.

[2]In the case of Mota Raja Udai Singh, the *patta* granted to Askaran Rathor contains the *rekh* figures of the villages granted to him in *jagir* (*Vigat*, i, 90). Apart from it, we do not find any instance to show that during his time *rekh* was having any meaning. As these *rekh* figures are the same as the *rekh* figures of Jaswant Singh's time, it seems that Nainsi wrote the same figures against the villages granted by Raja Udai Singh; *See* G.D. Sharma, Some land revenue grants of the time of Ajit Singh and Abhey Singh, *PIHC*, 1969, 184.

[3]*Rajputana Gazetteer*, (1879), ii, 24.

[4]*Report on the Administration of Jodhpur State*, (1885-86), 49.

[5]Dr. Narain Singh Bhati in the introduction of *Pargana-ri-Vigat*, refers to the term *rekh* in relation to the *jagir* villages. Dr. B.D. Sharma, in the *Journal of the Rajasthan Institute of Historical Research*, vi, 33, calls it the tribute paid by the *jagirdars*; Dr. G.N. Sharma (*Social Life*, 36) interpreted it (the *rekh*) as a military cess 'which was supposed roughly to be eight per cent of the gross rented value of the estate'. Such an approach is no doubt a result of neglecting the historical background of the state land revenue administration. Dr. G.N. Sharma has not cited any contemporary reference. It seems that his information was based on the account of the later half of the 18th century.

[6]Apart from the *Vigat*, which mentions *rekh* against *khalisa* and *jagir* villages, another contemporary work, *Hukumat-Bahi* records *rekh* for both the *khalisa* and *jagir* villages (f. 135a).

[7]*Mazmu-i-Halat-ve-Intezam Marwar* (1883-84) pp. 353-4.

[8]The figures are based on the data given at the end of the chapter.

[9]*Hukumat-Bahi*, ff. 120a-36b; Also *see*, "Some land revenue grants of the time of Ajit Singh and Abhay Singh". *op. cit.*

[10]*Hukumat-Bahi*, ff. 120a-36b.

[11]*Vigat*, i, 133, 147-8, 204-367, 409-18, 501-8, and ii, 12-31, 116-31, 221-87, 327-57.

[12]*Ibid.*

[13]*Hukumat-Bahi*, ff. 136b.

[14]G.D. Sharma, "Some land revenue grants of the time of Ajit Singh and Abhay Singh", *op. cit.*

[15]In A.D. 1668 (V.S. 1725) a *patta* was granted to Rathor Arsi Keshri Singh Bhagwandasot alongwith the right of *ghasmari*. The *rekh* of the *patta* was Rs. 16,000 (*Hukumat-Bahi*, MS, 187-90).

[16]The term *Tan* has been implied in territories of Amber and Kota. In Marwar the term implied was *rekh*.

[17]*Lag-bag* file No. 202, *Jodhpur Administration*, R.S.A.B. In the ancient and the early medieval chronicles the term *bhog* was used for customary state share of the agricultural produce. Normally the state derived its share at the rate of 1/6th of the produce. For details, *see* U.N. Ghosal, "Some Hindu Fiscal Terms Discussed", *Proceedings of the Fourth Oriental Conference*, ii, 202; Also see, *Land Revenue in India* (ed. R.S. Sharma) 6-7 and 24-6.

[18]*Bhog* or *mal* was the original tax while *lag-bag* represented the charges levied over and above the *bhog*, *Lag-bag* file No. 282. *Jodhpur Administration*, R.S.A.B.

[19]There is a distinction between *dastur-ul-amal* and *amal-dastur*. *dastur-ul-amal* was the compilation of the old rules and regulations which were approved by a ruler. These were the guidelines for the state officials according to which the work was done. *Amal-dastur* comprised the newly framed rules and regulations which commenced with the accession of a ruler. (*Supra. cit.*) Khwaja Yasin, *Glossary of Revenue and Administrative Terms*, British Museum Acc. 6603; Also *see*, *Lag-Bag Enquiry Committee Reports* (A.D. 1893) 29/4. R.S.A.B.

[20]*Vigat*, ii, 88-9.

[21]*Ibid.*, ii, 89-96.

[22]*Ibid.*, ii, 97.

[23]*Ibid.*, ii, 96.

[24]*Ibid.*, ii, 95.

[25]*Ibid.*, ii, 90-1.

[26]*Ibid.*, ii, 96-7.

[27]*Ibid.*, ii, 324-7.

[28]The tax levied on the Rajputs was known as *mukata*. *Vigat*, ii, 330, 339; Also see. *Hukumat Lags*, 29/4, Government of Jodhpur, R.S.A.B.

[29]*Vigat*, i, 396-7.

[30]*Ibid.*

[31]Although the *Banias* and *Mahajans* paid the land revenue at the rate of 1/5th of the *bhog*, it cannot be considered a standard rate.

[32]A study of the revenue documents of Eastern Rajasthan shows that the standard revenue demand in the area was 2/5th of the produce on *polaj* land and 1/3rd of the produce on the *banjar* land. cf. Satish Chandra and Dilbagh Singh, "Stratification and Structure in the village society in Eastern Rajasthan", *P.I.H.C.* 1972. Also *see*, Siddiqi, N.A., *Land Revenue Administration under the Mughals.*

[33]*Vigat*, ii, 225.

[34]The cultivable land (*ziraiti*) measured in that year was 2,39,641 *bighas* and the remaining was 26,129,59 (*Vigat*, ii, 97).

[35]*Vigat*, i, 396-7.

[36]The table is prepared on the basis of the statistics given in the *Vigat* (Vols. I & II) and *Hukumat-Bahi.*

[37]The term *lag* stands for the customary rights of the village officials while the term *bab* is used for the taxes imposed in addition to the regular assessment on the land. The term *abwab* is plural of *bab.*

[38]*Vigat*, ii, 89; G.D. Sharma, "Some agricultural taxes", *P.R.H.C.* 1972.

[39]*Lag-bag* file No. 902, *Mahkma Khas*, Jodhpur Government, R.S.A.B.

[40]*Lag-bag Enquiry Committee Report*, 1941, R.S.A.B.

[41]*Vigat*, ii, 89.

[42]*Hukumat Lag*, file No. 29/4, Part I, 45 (A.D. 1893), *Mahkma Khas*, Jodhpur Government, R.S.A.B.

[43]*Vigat*, ii,

[44]*Ibid.*, ii, 89, 92.

[45]*Ibid.*, ii, 92.

[46]*Ibid.*, ii, 97.

[47]*Ibid.*, ii, 88, 95.

[48]*Lag-bag*, file No. 202, Jodhpur Government, R.S.A.B.

[49]*Hukumat Lag*, file No. 29/4, 46-7, Jodhpur Government, R.S.A.B.

[50]*Ibid.*

[51]*Vigat*, ii, 88-91.

[52]*Hukumat Lag*, file No. 29/4, 86, Jodhpur Government, R.S.A.B.

[53]*Vigat*, ii, 89.

[54]*Ibid.*, ii, 92-3. These cesses were charged in the name of inkpot-ceremony, expenses incurred in purchasing papers for writing, *potdari*, and collecting the grain from the threshing floor.

[55]*Hukumat Lag*, file No. 29/4, I, 64, *Jodhpur Records*, R.S.A.B.

[56]*Hukumat Lag*, File No. 29/4, I, 71, *Jodhpur Records*, R.S.A.B.

[57]*Vigat*, ii, 326.

[58]*See*, *Supra*, 92-6.

[59]In his account of the year A.D. 1663 (V.S. 1720) of the *pargana* of Jodhpur, Nainsi mentions 14 cesses while in the list of the year A.D. 1658 (V.S. 1715) he named only 7 taxes (*Vigat*, i, 158-9).

[60]*Vigat*, i, 166.

[61] 40 *dogani* was equivalent to one rupee (*Ibid.*, ii, 88).

[62]*Ibid.*, ii, 88.

[63]*Vigat*, ii, 94.

[64]*Ibid.*, i, 133.

[65]*Lag-bag* file No. 202, *Jodhpur Records*, R.S.A.B.

[66]*Ibid.*

[67]*Vigat*, ii, 324-6.

[68]*Vigat*, ii, 325.

[69]One maund of cloth contained ten *farad* (*Ibid.*, ii, 325).

[70]*Ibid.*

[71]*Ibid.*

[72]*Ibid.*

[73]*Ibid.*

[74]*Vigat*, I, 167.

[75]*Vigat*, ii, 308.

[76]Tax on the production of *pani* was removed and the rate of *ghasmari* was reduced from 15 to 8 per cent *dogani*. *Ibid.*, ii, 92.

[77]We do not find an account of such taxes but the later descriptions make it clear that tax burden was increased during that period.

[78]*Vigat*, ii, p. 92.

[79]*Ibid.*

[80]*Ibid.*, ii, 93.

[81]*Ibid.*, ii, 93. These cesses were removed on the recommendation of the *Vakil* of Maharaja at the Mughal court, obviously on the order of the Emperor. But the text here is not clear whether the Emperor directly ordered the *Vakil* who in turn consulted the Maharaja or that the Maharaja was directly asked by the Emperor.

[82]*Vigat*, ii, 93.

[83]*Ibid.*, ii, 94.

[84]*Ibid.*, ii, 95.

[85]*Ibid.*

[86]*Basta* No. 12/53, *Jodhpur Records*, R.S.A.B.

[87]*Basta* No. 12/53, *Jodhpur Records*, R.S.A.B. When the Bhatis invaded Pokaran, Muhnot Nainsi was sent as the commander of the Rathor army.

[88]*Byav-Bahi*, i, 213; Basta No. 12/53, *Jodhpur Records*, R.S.A.B.

[89]Letter from Jaswant Singh to Muhnot Nainsi, *Basta* No. 12/53, *Jodhpur Records*, R.S.A.B.

[90]*Ibid.*

[91]*Vigat*, i, 126 and 128.

[92]Rajkarin, *Tiwari Purohit-ki-Khyat*, 43.

[93]*Vigat*, ii. 92.

[94]Under the *khalisa* there were the offices of *karori* or *amil* and *amin* in Merta. *Amin* was under *karori* and was sent in the survey party to carry out measurements for the purpose of assessment. But due to the change in the office of *karori* or *amil*, as a result of the appointment of *hakim*, the office of the *amin* assumed more power in a *pargana* under the control of the Rathor ruler. The change in the working of the *amin* was also seen in the *parganas* under imperial control. For details *see*, Irfan, *Agrarian System*, 276-7.

[95]In reference to Merta we find the existence of *faujdar*, *amil*, and *amin* in A.D. 1620 when it was in the *jagir* of Prince Khurram (*Vigat*, ii, 73-4).

[96]*Vigat*, ii, 77.

[97]Letter from Miyan Farasat to Muhnot Harchand of *Pargana* Jalor dated A.D. 1664 (*Ashadh sudi* 5, 1721) Basta No. 53/5, *Jodhpur Records*, R.S.A.B.: *Jodhpur-Khyat*, ii, 14-15.

[98]Letter from Miyan Farasat to Qanungo Muhnot Harchand. *Supra cit.*

[99]*Bilada Records*, Letter No. 5-15.

[100]*Bilada Records*, No. 10-13.

[101]*Vigat*, ii, 93-5.

[102]*Bilada Records*, No. 20, 25, 29; *Vigat*, ii, 97.

[103]*Vigat*, ii, 96-7.

[104]*Ibid*., ii, 93.

5

PATTADARI SYSTEM AND THE MARWAR NOBILITY

As has been discussed in Chapter 4, the system of *bhai-bant* was replaced by the *pattadari* system which led to the changes in the rights and position of the nobility. Accordingly, the old relationship based on the concept of *bhai-bant* was replaced by a new relationship based upon hierarchy of ranks. Thus the Rathor *sardars* had to accept certain obligations of service, and in lieu thereof, they were granted *pattas*. It may be noted that the assignment of the *patta* was made not only in favour of the *sardars* rendering the state service but also in favour of those who were exempted from the service obligations. Broadly, the *pattas* fell into two categories: (a) *chakari-ka-patta*,[1] and (b) *gair-chakari-ka-patta*.[2]

The *chakari-ka-patta* was granted in lieu of military and other services which a noble was required to render to the Maharaja. As per practice the state rarely paid the salary in cash; the amount of salary was adjusted in terms of the land revenue assignments. Since the *patta* was usually granted in lieu of salary, the state had to determine in each case an area that would yield revenue equivalent to the sanctioned pay.[3] Usually the amount stipulated in *patta* was equivalent to the revenue given in assignment. Whenever the assigned amount was less than the claim of the *pattadar*, the balance was recorded as *talab*.[4] The *talab* could be paid in cash, though the general practice was to assign the additional *patta* to cover the *talab*.[5] The *rekh* figures of each village formed the basis for the determination of the *patta* against one's salary. At the time of assignment of *patta*, the information was sent, along with the copy of *patta*, to the local officials clearly stating the precise rights and obligations of the *pattadars*.[6]

The *pattas* were granted under some specific conditions. The *pattadars* were obliged to render military service, within and outside Marwar. The number of followers and horsemen to be maintained depended upon the amount of salary and the rank of the *pattadars*. From a near-contemporary *Khyat* it is gathered that on the *rekh* of Rs. 1000 the *pattadars* had to maintain one horse and the same rule was observed with the increment of the *rekh*.[7] Rathor Ratan Singh, son of Pahad Singh of Mertia Rathors, held a *patta* of Rs. 4000 *rekh* and was maintaining four horses.[8] Similarly, Prem Singh, son of Hemraj of Chauhan clan, held a patta of Rs. 2000 *rekh* and maintained two horses.[9] In contrast to these examples there are instances where the practice of keeping one horse on every thousand *rekh* was not observed. In a *patta* amounting to *rekh* of Rs. 40,200 granted to Rawal Bharmal and Rawal Maheshdas, their obligations were: (a) Rs. 18,200 to be paid as *peshkash* in two equal instalments, (b) to maintain fifty horses for *zabta* (25 horses by Bharmal and 25 horses by Maheshdas), and (c) to serve by rotation and to maintain sufficient number of followers.[10] This shows that on the *rekh* of Rs. 40,200 the grantees were asked to maintain 50 horses. If we take the ratio of a horse and the figures of *rekh*, the amount would come roughly to Rs. 1,800. In another instance the the grantee was asked to maintain a horse and a camel on the *rekh* of Rs. 35, 000.[11] Another *patta* refers to a horse on Rs. 1000 *rekh*.[12]

These references show that the grantee had to maintain a horse on every thousand *rekh*, although in some cases such a rule was not observed when other obligations were also imposed. It seems that the rule was strictly implemented in a particular situation but could be relaxed with the changing circumstances. Apart from the horse or horses, the *pattadar* had to maintain camels and the *paidal* (foot). In the absence of any contemporary account it is difficult to determine the number of the camel and *paidal* which was to be maintained by a *pattadar*. On the basis of a near-contemporary source it could be said that the number of the camel, *sawar* and footmen was determined at the rate of one *sawar*, camel and footman on Rs. 1000, Rs. 700 and 500 *rekh* respectively.[13] There are references when a grantee could be exempted from maintaining an animal contingent after payment of a particular amount as *peshkash*.[14] This particular system enumerated above was to some extent similar to the *mansabdari* system in which the *mansabdar* was obliged to maintain a specific number of animal contingent upon his rank.

It is evident from the account of *pattas* that at the time of assignment the grantees were required to pay a lump sum amount as *peshkash*. The Raja had an option to accept *peshkash* in cash or in the form of horse or camel or both.[15] After receiving *peshkash, patta* was granted. In case of any lapse on the part of an assignee, the *patta* could be withdrawn, but the withdrawal could be postponed for a fresh *peshkash*, which the assignee was asked to pay.[16] From the details mentioned in the *Bahi* and the *Vigat*, it is difficult to determine any relationship between the *rekh*, *patta*, and the *peshkash*. Sometimes the amount of *peshkash* was half of the *rekh* and sometimes it was almost equal to *rekh*. There is hardly any evidence in favour of *peshkash* ever being more than the *rekh*. This suggests that the imposition of *peshkash* was dependent on the paying capacity of the grantee and the sources of his income, including the productivity of land. The *pattadars* were not expected to render service within Marwar (*desh*) alone but they could be asked to serve outside Marwar also. In the *pattas* this was specifically mentioned that the *pattadars* would not make any objection in serving within or outside Marwar.[17] The condition of service outside Marwar was made compulsory due to the obligations of the Rathor ruler towards the Mughal state. The Rathor ruler needed the services of the *sardars* not only to keep his contingent whenever he had to serve outside Marwar, but also to maintain his control over the *jagirs* granted to him.

Whenever a *pattadar* was required to serve in the *jagir* of the Maharaja granted by the Mughal Emperor outside his *watan jagir*, the necessary increment was made in the salary of the *pattadar*.[18] The increased amount was covered by assigning to him an additional *jagir* of the same amount within Marwar or outside Marwar where the grantee was posted. In case the state failed to assign to him any *jagir* the amount was paid in cash.[19] The increased amount continued to be a part of the salary of the *pattadar* as long as he was serving outside Marwar, but after his return the old terms were restored. The *pattas* granted to the Rathor *sardars* outside Marwar could be taken back as *jagirs* of the *mansabdar* (or the Raja) were transferable or could be cancelled by the Mughal Emperor.

The rights of the *pattadars* were defined in the grants issued to the *sardars*. In the account of the *pattas* granted to Rawal Bharmal and Rawal Maheshdas, the grantees were instructed not to assign any *sasan-khet* (field for religious purposes) out of the *patta* villages granted to them.[20] Similarly, the *patta* granted to Rathor Rinchhoddas mentions that the grantee should not assign any *sasan* land without the prior permission of the state.[21] Such information has not been given in the *Hukumat-Bahi* as it does not contain the full text of the *pattas*. The details of the *pattas* of the time of Maharaja Ajit Singh mention similar conditions as given in the above two *pattas*, which makes it clear that the rights of the grantee were specifically indicated in the *patta*.[22] He was granted the land revenue[23] of the territory mentioned in the *patta*. In some of the *pattas* mention is made of the right of *ghasmari* and *bab* along with land revenue.[24] It is obvious that the *pattadar* held the right of collection of *mal*, and the right of *ghasmari* and other taxes given additionally. Thus, it is implied that the claim of the *pattadar* was strictly limited to the land revenue of the assigned village and this fact was specifically stated in the *patta*. It also implied that the *pattadar* could not claim any right or title to the land in village or villages granted to him. In such a category of assignment the *pattadar* was entitled to the collection of land revenue from the *riaya* (Peasants) in his jurisdiction, but he was not the owner of the land. The ownership and the right of *riaya* remained undisturbed and they paid the state demand to the village officials who in their turn deposited it with the *hakim*. This was an important change in the nature of the *pattas*, in comparison to the *pattas* granted to the Rathor *sardars* earlier. However, while maintaining restrictions on the *pattadars*, the state could interfere in these *patta* lands.

These *pattas* were transferable and were known as *pher-badal-ra-patta*.[25] Accordingly, the amount of the *patta* remained the same but the possession over the villages was subject to change. Rathor Bhagwandas Sundardasot held a *patta* worth Rs. 6,800. In A.D. 1662 (V.S. 1719) he was granted village Bahdawas in *patta* in place of village Thomb. Later on, in A.D. 1675 (V.S.1732) village Thomb, along with other villages, was taken in *khalisa* and he was granted *tappa* Kodeno (in *pargana* Jodhpur) along with 23 villages.[26] In the *Bahi* many references occur which refer to the resumption of old villages and assignments of the new ones.[27] It seems that the transfers of the *patta*-villages were made when there was any fault from the side of the grantee. A study of the *pattas* suggests that although in principle the *pattas* were transferable, it would be wrong to presume that like the *jagirdari* system of the Mughals, the *pattas* were constantly transferred after three or four years. The *pattas* remained with the grantee as long as he was in the state service or till his death. Thus the *pattadars* did not live in a state of uncertainty like the *jagirdars* of the Mughal Empire who could be deprived of their jagirs any time.[28]

After the death of the grantee it depended on the will of the Maharaja to bestow the same *patta* upon the son of the deceased or not. As the amount of *patta* was determined on the basis of one's salary claim it was not necessary that while granting the *patta* to the son of the deceased he should get the same amount or the *patta* or the villages which his predecessor held. The worth of *patta*, whether higher or lower, depended upon the status of the grantee. The assignment could also be made in altogether different *parganas*. Thus these *pattas* were not hereditary and could be taken into *khalisa* or transferred to any other *pattadar*. It is noteworthy that even within Marwar the grantee was not given the villages in one *tappa*.[29] Some time these villages could be scattered over different *tappas* or *parganas*.[30] Such a practice was resorted, primarily, in order to keep control over the *sardars*. For internal stability the earlier arrangement of *bhai-bant* provided an opportunity to the nobles to function independently and to claim hereditary rights in land in one capacity or the other. To avoid such a situation the transferability of the *patta* became an important feature of the *pattadari* system.

Thikana

As has been stated earlier, the system of *bhai-bant* provided an opportunity to various Rathor princes or *sardars* belonging to the various Rathor or non-Rathor clans to maintain hereditary claims over their respective territories. It may be noted that the territorial claim of these various Rathor or non-Rathor *sardars* was recognized over the areas which had been conquered by their ancestors. Their respective territories were known after a capital town or village where they kept their families (*basi*). These were also known *thikanas* and the possessors of these *thikanas* were known as *thikanadars*.[31] The introduction of *pattadari* system reduced the territorial claim of these *thikanadars*. Accordingly, although the capital town or village remained with the descendants of the *thikanadars*, other adjacent villages became transferable as the *patta* villages. During the time of Jaswant Singh, Prithvi raj Bhati, son of Govinddas, served as *pradhan* and held the *patta* worth Rs. 40,000 along with the *thikana* of Lewera.[32] A study of the holdings of his ancestors reveals that during the time of Maldeo, Niba Bhati, the son of Anand Bhati, was granted the village of Lewera. Niba Bhati established his *thikana*[33] there. After the death of Niba, Lewera remained with his descendants. Govinddas Manawat, the grandson of Niba, held Lewera along with other villages in *patta* during the time of Raja Udai Singh and Sur Singh.[34] After the death of Govinddas, Lewera remained in the *patta* of his son Prithiraj Bhati. During Jaswant Singh's reign Prithiraj was holding Lewera in his *patta*. It may be noted that when Govinddas died in A.D. 1606 (V.S. 1663) (during Maharaja Sur Singh's reign) the *patta* of Lewera was granted to his youngest son, Prithiraj.[35] Though the *thikana* Lewera remained in the family, the right of primogeniture was no longer observed in this case. Lewera was treated as the hereditary *thikana* of the family. It was always granted in lieu of the salary of the grantee. The same practice is observed in case of Surtan Bhati, the son of Mana Bhati, who was granted

Kelwa in *thikana* by Maharaja Udai Singh. The said *thikana* was enjoyed by Ramchandra Bhati, son of Surtan, during the reign of Gaj Singh.[36] A study of *thikana* Asop and *thikana* Ahua reveals that during the time of Jaswant Singh, Rathor Raj Singh of Kumpawat clan and Rathor Maheshdas, son of Surajmal of Champawat clan, held the said *thikanas* respectively as their hereditary right.[37] But other villages remained transferable, although their claim over the *thikanas* was accepted as long as they were serving the state.[38]

Thus we see that the *thikanas* of the descendants of the old Rathor and non-Rathor *sardars* were recognized by the Rathor rulers. At the same time the Raja held the right of deciding the successor of the deceased *thikanadar* out of his sons. Thus it could be inferred that although in theory the Rathor ruler could resume the right of a particular *thikanadar* over his *thikana* village, in practice the *thikana* village always remained with the members of the same family. It may be noted that these *thikanas* remained with the holder so long as they rendered service to the Raja.

Grant of Thikana and Bhom

During Jaswant Singh's reign many *sardars* were granted *thikanas*.[39] Rathor Askaran of Pattawat sub-clan who fought in the battle of Dharmat was given a village Mayakor as *thikana*. Later on Askaran populated the village of Mayakor and kept his *basi* there.[40] In the year A.D. 1644 (V.S. 1701) Laxmidas Deorajot established a *thikana* and named it Kanedio.[41] Rathor Sur Singh of Kumpawat clan established a *thikana* in *pargana* Sojat in his own name and kept his household there. He invited the cultivators from the neighbouring areas and populated it.[42] Many other grants or the establishments of the *thikanas* were of similar nature. A study of these grants reveals that the Rathor *sardars* were granted the *thikana* villages separately from the *patta* villages. The grant of such *thikanas* was a reward to the grantee for his meritorious service to the state. It was not essential that only inhabited villages should be granted in *thikana*. Waste lands could be assigned for the purpose of habitation, leading to the establishment of a *thikana*. In case of the *thikana* where the grantee was given land without habitation, the *thikanadar* had to invite the cultivators from neighbouring areas and populate the village. The grant of a *thikana* could also be made out of villages which were already under settlement.

It may be noted that the *thikanadars* had to pay a fixed amount to the state or to the *pattadars* as the case may be. Rathor Ajab Singh Kumpawat held the *thikana* of Ajabwaragudo in the *pargana* of Sojat which was held in *patta* by another state employee. Ajab Singh used to pay a fixed amount of Rs. 40 per annum to the *pattadar*.[43] Similarly, Rathor Himmat Singh Rajawat held the *thikana* of Guddo in *pargana* Sambhar. He paid a fixed amount of Rs. 380 per annum to the *pattadar* (*jagirdar*).[44] The annual consolidated amount paid by the *thikanadars* was known as *bhugat-bhog*.[45] It appears that the amount was fixed after considering the services of the grantee and resources of the village.

Apart from *thikana* villages, the state also granted a village or a part of it as *bhom*[46] to the *sardars*. Rathor Hemraj, son of Rinmal, was given 500 *bigha* of land in village Taleda of *pargana* Merta in A.D. 1710 (V.S. 1767). He was depositing Rs. 37/7/- (Rs. 37.44) annually as *bhom-bab*.[47] Another *sardar* was granted $1\frac{3}{4}$ bigha of land as *bhom* in village Labado of Pali. He was depositing Rs. 9 annually as *bhom-bab*.[48] In another case we find that on 440 *bigha* of *bhom* land Rs. 139/11/- (Rs. 139.69) were charged as *bhom-bab*.[49] The contents show that the territory granted in *bhom* was clearly defined. The local officials were instructed to measure the given area and demarcate it in a particular village or anywhere in a *pargana*, as stated in the *pargana*. The *pattadars* and revenue officials on their part were naturally anxious that the grantees should confine their right to the area of their grant and do not occupy area in excess of it.

Although the grant of *bhom* was considered to be a special favour of the state, the *bhomia* had to pay a fixed amount known as *bhom-bab* to the state. The variations in the rates of the *bhom-bab* show that its rate was not standardized in Marwar. Even in the same *pargana* rates varied. The reason is quite obvious. In the areas where irrigation facilities were available, the rates of *bhom-bab* were higher in comparison to other areas where such facilities were not available.[50] In those areas where the *bhomia* was asked to populate the area, the rates were considerably lower. Sometimes the *bhomia* was even exempted from the payment of *bhom-bab*.[51] It seems that such exemption was made when the *bhomia* colonized the area at his own cost.[52] Thus it may be concluded that the amount of the *bhom-bab* was fixed on the basis of geographical and economic resources of the area, though in all cases the rates of *bhom-bab* were fixed concessionally.

A careful study of the nature of the grant of the *thikana* and *bhom* shows that both the tenures signified similar rights. Such grants were given as *mundkati* or reward for showing valour in war or rendering other meritorious services. These were revenue-free holdings but the retainee paid a quit-rent known as *bhugat-bhog* or *bhom-bab*. These holdings were hereditary and the state did not interfere in their affairs as long as their conduct was satisfactory.[53] Both *thikanadars* and *bhomias* were obliged to serve the state in suppressing dacoities and other crimes in their village and to protect the travellers.[54]

Apart from the *bhom* or *thikana* granted to the *sardars* by the state, references are there to such *bhom* villages which were known as *bhomi-chara-ra-gaon*.[55] Such villages were established by the Rathor princes or *sardars* and later on maintained by their descendants. Similarly there were *bhomi-chara* villages which had been inhabited prior to the advent of Rathors by the Rajput families other than the Rathors.[56] These Rajputs were later on known as *seerivi Rajputs*.[57] In the *parganas* of Sojat, Jaitaran and Sanchor, Nainsi recorded *bhomi-chara* villages which were mainly populated by the Rajputs.[58] The *hasil* figures of these villages suggest that a fixed amount was paid to *pattadar*.[59]

The grandsons of Rathor Jagmal Malawat held 30 villages on *bhomi-chara*.[60] It is mentioned that these Pokarna Rathors who were *bhomias* were neither rendering any service nor paying any *peshkash* or *nalbandi* (army tax) to the state.[61] It seems that *bhomias* were obliged to perform the state service or to pay *peshkash*. The reason as to why the state failed to force the *bhomias* to render the service is quite clear. As these villages were dominated by the members of the same family,[62] it seems that the area was *zortalab*. A study of the settlement of these villages reveals that majority of the members of the *bhomia* family were self-cultivators (*khud-kashtkars*).[63] The *bhomia*, being the descendant of the first colonizer, had the right of realizing land revenue from the peasants and also the right of allotting the uncultivated area to the cultivators. Almost similar privileges were enjoyed by the leaders of subdued tribes, Mers and Meenas, who were recognised as *bhomias*. In the *pargana* of Sojat, 19 villages were exclusively inhabited by Mers who held the *bhom* rights.[64] This account reveals that mostly the *bhomi-chara* holdings represented the last remnants of the Rajput chiefs and the holdings of the tribal leaders whose families had been displaced in the continual struggle for supremacy. The defeated families retained or were allowed to retain certain villages as *bhom* holdings out of consideration by the new conqueror, and being the older settlers having hereditary rights they were looked upon with great respect. The *bhomi-chara* villages were different from the *bhom* land granted by the state. In case of the former, the Raja had to recognize the *bhom* rights of the descendants of the chiefs of the old families, but in case of the latter the Raja made a fresh grant to a *sardar* giving him a definite area in *bhom*.

The account given above makes it clear that the holdings of newly granted *thikanas* and *bhom* were vested with similar rights. Both the grants were hereditary and the grantees were obliged to pay a lump-sum amount to the state annually. In spite of these similarities the two types of grants were different because the holder of the *thikana* was free to extend the area under cultivation by inviting cultivators from the neighbouring areas. Thus the cultivated area under a *thikana* village could be extended. But the holders of *bhom* (not *bhomi-chara*) could not extend their holdings to the cultivated area beyond the land specified. The practice of the grant of the *thikanas* and *bhom* did not imply the emergence of any new class of nobility. In fact, it was not the replacement of the old by the new but a case of individual favour shown towards the members of the same family. At the same time it would be wrong to presume that the old hereditary *thikanadars* had lost their position or influence in the state politics. A study of the holdings of the old *sardars* reveals that the Jaitawat, Kumpawat and Jodhawat Rathors remained in majority and retained their influence. Thus the clan domination remained as before, but now their position depended on the wishes and whims of the Rathor ruler.

It has been observed that a *bhom* or *thikana* generally comprised a village or villages or *patti* (portion) of a village. The *bhom* or *thikana*, therefore, signified a right which belonged to a rural class other than, and standing above, the peasantry. In the village where the peasants belonged to the family of the same clan, who held *bhom* rights, they enjoyed the *khud-kasht* rights. In those areas where the peasants engaged themselves in cultivation, the *bhomia* hardly interfered. He only realised his share from the peasants. Under these circumstances the proprietary right of the *bhomias* and peasants were inter-related. There is hardly any example to show that the *bhomia* had a right to take away the land from the peasants. Obviously, when large areas (or wasteland) remained still unploughed the main concern of a *bhomia*, in normal circumstances, was to keep his peasants rather than lose them. As these *bhoms* were granted by the Raja, the *bhomia* was also to look after the welfare of the peasantry. Since it was a right primarily associated with land, we may expect that it gave its possessor a share in the land produce.

Gair-Chakari-ka-Patta

The term *gair-chakari-ka-patta* implied the grant against which the holder was not obliged to perform state service.[65] It was also known as *ghar-baitha-ri-jagir*. Such grants comprised the *pattas* which were given in *badhara* or *Inam*. Many such grants were given by Jaswant Singh to his *sardars* after his return from the battle of Dharmat.[66] If a *sardar* died fighting in the battle, a *patta* could be granted to his family for maintenance. This was known as *jivika*.[67] Although the holder of such grant was exempted from all taxes, any increase in the size of his holding made it obligatory for him to render the state service.

Composition of the Nobility

The prevalence of the *pattadari* system does not imply that in the Rathor state the *pattadars* belonged to the Rathor clan only. A study of the *pattas* assigned during Jaswant Singh's reign shows that although most of the *pattas* were granted to the different families of the dominant clan (Rathors), the members of the different Rajput clans also figure in it in considerable number. The *sardars* of Rathor clan were mainly the descendants of Rao Jodha's fourteen sons aud twenty-three brothers. The holdings of the Marwar *sardars* above Rs. 1,000 under Maharaja Jaswant Singh from A.D. 1658 to A.D. 1662 reveal that out of 618 *sardars*, 525 belonged to the various Rathor sub-clans.[68] Among the Rathor *sardars* there were 80 Jodhas, 76 Mertias, 75 Kumpawats and 44 Udawats and 22 Champawats and thus the Rathors constituted the largest number.

A study of the *pattas* granted to the *sardars* of various Rathor sub-clans in various *parganas* of Marwar shows that the Kumpawats in *pargana* Jodhpur, Udawats in *pargana* Jaitaran, Jaitawats in *pargana* Sojat, Pattawats in *pargana* Phalodi, Mertias in *pargana* Merta, Narawats in *pargana* Pokaran, Balawats in *pargana* Siwana and Jodhas in *pargana* Jalor had the largest holding.[69] It may be noted that although the Rathor *sardars* of Kumpawat clan held the largest area in *pattas* in Jodhpur, their position in other *parganas* was not the same. It may also be noted that Rathor *sardars* belonging to a *khamp* (sub-clan) did not possess the largest numbers of *pattas* in other *pargana* at a time. This suggests that there could not be one dominant clan in two *parganas*. It seems that in the interest of the state a balance among the various clans of nobility was maintained. This can be supported by the fact that, as mentioned above, the holdings of a *sardar* were not centralized either in one *tappa* or *pargana*. Thus the provision of *daro-bast-jagir* was avoided to eliminate the possible hereditary claim of *pattadars*. The *pattadars* of the Rathor clan who were holding the *pattas* of *rekh* worth Rs. 100 to Rs. 1,000/- were comparatively less in number. The Kumpawat and Champawat Rathor *sardars* who constituted one of the largest groups among the *pattadars* of Rs. 1,000 and above had no *patta* of the latter category. Similarly, another important Rathor sub-clan, Mertia, also held only one *patta* worth Rs. 800. This suggests that the old Rathor families enjoyed the dominating position in the ruling class. Among the non-Rathor *sardars* who formed part of the Marwar nobility were Panwars, Solankis, Chauhans, Kachhawahs, Parihars, Gahilots, Tanwars and Bhatis who belonged to the various Rajput clans. A study of the numbers of the *pattas* of Rs. 1,000 and above further reveals that the number of the non-Rathor *pattadars* was 15 per cent of the total. Among these the number of holders was 25 Bhatis, 21 Chauhans and 18 Kachhawahs who comprised the largest number of the *pattas*. Among the remaining there were 8 Gahilots, 7 Parihars, 3 Muhatas, 3 Musalmans, 2 Gorhs, 2 Tawars, 2 Panwars and 1 Solanki. Obviously, these numbers were negligible in comparison to the number of the Rathor *sardars*. These figures suggest that among the non-Rathor *sardars*, the Rajputs of Bhati clan held the highest place. But Bhatis and the Kachhawahs were not holding any *patta* of the category lower than Rs. 1,000. This further reveals that those clans which held high position in the nobility maintained their superiority over other Rajput *sardars*. The total amount granted to other non-Rathor *sardars* was also very low. Thus the Rathor *sardars* held the highest revenue in both the categories.

Like *patta* villages, *thikanas* were granted in different villages to the members of a particular *khamp*. Thus we find that the *thikanas* of Jaitawat Rathors were scattered in the *parganas* of Jodhpur, Jaswantpura, Jalor, Sojat and Siwana. Similarly the Kumpawats were holding the *thikanas* in the *parganas* of Merta, Jodhpur, Nagaur, Jalor and Sojat.[70] Although, excepting those of the Chauhan *thikanadars*, the figures of non-Rathor *thikanadars* are not given in the table, yet it may be surmised that the same practice was adopted in the case of non-Rathor *sardars* also.

Nobility and Administration

The *sardars* who were granted the *pattas* were not only obliged to render military service but they could also be given administrative assignments. In the state, the *pradhan* was the chief officer and was directly responsible to the Maharaja.[71] The office of the *pradhan* under the Rathor rule could be traced back to the time of Rao Chunda.[72] Since then the *pradhans* had worked as chief advisers to the Rathor rulers. In the absence of the Rathor ruler, the *pradhan* used to be the chief commander of the army. After the acceptance of the suzerainty of the Mughals, the Rathor rulers began to serve outside Marwar and the *pradhan* became the over-all incharge of the state in their absence. The *diwan* and the *bakhshi* took decisions with the consultation of the *pradhan*.[73] Orders as well as the *pattas* granted to the *sardars* were issued by the *pradhan* on behalf of the Maharaja.[74] Thus the *pradhan* held the highest rank in the official hierarchy of the Marwar state.

As has been mentioned earlier, Raj Singh Kumpawat was given the office of *pradhan* at the time of the accession of Jaswant Singh. While holding a *patta* in Marwar he held the imperial *mansab* of 1,000/400. After his (Raj Singh's) death in A.D. 1638 Maheshdas Surajmalot of Champawat branch was appointed as *pradhan*. He held the imperial *mansab* of 1,000/500. In the year A.D. 1643 Maheshdas was removed from the office of *pradhan* and in his place Gopaldas Sunderasot of Mertia branch was appointed as *pradhan*. It may be noted that Gopaldas was not holding any imperial *mansab* and his post as the *vakil* of Jodhpur in the Mughal court had also ceased. It was felt that it would not be possible for him to discharge his duty as *pradhan* while living at the Mughal court.[75] After the removal of Gopaldas Sunderdasot in A.D.1648 Prithi (Prithvi) Singh Goinddasot of Bhati clan took over the charge as *pradhan*. In A.D. 1660 Prithi Singh was removed and in his place Rai Bhagwandas Jogidasot of Champawat branch was appointed. Thus it is apparent that no *pardhan* enjoyed the office for a long time. As soon as the Raja felt the necessity of the removal of *pradhan* he acted with impunity. It is clear that the post was neither hereditary nor confined to the members of a particular branch of the Rathor clan. The appointment of Prithi Singh Bhati, son of Goinddas Bhati, who enjoyed the office of *pradhan* during the reign of Maharaja Sur Singh, suggests that the office of the *pradhan* was not exclusively for the Rathor *sardars*. Non-Rathor *sardars* were also appointed for this office frequently.[76] It may be noted that the person who was appointed on the post generally used to have an experience of the office of the *diwan* and the *hakim*. This suggests that due consideration was given to the merit of the person, although a study of the social and political background of the persons appointed on this post reveals that each of them belonged to the privileged group of the nobility. The short tenure of these *pradhans* shows that it was a part of the policy of the Raja whose interest lay in keeping full control over the *pardhan* who, being the highest officer, enjoyed all the administrative as well as military powers in the state. There is no instance to suggest that after removal from the post of *pradhan* the retainee enjoyed any other post or the *patta* in Marwar. Generally, they accepted the imperial service and thus became the *mansabdar* of the Mughal court. As soon as a *pradhan* joined the imperial service his *patta* holdings were taken into *khalisa*.[77]

The offices of *desh-diwan* and *tan-diwan* were considered second and third in the rank of the administrative hierarchy. It may be noted that prior to Jaswant Singh's reign the office of *tan-diwan* was created to curb the power of *diwan*. Moreover, it was necessary to create a separate office in order to maintain an account of the claims of the *pattadars* and other officers related to the finance department of the state. His work was interrelated with the function of the *desh-diwan*. From a letter addressed to Nainsi by Raja Jaswant Singh[78] it is clear that the *desh-diwan* was not only incharge of the management of the state finance, but he also held the responsibility of the assignment of the *pattas* to the nobles and the general administration of the state.[79] Whenever needed he also discharged the duties of a military commander.[80] A study of the inner working of the office of *desh-diwan* reveals that the *desh-diwan* held a higher position than the *tan-diwan* but the latter cannot be taken as his subordinate. In the *darbar* of the Raja both of them had the right to appear and put matters related to their duties before the Raja, but the *desh-diwan* also enjoyed the position of offering suggestions on political and financial matters. He had the privilege of putting his seal upon *farmans* and other documents issued from his office.[81]

Sukhmal Subhawat Singhvi was *desh-diwan* when Gaj Singh died. He continued in office when Jaswant Singh ascended the throne. After his death in A.D. 1645 Pratapmal Singhvi assumed the office of *desh-diwan,* but later on he was given the post of *hakim* of Merta and in his place Miyan Farasat was appointed as *desh-diwan* in A.D. 1645.[82] He remained in office till A.D. 1657 except for a gap of a year in 1648-49 when he was replaced by Raghunath Bhati. In A.D. 1657 Muhnot Nainsi was appointed *desh-diwan* who remained in this office till A.D. 1666.[83] Raghunath Singh Bhati was then appointed on that post who remained till Jodhpur was taken into *khalisa* after the death of Jaswant Singh.[84] Thus like the post of the *pradhan*, the office of the *diwans* was also assigned only to such person, who had prior administrative experience. Significantly, the offices of the *diwans* always remained with the non-Rathor *sardars* as we find that during Jaswant Singh's reign not a single Rathor *sardar* was appointed to these posts. Among the *desh-diwans* appointed during that period, one was Muslim, one was Bhati Rajput and the rest belonged to the *Vaishya* community.[85] The appointment of Miyan Farasat, Muhnot Nainsi and Sundardas Nainsi and Bhati Raghunath, indicates that professional qualification in the matters of finance was an important factor in the appointment of *desh-diwan* and *tan-diwan.* During the tenure of Miyan Farasat many changes were made in the field of revenue administration. These changes were given definite shape during the tenure of Muhnot Nainsi who worked hard to reform the land revenue machinery.[86]

A significant feature which appeared during Jaswant Singh's reign was the introduction of the practice of *peshkash* for the office of the *desh-diwan.* This is apparent in relation to Muhnot Nainsi and his brother Sunderdas who were imprisoned on the ground that they failed to deposit the *peshkash* as demanded by the Raja. It may be noted that the demand was made when they were working on the posts of the *desh-diwan* and *tan-diwan* respectively. Although, the reason of the demand has not been mentioned in any of the contemporary works, it can be presumed that the office of *diwan* had become a source of profit[87] and, therefore, they were required to pay the amount of *peshkash* to atone for the profit they had gained.[88] It may be noted that as the office of *desh-diwan* dealt with all the revenue matters and decided the assignments to the *pattadars*, the malpractices should have become common.

The *peshkash* was demanded not only for the security but also to make up the balance recovered from the *diwan*.

The other officer of an equal rank was *bakhshi*. However, in the chronicles of Jaswant Singh no reference is made to a person holding that post. Other near-contemporary accounts show that in Marwar the office of *bakhshi* had been very much in existence since the time of Raja Sur Singh.[89] In the administration of Marwar the *bakhshi* was an official of high rank. He was the head of the military department, and, as such the chief representative of the *sardars*. Thus he was well acquainted with the family background of all the *sardars* and the *pattas* they held.[90] All orders related to the assignments of the *pattas* and the appointments to the high officers of the state, such as *hakim*, *amin*, *shiqdar* or *kotwal*, etc., passed through the *bakhshi*. The *bakhshi* was responsible to forward it to the *diwan* after indicating the amount of the *patta* and fixing the number of the *sawar* or footmen according to the rule of the state.[91]

Although *bakhshi* was head of the military department, a study of the various campaigns that took place during the time of Jaswant Singh shows that his position did not give him any supremacy in the army. He was not the supreme commander of the state army nor was he entitled to lead an expedition by virtue of his post. It was at the discretion of the Raja to make suitable arrangements according to the nature of the the expedition and take decision about the composition of the army and the generals to be selected. Thus we find that in an army sent against Jaisalmer, Muhnot Nainsi was given the command of that army, which he was maintaining while he held the office of the *hakim* at Phalodi.[92] As has been mentioned, in 1659 when Aurangzeb took Marwar from Jaswant Singh, the latter appointed Nainsi the commander of the army stationed at Merta against the imperial aggression. Apparently, on both the occasions, the command of the army was not given to the *bakhshi*, but to a person of Raja's choice. It seems that the function of the *bakhshi* in Marwar was very much similar to that of the imperial *mir-bakhshi* under the Mughals.[93] But in the absence of the names of the *bakhshi* serving Jaswant Singh's reign, it may be assumed that only one person might have served during this period. Thus, like the *mir-bakhshi* of the imperial court, the office of *bakhshi* was not subject to frequent changes.

Another important office to be mentioned was *hakim* and *shiqdar* or *kotwal*. As has been mentioned in the previous chapter, the *hakim* was in charge of the *pargana* and enjoyed both civil and military powers. A study of the appointments made during the time of Jaswant Singh reveals that considering a person for the office of *hakim* the merits of the individual weighed high and that his family antecedents were a secondary factor.

The *shiqdar* was another important functionary in the administration. In Marwar the term *shiqdar* was synonymous with the *kotwal* who was solely incharge of the town administration.[94] The appointment of *shiqdar* was made by the Raja with the consultation of the *pradhan* and the *desh-diwan*.[95] Although he had to follow the orders of the *hakims* in his *pargana*, he was directly responsible to the Raja. The primary duty of the *shiqdar* was to adopt security measures for the welfare of the town.[96] He kept an eye on the activities of the people and noted the details about every person coming in and going out of the city. He was answerable for all the thefts and other crimes committed within the town and if he failed to stop them he had to make good the loss.[97] Beside these police duties, the *shiqdar* had to supervise over the market arrangements and was responsible for the collection of the state dues in the town and its vicinity. Whenever a person died without leaving a male issue, the decision was taken on the basis of the enquiry of the *shiqdar*.[98] Thus the office of the *shiqdar* was similar to the office of the *kotwal* of the Mughal Empire.[99]

During the time of Maharaja Gaj Singh, the office of the *shiqdar* was held by Radhodas, son of Kumbhkaran of Champawat Rathor clan.[100] We do not have the names of the *shiqdars* of the time of Jaswant Singh. The reference that Radhodas held the *patta* during Jaswant Singh's reign suggests that he held the same office till his death. The account of the time of Ajit Singh reveals that Shobhawat Dayaldas of Mertia clan held the office of *shiqdar* of Jodhpur.[101] It is clear that Radhodas worked as *shiqdar* during the time of Gaj Singh and Jaswant Singh till the latter's death. During Ajit Singh's reign the office was held by Shobhawat Dayaldas of Mertia clan. This suggests that office of the *shiqdar* was permanent and the officer appointed on this post continued till his death. Although it was not hereditary, as we have seen that the above-mentioned *shiqdar* belonged to the Champawat and the Mertia clans of the Rathors, it remained in the possession of the Rathor *sardars*.

The above narration makes it clear that in spite of the majority of the Rathor *sardars* in the Mewar nobility, the administrative arrangements were not exclusively in their hands. Non-Rathor *sardars* were treated equally and enjoyed the highest administrative positions. Significantly, while the offices of *pradhan* and the *hakims* of the *parganas* remained mostly in the hands of the Rathor and non-Rathor *sardars,* the offices of the *diwans* always remained in the hands of non-Rathor *sardars* particularly those who belonged to the *Vaishya* community. This was perhaps to discourage the retention of the offices of both the *pradhan* and *diwan* by Rathor *sardars.* But an equally important factor behind the appointment of the *diwans* was their experience in the field of revenue administration.

APPENDIX 5:I

(A) Rathor sardars holding the pattas of Rs. 1000 rekh and above.

S. No.	Pattadar	Nos.	Holdings in Marwar *Rekh* in Rupees	Holdings outside Marwar	Total Rs.
1	2	3	4	5	6
1.	Fitak	1	(300)	—	(300)
2.	Bidawats	2	2,000	—	2,000
3.	Patawats	22	42,400	—	42,400
4.	Roopawats	8	17,500	—	17,500
5.	Jagmals	20	39,300	4,500	43,800
6.	Balawats	21	45,220	1,000	46,220
7.	Mandawats	16	44,900	2,000	46,900
8.	Uhad	6	31,600	—	31,600
9.	Dungrot	3	7,500	—	7,500
10.	Bhiwot	4	5,800	—	5,800
11.	Chaundawats	1	1,000	—	1,000
12.	Purbia Rathors	5	11,000	3,000	14,000
13.	Sindhals	3	4,200	—	4,200
14.	Baithwasia Rathors	1	1,200	—	1,200
15.	Sanda Raimalot	1	1,500	—	1,500
16.	Deorajots	2	8,000	—	8,000
17.	Chawada Rathors	1	1,900	—	1,900
18.	Gangadia	3	4,150	—	4,150
19.	Mahchas	7	99,900	—	99,900
20.	Champawats	22	4,00,300	97,300	4,97,600
21.	Mertias	76	3,66,800	84,200	4,51,000
22.	Kumpawats	75	2,86,650	1,51,650	4,38,300
23.	Jodhas	80	4,05,800	2,28,400	6,34,200
24.	Jaitawats	28	1,40,100	36,000	1,76,100

Appendix 5:1 (Contd.)

1	2	3	4	5	6
25.	Udawats	44	1,56,090	1,62,300	3,18,390
26.	Karamsot	30	90,300	10,900	1,11,200
27.	Raipal Jodhaut	1	1,100	—	1,100
28.	Narawat	3	49,150	—	49,150
29.	Bikawat	1	—	8,000	8,000
30.	Khangarot	1	—	10,000	10,000
31.	Khangor Jodhawat	2	7,000	7,000	14,000
32.	Sujawat	2	2,800	—	2,800
33.	Karnots	8	31,500	11,500	43,000
34.	Bhojrajots	3	17,000	5,000	22,000
35.	Mandnot	1	4,000	—	4,000
36.	Bharmalot	4	56,000	13,000	69,000
37.	Akherajot	24	33,700	8,500	42,000
38.	Tank	2	2,000	—	2,000
39.	Vaisa	1	5,000	—	5,000
	Total	525	24,35,760	9,42,240	33,78,010

Appendix 5:1 (Contd.)

(B) Non-Rathor sardars holding the pattas of Rs. 1000 rekh and above

S. No.	Pattadar (Clan)	Nos.	Holdings in Marwar *Rekh* in Rs	Holdings outside Marwar	Total Rs.
1	2	3	4	5	6
1.	Muhtas	3	5,000	—	5,000
2.	Panwars	2	1,800	—	1,800
3.	Solankis	1	2,700	1,000	3,700
4.	Chauhans	21	64,100	31,700	95,800
5.	Kachhawahas	18	28,950	1,24,600	1,53,550
6.	Parihars	7	12,200	—	12,200
7.	Gahlots	9	14,700	—	14,700
8.	Tanwars	2	—	16,000	16,000
9.	Gorhs	2	12,000	7,000	19,000
10.	Musalmans	3	6,500	—	6,500
11.	Bhatis	25	1,28,407	8,500	1,36,907
	Total	93	2,76,357	1,89,800	4,66,157

Numer of the Rathor *Pattadars* ... 525
Number of the Non-Rathor *Pattadars* ... 93

Total 618

APPENDIX 5:2

Rathor and Non-Rathor sardars holding the patta of rekh worth Rs. 100 to Rs. 1,000

S. No.	Pattadars (Clan)	Nos.	Holdings in Marwar *Rekh* in Rs.	Holdings outside Marwar
1	2	3	4	5
		(A)—*Rathor Sardars*		
1.	Fitak	2	600	—
2.	Patawats	6	2,900	—
3.	Roopawats	6	2,500	—
4.	Jagmals	8	4,000	—
5.	Balawats	7	4,700	—
6.	Uhad	2	1,100	—
7.	Dungrots	4	2,000	—
8.	Bhiwots	2	1,100	—
9.	Chaundawats	19	8,200	—
10.	Purbia Rathors	2	700	—
11.	Sindhals	3	900	—
12.	Gangadias	13	6,550	—
13.	Mertias	1	800	—
14.	Jodhas	4	1,600	—
15.	Jaitawats	4	2,200	—
16.	Udawats	1	900	—
17.	Karamsots	6	2,900	—
18.	Karnots	2	600	—
19.	Akherajot	5	3,200	—
20.	Vais	1	300	—
21.	Walisa	1	700	—
22.	Mandala	2	1,200	—
23.	Chahadda	1	600	—
24.	Jaisinghots	3	1,100	—
25.	Jeelua	2	850	—
26.	Jhunjharia	1	300	—
27.	Chanchenga	1	300	—
28.	Jaitmal	6	3,100	—

Appendix 5:2 (Contd.)

(B)—*Non-Rathor Sardars*

1	2	3	4	5
1.	Charans	2	500	—
2.	Muhta	5	2,500	—
3.	Panwars	24	10,500	—
4.	Solanki	1	400	—
5.	Gahlots	4	1,400	—
6.	Chauhans	16	7,700	—

(a)	Total Rathor Sardars	116	56,750
(b)	Total Non-Rathor Sardars	52	23,000

APPENDIX 5:3

I. (A) Holdings of the various Rathor sub-clans in parganas of Marwar

S. No.	Name of the clan	No. of holdings	Land Revenue
1	2	3	4
		Pargana Jodhpur	
1.	Bidawats	1	2,000-00
2.	-do-	3	3,000-00
3.	Patawats	15	27,000-00
4.	Roopawats	6	10,000-00
5.	Jagmal	3	6,000-00
6.	Balawats	8	20,400-00
7.	Mandawats	9	27,106-00
8.	Uhad	11	31,500-00
9.	Dungrots	3	5,500-00
10.	Bhiwots	4	5,800-00
11.	Chaundawats	1	1,000-00
12.	Purbia Rathors	6	21,200-00
13.	Sindhals	2	2,800-00
14.	Baithwasia		1,500-00
15.	Sanda Raimalot	1	1,990-00
16.	Deorajotswats	2	1,900-00
17.	Chaweda Rathors	1	
18.	Gangadia	2	3,050-00
19.	Mahcha	3	47,000-00
20.	Kumpawat	36	2,37,100-00
21.	Champawats	27	1,56,100-00
22.	Mertias	28	90,700-00
23.	Jodhas	17	58,600-00
24.	Jaitawats	4	5,900-00
25.	Udawat	7	36,500-00
26.	Karamsot	17	50,100-00
27.	Narawat	1	2,500-00
28.	Sujawats	2	2,800-00

Appendix 5:3 (Contd.)

1	2	3	4
29.	Karnots	5	21,000-00
30.	Bhojrajot	2	7,000-00
31.	Mandnot	1	4,000-00
32.	Bharmalot	2	3,500-00
33.	Akherajot	8	10,000-00
			9,07,146-00
	Pargana Jaitaran		
1.	Mertia	3	9,000-00
2.	Kumpawat	4	25,000-00
3.	Jodhas	16	32,700-00
4.	Jaitawats	1	1,500-00
5.	Udawats	12	79,690-00
6.	Akherajot	2	2,000-00
			1,39,890-00
	Pargana Sojat		
1.	Champawat	14	80,200-00
2.	Kumpawat	21	71,000-00
3.	Jodhas	2	23,500-00
4.	Jaitawats	25	85,700-00
5.	Udawats	8	20,800-00
6.	Karansot	1	2,000-00
7.	Bhojrajot	1	1,500-00
8.	Akherajot	14	23,300-00
			3,08,000-00

Appendix 5:3 (Contd.)

Pargana Phalodi

1	2	3	4
1.	Bidawats	1	3,000-00
2.	Patawats	10	15,000-00
3.	Roopawats	2	6,300-00
4.	Jodhas	1	2,000-00
5.	Karamsot	3	8,300-00
6.	Karnot	1	1,000-00
	Pargana Merta		
1.	Bidawats	1	3,000-00
2.	Pattawats	1	500-00
3.	Jagmal	3	10,600-00
4.	Sindhals	2	1,400-00
5.	Baithwasia	1	1,200-00
6.	Gangadia	1	1,000-00
7.	Champawat	15	50,000-00
8.	Mertia	40	2,40,300-00
9.	Kumpawat	9	25,300-00
10.	Jodhas	40	1,73,000-00
11.	Jaitawats	1	1,500-00
12.	Udawats	10	35,300-00
13.	Karamsot	2	4,000-00
14.	Khangor Jodhawats	1	2,000-00
15.	Bhojrajot	1	8,500-00
16.	Akherajot	1	2,500-00
17.	Take	1	1,000-00
	Pargana Pokaran		
1.	Narawats	1	41,150-00
	Pargana Siwana		
1.	Jagmalot	5	7,000-00
2.	Balawats	6	12,200-00
3.	Mahcha	1	3,400-00

Appendix 5:3 (Contd.)

1	2	3	4
4.	Champawat	1	2,000-00
5.	Jodhas	1	2,100-00
6.	Udawat	1	6,000-00
7.	Karamsot	1	1,400-00
8.	Karnot	1	5,500-00
	Pargana Jalor		
1.	Bidawats	1	2,000-00
2.	Jagmals	7	9,200-00
3.	Balawats	10	10,400-00
4.	Mandawat	8	18,400-00
5.	Uhad	2	8,800-00
6.	Mahewacha	3	4,200-00
7.	Champawat	6	8,200-00
8.	Mertia	4	7,900-00
9.	Kumpawat	5	9,800-00
10.	Jodhas	10	32,700 00
11.	Jaitawats	3	8,500-00
12.	Udawat	5	21,500-00
13.	Karamsot	6	8,200-00
14.	Raipal Jodhawats	1	1,100-00
15.	Narawat	1	3,000-00
16.	Khangor Jodhawat	1	5,000-00
17.	Karnot	2	3,000-00
18.	Bharmalot	1	500-00
19.	Akherajot	6	8,000-00

II. Non-Rathor Sardars' holdings in various parganas of Marwar

1	2	3	4
		Pargana Jodhpur	
1.	Solankis	1	1,100-00
2.	Chauhans	15	51,100-00
3.	Kachhawahs	1	3,000-00
4.	Parihar	6	10,200-00
5.	Musalman	3	5,500-00
6.	Bhatis	14	47,800-00
		Pargana Jaitaran	
1.	Chauhan	1	6,500-00
2.	Bhati	1	500-00
		Pargana Sojat	
1.	Solankis	1	1,600-00
2.	Chauhans	1	1,000-00
3.	Bhatis	3	12,000-00
		Pargana Phalodi	
1.	Parihars	1	2,600-00
2.	Bhatis	2	12,500-00
		Pargana Merta	
1.	Panwars	2	2,600-00
2.	Chauhans	1	2,200-00
3.	Kachhawahs	2	5,500-00
4.	Parihars	3	4,000-00
5.	Gaurh	1	12,000-00
6.	Bhatis	2	12,200-00

Appendix 5:3 (Contd.)

1	2	3	4
		Pargana Siwana	
1.	Chauhans	2	4,000-00
2.	Musalmans	1	1,000-00
3.	Bhatis	5	9,300-00
		Pargana Jalor	
1.	Chauhans	6	19,200-00
2.	Parihars	3	3,500-00
3.	Bhatis	4	11,500-00

(B) Position of the dominant clans in the parganas of Marwar

S. No.	Name of the clan	No. of the *Pattas*	Land Revenue
1	2	3	4
		Pargana Jodhpur	
1.	Kumpawat	36	2,37,100-00
2.	Champawat	27	1,56,100-00
3.	Mertias	28	90,700-00
		Pargana Jaitaran	
1.	Udawats	18	79,690-00
2.	Jodhas	16	32,700-00
3.	Kumpawats	4	25,000-00
		Pargana Sojat	
1.	Jaitawats	25	85,700-00
2.	Champawats	14	80,200-00
3.	Kumpawats	21	71,000-00
		Pargana Phalodi	
1.	Patawats	10	15,000-00
2.	Karamsots	3	8,300-00
3.	Roopawats	2	6,300-00

Appendix 5:3 (Contd.)

1	2	3	4
		Pargana Merta	
1.	Mertias	40	2,40,300-00
2.	Jodhas	40	1,73,000-00
3.	Champawats	15	50,000-00
		Pargana Pokaran	
1.	Narawat	1	41,150-00
		Pargana Siwana	
1.	Balawats	6	12,200-00
2.	Jagmals	5	7,000-00
3.	Udawat	1	6,000-00
		Pargana Jalor	
1.	Jodhas	10	32,700-00
2.	Udawats	5	21,500-00
3.	Mandawats	8	18,400-00

APPENDIX 5:4

Thikanas and Thikanadars[1]

S. No.	Clan	Name	Village	Pargana
1	2	3	4	5
1.	Karnot	Durgadas	Karno	Panchpadra
1.	Chauhan	Ram Singh	Jalotro	Jaswantpuro
2.	,,	Manohardas	Josiyad	Nagaur
3.	,,	Ajab Singh	Sankhwas	Nagaur

[1]The table is based on the information available in *Basta* No. 97/4, *Jodhpur Records*, R.S.A.B.

Appendix 5:4 (*Contd.*)

1	2	3	4	5
4.	,,	Harnath Singh	Dipawab	Jalor
5.	,,	Sabal Singh	Derapali	Jalor
6.	,,	Berisal	Nagani	Jalor
7.	,,	Dayaldas	Kalnedo	Jodhpur
8.	,,	Man Singh	Makraw	Parbatsar
9.	,,	Prithi Singh	Kurno	Pali
10.	,,	Dalpat Singh	Kadnot-Adena	Pali
11.	,,	Ramchandra	Pamaero	Sanchor
1.	Gangadia Rathors	Deidas	Jasia	Jodhpur
2.	,,	Jagsal	Leniamio	Jodhpur
3.	,,	Bhanu	Mukronini	Panchpadra
4.	,,	Kalyan Singh	Nero	Jaswantpuro
1.	Mehcha	Prithraj	Bhichalsi	Jodhpur
2.	,,	Bakht Singh	Nosaro	Jaswantpuro
3.	,,	Kaloli	Thob	Panchpadra
4.	,,	Manohardas	Thob	Panchpadra
5.	,,	Bhanuji	Muknorini	Panchpadro
6.	,,	Kalyan Singh	Naro	Jaswantpuro
1.	Narawat	Sabal Singh	Guhe	Nagaur and Bhudano
2.	,,	Man Singh	Bhrudyas	Parbatsar
1.	Sankhela	Gordhan	Bhatkorio	Jodhpur
1.	Patawat	Bithaldas	Khario	Phalodi
2.	,,	Mayajalji	Kelansar	Phalodi
3.	,,	Jodh Singh	Simanwo	Phalodi
4.	,,	Askaran	Mayakor	Phalodi
1.	Jaitawat	Dhirat Singh	Khand-adewel	Jaswantpuro
2.	,,	Himmat Singh	Uda	Jalor
3.	,,	Bhav Singh	Alasan (Half)	Jalor
4.	,,	Udai Bhan	Khutlio	Bilado

Appendix 5:4 (Contd.)

1	2	3	4	5
5.	„	Sadul Singh	Khutlio	Bilado
6.	„	Mowandas & Himmat Singh	Sarano	Jalor
7.	„	Ajab Singh	Bado Gudho	Sojat
8.	„	Naraindas & Sawaldas	Dundala Badho	Sojat
9.	„	Udaibhan & Partap Singh	Bali	Sojat
10.	„	Sadup Singh	Bahali	Sojat
11.	„	Sujan Singh	Khokhro	Sojat
12.	„	Deokaran	Bagadi	Sojat
13.	„	Jagram & Roop Singh	Sarang-was	Sojat
1.	„	Jait Singh & Raghunath Singh	Hungao	Bilado
2.	„	Puranmal & Sujan Singh	Jadan	Sojat
1.	Kuba	Rao Keshodas	Thur	Jaswantpuro
2.	„	Keshodas	Munthela	Jaswantpuro
1.	Malawat	Gordhan	Gudho Bijara	Sojat
1.	Bhayel	Askaran & Ramchandra	Modi	Siwano
1.	Mandela	Delpat Singh	Baswani (Half)	Nagaur
2.	„	Sundardas & Narhardas	Panwo	Jalor
3.	„	Dalpat Singh & Amar Singh	Bisroth	Jalor
4.	„	Sundardas	Barani	Jalor
5.	„	Narhardas (See No. 2)	Sirano	Jalor
6.	„	Kanji	Chopedi	Sojat

Appendix 5:4 (Contd.)

1	2	3	4	5
1.	Musalman	Bilkhan	Siwano	Jalor
2.	„	Sodaj Khan	Chhaldi	Sanchor
3.	„	Amir Khan	Medo	Sanchor
1.	Deorajot	Likhmidas	Kanedio	Shergarh
1.	Kumpawat	Narkhan	Nadaser	Jophpur
2.	„	Sabal Singh, Ajab Singh, Bharmal & Kumbh Karan	Lawanio (one-fourth each)	Bilada
3.	„	Keshri Singh	Khario Bado	Merta
4.	„	Kishen Singh	Khariari Basni	Merta
5.	„	Fateh Singh	Banas	Merta
6.	„	Nar Singh	Rajod	Merta
7.	„	Bhopal Singh	Budi	Godwar
8.	„	Mehkaran & Sirdar Singh	Khiwas	Godwar
9.	„	Dalpat Singh	Parasaro	Nagaur
10.	„	Shyam Singh	Bodin	Nagaur
11.	„	Sabal Singh	Suhano	Nagaur
12.	„	Shyam Singh	Uan	Jalor
13.	„	Sabal Singh	Katalio	Sojat
14.	„	Sur Singh	Sur Singh-ro-Gudo	Sojat
15.	„	Ajab Singh	Ajabaro Gudo	Sojat
16.	„	Meghraj	Chelawal	Sojat
17.	„	Madhodas	Ghando	Sojat
18.	„	Jagannath Singh	Uapli	Sojat
19.	„	Sabal Singh	Dorandi-sodo	Sojat
20.	„	Goindas	Melop	Sojat
21.	„	Nar Singh	Redawar (Half)	Sojat

Appendix 5:4 (Contd.)

1	2	3	4	5
22.	,,	Keshri Singh	Siriyari	Sojat
23.	,,	Gordhandas	Chedawal	Sojat
1.	Goingade Rathor	Champoji	Manarobas	Sergarh
2.	,,	Jai Singh	Metuhama	Sergarh
3.	,,	Kalyan Singh	Tebedi	Sergarh
4.	,,	Meng Singh	Galaiser	Sergarh
5.	,,	Bhagwandas	Khirji	Sergarh
6.	,,	Sadul Singh	Sekhalo	Sergarh
7.	,,	Sunderdas	Neto	Sergarh
8,	,,	Ram Singh	Bhojasobas	Sergarh
9.	,,	Dungar Singh	Asaro	Sergarh
10.	,,	Ugar Singh	Fateh Singh-ro-bas	Sergarh
1.	Saicha Rathor	Ajab Singh	Sindari	Malani
1.	Mertia Jagmalots	Amar Singh	Manari (6 villages)	Nagaur
2.	,,	Nar Singh	Samal	Jaitaran
3.	,,	Gokaldas	Achaldas	Merta
1.	Mertia Goindasot	Jaskaran	Itawo	Merta
1.	Mertia Chandawat	Murardas	Kupadawas	Merta
1.	Jodha Udai Singhot	Keshri Singh	Pisagan	Ajmer
2.	,,	,,	,,	,,
1.	Jodho Chandrasenot	Nar Singhdas	Tantodi	Ajmer
1.	Mertia Vithaldasot	Aidan	Jegiyar	Nagaur
2.	,,	Banmalidas	,,	,,
			Total — 101	

APPENDIX 5:5 (A)

The following charts show the emergence of various khamps (sub-clans) of tne Rathor clan*

1. Rao Asthan (A.D. 1273-1292)

- —Joop's sons
  - —— Sindhal = *Sindhal* Rathor
  - —— Joolu = *Joolu* Rathor
  - —— Joora = *Joora* Rathor
  - —— Uhad = *Uhad* Rathor
  - —— Mulu = *Mulu* Rathor
- —Dhandal—*Dhandhlot* (or Dhandal Rathor)
- —Chachig—*Chachig* Rathor

APPENDIX 5:5 (B)

2. Rao Chunda (A.D. 1394-1423)

- ——Randheer = *Randheerot*
- ——Aradkamal = *Aradkamlot*
- ——Kanha = *Kanhawat*
- ——Sahesmal = *Sahasmalot*
- ——Bhiv = *Bhivot*

*These charts are based on the information available in the *Nainsi Khyat*, *Jodhpur-Khyat* and *Dayaldas Khyat*.

APPENDIX 5:5 (C)

3. Rao Viram (A.D. c. 1374-1383)

- Devraj—*Devrajot*
  - Chahaddeo = *Chahaddeot*
- Gangode—*Gangodei* Rathor
- Jai Singh—*Jaisinghot* Rathor

APPENDIX 5:5 (D)

4. Rao Rinmal Chundawat (A.D. 1428-1438)

- Rao Akheraj—sons—Maharaj—son—*Kumpa* = *Kumpawats*
  - Panchayen—son—*Jaita* = *Jaitawats*
    Bhada = *Bhadawat*
  - Rana = *Ranawats*
  - Mala = *Malwats*
  - Nagraj = *Nagrajot*
- Rao Jodha—(*See* another chart)
- Kandhal—*Kandhlots*
- Champa—*Champawats* (Champa's son)—Goindas = *Goindasots*—Bherudas-son-*Jagmal* = *Jagmalots*
- Lakha = *Lakhawats*
- Bhakarsi—son—*Bala* = *Balawats*
- Dungarsi—son—*Dungarot*
- Jaitmal—Bhoj = *Bhojrajot*
- Mandal—*Mandlawat*
- Paat—*Patawat*
- Roopa—*Roopawat*
- Karan—*Karnoot*
- Sanda—*Sandawat*
- Mandal—*Mandelot*
- Ouda—*Oudawat*
- Vera—*Verawat*
- Hapa—X
- Admal—X

——Jagmal—Khetsi = *Khetsiot*
——Natha—*Nathut*
——Karamchand—X
——Sindha—X
——Tejsi—X
——Saver—X
——Sagata—X
——Govind—X

APPENDIX 5:5 (E)

5. Rao Jodha Rinmalot (A.D. 1453-1489)

——Neeba—X
——Satal—X
——Duda—(Succeeded to Rao Jodha)
——Karamsi—*Karamsiot*
——Raipal—*Raipalot*
——Vanveer—*Vanveerot*
——Jaswant—X
——Kumpa—X
——Chandrao—X
——Bika—*Bikawats*
——Bida—*Bidawat*
——Joga—X
——Bharmal—*Bharmalot*
——Duda—*Mertias*—(Grandsons)——
　　——Chanda = *Chandawat*
　　——Jaimal = *Jaimalot*
——Ver Singh—*Versinghot*
——Joga—son—Khangar = *Khangarot*
——Suja—sons————Shekha = *Shekhawat* Rathor
　　—Devidas = *Devidasot*
　　—Udaji = *Udawat*
　　—Prayagdas = *Prayagdasot*
　　—Sanga = *Sangawat*
　　—Mampa = *Mampawat*

REFERENCES

[1]*Chakari* (service) *ka* (of) *patta* (lease) stands for the grant conferred for service. *Hukumat-Bahi* contains a detailed list of such *pattas*.

[2]*Patta* granted without any service obligation was termed as *gair-chakari-ka-patta*.

[3]The *pattas* listed in *Hukumat-Bahi* and *Patta-Bahi* (Basta No. 97, *Jodhpur Records*, R.S.A.B.) mention the amount of salary of the grantee of the *patta*. After mentioning the *patta-rekh* or amount of salary, the revenue of the sanctioned *jagir* is given which was supposed to be equivalent to the *patta-rekh*. If the granted amount was less, the balance was shown as *talab* which was, in principle, paid in cash.

[4]*Talab* (request, petition), a demand of pay. According to the various documents given in *Hukumat-Bahi* and *Patta-Bahi* (R.S.A.B.) the term *talab* is used for the pay fixed by the Raja.

[5]*Hukumat-Bahi*, ff. 110a, 115b.

[6]*Bilada-Ke-Itihasik-patra*, No. 1-9, R.S.A.B.

[7]*Rathora-ri-pidia-ri-Khyat* (MS), 84.

[8]*Vigat*, ii, Appendix I (A), 408-10.

[9]*Ibid*. The account mentions of few more names who also maintained the horses at the same proportion.

[10]*Vigat*, i, 367-72.; *Hukumat-Bahi*, f. 152b.

[11]Rathor Durjan Singh held a *patta* worth Rs. 3,500 on condition that he would keep a horse and a camel and would pay Rs. 60 as *peshkash* (*Hukumat-Bahi*, f. 106a).

[12]*Hukumat-Bahi*, f. 104a.

[13]*Marwar-ra-Pedia-ri-Khyat* (SS), 85. Also *see*, *Chiefs and Leading Families in Rajasthan*, 7.

[14]Basta No. 97/4, *Jodhpur Records*, R.S.A.B.

[15]Rathor Parbat Singh who was granted a *patta* worth Rs. 1,000 was asked to pay Rs. 500 and a horse as *peshkash* (*Hukumat-Bahi*, f. 107b).

[16]*Hukumat-Bahi*, ff. 109b. It is mentioned that when Rathor Hardas was posted at *Thana* Shathalna some articles were stolen from the house of Pathan Husain Khan in A.D. 1670 (*Vs*. 1727). Consequently, his *patta* was withdrawn but later on it was restored after receiving from him Rs. 400 as *peshkash*.

[17]The words "सो चाकरी भली भात करसी,
मेलसी जठे जसी उजर करण पावे नही"
have been written in all the *pattas* issued to the *pattadars*. Basta No. 101/14, R.S.A.B.

[18]Basta No. 76, File No. 2, *Jodhpur Records*, R.S.A.B.

[19]*Hukumat-Bahi*, f. 126a.

[20]*Hukumat-Bahi*, f. 152a.

[21]*Basta* No. 7, File No. 2, *Jodhpur Records*, R.S.A.B.

[22]*Infra*.

[23]As the *rekh* represents the land revenue demand of a territory, it implied that the revenue from other sources was not a part of *patta-rekh*.

[24]Rathor Arsi, son of Kishan Singh, held a patta worth Rs. 16,000 which was granted to him in A.D. 1667 (*Ashadh vadi* 14, 1724) at Aurangabad. In A.D. 1668 (V.S. 1725) Rathor Arsi was given the right of *ghasmari* along with *mal* (*Hukumat-Bahi*, f. 145a). Rathor Sabal Singh Priyagdasot was given the revenue of *dan* and fairs along with *mal*. *vide*. f. 148a.

[25]*Vigat*, ii, 399.

[26]*Hukumat-Bahi*, f. 141a.

[27]*Hukumat-Bahi*, f. 123a.

[28]For the transfer of the *jagirs* and its impact on the peasantry, see, *The Mughal Nobility*, 89-92.

[29]The *pattas* mentioned in the *Hukumat-Bahi* clearly indicate the practice of assigning *patta*-villages in different *parganas*.

[30]Rathor Prithviraj Vithaldasot held the patta worth Rs. 12,400 in Marwar. He was granted Rs. 5,000 in 4 villages of *pargana* Jodhpur and Rs. 7,400 in 4 villages of *pargana* Merta (*Hukumat-Bahi*, f. 125a).

[31]*Lag-bag* File No. 202, *Jodhpur Administration*; Basta No. 97/4, *Jodhpur Records*, R.S.A.B.

[32]*Nainsi Khyat*, ii, 157.

[33]Sometimes the term *Rajasthan* has been used in place of *thikana*.

[34]*Nainsi Khyat*, ii, 154-5.

[35]*Ibid*., ii, 156-7.

[36]*Ibid*, ii, 157-8.

[37]Basta No. 11/49, *Jodhpur Records*, R.S.A.B.

[38]*Ibid*.

[39]*Basta* No. 97, Reg. No. 4 (R.S.A.B.) contains the list of the *sardars* who were granted village or villages as *thikana*.

[40]*Ibid*.

[41]*Ibid*.

[42]*Ibid*.

[43]Basta No. 97/4, *Jodhpur Records*, R.S.A.B.

[44]*Ibid*.

[45]Basta No. 97/4; *Lag-bag* file No. 202/4, *Jodhpur Records*, R.S.A.B.

[46]*Bhom* : Hereditary landed estate held free of assessment; though the holder paid a fixed amount to the state.

[47]Basta No. 76/4, *Jodhpur Records*, R.S.A.B.

[48]*Ibid*.

[49]*Ibid*.

[50]*Lag-bag* file No. 202, Jodhpur Records, R.S.A.B.

[51]Rathor Mukanddas was granted village Bankh in *pargana* Jalor. He was exempted from *bhom-bab*. *Basta* No. 76/4, *Jodhpur Records*, R.S.A.B.

[52]Rathor Badridas Mertia fought against the Mers and drove them out of village Jalsu in *pargana* Merta. Consequently, he was granted *bhom* in the same village. He inhabited the area and therefore exempted from the *bhom-bab*. Basta No. 76/4, *Jodhpur Records*, R.S.A.B.

[53]*Lag-bag* file No. 202, *Jodhpur Records*, R.S.A.B. Baden Powele, *Land System of British India*, i, 329-30. For the general characteristics of *bhom* tenure, *see* the *Imperial Gazeteer of India*, xiv, 195-6.

[54]A study of the records of *thikana* Bilada reveals that the holder of the said *thikana* was the *sirvi* Rajputs who enjoyed that land prior to the Rathors' advent. Later they engaged in cultivation and paid *bhom-bab* to the state. (*Bilada Records*, 1-5, *Thikana* Bilada).

[55]*Vigat*, ii, 347.

[56]*Ibid*.

[57]The Rajputs who held the villages on *bhomi-chara* were descendants of the subdued Rajput families. They later on engaged in cultivation. Since they started ploughing the land, they came to be called *Sirvi* Rajputs.

[58]*Vigat*, i, 461, 531-4, and ii, 340-400; *Basta* No. 76/4, *Jodhpur Records*, R.S.A.B.

[59]The Sirvi Rajput of village Ladpura of *Pargana* Sojat paid Rs. 60 per annum to the *pattadar* of Bagadi (*Vigat*, i, 461).

[60]*Vigat*, ii, 340.

[61]*Ibid*.

[62]*Ibid*., ii, 340-5.

[63]For the definition and characteristics of *Khud-kashtkar*, *see* Satish Chander, 'Some Aspects of Indian Village Society in Northern India during the 18th Century', *I.H.R.*, March 1974, pp. 53-6.

[64]Such villages were out of the revenue jurisdiction as we find that no assessment figures were given against these villages. *cf*., i, 532-5.

[65]Basta No. 97/5, *Jodhpur Records*, R.S.A.B.

[66]Basta No. 79/3, contains a list of such grantees, R.S.A.B.

[67]*Lag-bag Enquiry Committee Report* (1883), 95-6; *Reports on Jodhpur Constitutional Reforms* (1944), 49.

[68]*See* Appendices Nos. 1 and 2 given at the end of this Chapter.

[69]*See* Appendix No. 3, given at the end this Chapter.

[70]*See* Appendix No. 2, given at the end of this Chapter.

[71]*Ajitodaya*, 18/33; *Hukumat-Bahi*, f. 124b. The *pradhan* was also known as *Musahib* (*Mazmun-i-Halat-va-Intezam-Marwar*, 261).

[72]In reference to the account of Rao Asthan, Nainsi refers that Dhabi was the *pradhan* of Raja Partapsi, the ruler of Khed. (i, 12). For the names of the persons who were appointed as *pradhan*, see, *Ibid*., ii. Appendix Nos. 478-9; *History of Oswals*, 321-7.

[73]Letter from Jaswant Singh to Nainsi, Basta No. 12/53, *Jodhpur Records*, R.S.A.B.; *Mazmun-i-Halat-va-Intezam-Marwar*, 261.

[74]Letter from Jaswant Singh to Muhnot Nainsi, Basta No. 12/53, *Jodhpur Records*, R.S.A.B.; *Majmun-i-Halat-va-Intezam-Marwar*, 261.

[75]*Haqiqat-Khata-Bahi*, No. 1, pp. 2-4; cf. *Supra*.

[76]For the name of the non-Rathor *sardars* who enjoyed the post of *pradhan*, *see Vigat*, ii, 478-80.

[77]The charges made against Muhnot Nainsi and Muhnot Sunderdas, who were *desh-diwan* and *tan-diwan* respectively, show that for the wrong practices in the office both were jointly responsible.

[78]Basta No. 12/53, *Jodhpur Records*, R.S.A.B.

[79]*Ajitodaya*, 18/34-8; *Vyav-Bahi*, 213.

[80]When the Bhatis invaded Pokaran, Muhnot Nainsi was appointed the Commander of the Rathor army.

[81]Basta No. 12-53, *Jodhpur Records*, R.S.A.B.

[82]*Jodhpur-Khyat*, i, 255.

[83]*Jodhpur-Khyat*, i, 254; *Vigat*, i, 132.

[84]*Ibid.*

[85]Basta No. 101, Reg. No. 16 and Basta No. 43. Bahi No.5, 82, R.S.A.B. It has been argued that these families belonged to the Rathor Princes but later on became Jain and changed their profession, though some of them were still recognized as military commanders in their time. It furnishes an example of extensive inter-change of caste in medieval India on account of a change of profession or religious doctrine. Racial characteristics were not altogether lost by such a change.

[86]See Chapter IV.

[87]It was a general complaint that the *diwan* was unable to realize the revenue as per demand and for that he was solely responsible.

[88]In A.D. 1654 (V.S. 1711). Pancholi Balbhadra was asked to pay one lac rupees as fine. He was removed from the office of the *tan-diwan* and imprisoned where he died later on. (Basta No. 59/4, *Jodhpur Records*, R.S.A.B.).

[89]*Jodhpur-Khyat*, i, 254-5; *Byav-Bahi*, i, 213.

[90]*Byav-Bahi*, i, 214.

[91]Basta No. 12/52, *Jodhpur Records*, R.S.A.B.; *Byav-Bahi*, i, 214.

[92]Basta No. 97/4, *Jodhpur Records*, R.S.A.B.

[93]For details, see Ibn Hasan *Central Structure*, 213-33.

[94]*Byav-Bahi*, i, 215.

[95]*Farman* (order) of Chaitra Sudi 10, 1767 issued by Maharaja Ajit Singh to Dayaldas regarding his re-appointment as *shiqdar* of Jodhpur. Basta No. 76/2, *Jodhpur Records*, R.S.A.B. During the region of Maharaja Ajit Singh Shobhawat Dayaldas held the office of *shiqdar* A.D. 1709 (V.S. 1724) of *pargana* Jodhpur. The order of his appointment was issued by the office of the *Diwan* on behalf of the Raja.

[96]Letter from Maharaja Ajit Singh to *shiqdar* Dayaldas dated *Chaitra Sudi* 15, 1766. Basta No. 76/2, *Jodhpur Records*, R.S.A.B.

[97]*Byav-Bahi*, i, 215.

[98]*Byav-Bahi*, i, 215; *Muzmun-i-Halat*, 709-10.

[99]For the working of the *kotwal* in the Mughal administration, Thevenot (ii, 20) and Manucci (ii, 421) provide a detailed information. Also *see*, Sarkar, *Mughal Administration*, 68-9, *Provincial Government*, 236.

[100]*Basta* No. 6/66, R.S.A.B.

[101]*Ibid.*

6

PERIOD OF INSTABILITY AND THE MARWAR NOBILITY (A.D. 1678-1707)

Maharaja Jaswant Singh died on 28 November 1678 (*Pausha vadi* 10, 1735) at Peshawar while he was serving at the *thana* of Jamrud. As he had died without an heir the problem of succession to the *gaddi* of Jodhpur arose. The delay by Aurangzeb in granting the *tika* to Ajit Singh and later his decision to assign Jodhpur to Indra Singh, son of Rathor Amar Singh of Nagaur, caused conflicts between the Marwar *sardars* and the Mughals for about thirty years which could be termed as the Marwar war. Although much has been written about the causes of this war,[1] a study of the role and the attitude of the various *sardars*, their relations with the Mughal court and the attitude of Aurangzeb after the death of Maharaja Jaswant Singh enable us to draw a clear picture of the political developments of this period.

After the death of Maharaja Jaswant Singh the Rathor *sardars* in Peshawar held a meeting on 29 November 1678 (*Pausha vadi* 11, 1735) and sent a messenger to Jodhpur. In their message they asked Bhati Raghunath, the *pradhan*, and Pancholi Keshari Singh, the *diwan*, to maintain law and order, and not to create any disturbance in the *desh*[2] (Jodhpur—Marwar). It was also stated that if any Mughal officer arrived there to take over the administration they should not object.[3] A messenger was also sent to Shyamdas, the *vakil* of Jaswant Singh at the Mughal court, asking him to try to obtain permission for retaining Jodhpur under the Rathor control, and if that was not possible, to plead for the retention of Sojat, and Jaitaran.[4] Thus the Rathor *sardars* who accompanied Jaswant Singh to Jamrud agreed that in the absence of any male issue the Mughal Emperor had the right to keep Jodhpur under *khalisa* or to make alternative arrangements. The attitude of the Marwar *sardars* at Peshawar hardly made any impact on the *sardars* in Marwar. After receiving the news of the death of Jaswant Singh, the Rathor *sardars*, under the leadership of Raghunath Bhati, assembled at Jodhpur and decided to take defensive measures against the expected Mughal move. Thus Rathor Sonag Vithaldasot, Bhati Ram Kumbhawat, Rathor Sabal Singh, Uhad Bhagwandas, etc., stayed at Jodhpur along with 2,000 *sawars* for security arrangements. Bhati Raghunath, the *pradhan* of Jodhpur, Pancholi Keshari Singh, the *desh-diwan*, and other Rathor *sardars* proceeded to Merta where they started augmenting their ranks.[5] The Rathor *sardars* collected an army of 20,000 *sawars* and their strength continued to increase day by day.[6] In such a state of political uncertainty, some of the Rathor *sardars* started plundering the *parganas* of Jodhpur and Sojat, and realised the land revenue by force.[7]

At the court, when the news of the death of Jaswant Singh was reported, the reaction of Aurangzeb was not the same as had been generally presumed.[8] After receiving the news of the death of Maharaja Jaswant Singh and the pregnancy of the two *Ranis*,[9] Aurangzeb reacted favourably on the demand of the Rathor *sardars* at Peshawar. He issued a *farman* (December 1678) to the Rathor *sardars* at Peshawar which was duly received on 31 December 1679 (*Magh vadi* 13, 1735) at Attock. In the *farman* it was stated that the *desh* (Jodhpur) would be bestowed on the son of the deceased Maharaja, if born to one of the *Ranis*, on the condition that he appeared before the court.[10] Aurangzeb also agreed for the assignment of Jaitaran and Sojat which conformed to the proposal of *vakil* Shyamdas and the Rathor *sardars* at Peshawar. The *sardars* of Marwar were also aware of it. Following his decision, to which *vakil* Shyamdas had given his consent, Aurangzeb issued *farmans* to Bhati Raghunath, Pancholi Kesari Singh, Rathor Ram Singh and Miyan Farasat assuring them that their *pattas* and services would remain undisturbed.[11]

Mir Khan, the Mughal *subadar* of Kabul,[12] did not appreciate the delivery of the *farman* and therefore it was withdrawn. From the report of *vakil* Shyamdas sent to the Rathor *sardars* it appears that this was done on the representation of Mir Khan's brother who feared that on receipt of the *farman* the Rathors would be emboldened to create trouble while Mir Khan remained in the mountainous area fighting the Pathan tribesmen. According to *vakil* Shyamdas when Aurangzeb came to know that his *farman* and the *hasbulhukm* had been withdrawn by the *subadar* of Kabul he was highly annoyed, and declared that he had never wanted that imperial officers should try to seize the documents after their delivery to the Rathors. Apparently, Aurangzeb had ordered the withdrawal only if the messenger was still on his way to Peshawar. Indignant at the indiscreet act of withdrawal of documents, the Emperor ordered that Mir Khan's brother, who had created that confusion, should be removed. While these events were taking place at the court, the *vakils* of Rao Indra Singh, Raja Man Singh Rathor and Ram Singh Rathor had made representations to the Emperor for the grant of Jodhpur to them. However, Aurangzeb had told them that he would bestow the *desh* on the son of Jaswant Singh.[13]

The withdrawal of the *farman* annoyed some of the Rathor *sardars*. They were of the opinion that they should not allow the royal officers to seal the *karkhana* of the Maharaja. However, later on, they agreed that the imperial officers should be allowed to do it according to the Mughal custom and rules so that cordial relations with the Emperor might continue. Since Mir Khan was very much annoyed with the Rathor *sardars*, Aurangzeb ordered Mirza Niwaz Beg, the *faujdar* of Rohtas, to bring the family and treasury of Maharaja Jaswant Singh from Jamrud to the imperial court at Delhi.[14] Mir Khan turned down the request of Niwaz Beg to proceed to the court along with the Rathor *sardars*. This delay further upset the Rathors. On 11 January 1679 (*Magh sudi* 11, 1735)

Rathor Sangram Singh along with other *sardars* approached Mir Khan for permission to depart, but the latter told them that he had received no orders in this regard. But Sangram Singh insisted, and told him that the Rajputs had no provisions left, and if he did not sign the permit, they would indulge in looting and plundering which would annoy him. After much persuasion, Mir Khan agreed to sign the permit, stating that he was doing so on his (Sangram Singh's) responsibility.[15] On their way to Delhi, the Rathor *sardars* had a quarrel at Attock with the *darogah* of the river who refused to give them boats without the imperial permission. Possibly on the basis of this clash, Kamdar Khan, the *subadar* of Lahore, had sent complaints about the Rathors that they were indulging in plunder on their way to Delhi, and that this was being done after the birth of Maharaja (Ajit Singh). Although, the Emperor later received an *arzdasht* from Niwaz Beg in which he made recommendations favouring the Rathors and stated that they were faithful and would be reaching Delhi soon,[16] the adverse reports from the *subadar* of Kabul and Lahore irritated Aurangzeb. The hostile attitude and activities of the Rathor *sardars* in Marwar further increased this irritation and created a suspicion in the mind of Aurangzeb about their intentions.

From the above it is quite clear that in the beginning Aurangzeb was fully prepared to bestow Jodhpur on the son of the Maharaja, if born, and was not prepared to entertain the claims of other claimants. Aurangzeb had made no changes in the service conditions and *pattas* of the Rathor *sardars* in Marwar. It is hardly convincing that there was any conspiracy behind Aurangzeb's offer of the *pattas* or *mansab* to the Marwar *sardars*.[17] In fact, under *khalisa* control, the *sardars* could maintain their rights and privileges merely by accepting the imperial *mansab*. The confirmation of the services of the *sardars* was not anything new in their case. During the regency of Jaswant Singh, the appointment of the first two *pradhans* was made by Emperor Shahjahan. Further, keeping a Rajput State in the *khalisa* was again not a new approach to settling their affairs, particularly Jodhpur.

In order to keep Jodhpur in *khalisa* and to break the Rathor resistance, Aurangzeb sent Iftikhar Khan to take possession of it. Iftikhar Khan left Ajmer for Jodhpur via Merta.[18] From the contemporary accounts it appear that when Iftikhar Khan reached Merta he was opposed by the Rathor *sardars*. They had assembled at Merta and were fully prepared to resist the Mughal encroachment on Jodhpur.[19] To avoid the conflict Iftikhar Khan stayed outside Merta town. From there Iftikhar Khan sent a message to the Emperor informing him that the Rathor *sardars* had assembled there in large numbers and were preparing for a war. He mentioned that although he had asked them to accept the imperial service, they were not prepared to do so and were ready for a fight. They were also planning to plunder Ajmer, Sambhar and Didwana. Consequently, he had not entered the city of Merta and was waiting for further instructions.[20] It is said when the Emperor heard of the report of Iftikhar Khan he became furious.[21] About the same time Khwaja Agar[22] reported to Aurangzeb about the late Maharaja Jaswant Singh's treasure of rupees fifty-seven lacs which had been hoarded since the time of Mota Raja Udai Singh in the fort of Jodhpur and Siwana, and that it had been increasing at the rate of rupees one thousand every day.[23] It may be noted that Maharaja Jaswant Singh like most Mughal nobles owed money to the Mughal state. While holding *subadari* of Gujarat in 1672, he had been ordered to pay it back in annual instalments of two lacs of rupees.[24] Although it is difficult to assess the exact amount which he owed to the imperial treasury, the demand for the balance had been made many times when Jaswant Singh was in Jamrud.[25] The escheating of the property of a deceased noble, though a normal Mughal practice, had rarely been applied to Hindu Rajas. Aurangzeb took that extreme step on hearing about the hoarded treasure of Jaswant Singh.[26]

On 15th January 1679 Aurangzeb issued an order to Saiyid Abdullah Khan to proceed to Marwar and secure control over the forts of Jodhpur and Siwana.[27] At the same time he appointed Khidmat Guzar Khan as the *qiladar* of Jodhpur, Tahir Khan as the *faujdar*, Shaikh Anwar as the *amin* and Abdur Rahim as the *Kotwal*, and they were asked to proceed with Abdullah Khan.[28] It may be noted that the decision to occupy the fort of Siwana was taken when the Emperor was informed that the treasury had been shifted to Siwana fort.

From the messages sent to the Rathor *sardars* at Lahore by *vakil* Shyamdas, it appears that although in the beginning the Rathor *sardars* resented the march of Saiyid Abdullah Khan to Merta to assist Iftikhar Khan, the *faujdar* of Ajmer, the Rathor *sardars*, under the leadership of Raghunath Singh Bhati, unanimously decided to avoid any opposition to the Mughal army till the birth of the Maharaja. It seems that the Marwar *sardars* changed their earlier decision to resist when they came to know about the attitude of Aurangzeb who gave Merta to the Mughal army. Later on Rathor Roop Singh and Pancholi Keshari Singh reached Jodhpur accompanied by Iftikhar Khan and Abdullah Khan. Sonag Rathor was incharge of the Jodhpur fort. Many *sardars* of various Rathor clans were ready to fight with the Mughal army.[29] As no Rajasthani account refers to the role of Hadi Rani at this time, it is difficult to assess her influence on Sonag Rathor. But her presence in Jodhpur fort suggests that she supported the policy of Sonag Rathor. The attitude of the Rathor *sardars* staying at Merta indicates that a powerful group in the nobility was opposing the idea of Sonag Rathor. Abdullah Khan failed to get the possession of Jodhpur fort due to the opposition of Sonag Rathor and his followers. Therefore, he informed the Emperor that the Rathor *sardars* were preparing for an attack on Sambhar, Didwana and Ajmer.[30] It was also reported that Rana Raj Singh had decided to support the Rathors.[31] Hence Aurangzeb who had started for Ajmer sent (on 7 February 1679/*Phalgun sudi*) Khan Jahan Bahadur, Hussain Ali Khan, and other important nobles to take possession of Jodhpur.[32] Apprehending a more critical situation, Aurangzeb called Shahzada Akbar from Multan, Sardar Khan from Sorath, Bakhshi Sarbuland Khan and Shaista Khan from Agra, and Muhammad Azam Khan from Ahmedabad.[33] Apparently, the decision of a full-fledged campaign was taken only when Aurangzeb was convinced that the hostile activities of the Rathors had gone beyond tolerance.

Following the request of Abdullah Khan for reinforcements, Aurangzeb sent Nawab Bahadur Khan and Tahir Khan to Jodhpur. On 21 February 1679 (*Chaitra vadi* 7, 1735) *Nawab* Khanjahan Bahadur arrived at Merta. Rathor Roop Singh, Bhati Raghunath, etc., met him. The *Nawab* promised that the son of Maharaja, when born, would be given Jodhpur. For the time being Sojat and Jaitaran were granted to the Rathors on the condition that they would serve with 500 horses. It was agreed that the palace in the fort would remain under the control of the Rathors. In the city, the *faujdar*, the *kotwal* and the *qazi* would be appointed by the Emperor.[34] The *Nawab* agreed to these terms and asked the Rathor *sardars* not to create any trouble.[35] On February 24, 1679, the city was evacuated and various Rathor *sardars* with their clansmen went to their respective *thikanas*.[36] It has been stated earlier that Sonag Rathor and some other *sardars* along with Rani Hadi Jaswantde, were posted at Jodhpur for its defence. Even after the submission of Bhati Raghunath and others, Sonag Rathor was not ready to surrender. But on persuasion, he along with Rani Hadi and others left the fort.[37]

With the occupation of Jodhpur, the Mughal officers proceeded to take control of various other *parganas* of Marwar. *Kiroris* were sent to the *parganas* of Phalodi and Siwana with 300 *sawars* each. Gujar Khan was appointed the *qiladar* of Siwana and was entrusted with all the property therein. Mohammad Amin Khan was appointed *faujdar* of Jalor.[38] In the city (Jodhpur) Tahir Beg, Qazi Ahmad, Rahim Khan and Qasim Khan were appointed *faujdar*, *qazi*, *kotwal* and *kirori* respectively.[39] In Jodhpur various measures were adopted; prohibition was imposed on the use of *bhang* and wine; no one was allowed to enter the city after mid-night; and dancers were asked to leave the city. Changes were introduced in the measuring weights and the prices of articles. Accordingly, a maund was made equivalent to 42 *seers*. Levy on *dan* was fixed at the rate of one *taka* a rupee. Import of articles was banned. In *khalisa* villages the realisation of land revenue was made through *lata* (*latai*). In the *jagir* villages the amount of land revenue was fixed on each crop.[40] While leaving for Delhi, Aurangzeb ordered that the *Nawab* would stay at Ajmer for some more time and that his son would come to Jahanabad along with his followers and the booty he had captured from Marwar.[41] It is difficult to assess the intention of Aurangzeb behind these various measures. By appointing various officers in the *parganas* Aurangzeb did not dislodge any of the *pattadars* from their *pattas*. Thus their holdings remained unaffected even after the *khalisa* control over Jodhpur. It seems that he wanted to keep *khalisa* control over Jodhpur for a considerable period without making any change in the socio-political organization in Marwar.

Rathor *sardars* had agreed to these terms because they wanted to please the Emperor so that the Maharaja (son of Jaswant Singh) did not suffer due to their hostile activities.[42] Obviously, they were convinced that when the son of Jaswant Singh would be born the *Rajya* would be bestowed upon him by the Emperor. By now the news of this birth of the sons of late Maharaja had been received by the Emperor and Rathor *sardars* were also informed of it. After the agreement concluded between Bahadur Khan and the *sardars* and finding the latter's behaviour satisfactory, Aurangzeb decided to leave Ajmer. Thus he sent a *hasbulhukm* to the Marwar *sardars* then staying at Lahore which read as follows: "I am reaching Delhi from Ajmer and you should also reach there as soon as possible. Favours shall be granted to you and (you shall be) given leave after bestowing the *des* on you"[43]. Later, the Emperor left Ajmer for Delhi on 3 March 1679. It is difficult to say that Aurangzeb was motivated by a feeling of animosity in asking the newly born Maharaja to reach Delhi.[44] In fact, the Rathor rulers were granted the *gaddi* of Jodhpur by the Mughal Emperors either at Agra or Delhi. Therefore, the act of Aurangzeb was not unusual. He did not have any objection to the Rathor *sardars* accompanying the son of Bahadur Khan to the court with the expectation of getting the *tika* of Jodhpur for the newly born son of the deceased Raja.[45] Among the *sardars* who accompanied Bahadur Khan's son, Bhati Raghunath and Pancholi Keshari Singh deserve mention. Other Rathor *sardars* along with Sonag Rathor, Rani Hadi, and other family members remained in Jodhpur, waiting for the conferment of the *gaddi* on Ajit Singh. Apparently, when Aurangzeb left Ajmer he did not have any plan for depriving Ajit Singh of the *gaddi* of Jodhpur. It was only after his arrival at Delhi that his attitude became indifferent towards the Marwar *sardars* and their demand for the grant of Jodhpur in favour of Ajit Singh.

While staying at Delhi, the leading Rathor *sardars* approached the Emperor through Sarbuland Khan, Navsher Khan and Shaista Khan to concede their demand.[46] Even after their continuous representations the Emperor did not pay any attention to their demand, and repeated his earlier decision of granting the *parganas* of Sojat and Jaitaran, though it was a clear breach of *Nawab* Bahadur Khan's promise.[47] Aurangzeb not only neglected the claim of Ajit Singh but also took a drastic decision. He granted the *tika* of Jodhpur and the *mansab* of 3000/4000 to Indra Singh on 26 May 1679.[48] It has been mentioned that earlier Aurangzeb had refused to consider the name of Indra Singh and other Rajput *zamindars* for the *gaddi* of Jodhpur on the ground that the *tika* would be granted to the son of Jaswant Singh. Thus the decision of granting Jodhpur to Indra Singh was a notable change in Aurangzeb's policy towards Marwar and this created an unending political crisis.[49]

As has been mentioned that the Marwar *sardars* pleaded with the Emperor time and again for the grant of Jodhpur to Ajit Singh. Complications cropped up when Aurangzeb asked the Marwar *sardars* to submit the account and to hand over to him the treasury of the deceased Raja.[50] Bhandari Keshari Singh took all the responsibility on his shoulders, but instead of clearing the account he committed suicide.[51] The Marwar *sardars* also turned down the agreement made by Pancholi Jagannath with the imperial *qazi* according to which rupees twenty-six lacs had to be paid as *peshkash*.[52] It seems that Indra Singh had played an important role in raising the issue of the account of Maharaja Jaswant Singh. The breach of the agreement concluded by Pancholi Jagannath created suspicion about the motives of the Rathor *sardars*.[53] Indra Singh took advantage of the situation and succeeded in convincing the Emperor of the grant of Jodhpur in his favour.

The bestowal of the *gaddi* of Jodhpur on Indra Singh was a challenge to the claim of Ajit Singh. The Rathor's apprehension was that "acceptance of Indra Singh as ruler of Jodhpur would establish a precedent by which a direct descendant of a Raja could be divested by the Mughal ruler."[54] Sonag Rathor and other *sardars* who were then in Jodhpur along with Rani Hadi and other family members held the same opinion. Therefore, when Indra Singh reached Jodhpur he found that Rathor *sardars* under the command of Sonag Rathor were determined to offer him resistance. But soon after, when Indra Singh sent his son and other *sardars* to negotiate, Sonag Rathor and other Rathors went over to Indra Singh's side.[55] Most of the Rathor *sardars* along with Sonag were granted *pattas*.[56] Rani Hadi left Jodhpur along with some of her supporters. From the *Ajitodaya* it appears that Sanog Rathor and his followers were of the opinion that they should not come into conflict with Indra Singh as the latter also belonged to the same family. They argued that the Emperor intended to destroy the Royal family. It was suggested that in place of *khalisa*, the acceptance of Indra Singh would be favourable for them.[57] Rani Hadi did not favour the policy of Sonag Rathor. Thus, in Marwar, a group headed by Sonag Rathor was prepared to accept Indra Singh as ruler of Jodhpur in case the *gaddi* was not to be conferred on Ajit Singh. Although, the Marwar *sardars* under the leadership of Sonag Rathor had accepted Indra Singh as the ruler of Jodhpur, Durgadas Rathor and other *sardars* who had arrived from Delhi refused to follow the line of Sonag Rathor. After their arrival in Marwar, Durgadas Rathor was accepted the leader of Rathor *sardars*. They began strengthening their power under his leadership. Rao Indra Singh who had already won over a powerful group of Rathor *sardars*, invited Durgadas to help him, but Durgadas refused to do so.[58]

The presence of Durgadas Rathor and other Rathor *sardars*, and the fact that the young Maharaja was in Marwar provided a favourable atmosphere for the unity of the Marwar *sardars*. The Rathor *sardars* who were staying in their respective *thikanas*, after the submission of Sonag to Indra Singh were invited by Durgadas who granted the *pattas* to them and promised that these *pattas* would continue in future.[59] The activities of Indra Singh in Marwar further helped Durgadas in winning back Sonag Rathor and his fellow Rathor *sardars*.[60] From the contemporary accounts it appears that Indra Singh had to fulfil some commitments to the Mughal Emperor.[61] Thus, he destroyed temples, slaughted cows, opened a window towards the South and collected 37,000 rupees from the city.[62] It is doubtful whether Indra Singh himself was associated with these destructive activities or it was done by others to defame him. However, these activities annoyed Champawat Sonag and others who complained that he had gone back on promise.[63] Seeing this, Sonag and other *sardars* went over to Sirohi and met Durgadas. Durgadas Rathor blamed them for falling a prey to the inducement of Indra Singh and in the end all of them agreed to fight against the Mughals.[64]

Thus when Durgadas Rathor reached Marwar a powerful group of the Rathor *sardars* had already accepted Indra Singh as the ruler of Jodhpur. But Indra Singh, after securing the control over Jodhpur, engaged himself in destructive activities which ultimately united Durgadas Rathor and Champawat Sonag. After his control over Jodhpur, Rao Indra Singh appointed his own *sardars* to the various *thanas*. As mentioned above, Sonag Rathor and other Rathor *sardars* had gone to their respective *thikanas* and had accepted the service of Indra Singh. But after their withdrawal in favour of Durgadas, Indra Singh granted those *thikanas* which were under the control of Rathor *sardars* to his own followers. A study of the *sardars* holding the charge of these *thanas* shows that most of them were the relatives of Mertia, Udawat and Jaitawat clans who had joined the service of Indra Singh.[65]

The participation of Rana Raj Singh of Mewar in favour of the Rathors changed the whole political environment of Marwar. The factors leading to a breach between Aurangzeb and Rana Raj Singh have recently been studied in detail.[66] It would be wrong to assume that the Rana extended his support to the principle of legitimacy, or his support was a protest against the religious policy of Aurangzeb. As far as the legitimacy was concerned it is said that before the sons of Jaswant Singh were born, the claim of Indra Singh over the throne was the strongest; otherwise also while putting aside the claim of Ugra Sen, son of Chandra Sen, Akbar had established the precedence according to which the Mughal Emperor could grant the *tika* to any person belonging to the same family. For Rana Raj Singh, who had a long desire to establish the reputation among the Rajput Rajas, it was an opportunity to regain the leadership. At the same time inclusion of Marwar territory in *khalisa* would have led to further Mughal expansion towards Mewar. The Rana was fully aware of this danger and, therefore, his support to the Rathors was a political necessity.

Rana Raj Singh had not only given shelter to Ajit Singh, but he had also violated the limits of obedience by reconstructing the gates of Dabhari and Chittor.[67] Apart from building up a huge army under his command, the Rana had sent 5,000 *sawars* under the command of Sawaldas to help the Rathors.[68] The Rathor *sardars* became active and started plundering the imperial *thanas*. Sonag Rathor and Bhati Ram expelled Tahawur Khan (*faujdar* of Jodhpur and Ajmer) from Jodhpur and seized the city.[69] It may be noted that Bhati Ram was staying in the city along with some of his followers. The *sahukars, mahajans* and *raiyats* were angry with Indra Singh due to his behaviour.[70] Taking advantage of the situation Bhati Ram succeeded in securing the support of almost all the sections of the population. Likewise Dhawacha Sujan Singh also took possession of the fort of Siwana.[71] Durgadas Rathor with the help of the army of the Rana plundered the areas around Jalor and after a conflict with Fateh Khan, the imperial *qiladar* of Jalor, took possession of the city.[72] In Merta, Rathor Raj Singh and Pratap Singh also dealt a severe blow to the imperial *faujdar* Tahawur Khan.[73] The Emperor was informed about the situation prevailing in Marwar and Mewar. Consequently, Tahawur Khan, who had not displayed any valour in obstructing the rebels, was dismissed and deprived of the title of Khan. Indra Singh who was found too incompetent to rule the country and had failed in suppressing the disturbances was summoned to the court.[74]

Aurangzeb was kept fully informed about the deteriorating situation of Marwar and the threat posed by Mewar. He finally set out for Ajmer on 3rd September 1679.[75] He himself took over the general supervision while staying at village Palam and sent prince Akbar to Ajmer for future action. Akbar accompanied by Sarbuland Khan advanced to Jodhpur through Merta. After his arrival, Aurangzeb also deputed Hamid Khan, *subadar* of Allahabad, to help Akbar.[76] Although the Rathors at several places offered stiff resistance, the imperial army ultimately succeeded in establishing their hold over Marwar. *Faujdars*, *qiladars* and *kotwals* were oppointed in each *pargana* of Marwar. *Thanas* were established at various places to watch the activities of the Rathors. The following *faujdars* were appointed: Sujan Singh Rathor at Sojat and Jaitaran, Ajab Singh, son of Indra Singh, at Siwana, Priyagdas (Paragdas) Rathor at Jalor, and Chandra Sen at Pokaran.[77] Roop Singh Hada was assisting Inayat Khan, the *faujdār* of Jodhpur.[78] This suggests that in Marwar Aurangzeb did not dislodge the *sardars* who were working as *faujdars* in various *pargānas* even after the removal of Indra Singh.

In Mewar also Aurangzeb adopted the same policy and thus appointed the Rajput *sardars* in various *pargānās*: Pratap Singh Sisodia as *thanadar* of Sherpur, Mohkham Singh Mertia at Pur, Chandrabhan as *qānungo* of Mandal, Dolat Singh Sisodia as *thanadar* of Mandal, Man Singh Rathor as *thanādar* of Badnor, and Hati Singh as *thanadar* of Badmalgarh.[79] While appointment of these Rajput *sardars* was preferred, it would be wrong to say that there was no Muslim *thanadar* or *faujdar* in Mewar. The appointment of the *faujdārs* in all the *pargānas* of Marwar clearly indicates the inclusion of Marwar in *khalisa*. But the appointment of the Rathor *sardars* in most of the *parganas* as *faujdars* makes it clear that he wanted to maintain *khalisa* with the support of the local *zamindars* (*pattadārs*) or the persons who could be accepted by the local leaders or peasants.

Although Rana Raj Singh had openly entered the conflict with the Mughals in favour of the Rathors, he soon realized that he would not be able to continue the war against the Mughals who had not only established their hold over all the important places in Mewar but many known generals of the time were also working against him. At the same time, due to great devastation caused by the continuous conflicts, a serious economic problem had been created in Mewar. The Rana himself was plundering the areas which were parts of his own dominion. Politically the Rana had failed to gain the leadership of the Rathors. Sonag Rathor had plainly refused to work under the command of Prince Bhagwat Singh, son of Rana Raj Singh, and explained to him that their purpose was to defend Marwar.[80] After a bitter conversation Sonag Rathor left Mewar and went to Sojat.[81] The Rathor *sardars* were more concerned with their strategy in Marwar than in offering help to the Rana.[82] Many of Mewar *sardars* defected in favour of the Emperor.[83] From the *Waqai Ranthambhor* it appears that in March 1680 even the Rana had taken the initiative to make peace with the Emperor.[84] He sent Neel Kanth, a known *mahājan*, to Mohkham Singh, the *thānādar* of Pur, and through him the Rana expressed his willingness to make peace. Although Padshah Quli Khan promised Mohkham Singh to plead the case of the Rana,[85] the Emperor issued a *farmān* in which it was mentioned that the *vakils* of the Rana should be asked to leave the imperial camp. Padshah Quli Khan, therefore, had no other alternative but to ask them to leave the camp immediately.[86]

The death of Rana Raj Singh on 22 October 1680 changed the situation. Rana Jai Singh adopted a different attitude towards the Rathors. In fact, the prominent *sardārs* of the Sisodia clan were not in favour of keeping the Rathor *sardārs* in Mewar. They made it clear to the Rana that the Rathors were not trustworthy, and so they should be asked to leave Mewar. Consequently, Rana Jai Singh persuaded them to vacate Mewar.[87] It appears that most of the Sisodia *sardārs* were not in favour of war and it was against their will that they were fighting the Mughals. It was said that a group of the *sardars* led by Garibdas was responsible for the war. An investigation ordered by the Rana proved that the allegation of the *sardars* was correct. Garibdas was insulted by Jai Singh in open *dārbār*.[88] Thus a group of the nobility which favoured war against the Mughals and supported the Rathors was removed from power. It is noteworthy that even after being convinced that the support extended to the Rathors would be against the interest of Mewar, the Rana remained in favour of the Rathors. In fact, in the absence of any alliance with the Mughals, it was difficult for him to break away from the Rathors. As he had failed to get any favourable response from the Emperor, he along with the Rathors, approached Shah Alam and thereafter Prince Akbar for help. Although Rana Jai Singh was one of those who approached prince Akbar, after the latter's declaration as the Emperor of Hindustan, the former did not personally participate in the rebellion and withdrew his responsibilities after sending a contingent. Meanwhile the Rana had opened negotiations with Aurangzeb through prince Azam.[89] Both the parties were willing to restore peace. To avoid any misunderstanding the Rana addressed a letter to Durgadas forbidding the latter to bring prince Akbar in Mewar.[90] Apparently, Rana Jai Singh was no longer interested extending his support to the Rathors once the negotiations with the Mughals had started.

Marwar *sardars* under the leadership of the Durgadas Rathor got an opportunity to settle their score with Aurangzeb with the help of prince Akbar. But with the defeat of the combined army of Akbar and Marwar *sardars* in January 1681,[91] Aurangzeb established his control over Marwar.

Marwar between A.D. 1681 and 1707

The treaty concluded between the Maharana and the Mughal Emperor left the Rathor *sardars* alone to fight against the Mughals. Durgadas Rathor had gone to the Deccan along with prince Akbar. Emperor Aurangzeb had also left Marwar for Deccan in September 1681. Before his departure he had reorganized the administrative machinery in Marwar by making several changes in the appointments. Indra Singh, who had been deprived of the *gaddi*, was still holding the military charge of the area around Jodhpur. Now he was removed from Jodhpur on the ground that he was incapable of keeping his control over the area. His *mansab* was reduced from 3000/3000 to 1500/1500.[92] But his removal from Jodhpur deprived many of his followers of the *pattas* they held there.[93] Inayat Khan was appointed the *faujdar* of Jodhpur and Ajmer.[94] Shihabuddin Khan was given the *faujdari* of Sojat and Jaitaran but later on he was replaced by Sardar Tarfin. In August 1681 Saiyid Ibrahim was appointed on that post. Later, in September Sardar Tarfin was restored the *faujdāri* of Sojat and Jaitaran.[95] Kasim Khan was appointed the *faujdar* of Siwana. Apart from these appointments, the *faujdars* and *karoris* were appointed in each *pargana*. To maintain security of the trade routes, the Mughal *mansabdars* were also appointed at various places. Aurangzeb, being aware of the situation, made all these arrangements in order to continue *khālisa* over Marwar after his departure. Apparently, Aurangzeb made no change in his policy towards Ajit Singh. It is to be noted that even after the departure of Durgadas Rathor and the treaty with the Rana, the Mughal *faujdars* of various *parganas* in Marwar were facing a difficult situation.[96]

Sonag Rathor (Champawat) became the leader of the Marwar *sardars* after Durgadas's departure. After the death of Maharaja Jaswant Singh, Sonag Rathor had taken the command of the Rathor *sardars* on many occasions. Owing to his successful leadership he had earned a name as one of the leading *sardars* of Marwar. Thus in the absence of Durgadas Rathor, his leadership was accepted by all the sections of the Marwar nobility. The Rathor *sardars* of various *khamps* (sub-clans) assembled under his command,[97] and renewed their offensive action in the *parganas* of Merta, Sojat and Jodhpur. Rathor Harnath and Kanha Girdhardasot Champawat made a surprise attack on Sojat. In a battle fought between the Rathors and Sardar Khan who was the *faujdar* of Sojat, the Rathors were defeated but the Mughal army suffered a heavy loss.[98] Rathor Mohkam Singh of Mertia clan devastated the territory around Merta.[99] The *Rajrupak* mentions that Sonag Rathor surrounded Jodhpur and created a serious situation for Inayat Khan who was then in Jodhpur.[100] These Rathor *sardars* were not only engaged in plundering the imperial posts but also realized land revenue from the cultivators in various parts of Marwar.[101] Under these circumstances *faujdar* Inayat Khan was facing serious difficulty in retaining his control over Marwar. Therefore, with the tacit approval of the Emperor, he opened negotiations with Sonag Rathor. It was proposed that Ajit Singh would be granted Jodhpur and the *mansab* of 7000/7000.[102] Other Rathor *sardars*, along with Sonag, were also prepared to accept the *mansab*. But due to the death of Sonag Rathor the agreement could not be implemented.[103] It is difficult to determine the extent to which the proposal would have been implemented by the Emperor. The author of the *Ajit Vilas* holds that it was intended to deceive the Rathors and kill Sonag Rathor.[104] The death of Sonag was a severe blow to the Rathors. But to continue their resistance they nominated Ajab Singh Champawat (Rathor), the brother of Sonag, as their leader.[105] Champawat Ajab Singh died after a month. The *sardars* then nominated Udai Singh Champawat (Rathor), son of Dheer Singh, to be their commander.[106] The nomination of Champawat Ajab Singh and later Champawat Udai Singh makes it clear that after the departure of Durgadas, the Champawat *sardars* of the Rathor clan had established their leadership in the Marwar nobility. It is to be noted that there was unanimity among the Marwar *sardars* on the question of their leader. This was an important factor which enabled the Marwar *sardars* to continue their struggle against the Mughals.

At the time of Rathor Udai Singh's nomination as a leader, the number of the leading Marwar *sardars* was 59, among whom were 11 Champawats, 5 Karnots, 5 Jodhas, 5 Udawats, 6 Mertias, 2 Kumpawats, 4 Jaitawats, 2 Chauhans and 9 Bhatis.[107] These *sardars* who came from various parts of Marwar pledged themselves to fight against the Mughals. During the period when Durgadas remained out of Marwar, the Rathor *sardars* continued plundering and looting the imperial territories. From the details of battles which took place between Rathor *sardars* and the Mughal officers it appears that no united attempt was made to oust the Mughals from Marwar. In 1682 Rathor Udai Singh, after sufficient preparations, devastated the territory of *pargana* Sojat and plundered the territories of Mandal, Sarwarpur, and Toda.[108] Later on he marched towards Nagaur and looted it.[109] In the same year Jagram Udawat caused havoc in Jaitaran.[110] Jodha Udai Singh drove away the imperial army which attacked Bhadrajun. In A.D. 1683-4, Udai Singh forced Siddi, the *faujdar* of Sojat to pay Rs. 700 as *peshkash*.[111] The Bhils and Meenas were employed by the Marwar *sardars* against the Mughals.[112] Thus the Rathor *sardars* of Champawat, Udawat, Kumpawat, etc., and Bhatis, Chauhan, Sisodia and their relatives laid waste the whole of Marwar and made all trade routes impassable. It has been urged that during the absence of Durgadas (A.D. 1681-1686) the war fought against the Mughals was a people's war, because their (the Rathors) Raja was a child and their national leader Durgadas was absent in the Deccan.[113] A study of the above narration makes it quite clear that there was hardly a time when Marwar was without a leader. Rathor Sonag, Rathor Ajab Singh and Rathor Udai Singh had been nominated by the Rathor *sardars*. Although in the guerrilla warfare various clan leaders commanded their respective armies, whenever a serious fight took place the plan was chalked out with the advice of the above leaders of the Rathor clan. Udai Singh Rathor himself had rejected the idea that Durgadas was the only person who could assume the leadership. He equated Durgadas Rathor with many other Rathor *sardars*.[114]

But in spite of the leadership, the Rathor *sardars* were facing many difficulties. They had no arrangement for regular supply of arms and food. There was no treasury available wherefrom they could make regular payment to the soldiers. Due to continuous warfare the prices of wheat and *ghee* also went up from 24½ seers and 4¾ seers to 15 *seers* and 2½ *seers* a rupee.[115] Apart from the high rates of these two commodities there was a general increase in the price of grains.[116] The increase in the prices of the food commodities was also because of their short supply and decline in the production in Marwar. It may also be noted that due to the political instability the trade activities had become impossible. This caused the shortage of many commodities. In a state of perpetual warfare, the peasants were forced to pay the land revenue to the Rathor *sardars* as well as the Mughal officers.[117] As the payment of the land revenue to both these claimants was beyond the means of cultivators, it seems that there was no regular payment to any of the parties. The only possible way to make the payment regular was to secure the support of the local *zamindars*.

In 1683 prince Azam and Asad Khan left Marwar and the responsibility of maintaining peace and stability fell on the shoulders of Inayat Khan. He continued the old practice of securing the support of the local *sardars*.[118] The *Rajrupak* mentions that Inayat Khan asked his brother-in-law, Sikandar Khan, to win over the Rathor *sardars* by granting them the land on *ijara*.[119] As a result of this policy many Rathor *sardars* and others joined the imperial service.[120] Among them the names of Rathor Mohkam Singh and Anand Singh are worth mentioning.[121] The practice of *ijara* was a significant feature of the land revenue administration of Marwar. It suggests that as the regular machinery of the land revenue had collapsed due to continuous fighting, the adoption of the *ijara* system was the only alternative left to the Mughals.

Although the guerrilla warfare and destructive activities of the Rathors created a difficult situation for the Mughals, the

Rathor *sardars* themselves were passing through a hard time. However, the Rathors succeeded in securing the support of Hada Durjansal. Udai Singh Rathor gave in marriage one of his cousins, the daughter of Rathor Sujan Singh, to Handa Durjansal, who arrived in Marwar with 1000 horsemen.[122] It strengthened the opposition of the Rathor *sardars*. At the same time Udai Singh Rathor adopted a more practical approach. He was aware of the fact that the Rathor *sardars* would not remain for long on his side if the situation remained the same. Therefore, he thought it wise to bring out the Maharaja in public. The idea was welcomed by Tej Singh Idanot, Bhati Indra Bhan, Balo Akheraj, Udawat Jagram, Raj Singh Balramot, Mertia Balram and Jodha Udai Singh.[123] These Rathor *sardars* approached Khichi Mukanddas who was looking after the Maharaja. In the beginning Mukanddas showed his ignorance about the Maharaja and advised to keep patience till the return of Durgadas, but when the *sardars* pressed, he agreed to bring the Maharaja before them. On 18 March 1686 (*Chaitra sudi* 15, 1744) the Maharaja appeared before the Rathor *sardars*.[124]

It appears that Durgadas was not in favour of bringing out Ajit Singh from the concealment in his absence. For this Durgadas had instructed Khichi Mukanddas that the Maharaja would appear before the *sardars* in his presence alone.[125] While staying in Deccan Durgadas was worried about the appearance of Ajit Singh in his absence. He had told prince Akbar that if it was done he would lose his game.[126] Khichi Mukanddas had also informed him about the demand of the Rathor *sardars* and asked him to reach there (Marwar) as early as possible.[127] Accordingly, Durgadas had started from Deccan and Udai Singh Champawat, etc., were fully aware of his impending arrival.[128]

It seems that like Durgadas, Udai Singh Rathor was not ready to miss the opportunity. He had gained prestige and the unquestioned leadership in the absence of Durgadas. There were other Rathor *sardars* who also wanted to avoid Durgadas's intervention. They were fully conscious of the fact that in the presence of Durgadas it would be difficult for them to have any direct approach to the Raja as he would be under his control. In this period of hardship, they were fighting without any ruler. Now they were more willing to work under the supreme command of their Raja rather than Durgadas. For Udai Singh Rathor the return of Durgadas was distressing as he would have to work under the command of the latter. Therefore, he wanted to secure control over the Raja to maintain his position unchallenged.[129] The support of Hada Durjansal increased his strength.

The objective of Durgadas Rathor appears more personal than otherwise. He was not ready to allow the Raja to drift away from his guidance. This may be supported by the fact that as the Maharaja was brought out in public, Durgadas got so annoyed that after his arrival in Marwar he did not see the Maharaja personally for some time. It is also true that at the time of his arrival hardly a leader of any important clan, except his brother Khivkaran, was present. This suggests that when Rathor Durgadas reached Marwar, his arrival was not welcomed.

Raja Ajit Singh along with Udai Singh Rathor and other *sardars* went to Ahwa, Bagari, Rajpur, Bilada, Balunda, Riyan, Asop, Lavera, Hinwsar, Kolu and other places and accompanied by the *sardars* of these places proceeded to Pokaran.[130] After strengthening their position the Rathor *sardars* again attacked the Mughal posts. The Raja's visit to various *thikanas* enabled Udai Singh Champawat to increase his strength. Ajit Singh sent instructions to the *sardars* for the collection of the revenue from their villages.[131] Another tax, *faujbal* was also revived. It may be noted that it was similar to the tax levied during Jaswant Singh's time but now its rate was increased.

As has been noted earlier, after his arrival in Marwar, Durgadas Rathor did not see the Raja for a few months; he only informed him of his return through a letter.[132] It also seems that Durgadas Rathor was unwilling to indulge in clan rivalry and, therefore, he continued his own plan of action. But at the same time he made an attempt to consolidate his power by winning over Rathor *sardars* and others. He never refused to associate himself with other Rathor *sardars* against the Mughals. After his arrival from Deccan he met Ajit Singh for the first time in October 1687, but nothing came out of it.[133] Next year when Ajit Singh was invited by Shafi Khan,

Durgadas did not participate and the Raja was accompanied by Mukanddas Khichi and Mohkam Singh Champawat.[134] Thus it appears that it was not considered necessary to obtain Durgadas's consent even though he was in Marwar at that time. This makes it apparent that Udai Singh and his followers had established their influence over Ajit Singh. But it would be wrong to presume that Durgadas was having any ill-feeling against Ajit Singh, or his activities were motivated against the interests of Ajit Singh, though it is true that he was not in favour of the policy adopted by Ajit Singh towards the Mughals.[135] Durgadas Rathor, while keeping himself aloof from Ajit Singh, made efforts to consolidate his position through the support of the Rathor *sardars*. In 1687 Durgadas refused to help Thakur Raj Singh and Gajram against Sujan Singh, *zamindar* of Sojat. This attitude of Durgadas was not appreciated by Ajit Singh.[136] It seems that Durgadas was not interested in creating friction among the Rathor *sardars*, while at the same time he wanted to gain the sympathy of both the parties. It is evident that Durgadas Rathor had reached some understanding with Hada Durjansal.[137] Later on in February 1688 by the efforts of Durgadas, Daulat Singh, son of Durjansal, and Anup Singh (Rawal of Bundi) became friendly.[138] This enabled Durgadas to establish some contact with the Champawat *sardars*. Later, when in 1691 the Rathor army was sent to Udaipur to help the Rana, both Udai Singh Champawat (Rathor) and Durgadas led the army. The political crisis in Mewar had started as the eldest son of Maharana Jai Singh thought of usurping the state from his father. The Maharana with the advice of Mertia Gopinath sent a messenger to Ajit Singh soliciting the help of the latter. Thereupon Udai Singh Champawat and Durgadas Rathor were sent to help the Maharana. With their efforts peace was established in Mewar.[139] It is to be mentioned that the Maharana had sent a personal request to Ajit Singh to send Durgadas along with his army. The Maharana bestowed honour upon Durgadas by offering a horse, *siropao*, etc.[140] This enabled Durgadas to establish contacts with the Rana. Rathor Durgadas also availed the opportunity of the presence of Udai Singh Champawat and established cordial relations with him.[141] He had also secured the support from the Khangarot *sardars* of Amber.[142] There is sufficient evidence to show that Hari

Singh Khangarot (thakur of Diggi-Amber) had also collected a sufficiently large army to be presented to Durgadas whenever needed.[143] Thus, it can be said that till 1692 Durgadas had consolidated his position in Marwar.

From the contents of the letters of years A.D. 1693-1694 and A.D. 1697 it is evident that Durgadas Rathor after his arrival from Deccan, was still thinking in terms of securing Jodhpur in favour of Ajit Singh with the support of prince Akbar against Aurangzeb. Thus, he was in correspondence with prince Akbar who was expected to arrive in North India in A.D. 1694.[144] It may be noted that in 1694, a person who professed himself as Akbar had raised a rebellion at Deosuri pass in Mewar. From the study of the correspondence that took place between Durgadas and Hari Singh Khangarot, it appears that the rebellion of the imposter was the result of the failure of prince Akbar to arrive in time. It is significant to note that the man who raised the rebellion, against Aurangzeb professing himself to be prince Akbar, was getting the support of the local inhabitants of the *parganas* of Sojat (Marwar) and Godwar (Mewar) and also from the Rana. But the rebellion was crushed in a very short time by Muhammad Qazim, the *naib* of Shujat Khan.[145] It is not certain whether Durgadas extended his support to the imposter. But it is apparent that the name of prince Akbar could still command favour in Marwar and Mewar. Durgadas Rathor was fully prepared to extend his support to prince Akbar. However it is difficult to say whether Durgadas Rathor and prince Akbar had enough strength and resources to challenge Aurangzeb. The failure of prince Akbar to arrive led to some important political consequences in the politics of Marwar and the Mughal court. It is obvious that the power and position of Durgadas Rathor was increasing day by day of which the Mughal commanders were fully aware.

Changes in the Policy of the Mughals

The appearance of Ajit Singh and arrival of Durgadas Rathor compelled the Mughal commanders to change their policy in Marwar. The Mughal officers had realized that without a mass defection among the followers of Ajit Singh it would be impossible for them to maintain their hold in Marwar. The presence of Ajit Singh was expected to make the situation more difficult for the Mughals. Inayat Khan, *faujdar* of Jodhpur, agreed to grant one-fourth of the revenue of transit duties to the Maharaja.[146] But due to his sudden death in A.D. 1687 (V.S. 1744) the agreement could not be finalized. However, Rathor *sardars* collected the *chauth* (one-fourth of the land revenue) in the *pargana* of Jalor in A.D. 1668 (V.S. 1645).[147] After the death of Inayat Khan, Shujat Khan was appointed the *faujdar* of Jodhpur.[148]

Shujat Khan, after his arrival at Ajmer, adopted a policy of conciliation with the Rathor *sardars*.[149] Accordingly, he offered the *mansabs* to the Rathor *sardars* and asked them to take the *jagirs* on *ijara*.[150] Although many Rathor *sardars* joined the imperial service, most of them were the followers of Indra Singh.[151] This made but little difference to the position of Aijt Singh. Shujat Khan also sanctioned the *chauth* and the *rahadari* to Ajit Singh. But no official order was issued as Aurangzeb ordered him to withdraw such concessions.[152] In 1691-92 Shujat Khan tried to open negotiations with Ajit Singh and asked the latter to reach Ajmer so that he could be given the *mansab*. But the proposal did not materialise as the Mughal Commander was suspected of treachery.[153] Thus, like Inayat Khan, Shujat Khan was also in favour of giving concessions to the Rathor *sardars*, but nothing concrete came out.

Since Shujat had failed to arrive at any agreement with Ajit Singh, he initiated negotiations with Durgadas Rathor in 1694.[154] Till then Durgadas had strengthened his position in Marwar and it was feared that the arrival of prince Akbar would create more complications for the Mughals, particularly when the Emperor was in the Deccan. It seems that Aurangzeb realized the impending danger to Marwar. He wanted to avoid the danger which might have arisen after the arrival of Prince Akbar. He must also have thought that by winning over Durgadas in his favour he would be able to crush the rebellious activities of the Rathors and create dissensions between Durgadas and Ajit Singh. Thus, it seems, the negotiations by the Mughals in A.D. 1694 were necessitated by the political problem rather than the anxiety of Aurangzeb to bring back the sons and daughter of prince Akbar[155] who were staying in Marwar under the guardianship of Durgadas Rathor.

For Durgadas it was quite a favourable opportunity. It seems that after 1694 he was not certain about the arrival of Akbar, and at the same time he might have been conscious of the limitations of his strength against the Mughals. Thus he adopted a favourable attitude towards the Mughals, though he continued his attempts to strengthen his power. It seems that Durgadas was playing his cards well. On the one hand he was consolidating his power by securing the support inside and outside Marwar and waiting for Prince Akbar to re-start the revolt against Aurangzeb, while on the other he continued negotiations with Aurangzeb.

It is difficult to say as to what extent Durgadas was confident about his preparations for a war against Aurangzeb in case Akbar arrived. It is obvious that as soon as he received the *mansab*, he accepted the *faujdari* of Sorath and left Marwar in a state of uncertainty. He also accepted the terms of Aurangzeb for presenting Akbar in the court,[156] in case of the latter's arrival in India from Qandahar. That the agreement was favourable to Durgadas is obvious from the following table showing the *mansabs* granted to the various Rathor *sardars* including Durgadas and Ajit Singh.[157]

Mansabs granted by Aurangzeb[158]

Durgadas and his family members	*Ajit Singh and other Rathor sardars*
Durgadas son of Askaran 3000/2000	Ajit Singh 1500/500
Tejkaran son of Durgadas 500/300	Mukand Singh son of Sujan Singh 600/300
Mahkaran son of Durgadas 500/300	Raghunath Singh son of Sujan Singh 500/300
Abhai Karan son of Durgadas 400/200	Bhati Dada Chandra Bhan 300/200
Anup Singh son of Tejkaran 300/200	Rathor Maha Singh 200/100

Dalkaran son of Tejkaran	400/200	Mohkam Singh	200/100
		Rathor Prem Singh	150/50
TOTAL	5100/3200	TOTAL	3450/1450

Durgadas was granted the *jagirs* in the following *parganas*:[159]

Dams	*Jagir*
2,32,27,823	*Pargana* Merta, *darobast.*
40,00,000	*Pargana* Sojat
20,00,000	*Pargana* Siwana, *darobast*
1,28,86,258	*Parganas* in Gujarat.

On the basis of the above figures it can be safely stated that Durgadas succeeded in securing a very high *mansab* for himself and his family members while the *mansabs* bestowed upon Ajit Singh and other Rathor *sardars* were considerably lower in comparison. It could rightly be inferred then, that after his arrival Durgadas's motives were two-fold: (a) to raise rebellion with the help of prince Akbar, and (b) in failing that to carry on negotiations with the Mughals.

Although it is difficult to say to what extent he was sincere in his first motive, it is obvious that Durgadas took the advantage of the situation to further his interests. As soon as he received the *mansab* he left Marwar to its fate and went away to Sorath. This created a problem in the politics of Marwar. By granting an unusually high *mansab* to Durgadas, Aurangzeb ignored the claim of Ajit Singh and other Rathor *sardars*. Rathor *sardars* who had made equal sacrifices in the war against Aurangzeb were disappointed and started criticising Durgadas.[160]

Marwar between A.D. 1697 and 1707

It has been stated that Maharaja Ajit Singh was granted the *mansab* of 1500/1500. He was assigned *pargana* Jalor in *jagir* and was entrusted the *faujdari* of that *pargana*.[161] Durgadas Rathor went to Sorath. Other members of his family went away to their respective *thikanas*. The Rathor *sardars* who were fighting for the Raja were disappointed at the arrangements approved by Ajit Singh.[162] Obviously, it was difficult for Ajit Singh to safeguard the interest of all the *sardars.* He was unable to assign them *jagirs* or as an alternative to make cash payments. Consequently, most of the *sardars* left him at Jalor and went to their *thikanas* where they resumed former relations with the Mughals, i.e., started paying land revenue to them.[163]

It seems that Maharaja Ajit Singh, after taking possession of Jalor, took less interest in the affairs of the state.[164] He had appointed a number of officials to look after his *jagir.* The officials were to be paid by dividing the income of the *jagir* in the following manner:[165]

(1) One part to the Maharaja
(2) One part to Udai Singh Champawat
(3) One part to Durjan Singh Jaitawat
(4) One part to the other officials (*vyas, purohit,* etc.).

Thus, the Maharaja drew only one-fourth of the income for his expenses. The reference that the income of Jalor was calculated every day and was divided into four parts,[166] indicates that the *jagir* must have remained in *khalisa.* Since Ajit Singh was spending all his time with the *Ranis,* Udai Singh Champawat and his associates exercised all the powers.[167] Udai Singh's power had also increased because the Rathor *sardars* were the followers not of the Raja but of the former.[168] In disgust, some of them left the service of the Maharaja and went away to their *thikanas.* This further strengthened the position of the *pradhan.* Soon a rival group of nobles led by Mertia Kushal Singh emerged.[169] They suggested to the Maharaja that he should try to conquer Jodhpur.[170] They also wanted to return to the system of administration adopted by Jaswant Singh. As already stated, in Jaswant Singh's time, the Maharaja had given most of the villages in his *jagir* to the *sardars* as *pattas.* It would, thus, appear that Udai Singh was trying to exercise greater control over the entire *pargana.* The proposal of Kushal Singh and his associates was, therefore, opposed by Udai Singh Champawat and Durjan Singh, another *sardar* of the Jaitawat Rathor clan. According to the *Ajit Vilas,* in spite of the opposition of Udai Singh Champawat, Ajit Singh had agreed to make the changes in the administration of Jalor.[171] Consequently, Udai Singh Champawat and Arjun Singh opened negotiations with Rathor Mohkam Singh, son of Raja Indra Singh of Nagaur.[172] *Ajitodaya* mentions that Arjun Singh, *thakur* of Bagri, who was associated with Mohkam Singh, succeeded in inducing Champawat Udai Singh to defect in favour of Mohkam Singh in A.D. 1704.[173] It seems that Udai Singh Champawat who failed to maintain his position in the nobility might have thought in terms of joining the imperial service. This argument could be supported by the fact that Mohkam Singh's attack against Ajit Singh was supported by the Emperor.[174]

Although Udai Singh Champawat and his followers went over to the side of Mohkam Singh and their march against Ajit Singh was kept secret, they failed to gain any advantage against Ajit Singh. The Maharaja still enjoyed the support of the *sardars* belonging to the Champawat, the Kumpawat, the Udawat, the Mertia Rathors, and the other non-Rathor *sardars*.[175] As soon as the news of the defection of Champawat Udai Singh spread in Marwar, many Rathor *sardars* started from their *thikanas* and joined Ajit Singh.[176] Among them the names of Mertia Kushal Singh, *thakur* of Chandram, and Champawat Vijay Singh, *thakur* of Balunda are worth mentioning. These *sardars* were those who had earlier gone away to their *thikanas* because they were not happy with the manner in which Ajit Singh exercised his control over Jalor. They were dissatisfied not only because they failed to realize their desire as well as the reward for their sacrifices, but also because they failed to gain any stability in their respective *thikanas*. It is worth noting that apart from the Rathor *sardars* there were a number of other *sardars* who had gained confidence of the Maharaja. They were Chauhan Chatur Singh, Shiv Singh, Rawat Gokuldas, Gobinddas, Fateh Singh and Bhagwandas, Purohit Rinmal Singh, Mangalia Tej Singh.[177] Actually, the *sardars* whose names are mentioned above were those who had escorted the family of Ajit Singh. The position of the Rathor *sardars* became clear only when Udai Singh openly challenged Ajit Singh.

After defeating Mohkam Singh in 1705, Ajit Singh pursued him but on the intercession of the Mughal *faujdar* peace was concluded[178] and both Ajit Singh and Mohkam Singh went away to their respective *jagirs*. When these events were taking place in Marwar, Durgadas Rathor was also facing the attack from the imperial commander, Afzal Khan.[179] Therefore, Durgadas left Patan and took the route to Mewar in December 1705.[180] Thus again the Rathors abandoned their peaceful life and became active to regain their *watan jagirs*. Ajit Singh, who had earlier thought of reviving the system prevailing during the time of Jaswant Singh, hardly had time to implement it. In 1707, he received the news of the death of Aurangzeb.

Although after concluding peace with Ajit Singh in A.D. 1697 and creating conditions for Durgadas to leave Marwar, the Mughals succeeded in avoiding conflict with the Rathors, they could not establish their hold on Marwar. They had allowed the Rathor *sardars* to live in their *thikanas*. These *sardars* paid some lump-sum amount to the Mughal officials and continued their old rights. Such arrangements gave them opportunity to turn these *patta* villages into their *watan jagirs*. On the other hand, other Rathor *sardars* who were granted *jagirs* against their *mansab* failed to secure any confidence of the local *zamindars*.

Under such circumstances, the Mughal commanders could not secure support of the Marwar nobility. The arrival of Durgadas Rathor created more suspicion among those *sardars* who had accepted the imperial *mansab*. Thus the political situation of Marwar was quite favourable for Ajit Singh when he received the news of the death of Aurangzeb.

REFERENCES

[1]Sarkar J.N., *History of Aurangzeb*, (Calcutta 1924) iii, Bhargava, V.S., *Marwar and the Mughals*, (Delhi) 117; Athar Ali, 'Causes of the

Rathor Rebellion of 1679', *P.I.H.C.* (1961), 135-41; Satish Chandra, 'Mughal Relations with the States of Rajputana', contributed to the *Comprehensive History of India*, vii, Chapter viii(c) (in press).

[2]*Hukumat-Bahi* (MS). f, 154b; *Rathora-ri-Vamshavali* (ORIJ) 165.

[3]*Hukumat-Bahi*, f, 154b, *Jodhpur-Khyat* (ASLB) (I, 275) also narrates the same approach of the Rathor *sardars* staying at Peshawar.

[4]*Ajit Singh-ri-Khyat* (ORIJ), I, 2-3; *Hukumat-Bahi*, f, 154b; *Jodhpur-Khyat*, I, 283; *Waqai*, 90-1.

[5]*Rathora-ri-Vamshavali*, 166; *Ajit Singh-ri-Khyat*, I, 5-6; *Jodhpur-Khyat*, I, 276; *Ajitodaya*, 4/15-21; *Hukumat-Bahi*, ff, 164a, 165a-b.

[6]*Ibid.*

[7]*Hukumat-Bahi* (165a, 165b) mentions the names of the villages of the *parganas* of Jodhpur and Sojat where the Rathor *sardars* started the destructive activities and realized the land revenue by force. Also *see*, Satish Chandra, "Mughal Relations with the States of Rajputana" (*op. cit.*).

[8]Attempts have been made to show that Aurangzeb had already planned to include Marwar into *khalisa* and therefore when he got the news of the death of Jaswant Singh he availed that opportunity. *See*, Tod, I, 441; II, 44; *Jodhpur Rajya*, ii, 477; Asopa, R.K. *Sankshipt Itihas*, 212-13; Sarkar, *Aurangzeb*, iii, 325-9; *cf.* V.S. Bhargava, 117.

[9]*Ajitodaya*, 5/25; *Hukumat-Bahi*, f. 161b.

[10]*Ajit Vilas* (S.S.J.), 24; *Hukumat-Bahi*, f. 161b; *Jodhpur-Khyat*, i, 283; Mannucci, ii, 233.

[11]*Hukumat-Bahi*, f. 161b. The details of the *farmans* are not given in the *bahi*, but it may be presumed that they held out the same assurances given to the *sardars* at Peshawar. The Persian chronicles do not furnish this information given in the *bahi*.

[12]Muhammad Amir Khan remained the *Subadar* of Kabul till his death in A.D. 1682. But after his death whole of his moveable and immoveable property was confiscated (*Mirat* i, 310-11). For details *see* *Maasir-i-Alamgiri*, 226.

[13]*Hukumat-Bahi*, f. 162a.

[14]Ibid., ff, 161b, 162a-b, 163a.

[15]*Ibid.*

[16]Ibid., f, 172b.

[17]Athar Ali (Rathor Rebellion, *op. cit.* p. 136) and V.S. Bhargava (*op. cit.* p. 117n) hold that Aurangzeb had ulterior motives behind his offer of *mansabs* to the Rathor *sardars*. Also *see*, Athar Ali, *Mughal Nobility*, 100.

[18]*Waqai*, 90-1; *Ajitodaya*, 5/34-43.

[19]*Ajitodaya*, 5/29-37; *Hukumat-Bahi*, ff. 162a, 167; *Ajit Singh Khyat*, i, 7-8.

[20]*Ajitodaya*, 5/33-7; *Hukumat-Bahi*, ff. 167a, 171a; *Rathora-ri-Vamshavali* (ORIS) 166-7.

[21]*Ajitodaya*, 5/36-7.

[22]Khwaja Agar had been in the service of Jaswant Singh. But at the

time of the battle of Dharmat he defected and joined the service of Aurangzeb (*Hukumat-Bahi*. f, 162a).

[23]*Hukumat-Bahi*, f, 162a; *Ajit Singh-ri-Khyat*, i, 7-8.

[24]*Mirat*, i, 277; *Waqai*, 82; Satish Chandra, 'Mughal Relations with the Rajput States' (*op. cit.*).

[25]*Hukumat-Bahi*, f, 171a; *Ajit Singh-ri-Khyat*, i, 7-8.

[26]Satish Chandra has rightly argued that the escheating of Jaswant Singh's property was not unusual either as it was applied to all nobles who died in debt to the State (Mughal Relations with the States of Rajputana', *op. cit.*).

[27]*Maasir-i-Alamgiri*, 172; *Hukumat-Bahi*, f. 162. The *Bahi* date it on Magh Sudi 7.

[28]*Maasir-i-Alamgiri*, 172; *Hukumat-Bahi*, ff, 161a-b.

[29]*Hukumat-Bahi*, f, 167a.

[30]*Ajit Singh-ri-Khyat*, i, 9-10; *Waqai*, 131.

[31]*Waqai*, 131.

[32]*Maasir*, 172; *Hukumat-Bahi*, f, 167a; *Ajit Vilas*, 24.

[33]*Hukumat-Bahi*, f, 167b; *Jodhpur-Khyat*, i, 276.

[34]*Hukumat-Bahi*, f, 167a; *Ajit Vilas*, 24; *Rajrupak*, 25; *Ajit Singh Khyat*, i, 74, *Ajitodaya* (5/45-54) mentions that Bhati Ram Singh agreed to hand over the control on the condition that the state will be restored by the Emperor to the son of the late Maharaja, if born to any *Rani*.

[35]*Hukumat-Bahi*, f, 167a.

[36]*Ibid.*

[37]*Ibid.*

[38]*Ibid.*

[39]*Ibid.*

[40]*Ibid.*, ff, 173a, b.

[41]*Ibid.*, ff, 172a-b; *Maasir*, 175.

[42]*Rathora-ri-Vamshavali*, 167; *Ajitodaya*, Serg 5, sloka 42; *Ajit Singh Khyat*, i, 22-3.

[43]*Hukumat-Bahi*, ff, 171a-b.

[44]R.K. Asopa, (*Sankshipt Itihas*, 214) held that Aurangzeb wanted to convert the Rathor prince and, therefore, he issued orders to the Marwar *sardars* to reach Delhi along with them.

[45]*Hukumat-Bahi*, ff, 173b-174a; *Ajitodaya*, (6/56-57) and *Ajit Vilas* (24) mention that Rathor *sardars* along with Bahadur Khan first went to Ajmer and reached Delhi along with the Emperor.

[46]*Hukumat-Bahi*, f, 174a; *Ajit Singh-ri-Khyat*, i, 86-7; *Rathora-ri-Vamshavali*, 175. The account of *Waqai-Ajmer* like other contemporary Persian accounts do not give the details of the events that took place at the court after the arrival of Aurangzeb at Delhi.

[47]*Ajit Singh-ri-Khyat* mentions that the case of Ajit Singh was represented by Shaista Khan, Nawab Bahadur Khan, Raja Anup Singh of Bikaner and Raja Ram Singh of Ratlam; but the Emperor told them that at present he would grant only Sojat and Jaitaran to the sons of Jaswant Singh (*vide.*, I, 90-1). *Ajitodaya* (6/53, 54-64) also mentioned that instead of conceding the demand of the Marwar *sardars*, the

Emperor told them to accept the imperial Service. The Marwar *sardars* turned down the offer. Also, *Jodhpur-Khyat*, ii, 24-5.

[48]*Jodhpur-Khyat*, ii, 24-5.

[49]Cf. Athar Ali, 'Rathor Rebellion of 1679'; *op. cit*, *Marwar and the Mughal Emperors*, 121-7. Satish Chandra in his Chapter contributed to the Comprehensive History of India, (*op. cit.*) mentions in detail the various factors which caused the Marwar war.

[50]*Ajit Singh Khyat*, i. 90-1; *Jodhpur-Khyat*, ii, 24.

[51]*Ajit Singh Khyat*, i, 90-1; *Jodhpur-Khyat*, ii, 24. Kishan Singh committed suicide because the accounts were not systematic.

[52]*Jodhpur-Khyat*, ii, 24-5.

[53]*Ibid.*

[54]Cf. Satish Chandra, *op. cit*, No Rajasthani chronicle mentioned the position and role of Hadi Rani, chief Queen of Maharaja Jaswant Singh, during that period. The account of the *Waqai* mentions that Rani Hadi was leading a group of the Rathor *sardars* who were opposing the imperial control over Jodhpur. It seems that due to the presence of the Rani Hadi, the Rathor *sardars* who were then staying at Jodhpur under the leadership of Rathor Sonag, were not given much importance by the imperial *Waqai Nawis*. The Rathor *sardars* were, in fact the followers of Rathor Sonag and when the latter accepted the service of Indra Singh, Rani Hadi had to leave Jodhpur.

[55]*Maharaja Jaswant Singh-ri-Varta* 119/35; *Jodhpur-Khyat*, ii, 54-5. It appears from *Ajitodaya* (9/1-7) that Indra Singh came to Jodhpur via Nagaur, but the Rathors did not offer resistance because they did not think it proper to fight and weaken themselves by internecine conflict.

[56]*Ibid.* On *Bhadra sudi* 7, 1736 (2 September 1679) Indra Singh occupied Jodhpur.

[57]*Ajitodaya*, 9/5-7.

[58]*Ajit Vilas*, 32-3; *Jodhpur-Khyat*, ii, 54-5.

[59]*Achaldas Khichi-ri-Varta* (ORIJ) 119/35.

[60]Apart from Rathor Sonag other *sardars* were Pratap Singh Jaitawat, Rathor Harnath Champawat of Khario Fardera, Bhati Ram of Rampur, Rathor Hari Singh, etc., (*Jodhpur-Khyat*, ii, 54).

[61]*Ajit Singh Khyat*, i, 167-9; *Ajitodaya*, 7/80-1.

[62]*Ajit Singh Khyat*, i, 157, 158; *Ajit Vilas*, 34; *Ajitodaya.*

[63]*Ajit Vilas*, 33.

[64]*Ibid.*

[65]*Akhbarat*, 25 *Rabi*, *Sen.* 24/April 5, 1681.

[66]Cf. Satish Chandra, 'Mughal relations with the states of Rajputana', *op. cit.*

[67]*Futuhat-i-Alamgiri*, 78b, 79a. According to the treaty of 1615 the repairing of the fort of Chittor was forbidden by the Emperor. *See*, *Udaipur Rajya* i, 809.

[68]*Waqai*, 132; *Ajitodaya*, 9/37-40; *Jodhpur-Khyat*, ii, 56.

[69]*Ajitodaya*, 8/1-34.

[70]*Ajit Vilas*, 34.

[71]*Ajitodaya*, 8/30-2.

72*Jaswant Singh-ri-Varta*, 119-34-6; *Sankshipt Itihas*, 426.

73*Maasir-i-Alamgiri*, 179-80; *Ajitodaya*, 8/35-70; *Rajrupak*, 41-7.

74*Maasir-i-Alamgiri*, 179; *Dilkusha*, 165; *Ajit Singh Khyat*, i, 167-9.

75*Maasir-i-Alamgiri*, 180-1.

76*Ibid*, 181.

77*Akhbarat*, 6 *Shawwal*, 23 R.Y./1 Nov. 1679. 12 *Zul Quda*, 23 R.Y./5 Dec. 1679, 15 *Rabi*. 23 R.Y./15 April 1680; 24-5 *Jamadi* 23 R.Y./12-13 June 1680.

78*Akhbarat*, 12 *Rajab*, 24 R.Y./19 July 1680.

79*Waqai*, pp. 393, 438, 442, 460, 490, 508 and 515.

80*Waqai*, 427.

81*Ibid.*, 438.

82*Ibid.*, 547.

83Among them the name of Sawaldas and his family members holding the *mansab* are worth mentioning. *Ibid.*, 482-3.

84*Waqai*, 442-3, 461-2.

85*Ibid.*, 462.

86*Waqai*, 471-2. It is stated that the *vakil* explained that the prevailing disturbances were caused due to the rebellious activities of the various *zamindars* for which the Rana was not responsible (*vide*, pp. 417-2),

87*Waqai*, 602-4.

88*Ibid.*, 604.

89*Rajprashasti*, 23/31; *Vir Vinod*, 651-2, 655.

90Ojha, *Udaipur Rajya*, i, 897.

91*Ajit Singh-ri-Khyat*, i, 197-9; *Ajit Vilas* 40; Letter from Aurangzeb to Akbar, cit. in *Studies in Aurangzeb's Reign*, 91-2; *Vir Vinod* 653; *Marwar and the Mughal Emperors*, 132-4. Aurangzeb succeeded in creating a rift between prince Akbar and the Rathors which left them no alternative but to desert the camp at Kurki, a village in *Pargana* Jaitaran on 25 January 1681. Aurangzeb got a clear victory over Akbar without any losses on his side.

92*Akhbarat*, 15 *Rabi*, 24 R.Y./25 March 1681; *Ajit Vilas*, 41. According to the *Ajit Vilas* the Emperor also wanted to take away Nagaur from Indra Singh but due to the recommendation of Shah Alam, it was not done (*op. cit.*).

93Indra Singh had granted *pattas* to his *sardars* in Jodhpur. *Akhbarat*, 12 *Rabi*, 24 R.Y./March 23, 1681.

94*Akbharat*, 16 *Rabi*, 24 R.Y./27th March 1681. *Ajit Vilas*, 41. His *mansab* was raised from 1000/100 to 1500/100 (500×2-3h).

95*Akbharat*, 1 *Jamadi*, 24 R.Y./9 May, 1681; 13 Rajab 24; July 20, 1681; 19 *Shaban* 24/24 August, 1681 and 27 *Shaban* 24/1 September, 1681.

96Inayat Khan, the *faujdar* of Jodhpur was requesting the Emperor to raise his *mansab* so that he could check the activities of the Rathor *sardars*. He argued that the deceased Raja (Jaswant Singh) was able to exercise his control successfully as he was holding the *mansab* of 6000/6000 (actually his *mansab* was 7000/(500×2-3b). *Akbharat*, 29 *Jamadi* 24/6 June, 1681.

[97]A detailed list of the various clan leaders is given in the *Rajrupak*, pp. 182-94.

[98]*Ajit Vilas*, 41; *Rajrupak*, 190-4.

[99]*Ajitodaya*, 11/30,

[100]*Rajrupak*, 189-92.

[101]*Ajitodaya*, 11/30-4.

[102]*Ibid.*

[103]*Ajit Vilas*, 42; *Ajitodaya*, 11/32-3. From these accounts it transpires that the imperial commanders being tired of the harassment by Sonag were determined to conclude a treaty. But soon after his death they broke the promise.

[104]*Ajit Vilas*, 42.

[105]*Ajit Vilas*, 42; *Ajitodaya*, 11/33.

[106]*Rajrupak*, 209; *Ajit Vilas*, 42.

[107]*Rajrupak*, 209-11.

[108]*Rajrupak*, 213-26; *Maasir-i-Alamgiri*, 217.

[109]*Ajitodaya*, 11/47-8; *Ajit Vilas*, 43.

[110]*Ajitodaya*, 11/49-52.

[111]*Ajit Vilas*, 44, *Rajrupak*, 224.

[112]*Ajitodaya*, 12/2.

[113]Sarkar, *Aurangzeb* (2nd edn.), 219; Dr. Bhargava holds the same view.

[114]*Jaswant Singh-ri-Varta*, 120/35; *Ajit Vilas*, 54.

[115]*Waqai*, 14, 532.

[116]*Waqai*, 532.

[117]From *Ajitodaya* (11/40-52) it is revealed that the Rathor *sardars* claimed the land revenue from their respective *patta* villages while their *pattas* were resumed under the *khalisa* control.

[118]*Ajit Vilas*, 43.

[119]*Ijara*—A contract; a monopoly; a farm or lease of the revenue of a village or *pargana* or *mahal*; also of customs or collection of any description whether from government directly or from an intermediate payer of public revenue.

[120]*Ajit Vilas*, 44.

[121]*Rajrupak*, 233. *Ajit Vilas* mentions that the Mughal Emperor sent instructions to Inayat Khan to convince the Rathor *sardars* to accept the imperial service (*vide*, p. 45).

[122]*Ajit Vilas*, 52; *Ajitgranth*, 1444-93; *Rajrupak*, 296.

[123]*Rajrupak*, 395; *Ajit Vilas*, 52-3.

[124]*Ajit Vilas*, 53; *Rajrupak*, 296-7; *Sankshipt Itihas*, 445.

[125]*Ajit Vilas*, 53; *Sankshipt Itihas*, 445.

[126]*Ajit Vilas*, 50.

[127]*Ajit Singh-ri-Khyat*, ii, 145-6.

[128]*Ajitodaya*, 13/14.

[129]*Ajit Vilas*, 54.

[130]*Rajrupak*, 304; *Samkshipt Itihas*, 447.

[131]*Jaswant Singh-ri-Varta*, 120/36-7.

[132]*Ajit Vilas*, 58; *Samkshipt Itihas*, 447.

[133]*Jodhpur-Khyat*, ii, 81; *Ajit Vilas*, 59.

[134]*Rajrupak*, 326.

[135]*Rajrupak* (325-6) mentions that Ajit Singh had accepted the offer of Shafi Khan,

[136]*Ajit Vilas*, 62.

[137]Hada Sujan Singh died while fighting with Durgadas. (*Ajit Vilas*, 61).

[138]*Jodhpur-Khyat*, ii, 83-4.

[139]*Ajit Singh-ri-Khyat*, 220; *Ajit Vilas*, 66; *Rathor-ri-Vamshavali*, 220; *Suraj Prakash*, ii, 39.

[140]*Ajit Vilas*, 66-70; *Ajitodaya*, 15/2-4; *Rajrupak*, 332.

[141]*Ajitodaya*, 15/2-4.

[142]Letter dated *Asadh Sudi* 13, V.S. 1745/1 July, 1745, written by Hari Singh to Durgadas, *Jaipur Records*, Vol. X, 271-3. (Sitamau).

[143]G.D. Sharma, "Two unpublished letters", *Proc. Rajasthan History Congress*, 1970.

[144]G.D. Sharma, "Dao Aprakashit Patra", *Shodh Patrika, Versh* 22, i, 62-4; and 'Role of Durgadas Rathor in the Politics of Marwar', *Bengal Past and Present*, XCI, ii, 172, 176-81.

[145]*Akhbarat*, year 38, Jilkada 16/29 June, 1694.

[146]*Ajit Vilas*, 57; *Ajitodaya*, 13/23; *Rajrupak*, 332.

[147]*Ajit Vilas*, 62.

[148]Shujat Khan, in addition to his being the *faujdar* of Marwar, held the *subadari* of Gujarat. Thus he had an advantage over his predecessor Inayat Khan (Sarkar, *Aurangzeb*, v, 220-1).

[149]*Ajitodaya*, 15/44-5.

[150]*Rajrupak*, 336.

[151]*Ajitodaya*, 14/24.

[152]*Ajit Vilas*, 64.

[153]*Ajit Vilas*, 74.

[154]*Mirat-i-Ahmadi*, i, 317; *Ajitgranth*, 1518-26; *Ajit Vilas*, 64.

[155]Jadunath Sarkar held that with the growing youth of his captive grand daughter, his anxiety to get her back increased. The negotiations for this purpose, which had failed in 1692, were renewed in 1694. (*Aurangzeb*, v. 227).

[156]*Farman*, 10 Rajab, R.Y. 42. Copy available in the personal collection of Professor Satish Chandra.

[157]*Jodhpur-Khyat*, ii, 94-5; *Marwar-ke-Rathora-ri-Khyat*, 75; *Ajit Singh-ri-Khyat*, ii, 304-6.

[158]*Marwar-ke-Rathora-ri-Khyat*. 75; *Ajit Vilas* (text) 235/98; *Ajit Singh-ri-Khyat*, 304-5; *Vir Vinod*, 833.

[159]*Jodhpur-Khyat*, ii, 95.

[160]*Ajit Vilas*, 88.

[161]*Akhbarat*, 15 Rabiul, R.Y. 24/March 26, *Jodhpur-Khyat*, ii, 96.

[162]*Ibid*.

[163]*Ibid*.

[164]*Ajit Vilas*, 87.

[165]In A.D. 1697 Maharaja Ajit Singh married the daughters of

Chauhan Fateh Singh of Udaipur and Bhati Dal Singh of Darawar. Later Ajit Singh started living indulgent life and left all the administrative responsibilities in the hands of the *pradhan*, Champawat Udai Singh (*Ajitodaya*, 16/7-9).

166*Ajit Vilas*, 87.

167*Ibid.*, 16/9.

168*Ibid.*, 16/10, 13.

169*Ibid.*, 16/18.

170*Ajit Vilas*, 88.

171*Ibid.*

172*Ibid.*

173*Ajitodaya*, 16/20; *Jodhpur-Khyat*, ii, 65-7.

174*Rajrupak*, 388.

175*Ibid.*, 392.

176*Ibid.*

177*Rajrupak*, 392-3.

178*Ajitodaya*, 16/14.

179*Jodhpur Khyat*, ii, 98-9.

180In about 1705, Durgadas had taken village Sadari (*chhoti*) on *ijara* from the Rana (Reu., *Durgadas*, 43n).

7

REVIVAL OF THE OLD ORDER (1707-1724)

It has been mentioned that Ajit Singh's attempt to revive old administrative pattern in Jalor annoyed the *pradhan*, Udai Singh Champawat. Consequently, Udai Singh and his followers defected to the side of Mohkam Singh, the son of Rao Indra Singh and started a rebellion. The defection of Champawat Udai Singh did not however change the attitude of any sizeable section of the Champawat *sardars*, who, although unhappy with some actions of Ajit Singh, were not prepared to break their traditional bonds with him. Ajit Singh recognized the importance of the Champawats by conferring the post of the *pradhan* on Mukand Das (Champawat) Sujansinghot.[1] The Mertia and Udawat *sardars* who wanted to limit the power of the Champawats did not like the appointment of Mukand Das[2] and looked for an opportunity to oppose him.

After the occupation of Jodhpur (20 February 1707) Ajit Singh wanted to pacify the rivals of the Champawats. Therefore, he offered the post of *pradhan* to Durgadas Rathor.[3] Durgadas Rathor declined it and also refused to accept any *jagir* in Marwar. But he offered his services whenever required.[4] The reason behind Durgadas's indifferent attitude lies in the internal situation prevailing in Marwar. The acceptance of the office of the *pradhan* would have annoyed

Mukand Das who had held the office of the *pradhan* since the defection of Udai Singh Champawat and had considerable influence in state politics and among Champawat Rathors. Moreover, Durgadas did not enjoy the support of any powerful group in the nobility. He had reached the age of 67, and had neither any fascination for the office, nor desire for a *jagir* in Marwar.

It seems that there were other reasons as well which prompted Durgadas to take this action. Durgadas still had some influence at the Mughal court. After his arrival from Patan, though his *mansab* had been cancelled, he still expected the favour from the Mughal Emperor, Bahadur Shah.[5] As Maharaja Ajit Singh had secured control over Jodhpur, without the permission of the Emperor, Durgadas did not approve of it.[6] To avoid getting involved in the affairs he decided to leave Marwar and settle down in his *jagir* in Mewar.

After Durgadas declined the offer of *pradhanship*, Ajit Singh decided not to make any change in the position of Mukand Das Champawat who held this office. But this did not solve the problem. Bhav Singh Rathor and a number of other Kumpawat and Jaitawat *sardars* under the leadership of Arjun Singh Jaitawat, complained that Ajit Singh was the Maharaja of the Champawats only.[7] Incensed by Ajit Singh's favours for the Champawats these Rathor *sardars* collected some 300 to 400 *sawars* at Sojat and proclaimed a bogus person as Dalthambhan, the ruler of Jodhpur.[8] The Mughal *faujdar* of Sojat and the people of Bagari also extended their support to the fake Dalthambhan.[9] To quell this outbreak Ajit Singh marched in person to Sojat and secured his control over it by ousting the Mughal *faujdar*.[10] Arjun Singh Jaitawat and Bhav Singh Kumpawat fled along with the fake Dalthambhan. *Jadhpur-Khyat* mentions that Bhav Singh and Arjun Singh went to Delhi and Agra but could not get the support of the Emperor,[11] though Bahadur Shah was extremely annoyed at the action of Ajit Singh in occupying Jodhpur. Thus the attempt of the Rathor *sardars* to build up opposition against Ajit Singh failed.

Apart from this, Ajit Singh faced another challenge from the side of Mohkam Singh, the son of Indra Singh. After his defeat at the hands of Ajit Singh in A.D. 1705 (V.S. 1762),

Mohkam Singh had continued intriguing against the latter. He had given shelter and *pattas* to those Rathor *sardars* who were disgruntled with Ajit Singh.[12] After the occupation of Jodhpur by Ajit Singh in 1707 Mohkam Singh, who was holding charge of Merta,[13] went to the court of Bahadur Shah and revived the old claims of his family for the grant of Jodhpur.[14] Having secured his control over Sojat, Ajit Singh decided to expel Mohkam Singh from Merta. Due to his preoccupation with consolidation of his power in Marwar, Ajit Singh did not care to send a *nazar* or even a message of congratulations to Bahadur Shah on the occasion of his accession to the throne. It may be noted that at the time of Aurangzeb's death, Ajit Singh was an imperial *mansabdar* and held Sojat in *jagir*. His occupation of Jodhpur without the permission of the Emperor, his failure to send any *nazar* or presenting himself in the Mughal court was taken by the Emperor as an act of defiance.

As is well known, Bahadur Shah decided upon a campaign to rectify the position. While staying at Bhusawar[15] (25 November to 24 December 1707) he issued an order to Mihrab Khan[16] to proceed to Jodhpur and to take possession of it. The news of Bahadur Shah's march towards Jodhpur created a serious problem for Ajit Singh. As mentioned above, the Rathor ruler was facing the opposition of some of the Rathor *sardars*, while at the same time, Rathor Mohkam Singh, son of Raja Indra Singh, was also intriguing to oust him from Jodhpur. Under these circumstances Ajit Singh's choice of retaining Mukand Das Champawat as *pradhan* was unavoidable.

Durgadas Rathor was keen to bring about compromise between Ajit Singh and the Emperor and so he advised the former to evacuate Jodhpur and to attend on the Emperor.[17] Durgadas was perhaps also actuated by the motive of securing a *mansab* for himself.[18] Thus when Bahadur Shah was staying at Merta,[19] Durgadas sent a petition (*arzi*) to him.[20] In response to the letter of Durgadas, the Emperor sent a *farman* and three *hasbulhukms* to Durgadas Rathor on 30 January 1708. On 2 February 1708, he made enquiries about the *jagir* of Durgadas.[21] On 3 February 1708, another petition (*arzi*) from Durgadas was received by the Emperor in reply to a *farman* sent to him four days before.[22] Two days later, Ajit Singh's *ārzi* was also received. That was an indication of submission on the part of Ajit Singh. Therefore, Bahadur Shah sent Khan-i-Zaman, the son of *wazir* Munim Khan, to persuade Ajit Singh to come to the court. Ajit Singh met Khan-i-Zaman on 11 February at Pipal and it was agreed that Khan-i-Zaman and Mihrab Khan could establish *thānas* at Jodhpur.[23] Ajit Singh, along with Khan-i-Zaman reached the imperial camp on 13 February 1708.[24] It may be noted that Durgadas had an audience with the Emperor on 29 February 1708.[25] Obviously, Durgadas represented his own case before the Emperor.

Later on Ajit Singh was granted the *mansab* of 3500/3000, of which 1000 *sawārs* were *du-aspa sih-aspa*, with the three *pargānas*, Sojat, Siwana and Phalodi in *jagir*.[26] At the same time Durgadas was also granted the *mansab* of 3000/3000 and Jalor in *jagir*.[27] These arrangements did not satisfy Ajit Singh who, after his submission, had expected that Jodhpur would be granted to him. In the meantime Mihrab Khan had secured control over Jodhpur. After making necessary arrangements Bahadur Shah returned to Ajmer from Merta[28] and later on proceeded to Deccan to meet the challenge of Kambakhsh.

Much has been written on the flight of Maharaja Ajit Singh (20 April 1708) from the imperial court and the reoccupation of Jodhpur by Ajit Singh with the help of Maharana Amar Singh, Jai Singh, and Durgadas.[29] It is noteworthy that during this period Durgadas Rathor remained with Maharaja Ajit Singh and Jai Singh, but he mainatined his independent status. From the letter of Durgadas written to Pancholi Bihari Das on 3 September 1708,[30] it is clear that Durgadas's motive was to help these *Rājās*. It seems that the *mansab* granted to Durgadas Rathor also remained unimplemented and, therefore, he accompanied the Emperor to the Deccan. It would be seen that Durgadas Rathor had no personal interest in Marwar, though he helped Ajit Singh in securing control over Jodhpur due to the desire of Rana Sangram Singh II.

Maharaja Ajit Singh, after occupying Jodhpur (in July 1708) for the second time made no changes in the official assignments. The office of the *pradhan* remained with Mukand Das as before.[31] Raghunath Singh Champawat was appointed the *hakim* of Jodhpur.[32] The other officials were as follows:

1. Bithal Das Bhandari was appointed the *desh-diwan*.
2. Raghunath Bhandari was appointed the *tan-diwan*.
3. Harkisan Pancholi was given the office of the *bakshi*.
4. Champawat Shiv Ram Kalyandasot was appointed *daroga-i-daftar*.
5. Sobhawat Dayaldas Bainidasot was given the office of *shiqdar* (Jodhpur).

It may be noted that these appointments were made in February 1707 when Ajit Singh had occupied Jodhpur for the first time. The appointments of Mukand Das Rathor and other Champawat *sardars* were not to the liking of the Bhandaris and Rathor *sardars* other than the Champawats. Immediately after making these appointments Ajit Singh marched against Amber with Jai Singh. But the opposition to these appointments did not die down. In February 1709 when Ajit Singh returned to Jodhpur, Champawat Mukand Das[33] and his brother, Raghunath Singh were killed by Udawat Pratap Singh and Bhav Sabal Singhot.

It is said that Ajit Singh also nursed an ill-will against Mukand Das because he held an imperial *mansab* and *thikana* Pali in *jagir*.[34] From the contemporary accounts it is revealed that Mukand Das Champawat had conspired against Ajit Singh. The fact came to light when Bhandari Khivsi got hold of a letter written by Mukand Das Champawat to Mohkam Singh of Nagaur.[35] The letter indicated the exchange of correspondence between the two and constituted a positive evidence of conspiracy against the Maharaja.[36] It seems that like his predecessor Udai Singh Champawat, Mukand Das had planned to dislodge Ajit Singh from the *gaddi* of Jodhpur. Mukand Das thought that after the occupation of Jodhpur the Emperor would favour Mohkam Singh and his own support would strengthen the imperial position at Sambhar. By acting in this manner he could show his loyalty to the Mughal Emperor also. But Maharaja Ajit Singh could have never tolerated such an act of defiance. Earlier he had allowed Udai Singh Champawat to leave Sojat unharmed because of the latter's services to the cause of the Rathor rule in Marwar. Moreover, the rebellion of Udai Singh Champawat did not enjoy the support of the Mughals. But in the case of Mukand Das, Ajit Singh could see the impending danger which could have engulfed him after the arrival of Bahadur Shah in Marwar. The popular discontent against Mukand Das also provided him a favourable opportunity to get rid of him. It is possible that like Jaswant Singh, Ajit Singh was also not in favour of keeping an imperial *mansabdar* as a *pradhan*. The involvement of Ajit Singh in the murder of Mukand Das Champawat can be supported by the contents of the letter which was written by him to Gusai Neelkanthgiri.[37]

After the murder of Mukand Das Champawat, the office of the *pradhan* was entrusted to Bhandari Bithaldas who then held the office of *desh-diwan*.[38] The offices of *tan-diwan*, *desh-diwan*, and *hakim* (of Jodhpur) were given to Bhandari Maidas, Bhandari Khivsi and Bhandari Raghunath respectively.[39] It is to be noted that after the murder of the Champawat *sardars* none of the Rathor *sardars* other than the Champawats got any office. But the Bhandaris could not maintain their monopoly on all these offices. In October 1709 Bhandari Bithaldas was imprisoned and in his place Rai Bhagwandas Champawat was appointed *pradhan* of Jodhpur.[40] The appointment of another Champawat *sardar* after a gap of seven months was important, particularly when many Rathor *sardars* had expressed their resentment against the Champawats. By doing so Ajit Singh not only overlooked the claims of Bhandari Khivsi, the *desh-diwan*, but also rejected the possibility of the appointment of any other Rathor *sardar*. Rai Bhagwandas held a respectable position in the Rathor nobility. He had refrained from seeking any office in the state. In A.D. 1693 (V.S. 1750) Rana Jai Singh granted him some villages in *pargana* Gorwar[41] and the title of the *Rai*.[42] Although he enjoyed a *jagir* in Mewar, unlike Durgadas he remained in Marwar and continued his services under Ajit Singh.[43] Thus his appointment hardly met any opposition from any of the *sardars* and also fulfilled the need of the time.

After the death of Bhagwandas Champawat (A.D. 1715) the office of the *pradhan* was given to Bhandari Khivsi who remained in office till the death of Ajit Singh in 1724.[44] It may be noted that before assuming this office, Bhandari Khivsi had been working as *tan-diwan*.[45] Thus the appointment of Bhandari Khivsi was considered on the basis of his capability. The *pradhans* remained the most powerful officers in the administration and politics during the reign of Ajit Singh. Bhagwandas Champawat and Bhandari Khivsi enjoyed full confidence of the Maharaja. In the absence of the Maharaja they were responsible for maintaining over-all supervision of the political and administrative affairs of the state. They entrusted the right of granting *patta* to the *sardars* on behalf of the Raja.[46] They issued orders to the *hakim*s or other *sardars* for military activities, whenever it became necessary. Obviously as *pradhans*, they had to look after both the civil and military affairs. But they became more effective because of the continuous engagement of Ajit Singh in the politics of the Mughal court.

Other important offices of the state administrative organisation were the offices of *tan-diwan* and *desh-diwan*. Bhandari Bithaldas was appointed as *tan-diwan* after giving *peshkash* of rupees 2500 in A.D. 1707 (V.S. 1764). But in October 1708 when Bhandari Bithaldas was appointed *pradhan*, the office of the *tan-diwan* was given to Bhandari Khivsi.[48] Later in A.D. 1712 the office of *tan-diwan* went to Bhandari Maidas. But again in A.D. 1714 the post of the *tan-diwan* was given to Bhandari Khivsi.[49] During the period A.D. 1712 to 1714 Bhandari Khivsi was in prison and could secure his release only after paying some money to the Raja.

Almost a similar situation can be noticed in the case of *desh-diwan*. In A.D. 1707 (V.S. 1764) Sighvi Bakhtawar Mal was appointed *desh-diwan* after paying rupees 2,000 as *peshkash*.[50] In A.D. 1708 Bhandari Khivsi became the *desh-diwan*, retaining the post for only a short period. He was succeeded by Bhandari Raghunath.[51]

Thus the office of the *tan-diwan* and *desh-diwan* remained with the Bhandaris. There are references to the payment of *peshkash* by *desh-diwan* at the time of his appointment. A study of the various incumbents of these offices shows that most of them were imprisoned and released only when they paid an amount fixed by the state. For example, Bhandari Bithaldas was asked to pay Rs. 6,40,000 to get himself released from prison (in A.D. 1709/V.S. 1766).[52] In the year

A.D. 1714 (V.S. 1771) *tan-diwan* Bhandari Khivsi and *desh-diwan* Bhandari Raghunath were imprisoned.[53] Later, both secured their release after paying the *peshkash*. In A.D. 1715 (V.S. 1772) Bhandari Khivsi and Bhandari Raghunath were appointed as the *pradhan* and the *tan-diwan*.[54] The imprisonment of the officers working as *desh-diwan* and *tan-diwan* was not unusual. During the time of Jaswant Singh both Muhnot Nainsi and Muhnot Sundardas were imprisoned and they were asked to pay Rs. 1,00,000 to resume their posts. In the case of the *diwans* mentioned above, even after their imprisonment their services were not terminated and they resumed their office after making the payment demanded of them. Significantly, they were even promoted to higher posts. In the absence of details it is difficult to draw any conclusion about the nature of charges levelled against these high officials. As the offices of *tan-diwan* and the *desh-diwan* managed the finances of the state, they were held personally responsible if the realization was low and thus, it is just possible that they were held responsible for it and asked by the Raja to make good the loss.

Following the administrative pattern of his predecessors Ajit Singh appointed *hakims* in all the *parganas* of Marwar. In February 1707 Bhandari Naraindas, Bhandari Deokaran, Bhandari Raghunath and Bhandari Pomsi were appointed *hakims* of the *parganas* of Merta, Jaitaran, Jodhpur and Jalor respectively.[55] After the re-occupation of Jodhpur in A.D. 1709 the above *hakims* continued in their respective places.[55] In A.D. 1716 (V.S. 1773) Bhandari Pomsi was appointed as *hakim* of Nagaur.[56] Bhandari Girdhardas was appointed *hakim* of Merta.[57] In the same year Muhnot Sangram Singh and Muhnot Sawal Singh were appointed the *hakims* of the *parganas* of Maroth-Parbatsar and Jalor.[58] The account of the year A.D. 1724 reveals that the offices of the *hakims* in the *parganas* of Jodhpur, Merta, Sojat and Jaitaran were held by Bhandari Anup Singh, Raghunathot, Bhandari Manrup, Bhandari Dhanrup and Bhandari Gordhan.[59] It is evident that since the beginning of the reign of Ajit Singh, till his death, the Bhandaris were appointed as *hakims* in almost all the *parganas* of Marwar. The only exception was Muhnot Sangram Singh and Muhnot Sawal Singh who held that office in the *parganas* of Parbatsar and Jalor. But it may be noted that the appointment of these two Muhnot *sardars* was made on the recommendation of Bhandari Khivsi.

Apart from these higher offices, the office of the *shiqdar* and *bakshi* remained with non-Bhandaris, and with non-Rathor *sardars*. Sobhawat Dayaldas Vainidasot was appointed *shiqdar* when Maharaja Ajit Singh occupied Jodhpur with the help of Rana Jai Singh and Durgadas Rathor. Since then he remained on that post till the death of Ajit Singh.

The letters of the year A.D. 1709 (V.S. 1766) sent by Maharaja Ajit Singh to *shiqdar* Dayaldas indicate that in the beginning, when Ajit Singh was fighting against Bahadur Shah for his recognition, the *shiqdar* was enjoying unlimited powers. He was looking after the security arrangements of the city of Jodhpur and pursuading the inhabitants not to go out of the city.[60] He was responsible for implementing the orders of the Maharaja regarding the assignment of the *pattas* and other rights.[61] When Bhandari Bithaldas and Bhandari Khivsi, the *pradhan* and the *tan-diwan*, were under imprisonment, Dayaldas was instructed to release them only after realizing Rs. 69,000 in cash and not to free them if they delayed the payment.[62] These references suggest that even in a state of political uncertainty, internal as well as external, *shiqdar* Dayaldas was enjoying a stable position and also the confidence of the Maharaja. During Ajit Singh's reign he held the office of the *shiqdar* but due to the existence of powerful *pradhans* his earlier position was somewhat weakened. From the *patta* granted to Shobhawat Dayaldas,[63] it is apparent that with effect from his employment he was granted village Sangrio of *haweli* (Jodhpur) in *patta* for Rs. 31,000 of *rekh*. He was enjoying the right of *mal* and *ghasmari* while the right of *dan* and *bab* remained with the state. It seems that the salary fixed for him was Rs. 3,100 per annum.[64]

From the above account it is clear that the Rathor *sardars* failed to gain control of the various high State offices for which they had aspired after the removal of the Champawat *sardars*. Although the Champawats lost their influence in the State administration, the Mertia, Udawat, Jaitawat and Jodha Rathor *sardars*, who formed the bulk of the Marwar nobility, hardly gained any advantage out of it. They remained out of state administration.

The significant effect of this political development was that the Bhandaris gained the monopoly of all important state offices. Although before Ajit Singh, the Bhandaris had enjoyed the office of the *pradhan*, the *diwan*, the *hakim*, etc., they never held so many important posts at the same time. The Bhandaris were also appointed as *hakims* in various *parganas* of Marwar during the time of Jaswant Singh but these posts were mostly held by the Rathor or Bhati *sardars*. It is to be noted that the Bhati *sardars* who since the time of Raja Udai Singh held a respectable position in the administration were also eliminated during Ajit Singh's reign. The Muhnot *sardars* were again assigned administrative responsibilities. It has been recorded that since Muhnot Nainsi and Muhnot Sundardas had committed suicide, the members of the Muhnot family had been eliminated from the State services. In the year A.D. 1716 on the recommendation of Bhandari Khivsi and Bhandari Raghunath, Muhnot Sangram Singh and Muhnot Sawaldas were appointed the *hakims* of the *parganas* of Maroth-Parbatsar and Jalor respectively.[65]

Thus during the reign of Maharaja Ajit Singh the Rathor *sardars* and other *sardars* of various Rajput clans were eliminated from the state administration which after his death caused a serious political crisis in the politics of Marwar.

Rathor Nobility

Although all important administrative offices remained in the hands of non-Rathor *sardars*, the position of the Rathor *sardars* in the Marwar nobility remained predominant. In A.D. 1705 (V.S. 1762) Maharaja Ajit Singh forced Mohkam Singh to surrender. At that time the Rathor army consisted of 20,000 men while the Rathor *sardars* of 8 *misls*[66] (wings), Champawat, Kumpawat, Jaitawat, Karnot, Jodha, Udawat, Mertia and Karamsot, were present there.[67] At the time of the occupation of Jodhpur (February 1707) the strength of Ajit Singh's army had reached 30,000.[68] The number of *sardars* of the Rathor and non-Rathor clans who joined Ajit Singh on that occasion included 12 Champawats, 6 Kumpawats,

2 Jaitawats, 7 Jodhas, 8 Udawats, 12 Bhatis and 3 Cauhans.[69]

Of the later years we do not have any systematic account of the Rathor *sardars* who were holding the *pattas* during Ajit Singh's reign. Therefore, it is difficult to examine the exact position of the various clans of the *sardars* forming the Marwar nobility. It is related that when Saiyid Husain Ali Khan marched against Marwar in A.D. 1713 Champawat Bhupal Singh Jogidasot was given the charge of the defence of Jodhpur city and the fort. Among others, Champawat Hari Singh, Ugado; Udawat Subhram; Kumpawat Kisan Das, Tej Singh; Uhad Hari Singh; Indra Bhoj, Ram Singh and Dedo; Jodha Hari Singh, Dayaldas, Raj Singh, and Bhagwan Das were also there to defend the fort.[70] The army sent against Nagaur in A.D. 1716 (V.S. 1973) included Jodha Bhav Singh Rinchhodedasot, Udawat Amar Singh Kushal Singhot, Champawat Hari Singh and Kisan Singh Jaswantot, Bhati Indra Bhan Bhivot, and Hari Singh Madhosinghot.[71] Apart from these *sardars* Bhandari Sarangdhar, *hakim* of Merta and Bhandari Pasmi, *hakim* of Nagaur were also sent to seize Nagaur.[72] It has been mentioned that Maharaja Ajit Singh finally succeeded in killing the impostor Dalthambhan and Jaitawat Arjun Singh in A.D. 1717. The Maharaja had entrusted that task to Khetsi, Jiwan Das, and Hardas of Bhati clan; and Hari Singh Kisan Singh, Kesari Singh, Suja Hari Singhot and Rasa Sahasmalot of Champawat clan.[73]

A list of the *sardars* sent along with prince Abhay Singh against Muzaffar Khan in A.D. 1721, indicates that in the army the Rathor *sardars* were in majority.[74] When Abhay Singh was sent to the court in A.D. 1723 his army included 9 Champawats, 3 Karnots, 11 Bhatis, 4 Udawats, 8 Jodhas, 6 Mertias, 5 Kumpawats, 3 Chauhans, 6 Karamsots, 8 Jaitawats, 1 Meheha, 1 Mehcha, 1 Uhad, 1 Inda, 1 Manglia, 1 Khumaur, 1 Khichi, 1 Dhandal, 3 Parihars, 2 Dhawals, 2 Muhata, 1 Bareth, 1 Purohit, and 2 Hawat *sardars*.[75]

Although the participation of the *sardars* on various occasions is, in fact, not a true indication of the strength of the various classes of Rathor nobility even then some general idea may be formed about their position in the Marwar nobility. The foregoing account suggests that the number of the Rathor *sardars* was considerably higher than that of the non-Rathor *sardars* and others. Among the Rathor *sardars*, the Champawats held the highest position in the nobility. This suggests that in spite of strong opposition, the position of the Champawat in the Marwar nobility remained intact. Among the non-Rathor *sardars*, the Bhatis and the Chauhans had an edge over the other non-Rathor *sardars*. In this respect a comparison with the nobility of the time of Jaswant Singh reveals that among the non-Rathor *sardars*, the Bhatis and Chauhans retained their position. The Kachhawahs who held third position among the non-Rathor *sardars* were eliminated from power during Ajit Singh's reign. It seems that as the Kachhawah *sardars* held their *pattas* only in the *jagirs* of Jaswant Singh outside Marwar, they did not participate in Marwar war and consequently were excluded during Ajit Singh's time. But in the case of the Bhatis and Chauhans the situation was quite different. They had their *thikanas* and *bhom* in Marwar and served Ajit Singh during the time of adversity.

Administrative Pattern

As mentioned earlier, with the advice of some of the Rathor *sardars*, particularly the Mertia *sardars*, Ajit Singh had started granting *pattas* to the Rathor *sardars* against their service, leading to the restoration of the *pattadari* system prevailing during the time of Jaswant Singh. It has also been stated that when he occupied Jodhpur in February 1707, the Rathor *sardars* of eight *misls* (wings) were in his army. After securing possession over Jodhpur and other *parganas*, Ajit Singh took a stern attitude towards the *sardars* who had not supported his cause during the period of adversity. Such *sardars* were holding *pattas* since the time of Jaswant Singh and later, their *pattas* were recognized as *watan-jagirs* by the Emperor. Those who were either paying the land revenue to the Mughal officers or were engaged in the Mughal service were granted the right of realizing land revenue of their respective *patta* lands by the Mughal Emperor.[76] Many of the Rathor *sardars* who had not joined the service of Ajit Singh were deprived of their *thikanas* as well as *patta* land.[77] But in most of the cases after the confiscation of the *patta* or the *thikanas* it was granted to a *sardar* belonging to the same family. Thus the clan rights over the *patta* lands were in general recognized by the state.

Many of the *pattas* granted during the time of Ajit Singh are available and their study indicates the nature of rights and obligations of the *pattadars*. The *patta* dated 26 March 1688 (*Chaitra sudi* 5, 1744) issued in favour of Sobawat Dayaldas was granted against his services to be rendered to the state. It makes it obligatory for him to serve as required by the state and not to assign *sasan* land without prior permission. He was given village Malinatho of *Pargana* Jodhpur worth Rs. 400. The village was transferred from Dhani Ramdas.[78]

According to the *patta* issued on Monday, 9 October 1710, (*Kartik badi* 13, 1767)[79] Maharaja Ajit Singh had employed Surat Singh and Sawai Singh Rathor of Mertia sub-clan on the condition that they would serve with loyalty wherever they were sent and would not put forth any fresh demands. They were forbidden to assign *sasan* or *doli* out of the village without permission and to establish relations with others. The *patta* consisted of 12 villages and 1/3 of another village. It was to come into effect from *Shrawan sudi* 1767 V.S. and the rights of realizing *ghasmari, dan* and *bab*, etc., were to be retained by the state.

Patta issued on Friday, 24 April 1718 (*Baisakh sudi* 5, 1774)[80] on behalf of Maharaja Ajit Singh to Bhandari Vijay Raj mentioned the assignment of villages (as detailed below). It was stated that the right of *bab*, etc., would remain with the state. Rs. 400 was settled as *peshkash* to be deposited in the *taaluqa*. Eleven villages worth Rs. 25,250 from *pargana* Parbatsar, which was in *khalisa*, were assigned in the *patta*.

5000	village	1 Khalad	5000	village	1 Badgot
1000	village	1 Chetawo	1000	village	1 Kalavad
2000	village	1 Dehodio	2000	village	1 Chetai
2000	village	1 Ladoli	3500	village	1 Gigalio
2000	village	1 Rainsio	500	village	1 Pinawo
1250	village	1 Dabdio			

Total, *rekh* 25,250.

In addition to the above-mentioned villages one village of

5000 *rekh* from *pargana* Bachalero, which was in the *khalisa* was also bestowed on the Bhandari Vijay Raj. The total *rekh* of 12 villages amounted to Rs. 30,250.

The contents of the *pattas* mentioned above indicate the nature of the *pattadari* system. In the *patta* granted to Sobawat Dayaldas it is clearly mentioned that it was transferred from Danis Ramdas Kachhawatari. It reveals that the practice of the transfer of the *pattas* was prevalent during the time of Jaswant Singh and was continued by Ajit Singh during his reign. Similarly, the *patta* villages of a grantee were not centered at one place, but were scattered over various *tappas* or *parganas*.

The *pattadar* was granted the land revenue of the area indicated in the *patta* and no additional claim could be inferred. The grant of the right to collect any other tax or cess was indicated in the *patta* itself and obviously such additional rights were regarded as a special favour from the state.

As before, the *pattadar* was obliged to maintain the specific number of horses and footmen. In the *patta* given at the end of the chapter, the grantee was asked to keep 25 horses on the *rekh* of Rs. 25,000. This indicates that a *pattadar* had to maintain one horse on the *rekh* of each Rs. 1,000. It may be noted that many of the *pattas* of the time of Ajit Singh do not contain the number of horses to be maintained by a *pattadar*, though it can be well maintained that under the service conditions every *pattadar* was obliged to keep a particular number of horses.

A significant feature that appeared during the time of Ajit Singh was the realization of a lump-sum amount known as *tagirat-bal* from the *pattadars* along with the amount of *peshkash* or *hukamnama*.[81] *Tagirat-bal* began to be recovered from the *raiyats* of the *jagirdars*. The origin of the *tagirat-bal* dates from the time of Maharaja Ajit Singh. During the period of adversity the *raiyat* of Marwar used to pay a lump-sum amount to the Raja to help him against the Mughals. For rendering this help during the imperial control, this nominal help came to be called as *tagirat* or help rendered during the period of suspension.[82] This *tagirat* was a sort of extra tax paid to the Maharaja or the *pattadars* in addition to the ordinary revenue to the Mughals.[83] It seems that the purpose behind the payment of *tagirat-bal* was to maintain the right over their land when the condition changed. At the same time they (*raiyat*) had an advantage too. Keeping in mind the income from this source the Rathor army did not plunder their territory. But after establishing his control over Jodhpur and other *parganas* of Marwar, *tagirat-bal* was made permanent and added to the amount of *hukamnama*. Since then this amount was recovered with the *hukamnama*.

Juni Jagir and Bhom

As the *patta* was granted in lieu of the service, the grantee held the *patta* as long as he remained employed in the state service. When the *pattadar* was removed from the service his *patta* was also cancelled. At times, on confiscation of the *patta* villages, the Raja could, if he so pleased, permit the *pattadar* to retain a few fields just to save him from becoming homeless and destitute. Such territory was known as *juni-jagir*.[84] Maharaja Ajit Singh, as has been mentioned earlier, had cancelled the *pattas* of those Rathor *sardars* who did not serve him during the period of his adversity. *Pattas* were also cancelled on failure to render the stipulated service or for some other similar reasons.

Rathor Kisan Singh, son of Lajraj, held village Godwan in *pargana* Merta in *patta*. As he did not serve the Raja during his days of hardship, his *patta* was cancelled and his *jagir* was taken in *khalisa*. But, he was given 5300 *bighas* of land in *juni-jagir*.[85] Against this, Chundawat Kalyan Singh who had served Ajit Singh during his hard days was granted the *patta* of village Bhadsia of *pargana* Parbatsar in A.D. 1708. Later on, this *patta* was confiscated and he was granted land for cultivation.[86] These instances make it clear that the assignment of the *juni-jagir* was made when the grantee was divested of his *patta*. It seems that the grant of *juni-jagir* was a sort of subsistence allowance for the family of the old *pattadars*, although the state was not obliged to assign such *jagirs* to all the *sardars* whose *pattas* were confiscated.

A study of the extracts of the *bhom* grants of the period of Ajit Singh[87] reveals that most of the *bhoms* were granted to those *sardars* who had fought in favour of Ajit Singh during the period of instability. Rinmalot Hem Singh was granted 500 *bighas* of land as a *bhom* for the service he rendered during adverse days.[88] Kesavdas of Siwencha Jaitawat clan was granted *bhom* in village Kartosan of *pargána* Jalor in A.D. 1708 (V.S. 1765) as a reward for his services rendered during the time of adversity.[89] *Bhoms* were also granted to the sons of those *sardárs* who died in a quarrel, for example, Kumpawat Sabal Singh died in a duel which took place in Delhi in A.D. 1678 (V.S. 1735). After the occupation of Jodhpur, Ajit Singh granted the *bhom* to the three sons of Sabal Singh in three different villages.[90]

These *bhom* grants were rewards for the services rendered by a *sardar*. But the holder of these lands were required to pay the *bhom-bab*. Udawat Sunderdas held 1000 *bighas* of land in village Babalio of *párgana* Parbatsar and was paying Rs. 165 annually.[91] In another case, Rathor Sardar Singh held $1\frac{3}{4}$ *bigha* of land and was paying Rs. 9 per annum.[92] The rates of the *bhom-bab* differed according to the irrigation facilities, nature of services rendered and the status of the grantee. This can be supported by the fact that many of the *bhomias* were exempted from *bhom-bab*.[93]

The above description makes it clear that though many new *bhoms* were granted and *patta* land were changed into the *bhom* lands,[94] the nature of the system prevailing during Jaswant Singh's time remained the same.

The system of land revenue grants regulated the other factors related to the land revenue administration. The details available in a *parwána* of the year A.D. 1717 (V.S. 1774) and the references in the *Khyats*, enable us to understand the changes made during the time of Ajit Singh. The *párwana* issued on behalf of Ajit Singh contains the following instructions:[95]

1. The representatives of the *hakim*, *amin* and *kárkun* who collect the state share of land revenue through the method of *latai* or *kankut* shall not collect any extra money for their expenses.

2. The *kanwaris* (those who were engaged in collection of land revenue) shall not charge the *gughari* from the cultivators because the latter had been paying *kanwara-ro-bab* to the state.

3. The *kanwaris* shall collect the state share of the *kharif* crop in the month of November and the *rabi* crop in the month of April.

4. The *dastur* (customary charge) of the *qanungo* shall remain the same as it prevailed earlier.

5. In the towns and *khalisa* villages the *chaudharis*, the *mahajans* and the *raiyats* should pay the land revenue to the state, and hence no charges should be made from them in the name of punishment or *firohi* without sufficient enquiries.

6. On the production of rice the state demand would be the same as in the case of other grains.

7. The *mutasaddis* (*kanwaris*) shall not receive the *aata* (flour) from the village. They were asked to collect Rs. 5/- per village. The other dues remained the same as they prevailed earlier.

8. The *izafa* on various articles shall remain the same if it had been paid regularly earlier.

The contents of the *parwana* indicate that in the year A.D. 1717 (V.S. 1774) the state prohibited many of the cesses which were levied on the cultivators. These were the cesses which were paid to the *kanwaris* and other village officials. It appears that these officials collected the *gughari* and other cesses for their own expenses, although the state had collected the extra cesses for their expenses from the cultivators. Thus, under such a practice the amount paid by the cultivators was double than what they actually had to pay. It seems that the practice of the collection of these unauthorized cesses was not abandoned during the early half of Ajit Singh's reign. It may be noted that the same situation had prevailed during the early years of Jaswant Singh's reign and only later in A.D. 1657 (V.S. 1714) these practices were stopped by introducing new rules.[96]

No changes were made in the *dastur* of *qanungo* and *kanwaris*. It is mentioned that the *izafa* made on various articles, if paid regularly, was to remain the same. Although no specific reference is made about the period whose rates were followed, it seems that the rates of cesses as fixed during the time of Jaswant Singh were accepted.[97]

References to the *latai* and *kankut* make it obvious that both were prevailing as methods of realizing land revenue of the state. However, no specific mention is made regarding the nature of the land revenue demand. The contents of the *parwana* suggest that the rates of various cesses remained as before and only those practices were checked which were illegal. It seems the land revenue demand was also the same as it prevailed during the time of Jaswant Singh.

An important aspect of these rules was the time of their introduction. In the year A.D. 1715 Bhagwandas Champawat died and the post of *pradhan* was conferred on Bhandari Khivsi. In the preparation and implementation of these rules Bhandari Khivsi must have played an important part. Thus in the field of revenue administration attempts were made to regularize the rules and regulations which prevailed during the reign of Jaswant Singh, though due to lack of information it is difficult to assess to what extent they were implemented.

REFERENCES

[1]*Ajitodaya*, 117/11; *Jodhpur-Khyat*, ii, 111; *Rathora-ri-Khyat*, (S.S.) 70; *Ajit Singh-ri-Khyat*, iii, 462.

[2]*Ajit Singh Khyat*, iii, 163-5; *Rathora-ri-Vamshavali*, (ORI) 168.

[3]*Rathora-ri-Pidia-ri-Khyat* (S.S.), 169; Rathor Durgadas was offered the post of the *pradhan* as well as *diwan*. (*Jodhpur-Khyat*, ii, 106).

[4]*Jodhpur-Khyat*, ii, 106; *Ajit Singh-ri-Khyat*, ii, 356-7.

[5]*Ajit Singh Khyat*, ii, 352-4.

[6]Although at the time of Ajit Singh's control over Jodhpur Durgadas was in Marwar, he did not accompany Ajit Singh during his action against Jodhpur.

[7]*Juni Bahi*, 81.

[8]*Ajitodaya*, 1713-16; *Jodhpur-Khyat*, ii, 113. Dalthambhan, the son of Jaswant Singh, had died on his way to Marwar from Delhi in July 1679.

[9]*Jodhpur Rajya*, ii, 402.

[10]*Juni Bahi*, 82; *Jodhpur-Khyat*, ii, 111-12.

[11]*Jodhpur-Khyat*, ii, 112. *Arzedast* of Dhabhai Rup Ram and Himmat Ram to Maharaja Jai Singh, Jaipur Records (Hindi), Vol. i, 122, 36; *Jodhpur-Khyat*, ii, 113.

[12]*Ajitodaya*, 18/2-5.

[13]*Ajitodaya*, 13/28.

[14]*Ajit Singh-ri-Khyat*, ii, 340-2.

[15]Bahadur Shah left Agra on 24 October 1707. Khafi Khan, vii, 405.

[16]Mihrab Khan was appointed *faujdar* of Jodhpur on 9 October 1707.

[17]*Akhbarat*, 4 *Shaban*, A.H. 1119/18 December 1707. R.S.A.B.

[18]In a letter written by Maharaja Jai Singh to Durgadas Rathor the latter was asked to exercise his influence in relation to Amber. Letter dated Margshir sudi 1, 1764/14 November 1707. *Jaipur Records* (Sitamau), xiii, 144-8.

[19]Bahadur Shah reached Merta on 21 February 1708.

[20]Reu, *Durgadas*, 44.

[21]*Akhbarat*, 31 *Zil*, A.H. 1119.

[22]*Akhbarat*, 1 *Zilhizza* 1119/12 February 1708.

[23]*Ibid.*

[24]*Akhbarat*, Bahadur Shah, year 1 (443-5), *Jodhpur-Khyat*, ii, 120-1.

[25]*Akhbarat*, Bahadur Shah, year 2 (25-31); Raghubir Singh, 'Virvar Durgadas Rathor ke Jiwan ke Antim Bareh Varsh', *Nagari Pracharini Patrika*, 72, i-iv, 422-3.

[26]*Jodhpur-Khyat*, ii, 125, 126, B.N. 82. The grant was made on 13 April 1708; *Rathora-ri-Vamshavali* 200 (ORIJ).

[27]*Karnawata-ri-Khyat*, Basta No. 97/5, R.S.A.B.

[28]Bahadur Shah arrived at Ajmer on *Chaitra Sudi* 14, 1765/24, March 1708; Ojha, *Jodhpur Rajya*, ii, 534.

[29]For details *see*, Satish Chandra, *Uttar Mughal Kalin Bharat*, 48-50. The problem relating to these Rajput *rajas* would be discussed in the following chapter.

[30]*Shyamaldas Collection*, Nos. 50-1. R.S.A.B.

[31]*Ajit Singh Khyat* iii, 168.

[32]*Jodhpur-Khyat*, ii, 147; *Rathora-ri-Pidia-ri-Khyat*, 168.

[33]*Champawata-ri-Khyat*, *Batsa* No. 27/101, R.S.A.B : Ojha, *Jodhpur Rajya*, ii, 544. Rathor Mukand Das had served the Maharaja during the period of adversity. In A.D. 1691 (V.S. 1748), he was sent as one of the commanders of the Rathor army to restore peace in Marwar. When Ajit Singh was granted the *mansab* and got Jalor in *jagir*, Mukand Das Champawat was granted the *mansab* of 600/300 and Pali in *Jagir*. He had gained the confidence of the Maharaja to such an extent that after the flight of Udai Singh Champawat, he was given the post of the *pradhan*. Mukand Das Champawat had been with Ajit Singh when he along with Jai Singh reached Mewar. The Maharana gave him honour at the time of reception.

[34]*Vir Vinod*, 764.

[35]Ojha, *Jodhpur Rajya*, ii, 544-5.

[36]*Ajit Singh Khyat*, iii, 468; *Jodhpur-Khyat*, ii, 154.

[37]Letter cited in *Vir Vinod*, 764.

[38]*Jodhpur-Khyat*, ii, 149-50.

[39]*Rajrupak*, 444; *Jodhpur-Khyat*, ii, 150.

[40]*Ibid.*

[41]Copper plate dated Kartik Sudi 4/1750 issued by Maharana Jai Singh to Bhagwandas. *Bilada Archives*, Bilada.

[42]*Basta* No. 97/4, p. 4, *Jodhpur Records*.

[43]*Ibid.*

[44]*Jodhpur-Khyat*, ii, 165; *Rathora-ri-pidia-ri-Khyat*, 178; *Rathora-ri-Vamshavali*, 146; *Mundiya-ri-Khyat* (ORI), 171.

[45]*Jodhpur-Khyat*, ii, 133.

[46]Letter dated *Magha Sudi* 2, 1772 written by Bhandari Rai Shri to Rai Bhagwandas. Basta No. 97/4, 41. R.S.A.B.

[47]*Jodhpur-Khyat*, ii, 148.

[48]*Ibid.*, ii, 186.

[49]*Ibid.*, ii, 163.

[50]*Ibid.*, ii, 148.

[51]*Ibid.*, ii, 165; *Rathora-ri-pidia-ri-Khyat*, 178.

[52]Letter dated *Vaisakha Badi* 13, V.S. 1766 addressed to *Shiqdar* Dayaldas from Maharaja Ajit Singh. *Basta* No. 76/2, R.S.A.B.

[53]*Jodhpur-Khyat*, ii, 163; *Ajit Singh Khyat*, iii, 517-18.

[54]*Ibid.*

[55]*Ajit Singh Khyat*, iii, 463-4; *Rathor-ri-Pidia-ri-Khyat*, 168; *Jodhpur-Khyat*, ii, 147.

[56]Bhandari Pomsi had commanded the army sent against Nagaur in A.D. 1716. He captured Nagaur and it was recommended that he should continue there as the *Hakim* of Nagaur. *Ajit Singh Khyat*, iii, 518-23.

[57]*Jodhpur-Khyat*, ii, 166.

[58]*Ibid.* After the murder of Muhnot Karamsi at Nagaur, his sons Sangram Singh and Mohan Singh had gone to Kishangarh and were staying there. Maharaja Jaswant Singh had taken an oath not to give any employment to the family of Muhnot Nainsi and Sunderdas. But, now, on the recommendation of Khivsi both the descendants of Nainsi were taken in the state service.

[59]*Rathora-ri-Vamshavali* (*Bahi*), 146; *Mundiyari-Khyat* (ORI) 171; *Rathora-ri-Khyat*, (ORI), 268.

[60]Letters dated *Chaitra sudi* 15, 1766 and *Baishakh vadi* 13, 1766, written by Maharaja Ajit Singh to *Shiqdar* Dayaldas. *Basta* No. 76, *Jodhpur Records*, R.S.A.B.

[61]*Ibid.*

[62]*Ibid.*

[63]Letter of *Bhadrapad vadi* 4, 1764 sent to Shobhawat Dayaldas. *Basta* No. 76/2, *Jodhpur Records*, R.S.A.B.

[64]On *Chaitra sudi* 10, 1767 by an order Shobhawat Dayaldas was again appointed as *shiqdar*. It may be noted that he already enjoyed that office and the reissuing of the order of his appointment perhaps meant confirmation which is clear from another letter of *Baisakh Badi* 13, 1766. Probably other appointments made on various posts were confirmed after the assignment of Jodhpur to Ajit Singh by Bahadur Shah. Basta No. 76/2, *Jodhpur Records*, R.S.A.B.

[65]*Rathora-ri-Pidia-ri-Khyat*, 178; *Jodhpur-Khyat*, ii, 165.

[66]Dayaldas, *Aryan Khyankalp* (A.S.L.B.) f. 21.

[67]*Rajrupak*, 430-2.

[68]*Ibid.*

[69]The names of these *sardars* were: *Champawat* Bhagwan Das, Hari Singh, Udai Singh, Vijay Singh, Achal Singh, Sakat Singh, Muhkam Singh, Raj Singh, Kisan Singh, Kesari Singh, Hari Singh, Kumbh Karan; *Kumpawat* Vijay Singh, Ram Singh, Kesari Singh, Bhim Singh, Fateh Singh and Harnath Singh; *Jaitawat* Fateh Singh and Roop Singh; Jodha Bhiv Singh, Chandrabhan, Mohan Singh, Jogidas, Sakat Singh and Prithi Singh; *Udawat* Jagram Singh, Rede Ram, Partap Singh, Man Singh, Vijay Singh, Dalel Singh, Jujhar Singh and Harnath Singh; *Bhati* Harnath Singh, Bhan, Amar Singh, Khan Singh, Rinchhodh Das, Surajmal, Jeevan Singh, Khet Singh, Soor Singh, Lal Singh and Akhe Singh; *Chauhan* Fateh Singh, Lal Singh and Ajab Singh. (*Rajrupak*, 428-32).

[70]*Rajrupak*, 461-2.

[71]*Ibid.*, 478-9.

[72]*Ibid.*

[73]*Ibid.*, 482-3.

[74]*Ibid.*, 528-34; *Suraj Prakash*, 100-2.

[75]*Ibid.*, 565-75.

[76]Kumpawat Kirat Singh who had joined the Mughal service held Asop in *patta*. After the occupation of Jodhpur, Ajit Singh resumed Asop from Kumpawat Kirat Singh and later on granted it to Kumpawat Bhiv Sabalsinghot. During the period of instability Narawat Chandra Sen had helped the Rathor *sardars*, though he was in the Mughal service. Hence after his death, Pokaran remained in *patta* with his son. *Jodhpur-Khyat*, ii, 153.

[77]*Jodhpur-Khyat*, ii, 148. In the same *Khyat* names of some of the *sardars* who were deprived of their *thikanas* and *pattas* are mentioned.

[78]*Basta* No. 7/23, *Jodhpur Records*, R.S.A.B.

[79]*Basta* No. 76/9, *Jodhpur Records*, R.S.A.B. For detail, *see* Appendix i, given at the end of the Chapter.

[80]*Basta* No. 76/2. R.S A.B.

[81]*Jodhpur Administration*, R.S.A.B. Maharaja Ajit Singh had changed the name of *peshkash* to *Hukamnama* on the conferment on him the title of Raj-Rajeswar in A.D. 1711. Bandal No. 34, (List No. 202).

[82]*Intezam-Marwar*, 440-1.

[83]*Ibid.*

[84]Jodhpur Administrative Report, year A.D. 1883. *Jodhpur Records*. S.A. Sudhalkar, *Report on Jodhpur Constitutional Reforms*, 1944, p. 49.

[85]*Juni-Bahi*, *Basta* No. 76/4, R.S.A.B.

[86]*Ibid.*

[87]*Basta* No. 76/4. R.S.A.B. The *bahi* contains the extracts of some of the *bhom* grants made by Ajit Singh.

[88]*Basta* No. 76/4, R.S.A.B.

[89]*Ibid.*

[90]*Ibid.*

[91]*Ibid.*

[92]*Ibid.*

[93]Jodha Ratan Singh Mukandssinghot held village Barwa of *pargana* Jalor as a *bhom*. He was exempted from *Bhom-bab*. (*op. cit.*)

[94]Chauhan Narain Singh held village Bhagal of *pargana* Jaswantpura in *patta* in A.D. 1708 (V.S. 1763). The same village was granted to him in *Bhom*.

[95]*Rukka-Parwana Bahi*, No. 1, R.S.A.B.

[96]*See* Chapter 4.

[97]Jaswant Singh had also imposed the same checks on *kanwaris*.

APPENDIX 7:I

Transcribed copy of the Patta available at the State Archives, Bikaner (Basta No. 76/2)

पट्टा दिनांक कार्तिक बदी १३, १७६७, सोमवार (अक्टूबर ६, १६६०)

स्वरूप श्री अनेक सकल सुभओपमा विराजमानान महाराजाधीराज महाराजा श्री अजीतसिघजी महाराज कवर श्री अभयसिघजी देवसु तथा राठौड़ सुरतसिघ, सवाई सिघ केसरीसिघोत खापमेड़तीया आसामिया दोय नु माया कर चाकर राषीया, चाकरी भली भात कर सी मेलसी जठे जावसी उजर नही करे मोहम सिर नवी अरजकरया न पावे, बिना हुकम गाव में सासण डोली देण नह पावे कीसा सु पुकारो इत्तफाक करण नही पावे।

गाव १२ न गाव १री हेस तीजी पटे इनायत कीया है सुसंवत १७६७ रा सावणु माल घासमारी था अमल देजो उण वगेरे बाब सिरकार रा छै।

विगत

१२ गाव न हेस तीजो गाव व एक री परगने मारोठ रा ता ॥

षालसा री रेष २५००० हजार री तिणरी दाम ७०५६२०।

गांव लैणवे	१६०६४३।	गांव रावो	३६०००।
गाव पीपराली	१२८०४६।	गाव टीकरीयो खुडद	४३३४०।
गाव हरीयाजुण	३३०००।	गाव कांतियो	३३०४०।
गाव घड़वांसी	४३५३०।	गाव गोझरो, वट तीसरो	१८७३०।
गाव चांवड़ीयो	६०४८०।	गाव नादड़ो	३५०००।
गाव लौडीयाणौ	५७०००।	गाव आबावास	५१८११।
		गाव जायवाड़ो	५०००।

गाव में हेस एक तीजो दाम ७०५६२०। रेष २५०००। घोड़ा २५ जाबता रा राषसी आसामी २ ।

२० घोड़ा सुरतसिघ सेरासिघोत राषसी
५ घोड़ा सवाईसिघ केसरीसिघोत राषसी
२५ घोड़ा कुल

पैंसकसी रा रुपया ७००१ सात हजार एक माते किया। संवत १७६७ काती बद १३ मुकाम पायतखत गढ़ जोधपुर हुवो। श्री मुख परवानगी राठौड़ भगवानदास जोगीददासोत ।

8

INTER-STATE POLITICS AND RELATIONS WITH THE MUGHALS UNDER MAHARAJA AJIT SINGH

As has been mentioned, the occupation of Jodhpur by Ajit Singh in February, 1707 without the consent of the Emperor and his failure to send any *nazr* (present) or presenting himself in the Mughal court were taken as acts of defiance against the Emperor. The arrival of Emperor Bahadur Shah at Ajmer left no other alternative before Ajit Singh but to offer his submission to the Emperor. Although Bahadur Shah granted him the *mansab* of 3500/3000, of which 1000 *sawars* were *du-aspa sih-aspa* and the *parganas* of Sojat, Siwana and Phalodi, Ajit Singh remained dissatisfied without the grant of Jodhpur.

While these events were taking place, the various Rajput *Rajas* maintained close contact with each other through letters. As is known, Bahadur Shah had deprived Jai Singh of his *watan jagir*, Amber, on the plea that as there was a dispute for the Kachhawah throne between the two brothers, Jai Singh and Vijay Singh, the state should be taken in the imperial *khalisa*. Orders were issued that the name of the town should be changed to Islamabad and a new *faujdar* Saiyid Ahmad Khan Barah should be sent there.[1] The reason of the inclusion of Amber in *khalisa* was actually different from what had been given by the Emperor. In the letters addressed to Maharana Amar Singh, Jai Singh wrote that Emperor Bahadur Shah had taken over Amber in *khalisa* on account of displeasure for his (Jai Singh's) joining Azam's side. He added that Amber had been in their possession for a long time and such order had never been issued before. Jai Singh sought advice from the Maharana.[2] Rao Budh Singh of Bundi stated the same reason in his letter to Maharaja Ajit Singh. After giving the reason of the inclusion of Amber in *khalisa*, Budh Singh requested him to consider the problem seriously and to take a decision in consultation with the other Rajput rulers. Budh Singh also stated that the policy of the Emperor was anti-Hindu.[3] The letter written by Budh Singh was significant as it shows that he was not in favour of the action taken by the Emperor against Jai Singh, although he (Budh Singh) had fought on the side of Bahadur Shah against Azam Shah and was consequently granted 54 *parganas* including Kota.[4] It seems that Budh Singh had sympathy with Jai Singh as the latter had married his sister to the former just before the imperial control over Amber.[5] Apparently for Jai Singh the reason of Bahadur Shah's resentment was his participation in favour of Azam in the war of succession.[6] It is worth noting that Jai Singh had not referred to the disputes with his brother on account of which the Emperor had justified his action against Amber. It seems that by raising the issue of his participation against Bahadur Shah, he wanted the help of these Rajput rulers. But both Amar Singh and Ajit Singh made no active response to the letters of Jai Singh.[7] It was after the failure to get any support from Maharana Amar Singh and Ajit Singh that Maharaja Jai Singh wrote a letter to Durgadas Rathor requesting the latter to intercede on his behalf.[8] However, Durgadas made no effort to help Maharaja Jai Singh. The fact that in spite of the repeated request for help and raising the slogan of Hinduism being in danger none of these Rajput rulers paid any heed to the problem of Amber shows that the religious factor was not important in the calculations of the Rajput *Rajas*. Ajit Singh favoured united action against the Mughals only when he himself was dislodged from Jodhpur. Following the order of the Emperor, both Ajit Singh and Jai Singh remained at the imperial camp while he proceeded to the South to deal with Kam Bakhsh. These Rajas were left with Khan-i-Zaman. No definite instructions were issued for them, though both Ajit Singh and Jai Singh were expecting that the Emperor would restore their *watan jagirs* soon.[9]

Agreement among Rajput Rajas

The attitude of the Mughal Emperor forced the two Rajas to come to an understanding. Finding that the Emperor was lukewarm in restoring their *watans* and also due to the suspicion of Ajit Singh that Bahadur Shah might grant Jodhpur to Mohkam Singh of Nagaur in order to create a further division among the Rajputs,[10] they abruptly broke away from the imperial army near Mandsor on 20 April 1708 and came to Udaipur.[11] On Friday 12 May, 1708 Rana Amar Singh received Ajit Singh, Jai Singh and Durgadas at Dawda village (Udaipur), and conducted them to the Palace.[12] On the basis of *Jodhpur-Khyat* it is generally affirmed that at Udaipur the three *Rajas* decided not only to recover their *watans* but also to bring the whole of Hindustan under their sway,[13] which was something beyond their means. It is significant to note that till then Maharana Amar Singh had not shown any indication of his desire to help these *Rajas* against the Mughal Emperor. But to Ajit Singh the Maharana was morally obliged. In A.D. 1692-93 when there was a crisis following the rebellion of prince Amar Singh, Ajit Singh had rendered help to Maharana Jai Singh. Both Durgadas Rathor and Mukand Das Champawat were in the army which restored peace in Mewar and helped to establish cordial relations between father and son. However, due to the interference of Ajit Singh in the affairs of Sirohi which was granted to Maharana Amar Singh in A.D. 1702,[14] the relations between the two had become strained. In A.D. 1706 the misunderstanding was removed[15] and their relations were further strengthened by the mediation of Durgadas Rathor and Rai Bhagwan Das.[16] Durgadas Rathor had accepted the service of the Maharana and, therefore, on 27 April 1707 he left Jodhpur for Udaipur.[17] Rai Bhagwandas maintained cordial relations with the Rana and held a *jagir* in Mewar. Thus when Ajit Singh and Jai Singh accompanied by

Durgadas reached Mewar, the Rana received them warmly. It seems that after having failed to persuade the Emperor, they decided to get the help of the Rana.[18] Perhaps the Rana himself wanted to get into prominence by playing the role of a mediator. This, in fact, happened when the Rana received a *nishan* of 24 April, 1708 from prince Jahandar Shah in which he was asked not to assist the two Rajput rulers, but to send their *arzis* to the Emperor for pardon. The prince gave the assurance that he would obtain the *sanads* of the *jagirs* and the payment of salaries which though already sanctioned had been delayed because of the *ahalkars* (office staff).[19] The Maharana then sent the *arzis* of Ajit Singh, Jai Singh and Durgadas to the court in which they sought forgiveness for leaving the court without permission.[20]

The attitude of the Rana could be assessed on the basis of the contents of the above correspondence. He was in favour of the restoration of the *watan-jagirs* to these Rajas and thus he was pleading their case in the Mughal court. Both Ajit Singh and Jai Singh had also sent their *arzis* with the same object in mind. Apparently Ajit Singh and Jai Singh were waiting for a favourable response even after their flight from the imperial camp. The Rana was using his own influence for getting back their *watans*. But failing to get any encouraging reply from the side of the Emperor they decided to regain their *watan* lands by force. Although Rana Amar Singh was one of the parties sponsoring the joint expedition, he himself did not participate in it, but sent 7,000 Mewari troops under Shyamaldas and Mahasahani Chaturbhuj as military aid.[21] The combined army headed by four separate commanders, i.e., Ajit Singh, Jai Singh, Durgadas Rathor and Shyamaldas marched towards Jodhpur. This army was not commanded by a single commander; rather each one of them was free to take his own decision for operations. This actually happened when Ajit Singh after the occupation of Jodhpur, made no haste to march against Amber. Thus the unity of these Rajput states was disrupted; their primary object being to regain their respective *watan jagirs*. The military help rendered by the Rana and the participation of Durgadas Rathor were aimed at achieving the above objective rather than challenging the Mughal authority.

For Ajit Singh and Jai Singh the internal situation of Marwar and Amber was favourable. In Marwar, Rai Bhagwan Das and Raghunath Bhandari were active and apart from Jodhpur and Merta, where the Mughals had established their *thanas* in *parganas* such as Siwana, Sojat and Phalodi, the number of Ajit Singh's followers was increasing considerably.[22] The combined army besieged Jodhpur on 29 June 1708. After five days of the siege and on the suggestion of Durgadas,[23] Mihrab Khan, the *faujdar* of Jodhpur evacuated the fort; he was allowed to retreat unharmed on 3 July 1708.[24] Durgadas Rathor remained with Ajit Singh till he had secured control over Jodhpur; after that, finding him preoccupied with Jodhpur affairs, he went away to his *thikana* Samdari where he waited to join Jai Singh in his campaign against Amber.[25] Maharaja Jai Singh stayed at Jodhpur, but when he found that Ajit Singh was delaying the expedition against Amber, he moved to Pipad which was situated at a distance of 17 miles from Jodhpur. When Durgadas came to know that Jai Singh had started from Jodhpur, he himself set off from Samdari and met Jai Singh at Pipad on 22 August 1708.[26] Durgadas Rathor was prepared to march with Maharaja Jai Singh even if Ajit Singh failed to arrive.[27] The letter written by Durgadas to the Rana clearly indicates that after securing their control over Jodhpur, the combined army was to march for Amber.[28]

It is apparent that Durgadas's task was to help these Rajas in securing their *watan* lands. He had no personal ambition in Marwar. He participated in the combined expedition because the Rana asked him to do so.[29] This explains the policy of the Rana who was not ready for any united resistance against the Mughals and only wanted to help these Rajput Rajas in regaining their *watan* lands. Maharaja Jai Singh and Durgadas were waiting for Ajit Singh when he arrived at Pipad with his contingent.

Meanwhile, in the region of Amber the followers of Jai Singh had become very active and were launching attacks on Amber. Finally, in the beginning of July 1708 *diwan* Ram Chandra Muhta and Shyam Singh Kachhawah succeeded in securing their control over Amber and the Mughal *faujdar*, Husain Khan Baraha, was forced to leave Amber.[30]

War of Sambhar

At the end of August 1708, Ajit Singh, Jai Singh and Durgadas assembled at Pushkar to decide the future course of action. Here it was decided that the Rana should also come and participate. Accordingly, the Rajput rulers persuaded Durgadas Rathor to go to Udaipur, but the decision had to be changed later on.[31] Although the reason of concealing Durgadas's visit to Udaipur is not mentioned in any of the contemporary sources, the political events explain the necessity of it. Saiyid Husain Khan, the defeated *faujdar* of Amber, after collecting sufficient army, had advanced towards Amber from Narnol to regain control over Amber. The Rajput Rajas, therefore, decided not to give any chance to Husain Khan to achieve his goal. The absence of Durgadas would have delayed the action of the Rajput Rajas and provided enough time to the Mughals to strengthen their position. It was also doubtful that the Rana himself would have agreed to come personally to help Jai Singh and Ajit Singh against the Mughals.

Both the Rajas and Durgadas Rathor proceeded towards Sambhar and they reached there on 30 September 1708. Anticipating the Rajput movement Saiyid Husain Khan, with his brothers who were the *faujdars* of Merta and Narnol, hurried to Sambhar with the object of barring the path of the Rajputs.[32] A battle took place on 3 October 1708 in which Saiyid Husain Khan and his brothers were killed and the Rajputs came out victorious.[33] It may be noted that when Durgadas arrived at Sambhar, he pitched his camp separately. When the Maharaja asked the reason for doing so, he very politely replied that being an old man he expected to remain in this world only for short time and, therefore, he should be allowed to have his way.[34] The reply of Durgadas Rathor was not surprising. He had acted independently at the time of Ajit Singh's occupation of Jodhpur. In fact he came out in favour of these Rajput Rajas because he was asked by the Rana to do so. After the victory at Sambhar, Durgadas did not stay for long and proceeded to Mewar.[35] It appears that Durgadas was not ready to involve himself in the activities of Ajit Singh who had decided to keep control over Sambhar and Didwana and wanted to invade the imperial territory towards Narnol. Ajit Singh and Jai Singh stayed at Sambhar for a few weeks to make necessary administrative arrangements. It was agreed that the revenue of the conquered territory would be equally divided between the two. Both of them shared the responsibility of administration equally.[36] Maharaja Ajit Singh appointed the son of Bhandari Khivsi as *hakim* and Jagram as a *kotwal*. The purpose of making these administrative arrangements was to keep joint control over that territory for a long period.

Ajit Singh's Activities after the Battle of Sambhar

The victory at Sambhar infused a new spirit in Ajit Singh who, after making some security arrangements at Sambhar, proceeded to Jodhpur.[37] He did not spend much time in Jodhpur and after effecting necessary administrative changes, marched against Nagaur. When Mohkam Singh heard of the approach of Ajit Singh he fled to Ladnu and Rao Indra Singh had to take shelter in the fort. On Ajit Singh's arrivat at Nagaur, the mother of Indra Singh came to see him and persuaded him to leave Nagaur with Indra Singh. Mohkam Singh agreed to accept Ajit Singh's overlordship.[38] In accepting Mohkam Singh's submission Ajit Singh was only following the principle of '*bhai-bandh-chakar*' and accordingly he was ready to accept Mohkam Singh as a ruler of Nagaur as long as he obeyed his command.[39] Ajit Singh thereafter returned to Jodhpur.[40] Now apart from Jodhpur Ajit Singh had secured his control over Merta, Sojat, Jaitaran and Phalodi which were parts of Marwar.[41] Thus he had achieved his long-cherished desire, though its recognition by the Mughal Emperor was still lacking.

The Emperor till now had not shown any inclination of granting him Jodhpur. In the first week of February, 1709 Ajit Singh left Jodhpur and reached Merta from where he was to march on Ajmer.[42] Jai Singh had earlier promised to march from Amber to Ajmer as soon as he heard of the advance on Merta.[43] Ajit Singh did not wait for Jai Singh for a long time and on 5 February, he reached Ajmer and besieged the provincial capital for fifteen days. The Mughal *subadar*, Shujat

Khan, agreed to pay Rs. 80,000 whereupon Ajit Singh returned to Jodhpur in the middle of March, 1709.[44]

It is doubtful whether Ajit Singh wanted to extend his control over Ajmer. If that was his motive he could have postponed his attack till the arrival of Jai Singh. It seems that Ajit Singh wanted to terrorize the Mughal *subadar* of Ajmer so that the decision of granting him Jodhpur could be speeded up. The failure of Jai Singh to arrive at Ajmer could be examined in the same context. During all this period, Amber's *vakil*, Jagjiwandas, was carrying on negotiations with the Mughal officers. He pleaded through prince Azim-us-shan and Sarbuland Khan for the grant of a *mansab* of 5000/5000, title of Mirza Raja, *Noubat*, and restoration of *watan* for his ruler (Jai Singh).[45] But the Emperor did not agree to grant a *mansab* above 3000/3000. He offered to restore to Jai Singh all other *parganas* of Amber state save the city (*kasba*) of Amber, and to bestow all land to Ajit Singh save the city (*kasba*) of Jodhpur.[46] Shortly afterwards, Mewar's *vakils* Kanha Pancholi and Maya Ram prevailed upon the Emperor to restore *pargana* Amber to Jai Singh and to grant him a *mansab* of 3500/3000.[47] Thus it is obvious that while these negotiations were going on Jai Singh avoided attacking the imperial *thanas*. Jai Singh also wanted to secure the favour of the Emperor as is obvious from the fact that Shujat Khan praised Jai Singh for his non-cooperation with the Rathors and for persuading Ajit Singh to return from Ajmer.[48] Further, Jai Singh was aware that Vijay Singh was pressing the Emperor for granting him Amber also.[49] Thus while both Ajit Singh and Jai Singh were exchanging cordial letters, each of them was making individual efforts to get back his *watan*.

Since Bahadur Shah failed to satisfy the Rajput Rajas regarding their *watans*,[50] Ajit Singh and Jai Singh continued their united opposition. But the Rajput rulers persisted in pleading there case before the Emperor through the Maharana as well as through their respective *vakils* at the court.[51]

Ajit Singh took the lead in inviting the Maharana with his army to invade the imperial territory. The Maharana sent an army under the command of Durgadas Rathor.[52] While Ajit Singh was preparing to demonstrate his strength, Maharaja Jai Singh was persuading the former to have an audience with the Emperor. The letter of Bihari Das explains that Maharaja Jai Singh was not willing to participate in any activity which would cause further complications.[53] In fact, Jai Singh and Ajit Singh were suspicious of one another and were not ready to come into conflict with the Mughal Emperor. Thus, the united front against the Mughals had been virtually defunct. At the same time it was obvious that these Rajput Rajas would continue their struggle till they got their respective *watans*.

It is to be noted that a powerful section of the nobility led by Asad Khan, the former *wazir* of Aurangzeb, and his son, Zulfiqar Khan, the *mir-bakhshi*, held a sympathetic attitude towards these Rajput Rajas.[54] Bhandari Khivsi, the *vakil* of Maharaja Ajit Singh at the court, was engaged in negotiations with Emperor Bahadur Shah through prince Azim-us-Shan who was high in his father's favour. Prince Azim-us-Shan told Bhandari Khivsi that nothing could be expected unless both the Rajas attended the court personally.[55] The *vakil* of Maharaja Jai Singh was repeatedly asking the latter to come to the court immediately without waiting for Maharaja Ajit Singh.[56] In the letter written to Maharaja Ajit Singh, Jai Singh expressed his desire to appear in the court without any delay.[57] Obviously, Jai Singh wanted to establish that he had every intention to attend the court and, therefore, he sent his consent without waiting for Ajit Singh's reply.

The reason behind the delay on the part of Ajit Singh was his preoccupation with internal problems. He could leave the territory only after making the administration effective in Marwar. But the rapid march of Bahadur Shah towards Ajmer left no alternative for Ajit Singh except to attend the court personally. On 4 May, 1710 the Emperor ordered Mahabat Khan to proceed along with Chhatrasal and Raja Budh Singh to bring Jai Singh and Ajit Singh to the court.[58] The *farman* of 19 May, 1710 addressed to Ajit Singh stated that his faults were being pardoned and that Jodhpur was being conferred on him on condition that he would serve the Emperor and would attend the court with *Bakhshi-ul-Mamalik* (Zulfiqar Khan).[59] Bahadur Shah was keen that Maharaja Ajit Singh and Jai Singh should join him to meet the growing Sikh menace.[60] But Maharaja Ajit Singh, being engaged in internal disturbances, wanted to stay for some time to establish order in his state and, therefore, he, as well as Maharaja Jai Singh were given leave for six months.

In spite of repeated summons from the court, Maharaja Ajit Singh arrived at the court only on 17 October, 1710 after a lapse of about fifteen months.[61] Pleading for the *subadari* of Malwa or Gujarat, Maharaja Ajit Singh wanted to keep his control over Sambhar and Didwana.[62] He had not thus so far received any order regarding his *mansab* and hence he delayed his appearance in the Mughal court. This delay by Maharaja Ajit Singh was not appreciated by Maharaja Jai Singh who showed his inclination to attend the court, thereby leaving Ajit Singh alone to become the target of imperial displeasure.[63] In the court, Bhandari Khisvi was repeatedly urging that Ajit Singh would be starting immediately.[64]

When Ajit Singh had an audience with the Emperor, he was finally recognized as the ruler of Jodhpur. He was granted the *mansab* of 4000/4500 and Jodhpur along with the *parganas* of Sojat, Siwana and Phalodi. Outside Marwar, Ajit Singh was granted the *faujdari* of Sorath.[65] Ajit Singh was not given Merta and it remained in *khalisa*. Perhaps, the Emperor wanted to keep his control over Merta so that he could check Ajit Singh's activities against Nagaur. But Merta did not remain in *khalisa* for a long time. Finding it difficult to maintain peace over it, Merta was granted to Ajit Singh in *ijara*.[66] It is implied from the document that Ajit Singh would pay half of its *jama* to the Emperor, and that it was not to be treated as one of the *jagirs* granted to Ajit Singh.[67] This was a significant event in Rathor-Mughal relations. For the first time a *pargana* was given in *ijara* to the Raja who held the *watandari* claim over it.

Although Ajit Singh was granted Jodhpur, the *mansab* granted to him was not commensurate with his ambitions. When the *mansab* was granted to Ajit Singh, he had control over all those *parganas* in Marwar which were later on granted to him in *jagir*. Besides, he had control over Sambhar and Didwana. The *mansab* granted to him implied that he had to evacuate Sambhar and Didwana. However, Ajit Singh maintained his control over these two *parganas* even after getting back Jodhpur. This indicates that Ajit Singh was discontented with the *mansab* and the *jagir* he held. Thus during the reign of Bahadur Shah, the demands of Ajit Singh could not be satisfied. Jai Singh met the same fate. Hence, their mutual association continued, though at the court their representatives were pleading that their interests were separate.

After the death of Bahadur Shah (17 February 1712), Maharaja Ajit Singh's *mansab* was increased to 7000/7000 and he was appointed the *subadar* of Gujarat.[68] At the same time, Rathor Durgadas was also granted the *mansab* of 4000/3000 and *pargana* of Idar in *jagir* on the recommendation of Zulfiqar Khan.[69] The *mansab* and the assignment of the *subadari* of Gujarat were highly appreciated at the court as well as in Jodhpur.[70] Maharaja Jai Singh had also been granted the *mansab* of 7000/7000 and the *subadari* of Malwa, Emperor Jahandar Shah being himself favourably inclined towards the Rajput Rajas.[71] Thus the policy of Bahadur Shah was abandoned soon after his death.

The grant of *mansab* to Maharaja Ajit Singh and his appoinment to the *subadari* of Gujarat could not be implemented due to the murder of Jahandar Shah and Zulfiqar Khan, and the succession of Farrukh Siyar (February 1713). The political uncertainty at the Mughal court enabled Ajit Singh to extend his influence over neighbouring states Raj Singh, the ruler of Kisangarh, had taken sides with Azim-us-Shan against the Emperor. After his arrival at Kisangarh, Raj Singh wrote to Ajit Singh to help him in case he was persecuted.[72] Ajit Singh, considering that Raj Singh was his nephew, agreed to do so. But Raj Singh had to pay the price of this assurance. With the intention of bringing the adjoining territories under his control, Ajit Singh wrote to Raj Singh to come with an army. But Raj Singh did not pay any heed. Therefore conquering Banderwara, Bhinai and Vijaigarh, Maharaja Ajit Singh reached Deogarh.[73] When he was camping at Deogarh he again called Raj Singh but the latter gave no response. Therefore, Ajit Singh invaded Kisangarh and took possession of it. At first Raj Singh offered a stiff resistance, but later on made submission and concluded an agreement with Ajit Singh according to which Ajit Singh incorporated some of his areas into his own territory.[74]

Taking advantage of the political instability at the Mughal court during the war of succession, Maharaja Ajit Singh delayed the evacuation of Sambhar and Didwana. Since the restoration of *watan jagirs* to Ajit Singh and Jai Singh, Asad Khan had written many times to Ajit Singh to remove his *thanas* from Sambhar and to hand over their control to imperial officers.[75] It seems, Ajit Singh wanted to keep his control over Sambhar and Didwana till he had been assured of the intention of the Emperor.[76] Perhaps he was interested in retaining these *parganas* in his *jagir* because he was not interested in getting his appoinment either at Kabul or Maroth.[77] It is quite possible that by keeping his control over these areas he wanted to keep a good source of income with him. After the death of Bahadur Shah, the Rajput Rajas continued their control over Sambhar and Didwana. Zulfiqar Khan adopted a more strict attitude over the control of these *parganas* by the Rajput Rajas. This action of the Rajas, which amounted to disobedience, led to a political crisis. In these *parganas* the Mughal Emperor had assigned the *jagirs* to his *mansabdar* but none of them could get hold over them. Zulfiqar Khan, after the accession of Jahandar Shah, strongly told the *vakil* (Pancholi Jagjiwan) of Maharaja Jai Singh that he should ask both the Rajas to remove their *thanas* immediately, otherwise they would be punished. The *wazir* warned that in case of an imperial march, Ajit Singh could save himself by taking shelter in the hill areas but Jai Singh would not get any place to hide. He also demanded that Jai Singh should persuade Ajit Singh to behave like a Raja and not like a dacoit.[78] Later, after taking over the charge, the new *wazir* of Farrukh Siyar, Saiyid Abdullah Khan, again asked Pancholi Jagjiwan Ram to ask Jai Singh and Ajit Singh to remove the *thanas* from Sambhar.[79] Ajit Singh was also asked to deposit the amount which he had collected from the *haweli*[80] of Ajmer.[81] Ajit Singh did not take these instructions very seriously. He wanted the restoration of his *mansab* of 7000/7000 and repeated his claim for the grant of the *subadari* of Gujarat or Malwa through his *vakil*, Bhandari Khivsi.[82] Maharaja Jai Singh also approached the Emperor with a similar request.[83]

While these claims were being pressed, Ajit Singh continued his offensive activities which caused great concern at the court. Maharaja Ajit Singh had been nursing for long the foul desire to kill Rathor Mohkam Singh (son of Indra Singh) who had been pressing his right for the *gaddi* of Jodhpur. After the succession of Farrukh Siyar, Mohkam Singh repeated the old claim. Ajit Singh entrusted to Rathor *sardars*, mainly Durjan Singh Jodho, Amar Singh Bhati, etc., the task of assassinating Mohkam Singh. They killed Mohkam Singh in August 1713, while he was on a visit to Abdullah Khan.[84] In the meantime, Ajit Singh occupied Merta after the flight of Indra Singh who was then staying there. The occupation of Merta was clearly a violation of the conditions on which it had been given to Ajit Singh by Bahadur Shah. Indra Singh complained to the Emperor and repeated his claim over Jodhpur.[85] Although the Emperor did not give much weight to the claim of Indra Singh, it became necessary for him to check the activities of Ajit Singh.[86]

Although it is difficult to determine the exact motives behind Ajit Singh's aggressive activities, it seems that he wanted to demonstrate his power and compel the Emperor to concede his demand. However, a study of the reports sent by Pancholi Jagjiwan Ram to Jai Singh, shows that as early as June 1713, Farrukh Siyar had accepted the claims of the two Rajas over their respective *watan jagirs*. The question of granting them *jagirs* outside their *watan* territories was delayed as Abdullah Khan wanted a reassessment of their *jagirs*. It was, therefore, stressed that an assignment to the Rajas of the *jagirs* outside their *watans* could be made only after they had submitted a statement of the *jama* of their respective *parganas*. The *vakils* of Jodhpur and Amber on the other hand held that the assignments should be made on the basis of the old *jama* figures.[87] This was the main cause of contention. The attempt for a reassessment of the *watan jagirs* may also be looked upon as a part of the *jagirdari* crisis. The practice of assigning *jagirs* on the basis of the old *jama* figures would have compelled the *wazir* to grant additional *jagirs* to the Rajas outside their *watans* which the Mughal court was reluctant to do. Pancholi Biharidas, the *vakil* of Jai Singh at the Mughal court, was able to persuade the Emperor to confer the title of Mirza Raja Sawai on Jai Singh in July 1713.[88] Politically, it was a significant development in the policy of Farrukh Siyar as no such favour was shown to Ajit Singh. The reasons for the failure of Ajit Singh to get an equal consideration were his marauding activities which caused great concern at the court. Khivsi Bhandari while pleading the cause of Ajit Singh for a high *mansab* and *jagirs* was, however, able to establish close relations with the Saiyids.[89] But the Saiyids and the Emperor created a rift between Ajit Singh and Jai Singh. This allowed the Emperor to take advantage of the situation. It was decided that Ajit Singh and Jai Singh should not be appointed to contiguous *subas*. In the month of October 1713, Ajit Singh and Jai Singh were restored the *mansab* of 7000/7000, and were granted the *subadaris* of Thatta and Malwa respectively.[90] As was expected, Maharaja Ajit Singh refused to accept the *subadari* of Thatta. The disobedience of Ajit Singh in accepting the imperial order gave additional support to the anti-Ajit Singh attitude of Farrukh Siyar who was annoyed with him due to the murder of Mohkam Singh, and his delay in evacuating Sambhar and Didwana.

To settle the score with Ajit Singh, Farrukh Siyar sent an army against Marwar on 6 January 1714 under the command of Saiyid Husain Ali.[91] A letter addressed to Maharaja Jai Singh by Jagjiwan Das indicates that even before Husain Ali Khan's arrival at Merta, Maharaja Ajit Singh had come to an understanding with him. Husain Ali showed favour to him by stating that the murder of Mohkam Singh was not done at the instance of Ajit Singh.[92] Knowing the favourable inclination of Husain Ali towards him and the group politics of the Mughal court, Ajit Singh tried to win his sympathy. He showed him the letters written by the Emperor promising him favours if he fought and defeated Husain Ali.[93] Hence, no battle took place and in March 1714, a treaty was concluded between Husain Ali Khan and Ajit Singh. According to it, the latter submitted to Husain Ali and in proof of his loyalty agreed to marry his daughter to Farrukh Siyar. A *mansab* of 7000/7000 was conferred on him together with the *faujdari* of Thatta.[94] His son Abhay Singh was granted a *mansab* of 3000/2000 and the *faujdari* of Sorath.[95] Significantly, according to this treaty Maharaja Ajit Singh agreed to follow the earlier order of the Emperor to go to Sorath which he had not followed.

It is said that apart from the official declaration, Husain

Ali Khan and Ajit Singh concluded a secret pact according to which the former promised that Ajit Singh would be appointed to the *subadari* of Gujarat as soon as he had marched towards Thatta, thus publicly demonstrating his obedience to the imperial orders.[95] His demand for all the *parganas* which had been under Jaswant Singh was practically conceded. The question of reassessment of the *parganas* of Marwar was also dropped, and the *jagirs* were given on the basis of the old *jama* figures. It is noteworthy that the same concessions had already been made to Jai Singh when Amber was conferred upon him along with other *parganas* in his *watan* in October 1713.

During this period the relations between Ajit Singh and Jai Singh became strained. A study of the *Vakil-Reports* shows that Ajit Singh and Jai Singh differed on the question of Sambhar and Didwana. It has been mentioned above that Maharaja Jai Singh made it clear to Abdullah Khan that the delay in handing over the charge of these *parganas* was due to Ajit Singh who held control over them. It is apparent that Maharaja Jai Singh was no longer interested in opposing the Mughals jointly with Ajit Singh if the Emperor agreed to appoint him (Ajit Singh) the *subadar* of Gujarat or Malwa. This fact became more obvious when after his appointment in Malwa, Jai Singh left Ajit Singh alone to face the Mughal army. In fact, Jai Singh joined the Mughal army sent against Ajit Singh.[97] Apparently the favour shown to Jai Singh by granting the *subadari* of Malwa led to his disassociation from Ajit Singh. A study of the *Vakil-Reports* shows that since the succession of Farrukh Siyar, Jai Singh remained neutral and did not associate himself with the activities of Ajit Singh.

The appointment of Ajit Singh as the *subadar* of Gujarat was made on the recommendation of the Saiyid brothers and therefore his association with them became quite intimate. But Maharaja Jai Singh, who had succeeded in getting the *subadari* of Malwa through Khan-i-Dauran, had direct access to the Emperor. Thus, while Jai Singh associated himself with Farrukh Siyar, Ajit Singh became a partisan of the Saiyids. The growing animosity between Jai Singh and Ajit Singh was due not only to the factional rivalry at the Mughal court but also because both of them wanted to extend their influence over Rajputana. Ajit Singh felt that he had been deprived of Sambhar and Didwana due to Jai Singh, who put all the responsibility of disobeying the imperial orders on him in order to gain goodwill at the Mughal Court.

Ajit Singh and Saiyid Brothers

With the support of the Saiyid brothers, Ajit Singh retained his *mansab* of 7000/7000 and apart from the *subadari* of Gujarat, held the *parganas* of Sojat, Jaitaran, Phalodi, Siwana, Merta and Gajsinghpura along with Jodhpur.[98] Ajit Singh now took advantage of the situation prevailing at the Mughal court in expanding his territorial control around Marwar. While proceeding to Gujarat in A.D. 1715 (V.S. 1772), he occupied Bhinmal and Jalor which had been in the Rathor domain during the time of Maharaja Jaswant Singh.

Before leaving for Ahmedabad, Ajit Singh had also ordered Pemsi Bhandari to conquer Nagaur.[99] Pemsi invaded Nagaur and seized it. Indra Singh's defeat was certain, since he no longer enjoyed imperial support. His *sardars* started defecting in favour of the Jodhpur army. Even though the fort of Nagaur had fallen, the Champawat *sardars*, Bhagwandas Jogidasot, etc., were of the opinion that Indra Singh should not be killed.[100] At their instance Indra Singh was allowed to evacuate the fort and take shelter at the Mughal court.[101] There, he again began to poison the ears of the Emperor against the Maharaja, but this time he was not able to achieve much success. On the contrary, the Emperor granted Nagaur to Ajit Singh[102] in February 1717. The acceptance of the right of Ajit Singh over Nagaur was a significant factor in the consolidation of the Rathor power. Ajit Singh's control now extended over the areas which were once dominated by the Rathor clan. The political crisis at the Mughal court and the participation of Ajit Singh with the Saiyid brothers in dislodging Farrukh Siyar provided further opportunity to the former for extending his influence over the Rajput states as well as at the court.

After the assassination of Farrukh Siyar in February 1719, Ajit Singh gained the most advantageous position. He was granted the *subadari* of both Ajmer and Gujarat.[103] From a contemporary account, it appears that the award of the *mansabs* granted to Ajit Singh, his sons and other Rathor *sardars*, was a high watermark in the history of Marwar as well as of other Rajput states. The details of the *mansab* and salaries including *inam*, may be summarized as follows:[104]

Mansabdar	*Mansab* Zat	Sawar	*Salary* Dam
Ajit Singh	7,000	7,000 (5,000 × 2-3h)	11,00,00,000
Abhay Singh	5,000	4,000	4,20,00,000
Bakht Singh	2,000	2,000	2,00,00,000
Anand Singh	2,000	2,000	2,00,00,000
Kishore Singh	2,000	2,000	2,00,00,000
Rai Singh	1,500	1,000	1,20,00,000
Partap Singh	1,500	1,000	1,10,00,000
Ratan Singh	1,500	1,000	1,10,00,000
Total	22,500	20,000 (5,000 × 2-3h)	24,60,00,000
Rathor Sardars and others Nos. 44.	18,800	7,310	4,69,70,000

A study of the *mansab* and the amount of the salary sanctioned against Ajit Singh's *mansab*, indicates that the amount was fixed on the same principles which were followed during the time of Aurangzeb. Apart from the *jagirs* in Marwar, Ajit Singh was granted *jagirs* outside Marwar also. The most significant feature was the increase in the number of Marwar *sardars* which rose from seven, holding the imperial *mansabs* in the reign of Jaswant Singh, to 44. Even in A.D. 1697 when Aurangzeb had granted *mansabs* to Ajit Singh and Durgadas, the total number was 8 including Durgadas himself.

After being secured from the side of the Mughal court, Ajit Singh further tried to extend his power in Rajputana. Although he had been appointed *subadar* of Gujarat and the deteriorating political and administrative conditions required his presence there and in spite of the fact that Abdullah Khan repeatedly wrote to him about this, he paid no heed.[105]

Earlier, Ajit Singh had tried to help Jai Singh in retaining the *gaddi* of Amber. Since the latter had been hostile to the Saiyids, and had given shelter to his opponents,[106] Saiyid Abdullah Khan marched towards Ajmer along with Emperor Rafu-ud-Daulah and Ajit Singh with the intention of dislodging Jai Singh from the *gaddi* of Amber.[107] The Rajasthani chronicles record that Maharaja Ajit Singh interceded on behalf of Jai Singh and that it was due to his persuasion that Abdullah Khan agreed to pardon Jai Singh.[108] The Saiyids showed their generosity and granted Jai Singh a large sum of money and the *faujdari* of Sorath.[109] At a meeting with Jai Singh at Kaladera on 16 November 1719 Ajit Singh tried to strengthen the bonds of good-will between Jai Singh and the Saiyids.[110] Later, Maharaja Jai Singh accompanied by Ajit Singh reached Jodhpur on 10 December 1719. While staying there, Jai Singh was married to the daughter of Ajit Singh, the celebration being performed in May 1720.[111] The matrimonial relationship between the two houses was also in the interest of the Saiyids who wanted to win Jai Singh over to their side. But it would be wrong to presume that by entering into a matrimonial alliance with Jai Singh, Ajit Singh wanted to form a united front of the Rajput Rajas. Perhaps he was motivated by a desire to use the alliance with Jai Singh to consolidate his position in Ajmer. That is why, even after the marriage ceremony, he avoided departure for Gujarat, despite pressing letters from Saiyid Abdullah Khan.[112]

Jai Singh on his part was also clear about the intention of Ajit Singh and continued intriguing with the opponents of the Saiyids.[113] In spite of the cordiality established between the two Rajas, Jai Singh secured the clandestine support of Emperor Mohammad Shah. Maharaja Jai Singh was not satisfied with the position granted to him by the Saiyids. Although he held the *mansab* of 7000/7000 and the *faujdari* of Sorath, he could not forego the *subadari* of Malwa, which he had held during Farrukh Siyar's reign. However, when in the month of October 1720, Abdullah Khan sent him a letter through Ajit Singh,[114] conveying the grant of the *subadari* of Malwa, Jai Singh ignored the order of the *wazir* since it would have embroiled him with Nizamul-Mulk, the *subadar* of Malwa. Obviously, Maharaja Jai Singh had no faith in Saiyid

Abdullah Khan. At the same time, he could not ignore the influence of Ajit Singh which was increasing day by day. A study of the letters written by Jai Singh to the Maharana, the rulers of Bikaner, Kota and Indra Singh, reveals that he was trying to rally these Rajput Rajas in favour of Mohammad Shah and against Saiyid Abdullah Khan.[115] However, none of them responded to the suggestion of Jai Singh. Maharaja Sujan Singh of Bikaner had his own policy. In a letter dated 7 November 1720 (*Margsir vadi* 3, 1777) Raja Sujan Singh expressed apprehension of the encroachment by Ajit Singh on Bikaner as the latter had advanced to Nagaur. The ruler of Bikaner was also engaged in internal problems caused by factions in his nobility.[116] The Maharana of Mewar was not approached to extend open support to Mohammad Shah since it would have led to friction with Ajit Singh who was openly supporting the cause of the Saiyids. Similarly, the ruler of Kota was also not in a position to extend any kind of open support to the Emperor. Under these circumstances, Maharaja Jai Singh, without waiting for the return of Ajit Singh, left Jodhpur and reached Jahanabad in the later half of November 1720.[117]

Ajit Singh after the Murder of Husain Ali Khan

Maharaja Ajit Singh could not enjoy a supreme position for long. The murder of Husain Ali Khan on 8 September 1720 and the imprisonment of Abdullah Khan on 3 November 1720 had a direct impact on Ajit Singh who was then the most influential Rajput *mansabdar* at the Mughal court. Till then, he had retained the *subadari* of Gujarat and had appointed Bhandari Anup Singh as his *naib* there.[118] When the news of the defeat of Abdullah Khan at Husainpur on 4 November 1720 became known to Ajit Singh, he proceeded to Ajmer and made defensive arrangements.[119] In fact, Ajit Singh knew it well that due to the change in the court politics, he would not be allowed to continue as the *subadar* of both Gujarat and Ajmer. This proved true when soon after the defeat of Abdullah Khan, he was removed from the *subadari* of Gujarat and Ajmer.[120] In retaliation, he started plundering the imperial territory and sent out prince Abhay Singh and

Bhandari Raghunath towards Sambhar.[121] Likewise, the armies of the Maharaja got hold of Didwana, Toda, Jhadod, Bhinai and Amarsar.[122] In the meantime, Mohan Singh Jat, son of Churaman Jat, reached Sambhar where he was given shelter by Ajit Singh.[123] Abhay Singh now marched towards Narnol. At first Bayazit Khan Mewati, the *faujdar* of Narnol, tried to oppose him, but he had to retreat to Mewat as he could not withstand the onslaught of the Rathor forces. Abhay Singh, after sacking Narnol, plundered Tijara and Shahjahanpur.[124] Maharaja Ajit Singh also tried to gain control over Bikaner, but he failed in his efforts.[125] However, he conquered the following areas while the court was still planning an expedition against him:[126]

1. Ajmer
2. Bhinai
3. Toda
4. Maharoth
5. Bherudi
6. Babal
7. Nagaur
8. Parbatsar
9. Harsur
10. Tosina
11. Sambhar
12. Didwana.

The activities of Ajit Singh were a direct challenge to the imperial authority. Khan-i-Dauran suggested that Ajit Singh should continue as the *subadar* of Gujarat on the condition that he evacuated Ajmer.[127] This suggestion could have avoided the imperial march against Ajit Singh, but it was not accepted due to the opposition of Haidar Quli Khan and others.

It would be wrong to presume that Ajit Singh's intention was to remove the Mughals from Rajputana or the Emperor from his position. He was only repeating his old policy of demonstrating his strength in order to force the Emperor to accept his terms and conditions. But the offensive launched by him created suspicions against his motives. Much has been written on the court activities and the assignment of the *subadari* of Ajmer to various Mughal commanders who one after another failed to bring order to the region plagued by the defiant activities of Ajit Singh.[128] The determination of the Emperor to force Ajit Singh to evacuate Ajmer and the other imperial territories, ultimately changed his attitude and compelled him to withdraw to Jodhpur from Ajmer in March 1722, leaving Udawat Amar Singh at the fort of Garh Bitali (Ajmer), pending settlement with the Emperor.[129] He also sent an *arzadast* to the Emperor seeking pardon for his faults and pleading for the retention of Ajmer.[130] The departure of Ajit Singh from Ajmer after leaving behind his troops, indicated clearly that he was confident of retaining the *subadari* of that province.[131]

But the appointment of Nahar Khan as *diwan* of Ajmer and *faujdar* of Sambhar in December 1722 renewed the hostility of Ajit Singh who did not allow him (Nahar Khan) to secure control over Ajmer and got him murdered when he entered the territory of Ajmer and camped near the Rathors on 6 January 1723.[132] Earlier, Ajit Singh had extended his support to Churaman Jat of Bharatpur by despatching a contingent against Jai Singh,[133] but later on, he withdrew this support. After the defeat of Churaman Jat he renewed his contact with Mohkam Singh Jat to whom he had given shelter.[134] These acts of Ajit Singh not only enraged the Emperor but also showed his enmity against Jai Singh. Obviously, Ajit Singh was not in favour of the expansion of Jai Singh's influence over Jat territory but he could do nothing to help Mohkam Singh Jat to regain his territory. Reacting to these actions of Ajit Singh, Emperor Mohammad Shah appointed Sharf-ud-Daulah as the commander of a huge army to be sent against him. The Emperor also ordered Haider Quli Khan, Jai Singh, Girdhar Bahadur, etc., to help the imperial army. A *farman* sent to Jai Singh on 10 January 1723, says that Ajit Singh, the fake child of Jaswant Singh, had been pardoned several times for his offences, but had again shown his obduracy and raised his head. The wretch had blackened his face by murdering Shaikh Nahar Khan. He (the Emperor) could not sit at rest till the villain was killed or arrested. Hence Jai Singh was ordered to reach Narnol at the earliest, either alone or in the company of Mohammad Khan Bahadur.[135]

A study of contemporary Rajasthani records reveals that when Ajit Singh came to know about the approach of the imperial army, he withdrew from Ajmer and left a Rathor contingent at Garh Bitali to face the imperial army.[136] Thus,

Ajit Singh was not prepared for a direct conflict with the imperial army and the stay of the Rathor army at Ajmer was merely a show. In fact, just after his withdrawal from Ajmer, Ajit Singh started making efforts to conclude peace with the Emperor through Jai Singh.[137] Although Jai Singh had doubts about the motives of Ajit Singh, as the former had occupied some of the parts of his territory also, he took lead in settling the matters.[138] Prince Abhay Singh appeared before Haider Quli Khan with the *arzadast* of Ajit Singh, according to which the former was to have an audience with the Emperor for his pardon.[139] An agreement was concluded in June 1723 according to which the Maharaja agreed to surrender the territories which he had occupied by force.[140] Nagaur was granted to Indra Singh. Although Ajit Singh was restored to the *mansab* of 7000/7000, he had to send Abhay Singh to court in order to pacify the Emperor.[141] The question of his appointment as *subadar*, however, remained pending. He was deprived of the territory he had held outside Marwar. The conditions to which Ajit Singh had to agree were humiliating for him and isolated him in the Mughal politics. This actually happened due to the presence of Abhay Singh at the Mughal court who was tipped by the Emperor to assume the *gaddi* of Jodhpur.[142]

As has been mentioned, Jai Singh had played an important role in restoring peace in Marwar.[143] He as well as the Emperor, were in constant fear and were looking for an opportunity to have Ajit Singh killed and thus become free from anxiety.[144] The Emperor began to develop close relations with prince Abhay Singh through Jai Singh. He won over Bhandari Raghunath who was the most influential noble of Marwar.[145] Prince Abhay Singh was told that the Emperor was not happy with Ajit Singh and, therefore, it would be in the interest of his ancestral land if he succeeded in killing his father. Bhandari Raghunath also supported the idea.[146] A letter with the signature of Abhay Singh was secretly sent to Bakht Singh, younger brother of Abhay Singh. In this letter, he was advised to kill the old Maharaja for the sake of the safety of the state. As soon as this letter reached Bakht Singh he was astonished and did not know what to do. But in the end after realizing the future trouble over the state, he became inclined to do what was asked of him. Bakht Singh was also assured that he would be given independent control of Nagaur.[147] Accordingly, on 23 June 1724 (*Ashadh sudi* 13, 1781) Maharaja Ajit Singh was assassinated by his younger son, Bakht Singh.

Thus the rule of Ajit Singh ended with an unprecedented tragedy which later caused a civil war in Marwar. The events witnessed some important changes in the external politics of Marwar. The repeated violation of imperial orders had become a general practice during the time of Ajit Singh. The co-operation among the Rajput Rajas was mainly motivated by their personal interests, and as soon as one achieved his target, the other was left alone to struggle for his demands. Such practices led to suspicions among the Rajput rulers against each other and pushed them into internal feuds. The Mughal Emperor failed to achieve any advantage out of this due to intrigues and group politics at the court. The death of Ajit Singh marked the decline of the position of the Rathors among Rajput rulers as well as at the Mughal court for the time being. It also set the trend which led to the disintegration of the Mughal empire.

REFERENCES

[1]*Later Mughals*, ii, 46; *Parties and Politics*, 30.

[2]Letters from Jai Singh to Amar Singh of 7 June, 1707 and 25 August 1707. *Kharitas and Parwanas*, No. 2, R.S.A.B.

[3]Letter from Budh Singh to Ajit Singh dated *Magha sudi* 9, 1764 (August 25, 1707). *Jodhpur Records* (Sitamau) viii, 131-2.

[4]*Kota Rajya*, i, 253-4; *Parties and Politics*, 121.

[5]*Vamsha Bhaskar*, 2999; *Kota Rajya*, i, 255.

[6]*Bahadurshahnama* justifies the action of Bahadur Shah against Amber as Jai Singh had sided with Azam. See, *Parties and Politics* 30-31n.

[7]In his letter written to the Maharana on 11 September 1707, Maharaja Jai Singh acknowledged the receipt of a letter from the former. The contents of this letter show that it was a formal letter and the Maharana showed only outward sympathy rather than offering any military help. *Kharitas and Parwanas*, Bundle No. 4, R.S.A.B.

[8]Maharaja Jai Singh's letter to Durgadas dated 14 November 1707. *Jaipur Records* (Sitamau), xiii, 143-4.

[9]*Marwar Khyat* (SS) 70. It is mentioned that while the imperial camp was at Sitamau, these rulers realized that Bahadur Shah was in no hurry to restore to them their *watan jagirs* (*vide*, 70-1).

[10]Mohkam Singh, son of Indra Singh, was also with the imperial army and it was thought that the Emperor could grant him Jodhpur in his (Ajit Singh's) absence from Marwar. *Marwar Khyat* (SS), 70-1.

[11]*Akhbarat*, Bahadur Shah, year 2, p. 23; *B.N.* 96-7; *Dilkusha*, 1726. From the available source material it is obvious that these Rajas left the imperial camp from the camp near Mandsor. Irvine calls it (i, 49, 67) as Mandleswar, while both Kamvar (ii, 310) and *Jodhpur-Khyat* (ii, 127) mention that they left from Mandsor. In some sources reference is made of Badoreda (38 miles) and Khachrod (47 miles). It may be inferred that they had not gone beyond Khachrod. Due to the similarity of the names of the places situated on the north bank of river Narbada, Ojha has confused Mandeswar with Mandleswar which is situated on the north bank of Narbada (*Udaipur Rajya*, i, 602). The later historians repeated the same mistake.

[12]*Marwar Khyat* (SS) 70-1; *Ajit Singh Khyat*, iii, 412-21. For a detailed account of Rajput deliberations at Udaipur, see *Vir Vinod*, 769-72.

[13]*Jodhpur-Khyat*, ii, 127-8; *Parties and Politics*, 34n; Bhargava, *Marwar and the Mughal Emperors*, 149.

[14]*Amir-ul-Umra Shaistah Khan-ki-Yaddasht*, dt. 26 March 1703, cited in *Vir Vinod*, 749; also see, *Jodhpur Rajya*, ii, 525.

[15]Letter from Ajit Singh to Gusai Neelkant of March 25, 1706, cited in *Vir Vinod*, 764-5; 766-7.

[16]*Basta* No. 97/4, *Jodhpur Records*, R.S.A.B.

[17]*Jodhpur-Khyat*, ii, 106, 110.

[18]Letter from Jai Singh to Rana Amar Singh cited in *Vir Vinod*, 768.

[19]The copy of the *nishan* cited in *Vir Vinod*, 773-4; Ojha, *Udaipur Rajya*, 914.

[20]*Vir Vinod*, 774.

[21]*Ibid.*, 774-5; *Udaipur Rajya*, i, 915

[22]*Ajit Singh-ri-Khyat*, iii, 407-10.

[23]*Vir Vinod*, 774.

[24]*Rajrupak*, 427-32; *Jodhpur Rajya*, ii, 537.

[25]Letter written to Pancholi Beharidas by Durgadas on *Ashoj Vadi* 2, 1765 (3 September, 1708), cited in *Vir Vinod*, 835.

[26]In a letter dated *Bhadra sudi* 5, 1765 written to the Maharana, Durgadas complained that Ajit Singh was delaying the matter unnecessarily. *Shyamaldas Collection* 14/99, R.S.A.B. *Jodhpur-Khyat*, ii, 131-3; *Rajrupak*, 427-32.

[27]*Rajrupak*, 428-31.

[28]Letter dated 3 September 1708 (*op. cit.*).

[29]*Ibid.*

[30]*Akhbarat*, August 14, 1708; *Vir Vinod*, 774-5; *Marwar Khyat*, ii,

135; *Parties and Politics*, 35; *Maasir-ul-Umra* (Hindi, vi, 504-5), wrongly mentions that at that time Durgadas was at Amber.

[31]Letter dated *Ashoj sudi* 8, 1765 (24 September 1708), written by Durgadas to Pancholi Biharidas, cit. *Vir Vinod*, 835-6; *Jodhpur-Khyat*, ii, 138-9.

[32]Earlier, Churaman Jat also accompanied Saiyid Husain Khan but it seems that Churaman managed to remain aloof at the crucial time as he is nowhere mentioned in the account of the battle.

[33]*Akhbarat*, Bahadur Shah, year 2, 146 (Sitamau); *Jaipur Records, miscellaneous*, i, 165-6 (Sitamau); *Rajrupak*, 434-41; *Jodhpur-Khyat*, ii, 138-9; *Vir Vinod*, 836.

[34]*Ajit Singh-ri-Khyat*, iii, 434-36; *Rathora-ri-Pidia-ri-Khyat*, (SS), 168-71; *Jodhpur-Khyat*, ii, 141-43, 185; Ojha, *Jodhpur Rajya*, i, 541-42n.

[35]Durgadas left Sambhar in the last week of October, 1708.

[36]Letter from Ajit Singh to Udai Singh dated *Ashoj sudi* 7, 1766 V.S. *Kharita Jodhpur*, 1/5; *Jaipur Records*, R.S.A.B.

[37]*Rajrupak*, 441; Ojha, *Jodhpur Rajya*, ii, 543-5.

[38]Letter from Ajit Singh to Jai Singh dated *Magha sudi* 10 (8 January 1709), *Kharitas Jodhpur*, 7/12, R.S.A.B.

[39]In his letter dated 20 January 1710, (*Magha sudi* 11, 1766) written to *Shiqdar* Dayaldas, Ajit Singh mentions that Mohkam Singh had agreed to serve the cause of the state whenever it was needed. *Basta* No. 76/2, R.S.A.B.

[40]*Ajitodaya*, 18/99-106.

[41]Letter dated 7 February 1709 (*Phalgun sudi* 8, 1765) from Chaudhari Bhagwandas to Maharaja Amar Singh informing the departure of Ajit Singh. *Shyamaldas Collection*, 33/99, R.S.A.B.

[42]Kushal Singh Rajawat's letter to Jai Singh dated 8 January 1706/ (*Phalgun sudi* 10, 1765). *Jaipur Records* (Hindi), ii, 14 (Sitamau).

[43]Letter from Jai Singh to Ajit Singh dated 8 February 1709 (*Phalgun sudi* 10, 1765). *Jaipur Records*, ii, 14 (Sitamau); *Ajit Singh-ri-Khyat*, iii, 439-40.

[44]*Jodhpur-Khyat*, ii, 149-50. According to *Vir Vinod*, Ajit Singh realized Rs. 45,000 from Shujat Khan as the expenditure for the army (*vide* 8, 38).

[45]*Vakil Reports*, dated *Magha vadi* 4, 1707.

[46]*Vakil Reports*, dated *Magha vadi* 8, 1767.

[47]*Ibid.*

[48]Report of Bhandari Khivsi to Jai Singh dated *Ashadh vadi* 14, 1767. Vakil Report of Kalyan Singh to Jai Singh dated *Magha vadi* 4, 1767. *Vakil Reports* No. 18, R.S.A.B.

[49]*Vakil Reports*, dated *Magha sudi* 3, 1769.

[50]Letter of Rawat Malji to Maharana Amar Singh dated 5 April 1709 (*Baisakh sudi* 7, 1766). *Shyamaldas Collection*, 33/99, R.S.A.B.

[51]Letter from Ajit Singh to Jai Singh dated 28 March 1709 (*Baisakh vadi* 14, 1766). *Kharitas Jodhpur*, Jaipur Records, 7/11, R.S.A.B.

[52]Letter from Ajit Singh to Jai Singh dated October 1709 (*Kartik sudi* 4, 1766). *Kharita Jodhpur*, 7/6, R.S.A.B.

[53]Letter from Bhikaridas to Jai Singh dated *Phalgun vadi* 13, 1767. *Khatut-i-Maharajgan*, Reg. 198. R.S.A.B.

[54]For detailed information regarding the policy of the various groups in the court, see, *Parties and Politics*, 35-6.

[55]Bhikaridas's letter to Maharaja Jai Singh dated *Phalgun vadi* 13, 1767. *Khatut-i-Maharajgan*, Reg. No. 198, R.S.A.B.

[56]Bhikaridas's letter to Maharaja Jai Singh dated *Phalgun vadi* 13, 1767. *Khatut-i-Maharajgan*, Reg. No. 198, R.S.A.B.

[57]*Kharitas and Parwanas* (Jaipur Records), *Bundle* No. 1/42, R.S.A.B.

[58]*Akbharat* 29, Rabi I, 1122 H.

[59]Copy of the *farman* available in *Reu's Collection*, Summer Public Library, Jodhpur.

[60]For details, see, *Parties and Politics*, 50-3.

[61]*Ibid.*, 37-9.

[62]*Ajit Singh-ri-Khyat*, iii, 470-2.

[63]In a letter dated *Magha sudi* 15, 1767, written by Bhandari Khivsi to Maharaja Jai Singh, the former complained that he should not write such letters to *Nawab Khan-i-Khana*, *Munim Khan*; *Vakil Reports*, *Bundle* No. 1, Letter No. 24 R.S.A.B.

[64]Letter dated *Magha sudi* 7, 1767 (*op. cit.*).

[65]*Arzadast* from Pancholi Jagjiwan Ram to Jai Singh dated 1 November 1711. *Vakil Reports*, Reg. No. 103, R.S.A.B.

[66]*Arzadast* from Didwana Bihari Das to Jai Singh, dated *Bhadrapada* 1768 (August 1711).

[67]*Ibid.*

[68]*Akhbarat*, November 25; *Vakil Reports*, *Magh sudi* 7, 1769 (1712 A.D.). *Parties and Politics*, 74.

[69]*Vakil Reports*, *Shravan sudi* 5, 1769 (1712 A.D.).

[70]*Vakil Reports*, *Magh sudi* 1, 1769 (1712 A.D.)

[71]*Ibid.*

[72]Letter dated *Magha sudi* 8, 1768, from Raj Singh to Ajit Singh. *Basta* No. 97/4, R.S.A.B. Reu *Marwar*, i. 304-5.

[73]Letter from Ajit Singh to Pancholi Balkisan in March 1713 (*Chaitra* 1770). *Kharita-Bahi* No. 2, R.S.A.B.

[74]Letter dated *Margsir vadi* 10, 1769 from Ajit Singh to *Shiqdar* Dayaldas. *Kharita-Bahi* No. 2, R.S.A.B.

[75]Maharaja Ajit Singh's letter to Jai Singh. *Jaipur Records* (Hindi), ii, 15 (Sitamau).

[76]From the *Vakil Reports* dated *Shravan vadi* 2, 1769, it appears that Ajit Singh was disinclined to vacate his control over these areas.

[77]Both the Rajas wanted to get their posting near their *watans*. Bahadur Shah wanted to appoint them in the eastern *suba* and Deccan but as a result of their repeated request, Ajit Singh was granted the *subadari* of Sorath and Jai Singh of Prayag. *Vakil Reports*, dated 1 November 1711 (*Kartik sudi* 13, 1768). R S.A.B.

[78]*Vakil Reports*, dated 9 July, 1712 (*Shravan vadi* 2, 1769), and 4 August 1712 (*Sharvan sudi* 15, 1769).

[79]*Vakil Reports*, dated *Shravan sudi* 15, 1769. R.S.A.B.

[80]*Haweli*: habitation; the tract of country adjacent to a capital town and originally annexed to it for the supply of the public establishment.

[81]*Vakil Reports* (*op. cit.*) *Ajit Vilas*, 98, *Ajit Singh Khyat*, iii, 508.

[82] *Ajit Singh Khyat*, iii, 493.

[83]*Vakil Reports*, dated *Magha sudi* 4, 1770.

[84]*Ajit Vilas*, 98; *Marwar Khyat* (SS), 76; *Vir Vinod*, 841.

[85]*Ajit Vilas*, 97-8; *Ajit Singh Khyat*, iii, 493.

[86]*Ajit Singh-ri-Khyat* mentions that the murder of Mohkam Singh prompted Farrukh Siyar to send an army against Ajit Singh. (*vide* 494-5).

[87]*Vakil Reports*, dated *Baishakh sudi* 9, 1770 and *Jyestha sudi* 5, 1770 (Nos. 195-6). R.S.A.B.

[88]*Vakil Reports*, dated *Ashadh sudi* 4; *Ashadh sudi* 7 and *Shrawan sudi* 13, V.S. 1770 (1713 A.D.). R.S.A.B.

[89]*Vakil Reports*, dated *Ashadh sudi* 4, *Ashadh sudi* 7, and *Shrawan sudi* 13, V.S. 1770. R.S.A.B.

[90]*Vakil Reports*, dated *Bhadrapad sudi* 7, 1770; *Parties and Politics*, 100.

[91]*Ajit Vilas*, 98; *Parties and Politics*, 101.

[92]*Arzadast* dated 26 August 1713 (*Bhadra sudi* 7, 1770) from Pancholi Jagjiwan Das to Jai Singh. *Khatut-i-Maharajgan*, Reg. No. 203 (R.S.A.B.).

[93]K.K. 738; Shivdas, 10; *Parties and Politics*, 101.

[94]*Vakil Reports*, *Jyeshtha sudi* 11, 1771 and *Baishakh sudi* 1, 1772.

[95]The salary due against the mansab of Ajit Singh was six crores and twenty lacs of rupees. *Vakil Reports*, dated *Baishakh sudi* 1, 1772.

[96]*Parties and Politics*, 102.

[97]*Jodhpur-Khyat*, ii, 135-40; *Ajitodaya*, 21/1-38.

[98]*Ajit Singh-ri-Khyat*, iii, 523; *Jodhpur-Khyat*. ii, 143-5.

[99]*Ajit Vilas* (MS), 239/102; *Ajit Singh Khyat*, iii, 528-9. *Jodhpur-Khyat* (SS), 79.

[100]*Ajit Vilas*, 99; *Ajit Singh Khyat*, iii, 140-1.

[101]*Rajrupak*, 475-9; *Rathora-ri-Pidia-ri-Khyat* (SS), 178. This event took place in July, 1716.

[102]*Ajitodaya*, 23/2-13; *Ajit Singh Khyat*, iii, 142-3.

[103]*Ajit Singh Khyat*, iii, 344; *Ajit Singh-ri-Varta* (ORIJ), 126/41. For the policy of the Saiyid brothers towards Ajit Singh, see *Parties and Politics* (2nd Edn.) 148.

[104]*Yaddast Mansab, Aswar, Dam-Bada Maharaja Ajit Singh-ri, Basta* No. 90/11. *Jodhpur Records*. R.S.A.B.

[105]Letter No. 21 and 31, cited in *Balmukandnama* (Ed. Satish Chandra). For details, see, *vide*, Introduction, 5.

[106]In a letter written to the Rana, Abdullah Khan, complained about the activities of Jai Singh and his anti-Emperor attitude. (*Balmukandnama*, L. No. 1). *Jodhpur-Khyat*, ii, 175-6. Khafi Khan, ii, 832. Jai Singh had shown his willingness to support Neku-Siyar (son of Mohammad Akbar) who raised a rebellion against the Saiyids. 'Jai Singh had been actually camping at Toda Tank, 80 *kos* from Agra'. Amber

became the centre of the opposition to the Saiyids. For details, see *Parties and Politics*, 146; *Sawai Jai Singh*, 88-90.

[107]*Jodhpur-Khyat*, ii, 175; *Ajit Vilas* (MS), 243/106; *Ajit Singh-ri-Khyat*, iii, 555; *Balmukandnama*. Intro. 4, L. Nos. 1, 24.

[108]*Rajrupak*, 44; *Ajit Singh-ri-Varta* (ORIJ), 126/30-40; *Ajit Vilas* (MS) 243/106. *Ajit Singh Khyat*, iii. 555, mentions that Jai Singh had sent his *Vakil* to save him from the displeasure of the Saiyids. (*Balmukand-nama*, 14).

[109]*Parties and Politics* (2nd Edn.), 148. Ajit Singh formed his own equation through matrimonial alliances. While staying at Manoharpur on his way to Jodhpur, Ajit Singh married the daughter of the family of Gorh of Manoharpur.

[110]*Ajit Vilas*, 101.

[111]*Jodhpur-Khyat*, ii, 176; *Byav Bahi*, i, 1; *Dastur Kamwar*, 24/573; *Vamsha Bhaskar*, 3057-76; *Ajit Singh Khyat*, iii. 559.

[112]*Balmukandnama*. 5, see L. Nos. 5, 31, 21.

[113]*Ibid.*, 1, No. 54 (p. 5).

[114]*Siah-Bakai Daftar*, October 9, 1720. R.S.A.B.

[115]*Kharita Bahi* No. 2. R.S.A.B.

[116]Letter from Sujan Singh to Jai Singh, dated *Margsir vadi* 3, 1777. *Jaipur Records*, Vol. V. (Sitamau).

[117]*Jodhpur-Khyat*, ii, 178. *Rajrupak* says that Jai Singh left Jodhpur with the consent of Ajit Singh (*vide* 45).

[118]*Mirat-i-Ahmadi*, ii, 38-9.

[119]*Ajit Singh Khyat*, iii, 567; *Jodhpur Rajya*, ii, 180-1.

[120]For the policies of the various groups at the court, see, *Parties and Politics*, 179-80.

[121]*Ajit Singh Khyat*, iii, 567; *Jodhpur-Khyat*, ii, 180-1; *Achaldas-Khichi-ri-Varta*. 126/41.

[122]*Ajit Singh Khyat*. iii, 568-9; *Achaldas Khichi-ri-Varta*, 126/42-3.

[123]*Rajrupak*, 46.

[124]*Ajitodaya*, 30/12-31.

[125]Letter written by Maharaja Sujan Singh to Jai Singh, dated *Margsir Vadi* 2, 1777 (November 7, 1720). *Jaipur Records*, (Sitamau).

[126]*Ajit Singh Khyat*, iii, 56; *Jodhpur-Khyat*, ii, 182; Ojha, *Jodhpur Rajya*, ii, 593-4; *Later Mughals*, ii, 108; Shivdas, ff 76b, 78s.

[127]*Later Mughals*, ii, 108.

[128]*Later Mughals*, ii, 108-9; cf. *Parties and Politics*, 179-80.

[129]*Ajit Vilas*, 105-7.

[130]*Arzadast*, dated *Chaitra sudi* 15, 1779 (March 21, 1722). Copy available at *Reu's Collection*, S.P.L.J.

[131]It is said that in the month of March, through the intercession of Khan-i-Dauran, Ajit Singh was pardoned and allowed to retain charge of Ajmer. *Parties and Politics*, 180-1.

[132]*Ajit Vilas*, 105; *Ajitodaya*, 30/31-4; *Later Mughals*, ii, 111-12; *Parties and Politics*, 181.

[133]Letter from Pancholi Ram Chandra to Jai Singh, dated *Kartik vadi* 1, 1779 (October 28, 1722); *Jaipur Records* (Hindi), Vol. 3.

[134]*Ajit Singh Khyat*, iii, 565-6.

[135]Transcribed copy of the *farman* available at *Reu's Collection*, S.P.L.J.

[136]*Ajit Vilas*, 105; *Ajit Singh Khyat*, iii, 572-80; *Rathora-ri-Vamshavali* (*Bahi*-ORIJ), 240-4.

[137]*Rathora-ri-Vamshavali*, 242-4.

[138]*Ibid.*

[139]*Ajit Vilas*, 107.

[140]The names of these *parganas* have been mentioned above.

[141]*Ajitodaya*, 30/66-85; *Ajit Vilas*. 107-8.

[142]*Tarikh-Muzaftari*, 337; *Rathora-ri-Vamshavali* (*Bahi*-ORIJ), 240-1.

[143]*Ajitodaya* mentions (see 30/53-65) that it was as a result of the intervention of Jai Singh that the settlement was concluded.

[144]*Ajit Singh Khyat*, iii, 562.

[145]*Ibid.*

[146]*Mundiyara-ri-Khyat* (ORIJ), 266-7; *Vir Vinod*, 842-3.

[147]*Ajit Vilas*, 107.

9

MAHARAJA ABHAY SINGH (A.D. 1724-1749)

At the time of Maharaja Ajit Singh's murder, Abhay Singh was at the Mughal court along with Bhandari Raghunath who held the office of the *diwan* in Marwar. When the assassination of Maharaja Ajit Singh was reported at the court, the Mughal Emperor, Muhammad Shah, put the *tika* on the forehead of Abhay Singh conferring on him the *gaddi* of Jodhpur along with 14 *parganas* of Marwar. He was also granted a *mansab* of 7000/7000.[1] The *parganas* granted to Abhay Singh included Nagaur, Kekari, Ghatiali, Maroth, Parbatsar, Phulia, etc., which had earlier been taken into *khalisa* in June 1723.[2] The *Khyats* of Marwar[3] mention that the Emperor's attitude towards prince Abhay Singh was favourable, while, at the same time, prince Abhay Singh had been maintaining good relations with Raja Jai Singh. This had caused some suspicion in the mind of Ajit Singh who had sent Prohit Jagu, the *thakur* of Rohit, and Sagar Singh Champawat to Delhi to bring back Abhay Singh. It has been said that Raja Jai Singh informed Abhay Singh that the Emperor was not happy with Ajit Singh because of the latter's association with the Saiyids, who had killed Emperor Farrukh Siyar, and instigated Abhay Singh to murder Ajit Singh in order to win the favour of Emperor Muhammad Shah. Bhandari Raghunath's endorsement of Jai

Singh's idea encouraged Abhay Singh.[4] Consequently, he advised his brother Bakht Singh, who was at Jodhpur, to kill Ajit Singh. Following the advice of his brother, Bakht Singh killed his father Ajit Singh, on 23 June 1724 (*Asadh sudi* 13).[5] This shows that Ajit Singh's murder was political in nature.[6]

Civil War and the Marwar Nobility

Abhay Singh, after being recognized as the successor of Maharaja Ajit Singh, left the court for Jodhpur at the end of July 1724. Staying at Mathura, on his way to Jodhpur, he married the daughter of Maharaja Jai Singh. The Rathor *sardars* suspected that Jai Singh had abetted the murder of Ajit Singh. Many of the Marwar *sardars* accompanying Abhay Singh were not in favour of this alliance and advised him to go to Jodhpur first. Abhay Singh, however, did not agree. The result was that a large number of the *sardars* deserted him, and returned to their *thikanas* disgruntled. Many of them later joined the camp of Anand Singh and Rai Singh, the sons of Ajit Singh.[8]

Jai Singh's role in the murder of Ajit Singh has been a matter of controversy.[9] The active military aid extended by Jai Singh to Abhay Singh and the subsequent marriage with his daughter so soon after the event, celebrated in a most unprecedented manner and in such haste do create, suspicion of his complicity, but these facts are not enough. It was popularly believed that Abhay Singh, Bakht Singh, Bhandari Raghunath were all in league with Jai Singh in the murder of Ajit Singh. However this was not the only cause for the displeasure of the Marwar nobility.

A close study of contemporary documents shows some important features of the disturbance caused by the civil war, particularly factors leading to the dissatisfaction among the Rathor *sardars* against the Bhandaris, consequent upon the death of Ajit Singh. The refusal to accept the advice of Rathor *sardars* by Abhay Singh with regard to his marriage at Mathura displeased the Rathor *sardars* who were with him on his way to Marwar. Annoyed with it, some of the Rathor *sardars* left him and went to Marwar.[10] Among them were 21 Champawats, 5 Kumpawats, 5 Jaitawats, 2 Karnots, 3 Mertias, 4 Jodhas,

4 Udawats, 3 Karmsot and 3 Bhandaris.[11] When these Rathor *sardars* reached Marwar, they found a favourable situation caused by the revolt of Anand Singh and Rai Singh, and the support of the Rathor *sardars* in their favour. In fact, even before the defection on the marriage issue of the *sardars* accompanying Abhay Singh, the trouble had already started in Marwar. Hence it is just possible that the marriage was performed with a view to strengthening Abhay Singh's position in Marwar, a highly discreet decision taken in advance to meet the challenge that had already posed a serious threat to his position. From this matrimonial alliance Abhay Singh could procure Jai Singh's military help to quell the trouble in Marwar.

When the news of Ajit Singh's murder spread in Marwar, the Rathor *sardars* surrounded the palace of Bakht Singh. Most of them joined hands with prince Anand Singh.[12] In *pargana* Sojat all the Rathor *sardars* deserted the Bhandaris and imprisoned their officers Manroop and Dhanroop. The rebellious Rathor *sardars* under the banner of Anand Singh secured their control over *pargana* Jaitaran; they were also expanding their influence over Merta.[13] Their strength had increased so much that it was certain that if Anand Singh and Rai Singh had marched to Jodhpur they would have received a warm welcome.[14]

These inferences lead us to believe that after the murder of Ajit Singh, the Rathor *sardars* rebelling against Abhay Singh had made the Bhandaris their target. Although Raghunath Bhandari was suspected of being a party to the murder of Ajit Singh, this could hardly provoke the Rathor *sardars* to take such an extreme step. Their demand was to dispossess them of their offices.[15] It has been mentioned in the previous chapter that during Ajit Singh's reign the Bhandaris were exercising control over almost all the higher administrative posts. At the time of Ajit Singh's death, the offices of the *pardhan* and the *diwan* were held by Khivsi Bhandari and Raghunath Bhandari respectively. Besides, in Jodhpur, Merta, Sojat and Jaitaran, the office of the *hakim* was also in the hands of the Bhandaris. Thus, the Rathor *sardars* had a general complaint against the Bhandaris; somewhat similar to the complaint made by the

Rathor *sardars* against the Champawat Rathors at the beginning of Ajit Singh's reign.

It seems that the *sardars* whose *pattas* were transferred during the time of Ajit Singh were not having any holdings to meet their basic requirements while the new power structure had deprived other Rathor *sardars* also of their earlier position. This fact is revealed by the proposal put forward by Abhaimal suggesting that the rebellious Rathors could be conciliated if they were granted suitable *pattas*.[16] But this suggestion was not considered in the beginning due to the influence of the Bhandaris. The Rathor *sardars* being aware of the attitude of Abhay Singh, which was influenced by the Bhandaris, had invited Anand Singh and Rai Singh to find an alternative solution of the problem. The Rathor *sardars* who had left Abhay Singh at Mathura, had also taken up the cause of Rai Singh and Anand Singh to form an opposition against the Bhandaris. Thus the primary cause of the rebellion, started at Sojat and Jaitaran just after the death of Ajit Singh, was the frustration of the dislodged *pattadars* and those who had been deprived of their earlier position. It may be termed as an economic-*cum*-political crisis. It was accentuated by other factors such as turning down the suggestion of the Rathor *sardars* by Abhay Singh regarding his marriage with the daughter of Jai Singh and Bakht Singh's unpopularity due to his being a party to the murder of Ajit Singh.

Attempts to establish Peace in Marwar

When Maharaja Abhay Singh came to know about the state of affairs in Marwar, he despatched an army under the command of Raghunath Bhandari.[17] The understanding between Abhay Singh and Jai Singh had been strengthened by the matrimonial alliance between the two. Maharaja Jai Singh extended his full cooperation to Abhay Singh to meet the situation created by Rai Singh and Anand Singh with the help of the Rathor *sardars*. When the news of the uprising reached Mathura, Maharaja Jai Singh directed Kesari Singh Naruka to reach Merta to help Raghunath Bhandari so that the rebellion could be crushed.[18] The Kachhawah contingent reached Merta on 29 October 1724 (*Margsir vadi*).[19] Again, at the request of Kesari Singh, a further contingent of 5,000 *sawars* was sent to Marwar under the command of Rai Shivdas.[20] Maharaja Jai Singh also requested Maharana Sangram Singh II to send an army to help Bakht Singh whose palace had been surrounded by the Rathor *sardars*.[21] Maharaja Sangram Singh was trying to get the *pargana* of Idar on *ijara* from Maharaja Abhay Singh who was holding it since his accession to the *gaddi* of Jodhpur. The Maharana was eager to get control over it[22] and, therefore, he agreed to send a contingent to help Abhay Singh. The Maharana was also interested in helping Abhay Singh because Rai Singh and Anand Singh were increasing their influence in the areas around Idar, which could create trouble for the Maharana.

The combined armies of Jai Singh, Sangram Singh and Abhay Singh re-occupied Sojat and Jaitaran and the neighbouring territories which had been conquered by Rai Singh and Anand Singh. The Kachhawah and Sisodia *sardars* won over many of the Marwar nobles and further weakened the position of Anand Singh and Rai Singh. Finding it difficult to resist the combined force of the Rathors, the Kachhawahs and the Sisodias, Rai Singh and Anand Singh left the Marwar territory and went towards Sirohi. Taking advantage of the situation, Bakht Singh occupied Nagaur and Indra Singh withdrew from it for ever.[23] With the occupation of Nagaur the armies of Amber and Mewar returned to their respective territories. But the ousting of Rai Singh and Anand Singh from Marwar did not eliminate the danger to Abhay Singh from their side. After their flight from Marwar, Anand Singh reached Sirohi and there he regrouped his followers to march against Sojat and Jaitaran. Rai Singh marched towards Siwana, expecting to plunder the areas of Phalodi and Jodhpur.[24] As would be explained in the following chapter, the report that Rai Singh had entered into matrimonial relations with the Marathas in order to secure their help for the occupation of Jodhpur raised a serious problem.[25] This changed the whole attitude of the Rajput Rajas towards them.[26] Jai Singh made a fresh request to Abhay Singh that he should assign Idar to both the princes in *jagir* and grant *pattas* to their fellow *sardars*.[27] Although the peace settlement with these princes remained unshaken for some time, their rebellion left a deep impression on the politics of Marwar.

State Administration and the Nobility

Although the danger from the side of Rai Singh and Anand Singh continued till 1728, Abhay Singh succeeded in avoiding the opposition of the Rathor *sardārs* by granting them fresh *pattas.*[28] After his arrival at Jodhpur Abhay Singh imprisoned Bhandari Raghunath and Bhandari Khivsi in order to please the Rathor *sardars.*[29] But Abhay Singh did not make any other change in the administrative set-up except the removal of Khivsi Bhandari from the office of *pradhan* and installing Champawat Maha Singh Bhagwandasot in his place. In the month of October 1725 Champawat Maha Singh, Muhata Gokuldas, Pancholi Ram Kishan, Purohit Rinchhod, Bhandari Anoop Singh Raghunathot, Bhandari Manroop Pemsiawat and Dayaldas Sobhawat were appointed as *prādhan, diwān, bakhshi, khānsāma, hakim* at Jodhpur, *hakim* at Merta, and *shiqdar* respectively.[30] These appointments make it clear that Abhay Singh was not prepared to throw the Bhandaris completely out of his administration because like his predecessors he was not ready to entrust all the administrative powers into the hands of his own clansmen. This policy had a political advantage, for unlike the Rathor *sardars,* the non-Rathor *sardars* were completely dependent upon the good-will of the Maharaja. In 1726 Abhay Singh re-appointed Bhandari Raghunath to the office of *diwan.*[31] Abhay Singh's success over Anand Singh and Rai Singh and his seizure of Nagaur led him to believe that he had brought the situation under control, and that there were no serious internal problems before him. Hence he decided to implement the imperial orders to march on Gujarat. This was also Jai Singh's advice to him. On 22 November 1725, Abhay Singh set out for Gujarat *via* Jalor. But he had to put off his departure due to a fresh outbreak of hostile activities by Anand Singh and Rai Singh.

Bhandari Raghunath remained *diwan* till A.D. 1728, when he was imprisoned at Delhi and in his place Bhandari Rai Khivsi was appointed as *diwan.* The reason for the imprisonment of Bhandari Raghunath is not known. Mention is made that Bhandari Raghunath was not on good terms with the Rathor *sardars*.[32] It seems that even after the solution of the problems of the Rathor *sardars*, Bhaṇdari Raghunath continued his hostile attitude towards them. After Khivsi's death, in the same year, the office of the *diwan* was given to Muhta Amardas.[33] It may be noted that Pancholi Laljit was appointed *diwan* of Nagaur by Abhay Singh in 1728. In 1739 Bakht Singh removed him from the office of the *diwan* of Nagaur. Abhay Singh did not like the action of Bakht Singh. The relations between Abhay Singh and Bakht Singh which became strained during this period, will be discussed separately. The former had proposed to remove the Bhandaris from high posts and to appoint Pancholis in their place.[34] In the same year Abhay Singh made changes among the officials of the state administration.[35] Accordingly Pancholi Lalji, Pancholi Balkishan, Pancholi Khem Karan, Ram Kishan and Pancholi Khem Karan, son of Lalji were appointed as the *diwan*, *bakhshi*, *hakim* of Jodhpur, *subadar* of Jodhpur and *hakim* of Merta respectively.

It may be noted that all these officers belonged to the family of Lalji Pancholi. Thus one family was replaced by another.[36] But to occupy the posts of the *diwan* and the *hakim* of Jodhpur was in itself a challenging task. As already observed, the office of the *diwan* was a very tough and difficult one and the *diwans* generally met a tragic end. The same happened to the Pancholis. In A.D. 1742 (V.S. 1797) Pancholi Lalji, Pancholi Ram Kishan and Bal Kishan were dismissed from their offices, and were imprisoned.[37] In their place Bhandari Rai Amar Singh Khivsot, Bhandari Manroop Pemsiot and Bhandari Daulatram Thanisot were appointed as the *diwan*, *shiqdar* and *hakim* respectively at Jodhpur.

In A.D. 1744, Bhandari Amar Singh died and the post of *diwan* was given to Bhandari Girdhardas.[38] In the same year Bhandari Manroop and Daulat Ram, both *bakhshi* and *hakim* of Jodhpur respectively, were removed. Bhandari Ratan Singh was appointed *shiqdar* of Jodhpur.[39] In the year A.D. 1749 when Abhay Singh died the offices of the *diwan* and the *shiqdar* were held by Bhandari Surat Ram and Bhandari Daulat Ram respectively.[40]

From the foregoing it is clear that during the reign of

Maharaja Abhay Singh, the office of the *diwan* was held successively by the Bhandaris, the Muhatas and the Pancholis for 11 years, 10 years and 1 year, respectively. The position of the Bhandaris always remained uncertain. This was a significant factor during that period. The Muhatas who had been kept out of the office of the *diwan* since A.D. 1665, when Muhnot Nainsi and his brother committed suicide, regained their earlier position in the state administration. It is difficult to say to what extent the opposition of the Bhandaris was responsible for keeping them out of the office. It has been mentioned that till 1728 the continuous opposition of the Rathor *sardars* against the Bhandaris compelled Abhay Singh to avoid appointing them to the office of the *diwan*. The opposition of the Rathor *sardars* continued even afterwards. In A.D. 1734, Abhay Singh released Bhandari Raghunath and others and appointed the former as the *diwan*.[41] Reacting to his release and appointment as the *diwan*, many of the Rathor *sardars* left the service of Abhay Singh. To normalize the situation the latter had to remove Bhandari Raghunath from the office of the *desh-diwan*.[42] This suggests that the nobility played an important role in keeping the Bhandaris out of the office of the *diwan*. But other factors also exercised considerable influence.

During the time of Maharaja Jaswant Singh, it had become a regular practice for the incumbent to deposit a considerable amount in the state treasuary as *peshkash*. The practice started by Maharaja Jaswant Singh later became a regular feature of the office of the *diwans*. Like the *diwans* during the reign of Ajit Singh, all the *diwans* of Abhay Singh were also imprisoned. The reason for the imprisonment of the Bhandaris may be considered political, but the fact that others were also imprisoned and were released after payment of a huge amount shows that they might have been guilty of abusing their office. There are numerous allusions to the effect that to secure the release of a *diwan*, a huge amount was required, and after payment of which the man was again allowed to hold the office.[43] There can be no doubt that such a practice must have led to corruption and induced the *diwans* to make money by irregular practices.[44] Such practices apparently increased due to the fact that during the time of Abhay Singh, the appointments to other higher offices were made from members of a specific family or a Rathor sub-clan.

The opposition of the Bhandaris did not improve the position of the Rathor *sardars* in the administration, except the Champawat Rathors who enjoyed the office of the *pradhan* during Abhay Singh's reign. In A.D. 1725 Bhandari Khivsi was given the office of the *pradhan* after the removal of Champawat Maha Singh. But Abhay Singh had to reinstate the latter due to the opposition of the Rathor *sardars*. During the later years of Abhay Singh's reign, the office of *pradhan* remained with Champawat Maha Singh and Champawat Pratap Singh.[45] It is significant to note that during the reign of Ajit Singh, the Rathor *sardars* had constantly opposed the Champawat Rathors' appointment to the office of the *pradhan*. Now as the opposition shifted against the Bhandaris, the Champawat Rathors regained their previous position.

The post of the *hakim* in various *parganas* was quite an important one as the incumbent held all administrative and military powers over the area. It has been mentioned that at the time of Ajit Singh's death, Bhandari Anroop, Bhandari Manroop and Bhandari Dhanroop were holding charge of the office of the *hakim* in the *parganas* of Jodhpur, Merta and Sojat-Jaitaran respectively.[46] It has also been noted that in the year 1725 the Bhandaris were appointed to the posts of the *hakim* of the *parganas* of Jodhpur and Merta. In 1728 Bhandari Girdhardas, Bhandari Bijairaj and Bhandari Manroop held that office in the *parganas* of Jodhpur, Maroth-Parbatsar and Merta. When, in 1739, Pancholi Lalji was given the office of the *pradhan*, the Bhandaris were removed from the offices of the *hakim* of Jodhpur and Merta. In the changes made in 1742 the Bhandaris were oppointed as the *hakims* of Jodhpur and Sojat. A study of the office of the *hakim* of these *parganas* indicates that, in general, the Bhandaris remained in the office of the *hakim* in various *parganas* of Marwar. Thus, in spite of the opposition of the Rathor *sardars*, Abhay Singh did not make any drastic change in appointments to the various offices. The substitute for Bhandaris were not the Rathors but either the Muhatas or the Pancholis. So the Rathors were eliminated from state administration. Thus, during the time of Abhay Singh the three families, the

Bhandaris, the Muhatas and the Pancholis remained in power in the state administration except for the office of the *pradhan*, which remained with the Champawat Rathors.

Rathor Nobility

It has been mentioned above that the office of the *diwan* remained with the Champawat Rathors. Thus except the Champawat Rathors, the *sardars* of other Rathor sub-clans were not given any position in the state administration. But it would be wrong to assume that the Rathor *sardars* had lost their power in the state political organization. Due to lack of adequate information, it is difficult to assess the number and the strength of the *sardars*—Rathors and non-Rathors. Stray references throw some light on their position in the Marwar nobility. The Rathor army which marched against Sarbuland Khan in 1731, included 44 Champawat Rathors, 45 Mertia Rathors, 36 Jodha Rathors, 31 Kumpawat Rathors, 28 Udawat Rathors and so on.[47] This strength of the Rathor *sardars* indicates that in 1731 the number of Mertia Rathors was the largest, although the difference between the Mertias and the Champawats was quite negligible. However, on the basis of these figures no definite conclusion can be drawn. From a near contemporary source[48] it is gathered that in the beginning of the 19th century the holdings of the *sardars* of various Rathor sub-clans in Marwar were as follows:

Rathors	*No. of villages*	*Rekh*
Mertia	517	10,51,669
Champawat	312	4,26,523
Jodha	220	3,47,550
Udawats	136	3,43,015
Kumpawats	60	1,51,118

The above data provides a tentative picture of the holdings of various Rathor sub-clans at the end of Abhay Singh's reign. This assumption is based on the fact that after the death of Abhay Singh, on account of political instability, the whole politico-administrative organization took a different turn.

Accordingly, the *pattadars* started paying a lump-sum annual amount to the state against their services. Under the circumstances the question of the transfer of the *patta* became redundant. Thus these changes enabled the *pattadars* to retain their *patta* villages as before. On this basis it may be concluded that hardly any change occurred in the position of the holdings of the various Rathor *sardars* after Abhay Singh's death. These figures of early 19th century can be used as an index to understand the composition of the Rathor nobility during Abhay Singh's reign.

The statistics given in the above table (p. 257) shows that at the beginning of the 19th century, the Mertia Rathors held the largest number of *patta* villages as well as revenue; the next in order were the Champawats, the Jodhas, the Udawats and the Kumpawat Rathor *sardars*. It is noted that the revenue enjoyed by the Mertia Rathors was more than double of that of the Champawat Rathors. It has been mentioned that during the time of Ajit Singh, the Champawat Rathors, in spite of the opposition of other Rathor *sardars*, constituted the largest number in the Marwar nobility. The Mertias were the third biggest *patta* holders and the Jodhas the second. A comparison between the *patta* holdings of the time of Ajit Singh with the holdings at the beginning of 19th century shows that Champawat Rathors were losing their position while the Mertia Rathors gained considerably. It seems that since the time of Abhay Singh the numerical strength of the Champawat Rathors had started decreasing. The reason behind it was perhaps the attitude of the non-Champawat Rathor *sardars* which might have influenced the State policy. It may be noted that during the reign of Jaswant Singh, the Mertia Rathors held the second largest number of *pattas* in Marwar.[49] Thus it can be inferred that the position of the Champawats which increased during the period of instability and which remained static during Ajit Singh's reign, decreased considerably and the Mertia Rathors regained their old position.

The number of non-Rathor *sardars* like the Bhatis, the Chauhans and the Sonagaras who participated in the war of 1731, fought against Sarbuland Khan, is worth mentioning. The number of the Bhatis, the Chauhans and the Sonagaras was

23, 13 and 13 respectively.[50] A study of the accounts of the *pattas* of the Bhatis and the Chauhans reveals that their number was 44 and 41 respectively.[51] Thus the Bhatis and the Chauhans were holding the largest number of *pattas* among the non-Rathor *sardars*. It is significant to note that in comparison to their numerical strength at the time of Jaswant Singh, they had increased their *patta* considerably in the days of Abhay Singh.

The *pattas* granted during the time of Abhay Singh contain the same text as during the reigns of Ajit Singh and Jaswant Singh.[52] A significant feature in the politico-administrative organization that appeared during the reign of Abhay Singh is the change in the position of the *pattadars*. With the decline of central power and the increasing attacks of the Marathas, *jagirs* granted to Maharaja Abhay Singh outside Marwar yielded only a meagre revenue and that too quite irregularly. At the same time, due to increasing Maratha incursions into the Rajput territories and also on account of internal feuds among the Rajput Rajas, constant presence of the Rathor ruler was needed in Marwar. As such he could not render any service to the Mughal Emperor outside Marwar. Thus after (c) 1740 the Marwar *sardars* were not required to perform any service outside Marwar.[53] These changes became more apparent after the death of Abhay Singh when Maharaja Bijay Singh started realizing a lump sum amount from the *pattadars* at the rate of Rs. 300[54] for every Rs. 1,000 *rekh* in A.D. 1755 (V.S. 1812). The amount fixed against the *rekh* was termed as *mutalba*.[55] Obviously, under the changing circumstances the *pattadars* assumed a different position, as now they had to pay a fixed amount or tribute to the Rathor ruler. Thus by paying a lump sum amount annually against their *patta* lands, the *pattadars* retained their control over their *patta* villages and thereby assumed the character of *peshkash-i-zamindar*. These changes were, in fact, introduced during the reign of Abhay Singh, who had realized lump sum amounts from the *pattadars* to pay a huge amount to the Marathas and to maintain his own internal establishments.[56]

The orders issued on behalf of *diwan* Bhandari Bijay Raj in A.D. 1733 (*Kartik sudi* 3, 1790) and *diwan* Lalji in 1739 (*Ashoj vadi* 9, 1796) to the *pattadars* (*jagirdars*), *bhomias* and State officials—such as *qanungos* indicate that the earlier *dasturs* relating to the *bhog*, *kharach-bhog* and *lag-bag* remained the same.[57]

Another change during the reign of Abhay Singh was the adoption of the practice of *ijara* by the state. The letter issued on behalf of the Raja to Bhandari Amar Singh authorized the latter to collect the revenue from two villages of *pargana* Sojat for a year.[58] The amount paid by the *ijaradar* was assessed on the basis of the *hasil* of the previous year. Thus the *ijaradar* paid Rs. 650 on the *rekh* of Rs. 1,200.[59] We do not have such information for the *patta* villages. The available account of the *ijara* of the *khalisa* lands suggests that at least in *khalisa* territory this had become the general practice. Apparently, the practice of the *ijara* stemmed out of the State's need for money to meet its expenses which increased as the State had to pay huge amount to Maratha commanders.

Thus, the organisation of the nobility which had assumed a definite form during the time of Sur Singh, started taking a different shape during the latter half of Abhay Singh's reign. Six years after his death the whole character and the composition of the nobility had changed.

REFERENCES

[1]*Rajrupak*, 579: *Abhayodaya*, 6/11-12; *Jodhpur-Khyat*, ii, 182-3; *Tarikh-i-Muzaffari*, 337.

[2]*See* Chapter VIII.

[3]*Ajit Singh-ri-Khyat*, iii, 561; *Achaldas-ri-Varta* (ORIJ), 126/41; *Jodhpur-Khyat*, ii, 181-2; *Rathora-ri-Vamshavali*, (ORIJ), 191-2.

[4]*Achaldas-ri-Varta*, 126/40-1; *Ajit Singh-ri-Khyat*, iii, 560-2.

[5]*Jodhpur-Khyat*, ii, 182-3; *Jodhpur Rajya*, ii, 600.

[6]William Irvine has accepted the story of Kunwar who held that soon after Ajit Singh had made peace and returned to Jodhpur, he fell in love with the wife of his son Bakht Singh and was guilty of an incestuous intercouse. Overcome with shame and touched at the tenderest point of his honour, Bakht Singh sought opportunity of revenge. One night when Ajit Singh drunk and stupefied, and was lying fast asleep, his son stabbed him to death (*Later Mughals*, ii, 116-17). It may be noted that

no Rajasthani account makes any reference to such a relationship as given by Irvine. No reference is ever made which shows any bitterness between Ajit Singh and Bakht Singh. The fact that in the murder of Ajit Singh, there was the consent of Abhay Singh, and of the Bhandaris, even to some extent of Jai Singh, makes it clear that Ajit Singh's murder was not personal but political in nature.

[7]The marriage was performed on August 1, 1724 (*Bhadra vadi* 8, 1781). *Rathora-ri-Pidia-ri-Khyat*, 188; *Mundiara-ri-Khyat*, 169; *Jodhpur-Khyat*, ii, 194-6.

[8]*Jodhpur-Khyat*, ii, 194; *Vivid-Rajya-Vamsha-ri-Khyat* (SSJ), 284/110; *Rathora-ri-Vamshavali*, 194-5; *Mundiyara-Khyat* (ORIJ) 261; *Vir Vinod*, 844; *Jodhpur Rajya*, ii, 606.

[9]Dr. V.S. Bhatnagar has held that Jai Singh was not among those who instigated Abhay Singh to kill his father. Although he claims that his argument is based on contemporary documents, he does not mention a single document or any other source for this. (*Jai Singh*, 117).

[10]*Rajrupak*, 598; *Jodhpur-Khyat*, ii, 194-5; *Rathora-ri-Pidia-ri-Khyat* (S.S.), 188.

[11]*Mundiyara-ri-Khyat* (ORIJ), 171; *Rathora-ri-Pidia-ri-Khyat*, (SS), 188.

[12]*Arzadast* sent to Maharaja Jai Singh by Kesari Singh Naruka, dated 31, October 1724 (*Margsir vadi* 11, 1781). Letter dated 11 November 1724 (*Margsir Sudi* 6, 1781), written by Sangram Singh. *Jaipur Records*, (Sitamau).

[13]*Jodhpur-Khyat*, ii, 203. In the letter written by Sivdas to Abhaimal on Magha sudi 7, 1781, one of the possible alternatives suggested was to ask the Bhandaris to quit their offices. *Amber Records*, Bundle No. 1 (R.S A.B.).

[14]*Mundiyara-Khyat*, 171-2.

[15]*Arzadast*, dated October 31, 1724, (*op. cit.*)

[16]In a letter of *Magha sudi* 7, 1781, written by Shivdas to Abhaimal, the Amber *sardars*, the former said that normal conditions could be established in Marwar if peaceful settlement was made with Anand Singh and suitable grants were made to the Rathor *sardars*. *Amber Records*, Bundle No. 1, 124/4, R.S.A.B.

[17]*Mundiyara-ri-Khyat* (ORIJ), 270-2.

[18]*Arzadast* sent by Kesari Singh Namha to Maharaja Jai Singh, dated 31 October 1724 (*Margsir vadi* 11, 1781). *Jaipur Records* (Hindi), Vol. V. (Sitamau).

[19]*Jodhpur-Khyat*, ii, 200; *Mundiyara-ri-Khyat*, 275.

[20]Letter from Abhai Karan to Maharaja Abhay Singh dated *Chaitra vadi* 3, 1781. *Amber Records*, 1, R.S.A.B.

[21]Letter from Jai Singh to Sangram Singh, dated *Margsir sudi* 6, 1781 (November 11, 1724). *Jaipur Records* (Hindi), Vol. V, (Sitamau).

[22]*Vir Vinod*, II, 967; Ojha, *Udaipur Rajya*, i, 927.

[23]Abhay Singh's letter to Jai Singh, dated 3, July 1725/*Ashadh sudi* 5, 1781. *Jaipur Records* (Sitamau), Vol. V, 49.

[24]Letter from Abhay Singh to Jai Singh, dated 14, February 1726

(*Phalgun vadi* 2). *Jaipur Records* (Sitamau), Vol. V, 74. Letter of Abhay Karan to Abhay Singh dated June 6, 1725 (*Ashadh vadi* 13). *Basta* No. 76/2, *Jodhpur Records*, R.S.A.B.

[25]Letter from Jai Singh to Bhandari Raghunath dated 17, August 1726 (*Bhadra vadi* 6, 1783). *Kharitas and Parwanas*, 3, R.S.A.B.

[26]In June 1725, a huge army under the command of Kanha Pancholi was collected by the Maharana when Marathas made their first incursion into the Mewar territory (Kanha Pancholi's letter to Jai Singh, dated 26, June 1725).

[27]Letter from Jai Singh to Bhandari Rai Raghunath, dated 4 August 1726 (*Bhadra vadi* 6, 1713). *Kharita & Parwana*, Bundle 3, 4/530, 3/452. R.S.A.B.

[28]*Jodhpur-Khyat*, ii, 200; *Mundiyara-ri-Khyat* (ORIJ), 275.

[29]*Ibid.* Earlier Maharaja Abhay Singh had ordered the imprisonment of Bhandari Raghunath while he was camping at Mathura. But when he arrived at Jodhpur he got Bhandari Raghunath released. This act annoyed the Rathor *sardars* who went over to the side of the rebellious princes. Thereupon the Maharaja again got Bhandari Raghunath Khivsi imprisoned in February 1725.

[30]*Rathora-ri-Vamshavali* (*Bahi*, ORIJ), 146; *Champawata-ri-Khyat*, 370-1; *Basta* No. 27/101, R.S.A.B.

[31]*Jodhpur-Khyat*, ii, 203; *Rathora-ri-Vamshavali*, 146-77.

[32]*Vivid-Rajya-Vamsha-ri-Khyat*, (SS), 249/112.

[33]*Mundiyara-ri-Khyat* (ORIJ), 274; *Jodhpur-Khyat*, ii, 204.

[34]*Rathora-ri-Vamshavali* (ORIJ), 297-9; *Vivid-Rajya-Vamsha-ri-Khyat* (SSJ), 249/112.

[35]*Mundiyara-ri-Khyat*, 175; *Jodhpur-Khyat*, ii, 137.

[36]During the time of Jaswant Singh, Muhta Nainsi and his brother, Karamsi enjoyed the office of the *tan-diwan* and *desh-diwan* respectively.

[37]*Mundiyara-ri-Khyat*, 317; *Jodhpur-Khyat*, ii, 254-5.

[38]*Jodhpur-Khyat*, ii, 157-8.

[39]*Ibid*, ii, 237.

[40]*Ibid*, ii, 267.

[41]*Rathora-ri-Vamshavali*, 295.

[42]*Ibid.*

[43]*Basta* No. 97/9, *Jodhpur Records*, R.S.A.B.

[44]Pancholi Lalji and his clanmen were imprisoned in 1742 along with their *Bastas*—the files relating to their accounts.

[45]*Champawata-ri-Khyat*, 101, 371-3; *Daspo-ka-Itihas*, 94.

[46]see Chapter VII, *supra*, p.

[47]*Rajrupak*, 717-57; *Champawata-ri-Khyat*, 104.

[48]*Marwar-ra-Patta-ri-Vigat* (MS), 180 (A.S.L. Bikaner). The table is prepared out of the data given in this account.

[49]Chapter IV, Index No.

[50]*Rajrupak*, 740-56.

[51]The account of the *pattas* held by the Bhatis and the Chauhans are available in *Basta* No. 97/3, *Jodhpur Records*, R.S.A.B.

[52]*Basta* No. 96/2 and *Hat Bahi* No. 4 (R.S.A.B.) containing the

text of many of the *pattas* of the time of Abhai Singh.

[53]Although during Abhay Singh's control over Ajmer, Sambhar and Didwana, the Rathor army was sent there; the possession of Abhay Singh over these areas remained disputed.

[54]*Rathora-ri-Vamshavali* (ORIJ), 198; *Basta* No. 92/7, *Jodhpur Records*, R.S.A.B.

[55]*Lag-bag file* No. 202, R.S.A.B.

[56]*Basta* No. 97/2 (R.S.A.B.) contains references to the amount realized from various *pattadars*.

[57]*Basta* No, 101/3 and 76/2, *Jodhpur Records*, R.S.A.B.

[58]Letter from Abhay Singh to Bhandari Amar Singh, dated *Margsir sudi* 8, 1786; *Jodhpur ka Parwana*, *Jodhpur Records*, R.S.A.B.

[59]*Ibid*.

10

MARWAR POLITICS DURING THE TWILIGHT OF THE MUGHAL EMPIRE (A.D. 1724-1749)

The civil war in Marwar which broke out as a result of the revolt of princes Rai Singh and Anand Singh led to far-reaching consequences in the external politics of Marwar. As has been discussed, Abhay Singh's marriage with the daughter of Maharaja Jai Singh, was more of a political nature than anything else, as the latter made a notable contribution to the restoration of peace in Marwar. With the help of the contingents of Amber and Mewar, Abhay Singh succeeded in regaining control over the *parganas* of Sojat and Jaitaran which had been conquered by the Rathor princes and forced them to leave the territory of Marwar.

Abhay Singh's relations with Rai Singh and Anand Singh

As already stated, after his flight from Marwar, Anand Singh reached Sirohi and there he collected his followers to regain control over Sojat and Jaitaran. Rai Singh marched towards Siwana where he was feared to have plundered the areas of Phalodi and Jodhpur.[1] The situation became more complicated when it was reported that Anand Singh had entered into matrimonial relations with the Marathas in order to secure their help for the occupation of Jodhpur.[2] After it became known that both Rai Singh and Anand Singh were negotiating a deal with the Marathas, Maharana Sangram Singh II of Mewar, Jai Singh and Abhay Singh became more anxious to settle their disputes with the Rathor princes. Maharaja Jai Singh made a request to Abhay Singh to assign Idar in *jagir* to these princes. He urged that the followers of these princes should also be given *pattas*.[3] Maharaja Jai Singh wanted to solve the problems of the Rathor princes which had taken a different shape as they had invited the Marathas to get possession over Marwar. However, Jai Singh himself did not stand by his proposal due to other political considerations.

Maharaja Jai Singh had his own interest in keeping the Marathas out of Rajasthan. It is said that in 1725 an attempt was made by Jai Singh along with the Rana to conclude an agreement with Shahu, but it failed due to their lack of confidence in the Marathas.[4] The purpose of the proposed agreement with the Marathas can be gathered from the correspondence that took place among the Rajput Rajas. Reacting to news of the possible march of the Marathas, Jai Singh wrote letters to Maharana Sangram Singh, Abhay Singh and Rawal Durjansal in which he asked them to send their armies to Udaipur to form a united front against the Marathas.[5] These efforts were obviously made after the failure to arrive at an agreement with the Marathas in A.D. 1725, but as Jai Singh failed to get any concrete response from Abhay Singh and Maharao Durjansal, the raising of any united army against the Marathas was not possible.

The Maharana for some time past had been desirous of obtaining the *pargana* of Idar from Jodhpur. He had personally expressed this desire to Jai Singh and also sent a letter to Maya Ram, *vakil* of Sawai Jai Singh, for the same purpose. The Maharana was interested in securing Idar not only because it formed part of his hereditary *jagir*, but also due to its strategic importance in checking the sallies of the Marathas into Mewar territory. In Dhabhai Nagraj's words, "addition of Idar to Mewar would make her secure from this (Gujarat) side too. . ."[6] In fact Maharaja Jai Singh had accepted the fact that the assignment of Idar to the Maharana would bar the entry of the Marathas. Therefore, he advised Abhay Singh to make over the *pargana* of Idar to the Maharana.[7] Abhay Singh accepted this advice and gave Idar to the Maharana on condition that he would take the responsibility of killing Rai Singh and Anand Singh.[8] Jai Singh also favoured this deal. He wrote to the Maharana either to conduct the campaign against Rai Singh and Anand Singh in person, or to send a strong force under Nagraj Dhabhai after eliminating all chances of their escape. Accepting these conditions, the Maharana sent a large army against Anand Singh but the latter managed to escape.[9]

However the expulsion of Rai Singh and Anand Singh from Idar failed to bring any solution. Both these princes went to Sirohi and from there started making raids on the villages in the territory of the Maharana.[10] Upon Abhay Singh's request,[11] Jai Singh wrote to the Maharana to make every effort to suppress the marauding activities of Anand Singh and Rai Singh. He also sent Joshi Shambhu Ram, his diplomatic representative, to Jaisalmer, asking the Rawal not to give protection to Rai Singh and Anand Singh.[12] The ruler of Jaisalmer agreed to do so, realizing the situation created by the Rathor princes. It seems that these princes could not get any substantial help from the Marathas at that time. Therefore, they agreed to submit to the Rana. It is worth noting that Maharana Sangram Singh did not put them to death, disregarding the agreement which he had made with Abhay Singh while receiving Idar, and kept them with him. Maharaja Jai Singh himself was not in favour of taking their lives. He still held that they should be given suitable *jagirs* to feed themselves.[13] Perhaps both Sangram Singh and Jai Singh did not want to invite trouble from the side of the Marathas who had already shown their inclination towards these princes. Abhay Singh was also worried about the increasing interest of the Marathas in Marwar. In A.D. 1728 Bajirao had granted the *saranjami* of Jodhpur to Malhar Rao Holkar.[14] In the same year the Maratha *sardars*, Kanthaji and Pilaji had entered the territory of Sojat. Now, for Abhay Singh, there was no other alternative but to buy peace from his brothers.[15] On the advice of Maharaja Jai Singh, Abhay Singh agreed to make concessions to Anand Singh and Rai Singh. Therefore, it was agreed that those villages of *pargana* Idar which were on

Mewar side were to remain with the Maharana, and *Kasba* Idar and the other remaining villages would be given to them. The *sardars* who were with Rai Singh and Anand Singh were also given *pattas*. But they were made to promise that they would remain at Udaipur under the Maharana and would not move out from there.[16]

Thus the initiative taken by Maharaja Jai Singh and the Maharana resulted in a peaceful settlement for Marwar. A study of the terms of the agreement, suggests that peace was established on the same ground as was proposed in 1724 by Kesari Singh Naruka, the commander of the Kachhawah army sent to Marwar. The problem of the assignment of the *jagirs* to the followers of Rai Singh and Anand Singh had been solved by assigning them *pattas* in Marwar. Although during the period of instability the Rajput rulers of Mewar, Amber, Kota and Jaisalmer extended their co-operation to Abhay Singh, the appearance of the Marathas on the territory of Mewar and Marwar paved the way for future inroads.

Maharaja Abhay Singh and the Mughal Court

Due to the trouble created by Rai Singh and Anand Singh along with other internal strifes, Maharaja Abhay Singh failed to comply with the imperial order[17] by which he was supposed to proceed to Gujarat under Sarbuland Khan. He had been posted under Sarbuland Khan in September 1725[18] and was granted leave only for a month. After the flight of Anand Singh and Rai Singh from Marwar, Abhay Singh had started for Gujarat, but when he reached Sojat, the news of the preparations of the rebel princes did not allow him to leave the territory. The trouble continued till A.D. 1728 and consequently his march for Gujarat did not materialise. A study of the *Kharitas* exchanged between Jai Singh and Abhay Singh relating to the delay in proceeding to Gujarat,[19] shows that Abhay Singh had been pressed to proceed to Gujarat through Jai Singh. The apparent reason given by Abhay Singh was not only the problem of rebel princes but also the shortage of money.[20] It is doubtful that even after getting the additional money for his army expenses, Abhay Singh could have left Marwar without solving the problem of the Rathor princes.[21] The failure in implementing the imperial orders incurred the displeasure of the Emperor.[22] But he was unable to take any action against Abhay Singh.[23]

Inter-State Feuds and Maharaja Abhay Singh (1728-34)

The period between A.D. 1728 and 1734, saw many political changes in Rajputana which increased bitterness among the Rajput Rajas. The above account shows that during this period Jai Singh had unreservedly supported Maharaja Abhay Singh in keeping law and order in Marwar and in resolving the problems caused by the revolt of Rai Singh and Anand Singh. Although the co-operation shown by Maharaja Jai Singh indicates that both the rulers had trust in each other, a study of the correspondence which took place between Abhay Singh and Jai Singh, reveals that even during this period there were many factors which strained their relations.

As early as March 1726, Maharaja Jai Singh was facing trouble in his territory caused by the Shekhawat and the Khangarot *sardars*. Shekhawat *sardar* Lal Singh, etc., had been ousted from Amber territory by Jai Singh. They were given shelter in Merta from where they were making raids on the territory of Amber. Maharaja Jai Singh asked Abhay Singh to take action against these Shekhawat *sardars*,[24] but the latter did not pay any heed. After an interval of four months, Maharaja Jai Singh again wrote to Abhay Singh informing him that the officials of Bakht Singh were encouraging the rebels.[25] The request of Maharaja Jai Singh was not acceded to in spite of his reminders. The Rathor ruler continued his support to these *sardars* mainly for political reasons. He was using these *sardars* against the Ladkhanis of Nagaur who were creating trouble in his territory. The Shekhawat *sardars* were granted *pattas* where the Ladkhanis were engaged in destructive activities.[26] But this situation could hardly be tolerated by Jai Singh. He counted upon the useful role he had played in negotiations with Rai Singh and Anand Singh on the basis of which he tried to persuade Shekhawat *sardars* to leave Marwar. Thus in September 1728 an agreement was concluded, according to which Maharaja Abhay Singh promised not to give shelter in future to any Kachhawah or

Rathor *sardar* who might revolt against the Jaipur Maharaja.[27]

In fact the agreement was violated by Jai Singh himself who had given shelter to Rathor Kishor Singh, the brother of Maharaja Abhay Singh. In A.D. 1728, Rathor Kishor Singh, who was till then staying at Jaisalmer, raised a rebellion and started plundering the territories of the *parganas* of Pokaran and Phalodi.[28] The reason for his rebellious activities was the denial of a suitable *jagir* to him[29]. Apparently when Rai Singh and Anand Singh were given the villages of *pargana* Idar, Abhay Singh did not consider the claims of Kishor Singh. On the contrary, he sent Bakht Singh to check his activities. Finding himself unable to face the army of Bakht Singh, Kishor Singh went to Jaisalmer and later to Jaipur[30]. Maharaja Jai Singh not only gave him shelter in his territory but also pleaded his case for the grant of a *mansab* before the Emperor. As this act of Jai Singh was a breach of the agreement he had made with Abhay Singh, the latter also made no efforts to follow its terms. On the other hand, he encouraged the Kangarots to create trouble in the territory of Amber. In a letter dated 17 November 1728 (*Margsir vadi* 19, 1785) to Jai Singh, Abhay Singh explains that he wanted to secure his control over Ajmer, Sambhar and Didwana. Abhay Singh had earlier protested against the appointment of Muzaffar Khan as the *faujdar* of Ajmer and suggested that the combined armies of Mewar, Marwar and Jaipur should form a united front to check the imperial control over these *parganas*.[31] The idea of regaining the *parganas* of Ajmer, Sambhar and Didwana, however, remained unimplemented. It seems that Maharaja Jai Singh was not ready to involve himself in a scheme which might annoy the Emperor. In fact he was pleading before Emperor Muhammad Shah for the grant of the *subadari* of Malwa which he secured in October 1729.[32] Thus Abhay Singh's dream of acquiring the *parganas* of Ajmer, Sambhar and Didwana remained unrealised.

Maharaja Jai Singh could not retain the *subadari* of Malwa for long.[33] He returned to Jaipur in the beginning of A.D. 1730 and got entangled in the affairs of Bundi. Encouraged by his repeated successes, he sent an army against Bundi and after ousting Budh Singh, gave the *gaddi* to Dalel Singh, son of Salim Singh Hada of Narwar (March-July

1730).[34] This caused great concern among the Rajput Rajas. Jai Singh's action was not liked by the Maharana and Maharao Durjansal of Kota. Durjansal helped Budh Singh in the battle of Panchola,[35] and Maharana Sangram Singh accorded a warm welcome to Budh Singh, when after suffering defeat in this battle, he went to Udaipur. Maharana Sangram Singh showed sympathy towards Budh Singh because he was unhappy with Jai Singh on the question of the succession of Madho Singh, the son of Jai Singh born from the Mewar princess. Budh Singh also received the favour of Maharaja Abhay Singh, who took his side[36] not because the injustice done to the latter was pricking his conscience, but because opposition to Jai Singh enhanced his own prestige. Although no military help to Budh Singh was given by the Rana or Abhay Singh at this time, it became clear that both wanted to check the power of Maharaja Jai Singh.

Appointment of Abhay Singh as Subadar of Gujarat

Maharaja Abhay Singh was trying to get Ajmer, Sambhar and Didwana, but he failed in his objective. In the beginning of 1730 he was appointed the *subadar* of Gujarat in place of Sarbuland Khan.[37] It may be noted that in spite of repeated reminders by Raja Jai Singh, Abhay Singh had not proceeded to Gujarat to assist Sarbuland Khan. Now that he had been given the charge of that *suba* and had no pressing internal problems left in Marwar, he was in a position to take up the task assigned to him by the Mughal Emperor.

The appointment of Abhay Singh as the *subadar* of Gujarat had far-reaching consequences for the politics of Marwar as well as of Rajputana. Abhay Singh's success against Sarbuland Khan in A.D. 1730[38] and his agreement with Baji Rao I at Ahmedabad in February 1731,[39] were no doubt his personal achievements, although due to lack of support from the Mughal court he failed to provide stability to Gujarat.[40] Leaving all the administrative responsibilities of Gujarat in the hands of his deputy Ratan Singh Bhandari,[41] Abhay Singh arrived in Marwar in the later half of A.D. 1733. The departure of Maharaja Abhay Singh from Gujarat after leaving all administrative responsibilities in the hands of his deputy, was significant for the external and internal politics of Marwar for it left the Maratha *sardars* free to re-establish their control in Gujarat.[42] And, their incursions into Rajputana via Malwa aggravated the situation there.

Abhay Singh after his return from Gujarat

After his arrival, Abhay Singh got engaged in extending his influence in Rajputana.[43] Bakht Singh diverted his attention towards Bikaner by invading it. It is said that in the month of August 1733, a dispute arose between Rajadhiraj Bakht Singh and Sujan Singh, ruler of Bikaner, over a boundary affair.[44] But the motive of Bakht Singh was primarily political. He was not satisfied with Nagaur and had complained that the income from Nagaur was not sufficient for him to render services to the Emperor.[45]

The contents of the letter written by Bakht Singh to Bhandari Amar Singh, reveal that after being dislodged from the *jagir* of Patan, Bakht Singh was not holding any *jagir* in addition to Nagaur. Maharaja Abhay Singh also helped him with an army-contingent against Bikaner. Fighting went on for some time, but at last the ruler of Bikaner made an offer of peace. He accepted the allegiance of the ruler of Jodhpur and agreed to pay rupees twelve lacs as indemnity. Out of these twelve lacs, eight lacs were to be given in cash and the remaining four lacs had to be paid through the revenue of the territories of Kharbuj and Sarda.[46] The withdrawal of the Jodhpur army, however, took place not because of this favourable agreement, but because this had become necessary, as the Marathas had posed a threat to the existence of the Rajput Rajas.

The Maratha activities in Rajputana became more serious because of the entry of Malhar Rao and Ranoji Sindhia into Bundi in March 1734.[47] The apparent reason for their arrival in the territory of Bundi was to place Rao Budh Singh on the *gaddi*.[48] The Maratha *sardars* succeeded in their objective and proclaimed Budh Singh as the ruler of Bundi.[49] Although Budh Singh could not maintain his possession for long, as the military intervention of Maharaja Jai Singh restored Dalel Singh on the *gaddi* of Bundi,[50] the presence of the Maratha army in Rajputana was taken very seriously. Maharaja Jai Singh sought Abhay Singh's help to drive out the Marathas from Rajputana.[51] In his letter to Bhandari Amar Singh at Jahanabad,[52] Abhay Singh asked him to seek instructions from Khan-i-Dauran whether he should help Jai Singh against the Marathas in Amber and its neighbouring areas or proceed to Gujarat. Abhay Singh also asked him to approach Khan-i-Dauran for the grant of Ajmer. It seems that he wanted to take advantage of the situation created due to Maratha incursions on Rajputana, to put forward his claim for the grant of the *subadari* of Ajmer.

Maharaja Abhay Singh who was preparing for his departure to Gujarat upon repeated reminders from the Mughal court, agreed to attend the coronation ceremony of Maharaja Jagat Singh at the request of Maharaja Jai Singh, to discuss ways to check the Maratha thrust in Marwar.[53] Besides Abhay Singh and Bakht Singh, the rulers of Kota, Bikaner, Kishangarh and Karauli were also present at Hurda.[54] All these rulers met at Hurda,[55] a village near Udaipur, where a meeting was convened. On 17 July (*Shravan vadi* 13) they came to an agreement according to which they pledged to honour the following commitments:[56]

(1) They shall remain united in all circumstances, good or bad, with a pledge to abide by the terms.
(2) No one shall help the defector of another.
(3) After the rains, the situation shall be discussed and the chiefs of all the parties shall assemble at Rampura, and if for any reason a chief cannot come, he shall send his heir or some other person or a *sardar*.
(4) Should such an heir commit any mistake out of inexperience, the Maharana alone shall be competent to correct it.
(5) In every campaign all shall unite to conduct it.

A study of the above terms makes it clear that these rulers had realized the danger posed by the Marathas' appearance in Rajputana. Although the superiority of the Maharana above all the rulers of Rajputana was accepted, the trend of later events shows that the unity among the Rajput Rajas was purely superficial. As has been mentioned, till March 1734 Maharaja Abhay Singh was trying to secure the *subadari* of Ajmer along with that of Gujarat. Abhay Singh also showed his readiness to proceed to Ahmedabad if it was desired by nawab Khan-i-Dauran. His departure to Gujarat remained postponed due to the Maratha incursion on the Amber territory. It seems that Abhay Singh was waiting for a favourable reply from the Mughal *wazir* (which he got in June 1734) when he accepted the request of Jai Singh to help him against the Marathas.[57] Later, both Abhay Singh and Jai Singh participated in the Hurda conference. The participation of Abhay Singh was made possible only after his disappointment from the Mughal court. But he was still in touch with the court and made it clear that his participation was aimed at opposing the Marathas rather than at forming any united front against the Mughals.[58]

The Rajput Rajas could not meet at Rampura as they had planned to take united action against the Marathas. On the other hand, Abhay Singh, Jai Singh, Durjansal and other Rajput rulers joined Khan-i-Dauran who had left Delhi in November 1734 to oust the Marathas from Rajputana.[59] The combined army under the command of Khan-i-Dauran reached Rampura in February 1735 where Holkar and Sindhia were expected to be ready for the counter attack.[60] The Maratha commanders, Malhar Rao Holkar and Ranoji Sindhia harassed the contingent of Abhay Singh, Jai Singh, Durjansal and Khan-i-Dauran after isolating them from each other. Later, Holkar and Sindhia left their opponents in the field and entered the defenceless territory of Jaipur *via* Bundi.[61] Sambhar was sacked by them on 28 February 1735, yielding a rich booty.[62] While the Marathas were plundering the territory of Jaipur, Abhay Singh did not render any military help to Jai Singh. Later, after the negotiations between Khan-i-Dauran and the Marathas in March 1735,[63] Abhay Singh proceeded to Delhi along with Khan-i-Dauran. Abhay Singh's presence at the court at that time when Marwar was still facing the danger of the Maratha encroachment was motivated by selfish considerations. A letter written by Rathor Kanhi Ram to Abhay Singh reveals that Abhay Singh had informed him about his removal from the *subadari* of Gujarat and the appointment of

Munim Khan there.[64] It is quite likely that while remaining at the court Abhay Singh was trying to secure the *subadari* of Ajmer in place of Gujarat. In fact the demand of the *subadari* of Ajmer was put forward by Abhay Singh at the time when Khan-i-Dauran succeeded in getting the order of the grant of Ranthambhor in favour of Jai Singh.[65] As the Emperor was not in favour of granting the *subadari* of Ajmer to Abhay Singh, the grant of Ranthambhor was also withdrawn.[66] This caused serious concern to Jai Singh. Abhay Singh's policy towards the Marathas also created differences with Jai Singh. At the court Abhay Singh joined *wazir* Qamar-ud-Din Khan who was in favour of active action against the Marathas.[67] Thus Abhay Singh associated himself in the court with the party which openly opposed the policy of Jai Singh.[68] This rivalry became apparent when on the advice of Jai Singh, Malhar Rao, Ranoji, etc., entered Marwar and conducted a fierce campaign which lasted for two months, culminating in the surrender of the Rathors before the Maratha commanders at Merta in April, 1736.[69] Although the Maratha *sardars* left the territory of Marwar after securing a handsome indemnity, it became quite clear that the treaty, concluded in July 1734, was of no avail and no combined Rajput action against the Marathas was to be expected in future. With a view to exploiting the situation, both Abhay Singh and Jai Singh were trying to get more and more concessions from the Emperor and, therefore, the rivalry between the two became inevitable.

The political events which occurred between 1736 and 1739 exposed the weakness of the Mughal Emperor and the increasing strength of the Marathas.[70] Although Abhay Singh remained associated with the pro-war party at the Mughal court, he continued his efforts to improve his position in Rajputana. Due to mismanagement and irregularities, he was removed from the *subadari* of Gujarat in 1737.[71] Maharaja Abhay Singh's demand of the *subadari* of Ajmer was not entertained, but he succeeded in securing the *faujdari* of Sambhar in the same year and left Jahanabad in April 1737 for Marwar.[72] The grant of the *faujdari* of Sambhar was significant, as we find that apart from Ajmer, Abhay Singh was also trying for Sambhar. Earlier, Maharaja Ajit Singh had tried to secure the grant of Sambhar, but in spite of his best efforts, he failed to get it.

Inter-State Politics after 1737

Maharaja Abhay Singh, after his arrival at Jodhpur concerned himself with extending his influence over the neighbouring territories. Although he had been deprived of Ajmer, he wanted to secure its possession by force. As the Mughal Emperor was not in a position to take any military action due to his engagement with the Marathas and frictions in the court, Abhay Singh asked Maharao Durjansal and Maharana Jagat Singh to send their contingents for an attack on Ajmer. Although Maharao Durjansal assured him of his loyalty, he expressed his inability at the moment.[73] The Rana too did not show any interest in Abhay Singh's scheme.[74] Apparently, both the rulers of Kota and Mewar were not ready to associate themselves in a move against the Mughal authority. Abhay Singh could not achieve his desire and had to postpone his plan for the time being because of internal troubles caused by his brother Bakht Singh.

As has been mentioned earlier, although Bakht Singh had been granted Nagaur almost as an independent *jagir*, he was not satisfied with it and wanted to secure more *jagirs* from the Mughal Emperor. He was also not happy with the interference of Abhay Singh in the affairs of Nagaur. On all administrative posts of Nagaur, Abhay Singh had either appointed his own nominees or the appointments were made with his consent. During Abhay Singh's absence from Marwar (1731-33), Bakht Singh held charge of administrative and military affairs. Availing himself of this opportunity, he strengthened his power and established direct relations with the Mughal Emperor. Bakht Singh's intentions became clear when he turned down the advice of Maharaja Abhay Singh in 1738 to remove all the Bhandaris from the state administration. He also dismissed *diwan* Pancholi Lalji who was loyal to Abhay Singh.[75] This attitude of Bakht Singh annoyed Abhay Singh, who later on appointed Lalji as *diwan* of Jodhpur,[76] and increased the bitterness between the two brothers. The friction between the two became quite obvious when in A.D.

1739 (V.S. 1796), Maharaja Abhay Singh sent his army against Bikaner. The aim was to establish his superiority over the ruler of Bikaner and to recapture the *thanas* which had been seized by Zorawar Singh in 1736, just after his accession.[77] Abhay Singh could not register any success against Zorawar Singh as he had to withdraw his army in order to march against Merta. In June 1739 Bakht Singh invaded Merta according to the agreement concluded with Zorawar Singh.[78] The Maharaja, therefore, left for Merta in order to teach Bakht Singh a lesson. After the arrival of the Jodhpur army at Merta, the nobles of both the sides realized the futility of the fight. Therefore, Khichi Harnath on behalf of Abhay Singh, and Chauhan Mohkam Singh on behalf of Bakht Singh held a meeting. Reconciliation was thus brought about between the two brothers,[79] but both remained suspicious of each other.

During Abhay Singh's operations against Bakht Singh, the latter opened negotiations with Zorawar Singh, the ruler of Bikaner. The support of Zorawar Singh to Bakht Singh could have created a serious problem for Abhay Singh. Thus in the month of April, 1740, Abhay Singh again invaded Bikaner and laid siege to the Bikaner fort. When after some days the provisions of the garrison were exhausted, Zorawar Singh sent Purohit Jagu to Abhay Singh requesting for suspension of hostilities to enable him to leave the fort. But Zorawar Singh was playing a trick. Keeping Abhay Singh busy with peace efforts, he sent Muhata Bakhtawarmal to Nagaur and solicited help from Bakht Singh. Bakht Singh responded favourably, but to make his own position stronger he directed Bakhtawarmal to Jai Singh to win him over to his side.[80] Maharaja Jai Singh was already on bitter terms with Abhay Singh and was discreet enough to realize the danger from Abhay Singh if he succeeded in securing control over Bikaner, as he could then attack his own territory, *i.e.*, Jaipur.[81] It is said that to prove his sincerity in his promise to the ruler of Bikaner, Bakht Singh invaded Merta.[82] At the same time Jai Singh also reached there. This was an extreme step taken by Maharaja Jai Singh. The circumstantial evidence shows that Jai Singh's aggressive step was instigated by the Mughal Emperor and was a part of a bigger political game. The account of *Sawai Jai Singh-ri-Jodhpur per Chadhai* clearly indicates that Jai Singh marched against Jodhpur following the order of the Mughal Emperor.[83] He got a *farman* issued by the Emperor for the assignment of Merta to Bakht Singh.[84] Moreover, Maharaja Jai Singh proclaimed Ratan Singh, the brother of Abhay Singh, the ruler of Jodhpur.[85] Another brother of Abhay Singh, Raj Kishor, sieged Parbatsar.[86] Besides these two brothers of Abhay Singh, Jai Singh was also accompanied by Roop Singh Rathor, ruler of Roopnagar (Kisangarh), Surajmal Jat, Gopal Singh of Karauli, and an army contingent of Zorawar Singh of Bikaner.[87] Thus the intervention of Jai Singh isolated Abhay Singh and there was also the possibility that after the defeat of Abhay Singh the Mughal Emperor would recognize Rathor Ratan Singh as the ruler of Jodhpur. The assignment of Merta to Bakhat Singh by the Emperor had, in fact indicated the intention of the latter to check the activities of Abhay Singh in time.

As soon as Abhay Singh got the news of Jai Singh's arrival he raised the siege of Bikaner and returned to Jodhpur. Later he proceeded to Merta where both the armies took their positions. But Abhay Singh realizing the inferiority of his strength and the consequences of his defeat, initiated negotiations with Jai Singh. He released Bhandari Raghunath from prison and sent him to conclude terms. By that time it became clear that Bakht Singh was no longer inclined to support Jai Singh.[88] Bakht Singh might have anticipated the danger caused due to the recognition of Ratan Singh as the ruler of Jodhpur. This would have limited his control only to the *parganas* of Nagaur and Merta. Such an arrangement would have affirmed the division of the Rathor dominion of Jodhpur into various territorial units, which would have ultimately gone in favour of Jai Singh whose supremacy over Marwar would then become inevitable. In response to the peace offer of Abhay Singh, Jai Singh demanded a huge amount as indemnity. But, significantly, the claim of indemnity made by Jai Singh ignored Bakht Singh who was then fighting against his brothers along with Jai Singh. Under these circumstances Bakht Singh decided to support Abhay Singh and informed him about his decision. But Abhay Singh who had no faith in the sincerity of his brother paid no heed to his proposal and concluded peace with Jai Singh. According to the conditions, Abhay Singh agreed to pay rupees twenty lacs as indemnity to Jai Singh.[89]

The terms conceded by Abhay Singh were quite adverse, indicating his humiliation and the great triumph of the Kachhawah ruler. Therefore, soon after the agreement with Jai Singh, Maharaja Abhay Singh and Bakht Singh decided to recover their prestige by defeating Jai Singh. Bakht Singh tried to get the support of Maharao Durjansal of Kota informing him about his march against Jai Singh.[90] Bakht Singh advanced up to Dhundar, where he was defeated by Jai Singh. Later, the army of Bakht Singh reached Aleniyavas,[91] where Abhay Singh was staying. It is worth noting that in May 1741, Jai Singh extended an invitation to Baji Rao I to meet him at Dholpur, with a view to entering into an agreement of helping each other against common danger.[92] It is significant that instead of securing any help from the Mughal court, Jai Singh preferred to seek assistance from the Marathas. But his plan did not materialize. Jai Singh, along with Zorawar Singh of Bikaner, marched against the combined army of Bakht Singh and Abhay Singh. At Gangwara a severe battle was fought in May 1741.[93] But as a result of the intervention of Maharana Jagat Singh, both sides concluded peace in January 1742. They agreed not to interfere in each other's internal affairs.[94]

Thus the conflict with Bikaner moved on to Jaipur and for three years the armies of Jodhpur and Jaipur plundered each other's territories thereby sowing the seeds of instability in Rajputana. The Maharana remained neutral, but later, on the issue of the succession to the *gaddi* of Jaipur, he too entered the fray.

Maharaja Abhay Singh's Attempt to Revive his Position

Maharaja Jai Singh's death in September 1743 provided an opportunity to Abhay Singh to establish his superiority over the Rajput rulers. The political situation of the Kachhawah state was deteriorating due to a civil war on the issue of succession. The problem of succession was raised on the basis of the agreement of A.D. 1709, according to which the son of the Udaipuri Rani was to be installed on the *gaddi* after Jai Singh's death.[95] Although Ishwari Singh had been recognised as the legitimate successor of Jai Singh, the claim of his younger brother, Madho Singh, who was the son of the Udaipuri Rani was supported by Rana Jagat Singh. The involvement of the Rana complicated the situation. He invited Maharao Durjansal of Kota for help. Maharao Durjansal who felt offended due to the intervention of Sawai Jai Singh in the affairs of Bundi, responded favourably to the request of the Rana. Both the rulers met at village Megara and decided to march against Ishwari Singh. It was also decided that the *gaddi* of Bundi should be conferred on Ummed Singh, son of Budh Singh, who had been dislodged by Jai Singh.[96] Both the armies took their positions at village Jamoli of *pargana* Jahazpur. But the battle did not take place and the contending parties concluded peace agreeing to award Madho Singh the *pargana* of Tonk worth Rs. 5,00,000.[97] The agreement was made without the consent of Durjansal for whom it was a breach of the original agreement. It seems that the primary motive of the Rana was to settle the question of Madho Singh's succession and as soon as he had reached an agreement with Ishwari Singh, he stopped bothering about the Bundi affair. Maharao Durjansal who had helped the Rana on the condition that Bundi would be granted to Ummed Singh was thus disappointed. He, therefore, left the camp of the Maharana and went to Kota.[98] It may be noted that in spite of the enmity with the ruler of Jaipur, Abhay Singh did not render any help to the Rana during his campaign against Ishwari Singh. The succession of Ishwari Singh was favourable to Abhay Singh as the former could never be supported by the Maharana.

However, Maharaja Abhay Singh took advantage of the civil war in Jaipur. While Ishwari Singh was facing the Mewar army, Abhay Singh marched upon Ajmer and occupied it. At this time Bhatt Govind Ram arrived from Kota with 5000 *sawars* and joined the Maharaja.[99] Thus after leaving the Rana, Durjansal joined Abhay Singh. This suggests that the ruler of Kota was ready to join any camp which opposed Ishwari Singh and promised to correct the wrong done by Jai Singh regarding the *gaddi* of Bundi. On hearing about the seizure of Ajmer by Abhay Singh, Ishwari Singh marched towards Ajmer to settle the score with Abhay Singh. The fight did not take place and an agreement was reached between the two according to which Abhay Singh's control over Ajmer was recognised by Ishwari Singh.[100] Abhay Singh went a step further and established his control over Kisangarh. The interest of Raj Singh, the ruler of Kisangarh, could not be served by Ishwari Singh who failed to honour the promise made by Jai Singh.[101] In the meantime Hada Durjansal with the help of Fakhruddaullah succeeded in his attempt to dislodge Dalel Singh and install in his place Ummed Singh, son of Rao Budh Singh on the *gaddi* of Bundi.[102] But Ummed Singh could not maintain his position for long, as Dalel Singh recovered his possessions with the assistance of Ishwari Singh.[103] Although on the question of Bundi, Abhay Singh did not come into direct conflict with Ishwari Singh, the restoration of Dalel Singh was against Abhay Singh's wishes. Thus the old rivalry between the two houses continued. Internally, Abhay Singh's peace settlement with Ishwari Singh was opposed by his brother Bakht Singh who, without informing Abhay Singh, left for Nagaur.

The problem of Madho Singh's succession remained unsettled even after securing his possession of Tonk. The Rana was not satisfied with the agreement and he wanted to dislodge Ishwari Singh from the *gaddi* of Jaipur. Therefore, when Ishwari Singh was at the Mughal court, the Rana invited Holkar and promised him to pay rupees one crore if he seated Madho Singh on the *gaddi* of Jaipur.[104] Accordingly, Maharana Jagat Singh along with the Maratha army marched against Jaipur. But the whole plan was disrupted as Ishwari Singh reached Amber before the arrival of the joint forces and offered money to the Maratha *sardars* who were won over to his side. Consequently, the Maharana left for Udaipur without making any dent in Jaipur's strength.[105] Thus, after the death of Jai Singh, the rulers of Udaipur, Jodhpur and Kota continued fighting against Ishwari Singh and each of them tried to win over the support of the Marathas. It is significant to note that in no case did the rulers of Jodhpur and Udaipur unite against Jaipur, because Abhay Singh did not support the cause of Madho Singh and the Rana was not pleased with Abhay Singh's policy of expansion.

The increasing power of Maharaja Abhay Singh in the absence of a strong opponent like Jai Singh, led him to have designs over Bikaner. After the death of Zorawar Singh (May 1746), a dispute arose between Maharaja Gaj Singh and his elder brother, Amar Singh, on the issue of succession, which provided an opportunity to Abhay Singh to intervene in the internal affairs of Bikaner. He sent an army against Bikaner in support of Amar Singh.[106] It is said that Amar Singh went to Abhay Singh and solicited his help.[107] Other Bikaner *sardars* who were staying at Jodhpur, supported the cause of Amar Singh. Maharaja Abhay Singh availed himself of this opportunity and sent his army to help the dissatisfied prince. But after a decisive battle in July 1747, the Jodhpur army returned to its territory without achieving anything. Bakht Singh did not participate against Bikaner and on the invitation of the Mughal Emperor he joined the Mughals against Ahmad Shah Durrani. In fact, Maharaja Abhay Singh showed his inability to join the Mughal army against Ahmad Shah Durrani and also asked Bakht Singh not to attend the court.[108] The attitude of Abhay Singh only indicated the general trend of disobedience among the *mansabdars* who, taking advantage of the disintegration of the central power, started defying it.

Emperor Ahmad Shah after his accession in April 1748, adopted an indifferent attitude towards Abhay Singh which caused serious complications in the politics of Marwar. After his accession, the Mughal Emperor conferred upon Bakht Singh the *subadari* of Gujarat and Ajmer.[109] The intention of the Emperor behind the assignment of these *subas* is apparent as its ultimate result was the conflict between Abhay Singh and Bakht Singh. Abhay Singh already held control over Sambhar, Didwana and Ajmer. Bakht Singh was given Ajmer which meant control over Sambhar, Didwana and Narnol also.[110] The control over Sambhar and Didwana by Bakht Singh could never be accepted by Abhay Singh as the latter himself was interested in maintaining his control over there. Thus the assignment of the *subadari* of Gujarat and Ajmer was an open challenge to the rights of Abhay Singh. To secure control over these areas which fell under the control of Abhay Singh, a conflict between the two became inevitable. Abhay Singh sought the help of Malharrao Holkar through Durjansal with whom the Maratha *sardar* was staying. Abhay Singh agreed to pay Rs. 11,000 per day for humbling Bakht Singh. Bakht Singh got help from the ruler of Bikaner. The fight did not take place, as due to the revival of the conflict between Ishwari Singh and Mādho Singh, Holkar's march against Amber became necessary. However, Malharrao Holkar brought about a reconciliation between the two brothers.[111]

Holkar's march against Ishwari Singh in July 1748 marked a change in Abhay Singh's policy towards Jaipur. Maharaja Abhay Singh had always opposed the intervention of Jai Singh in the affairs of Bundi. However, after Jai Singh's death, Abhay Singh did not involve himself in the succession dispute at Jaipur. But since the military intervention of Holkar and Rana against Ishwari Singh had for its object the restoration of the *gaddi* of Bundi to Ummed Singh, son of Budh Singh, Abhay Singh sent 2000 *sawars* under the command of Mertia Sher Singh along with the Maratha and the Mewar armies. The combined armies of the Rana, Abhay Singh and the Marathas succeeded in defeating Ishwari Singh at Bagru on 1 August 1748 (*Bhadrapad vadi* 4). Ishwari Singh agreed to assign Bundi to Ummed Singh and four additional *parganas* of Tonk to Madho Singh.[112] Thus the Maratha interference in Rajputana politics became a dominant factor in deciding the disputes of the Rajput rulers. The Maratha commanders were paid considerable money by the parties which engaged them in their conflicts. Obviously the role of the Mughal Emperor in the matters of inter-state relations had shifted to the Marathas to some extent.

Although Bakht Singh could not secure control over Sambhar and Ajmer, yet due to the favour shown by the Mughal Emperor and the support of Bikaner, he had strengthened his position in Marwar. Maharaja Abhay Singh had realized his weakness and therefore, a few days before his death, he called a meeting of his *sardars*. Apprehending the possibility of the usurpation of the *gaddi* of Marwar by Bakht Singh, he asked his *sardars* to remain loyal to his son Ram Singh. The *sardars* agreed to defend the right of Ram Singh but they clearly reminded him that their support to Ram Singh would depend upon the latter's willingness to protect their interests and maintain their *thikanas*.[113] This attitude of the Rathor *sardars* marks a significant change in the nature of the relationship between the ruler and the nobility which was obviously the result of the political instability then prevailing in the Mughal Empire.

REFERENCES

[1]Letter from Abhay Singh to Jai Singh dated 4 February 1726 (*Phalgun vadi* 2). *Jaipur Records* (Hindi), Vol. V. 74 (Sitamau): Letter of Abhay Karan to Abhay Singh dated 6 June 1725 (*Ashadh vadi* 13). *Basta* No. 76/2, R.S.A.B.

[2]Letter from Jai Singh to Bhandari Raghunath of 17 August 1726 (*Bhadrapada vadi* 6, 1783). *Kharitas and Parwanas*, 3, 452. R.S.A.B. In the beginning of 1725, the Maratha armies were hovering over the border of Rampura and Kota-Bundi. Nizam-ul-Mulk had failed to check the Maratha incursions into the north. These were ominous developments, and the Maharana and Jai Singh realized that it was high time when the Marathas' growing influence should be checked. For Maratha penetration into Malwa, Gujarat and Bundlekhand, see, *Parties and Politics*, Chapter VIII.

[3]Letter from Jai Singh to Bhandari Raghunath, dated 4 August 1726 (*Bhadra vadi* 6, 1783). *Kharitas & Parwanas* (*op. cit.*).

[4]*Parties and Politics*, 201-3.

[5]Letters written by Jai Singh on *Ashoj sudi* 3, 1783. *Kharitas and Parwanas*, 3/261, R.S.A.B.

[6]Letter from Dhabhai Nagraj to Jai Singh, dated 31 August 1726 (*Ashadh sudi* 15, 1783). *Kharitas and Parwanas*, R.S.A.B.

[7]Jai Singh's letter to the Maharana dated 31 May 1727; cited in *Vir Vinod*, 968.

[8]Letter from Abhay Singh to Sangram Singh dated 30 May 1726 (*Ashadh vadi* 6, 1783). *Shyamaldas Collection*, R.S.A.B. (Also, cited in *Vir Vinod* ii. 969.

[9]Dhabhai's letter to Jai Singh dated *Ashadh sudi* 15, 1783. *op. cit.*

[10]Letter from Abhay Singh to Jai Singh dated 26 June 1727 (*Shravan vadi* 4). *Kharitas and Parwanas*, 6/31, R.S.A.B.

[11]Abhay Singh's letter to Jai Singh dated 26 June 1727 (*Shravan vadi* 4). *Jodhpur Kharitas*, R.S.A.B.

[12]Letter from Jai Singh to Sangram Singh dated 10 August 1728 (*Bhadrapad vadi* 2, 1785). *Jodhpur Kharitas*, R.S.A.B. The help of the

Rawal of Jaisalmer was sought due to the fact that Rathor Kishor Singh another brother of Abhay Singh, was staying there and it was feared that the Rawal might extend his support to the rebels on persuasion of Kishor Singh.

[13]Letter from Abhay Singh to Sangram Singh dated 10 August 1721 (*Bhadrapad vadi* 2, 1785). *Shyamaldas Collection*, I, R.S.A.B.

[14]*S.P.D.* (New Series), i, 6. The term *saranjami* denotes the revenue rights of an area for the maintenance of the army.

[15]*Mundiyara-ri-Khyat*, 276; *Jodhpur-Khyat*, ii, 209.

[16]Letter from Jai Singh to Maharana, dated 10 August 1728 (*Bhadrapada vadi* 13, 1785). (*op. cit.*); *Jodhpur-Khyat*, ii, 209.

[17]Letter from Jai Singh to Abhay Singh, dated 29 October, 1725 (*Kartik sudi* 4, 1782). *Kharitas and Parwanas*, 2, R.S.A.B.

[18]*Ibid.*

[19]*Kharitas and Parwanas*, Bundle No. 3 (R.S.A.B.) contains numerous letters exchanged between these two rulers.

[20]Letter from Abhay Singh to Jai Singh dated 4 February 1726 (*Phalgun vadi* 2, 1782). *op. cit.*, *Parties and Politics*, (2nd ed.), 302.

[21]Dr. G.R. Parihar holds that as the Emperor failed to fulfil his promise of financial aid, Abhay Singh showed his inability to proceed to Gujarat but agreed to send four to five hundred soldiers for imperial service (*Marwar and the Marathas*, 29).

[22]In his letter dated 2 December, 1725 (*Margsir vadi* 8), addressed to Abhay Singh, Jai Singh advised the latter to proceed to Gujarat warning him of serious consequences in case he failed to do so. *Jaipur Records*, (Sitamau).

[23]As at the court there were various groups led by influential nobles, no military action was possible. For group politics, see, *Parties and Politics*, 210-17.

[24]Letter from Jai Singh to Abhay Singh, dated *Vaisakh sudi* 15, 1726. *Kharitas and Parwanas*, No. 3/167, R.S.A.B.

[25]Letter from Jai Singh to Abhay Singh, dated *Bhádrapada* 10, 1783. *Kharita and Parwanas*, No. 3/256, R.S.A.B.

[26]Letter from Jai Singh to Abhay Singh, dated *Ashoj vadi* 8, 1783. *Kharitas and Parwanas*, No. 3/268, R.S.A.B.

[27]Letter from the Rathor *sardar* Anoop Singh to Jai Singh dated 5 September 1728 (*Bhadrapada sudi* 13, 1785). *Kapatdwara Records*, Reg. No. 1036C.

[28]*Jodhpur-Khyat*, ii, 131 (A.S.L.B).

[29]*Ibid.*

[30]*Rathora-ri-Vamshavali* (ORIJ), 215.

[31]Letter from Abhay Singh to Jai Singh dated 17 November 1728 (*Margsir Vadi* 12, 1785). *Jaipur Records*, Vol. III, 89. (Sitamau).

[32]*Parties and Politics*, 204; *Sawai Jai Singh*, 130.

[33]For the reasons of Jai Singh's removal from Malwa, see, *Parties and Palitics* 204-5.

[34]Budh Singh Hada of Bundi was married to the sister of Jai Singh. As Rao Budh Singh refused to accept the legality of the son of his

Kachhawahi Rani, Jai Singh forcefully dislodged Budh Singh and granted the *tika* of Bundi to Dalel Singh of Narwar. (*Vamsha Bhaskar*, IV, 3090-100, *Mundiyara-ri-Khyat*, 273; *Kota Rajya*, i, 340-1).

[35]In this battle Durjansal helped Budh Singh. The Hadas and Kachhawahs came into open conflict. (*Vamsha Bhaskar*, 3142-89; *Kota Rajya*, i, 342). Although Jai Singh won the battle, he lost the confidence of Abhay Singh and Maharana Sangram Singh.

[36]*Vamsha Bhaskar*, 3210.

[37]*Mirat*, ii, 115; *Siyar*, 462; *Servadeshma-Rajvioni*, 159; *Rajrupak*, 699; *Suraj Prakash*, ii, 242-55; Ashub, 371; *Parties and Politics*, 206.

[38]Letter from Abhay Singh to Bhandari Amar Singh dated 16 October 1730 (*Kartik sudi* 2, 1787). *Rukka Parwana Bahi*, No. 1/12, R.S.A.B.; *Rajrupak*, 707-811.

[39]Letter from Abhay Singh to Bhandari Amar Singh dated 10 April 1731 (*Chaitra sudi* 14, 1787). *Rukka Parwana Bahi* No. 1, R.S.A.B.; *Mirat*, ii, 134-5; *Jodhpur-Khyat*, ii, 139; *Uttar Mughal Kalin Bharat*, 180.

[40]*Mirat*, ii, 120-50; See *Parties and Politics*, 207, 297-8.

[41]*Mirat*, ii, 136-41; *Jodhpur Rajya*, ii, 629.

[42]For details, see, *New Maratha History*, ii, 131; Also see, *Jodhpur Rajya*, ii, 629-31.

[43]The argument that the danger of an invasion on Marwar by the ruler of Bikaner compelled Abhay Singh to reach Marwar (*Marwar and the Marathas* 48-9) cannot be accepted as we find that Bakht Singh attacked Bikaner when Abhay Singh was at Jodhpur. *Jodhpur-Khyat* (SS), 16; *Dayaldas Khyat*, ii, 61; *Rathora-ri-Vamshavali* (ORIJ), *Jodhpur Rajya*, ii, 631.

[44]Reu, *Marwar*, ii, 497.

[45]Letter from Bakht Singh to Bhandari Amar Singh, *vakil* of Jodhpur in the Mughal court, dated *Kartik sudi* 4, 1789. *Rukka Parwana Bahi* No. 1, R.S.A.B.

[46]Letter from Maharaja Abhay Singh to Bhandari Amar Singh, *vakil* of Jodhpur, dated March 3, 1734 (*Phalgun sudi* 10). *HRC*. December 1940, 202-3.

[47]*Vamsha Bhaskar*, iv, 3126-7; *Kota Rajya*, i, 345-6.

[48]According to Surajmal (*Vamsha Bhaskar*, iv, 3216) the Maratha *sardars* came at the invitation of the Rani Kachhawahi, the wife of Budh Singh, who offered Rs. 6 lacs in case they restored Bundi to her husband.

[49]*Vamsha Bhaskar* iv, 3220-1.

[50]For Jai Singh's military intervention in Bundi, see, *Life and Times of Sawai Jai Singh*, 221.

[51]Letter from Abhay Singh to Bhandari Amar Singh, dated *Phalgun sudi* 10, 1790.

[52]Letter from Abhay Singh to Amar Singh, dated 3 March 1734 (*Phalgun sudi* 10 1790). *Reu Collection*, Sumer Public Library, Jodhpur; Letter from Abhay Singh to Maharana Jagat Singh, dated *Jyeshtha vadi* 1, 1790. *Kharita Bahi*, 1-2.

[53]Letter of Maharaja Jai Singh to Kesari Singh dated c. early 1734.

Jaipur Records (Hindi), Vol. II, (Sitamau). *Jodhpur-Khyat*, ii, 228-9; *Mundiyara-ri-Khyat* (ORIJ), 296-7.

[54]*Ibid.*

[55]Hurda is about three miles from Barl Station on Chittor-Ajmer line of Western Railway.

[56]Transcribed copy of the agreement of 17 July 1734 (*Shravan vadi* 13). *Jaipur Records* (Hindi-Sitamau), iii, 54; *Jodhpur-Khyat*, ii, 229: *Vamsha Bhaskar*, 3227-8; *Vir Vinod*, 1218-21; *Udaipur Rajya*, i, 939; Tod, i, 482-3. According to *Vir Vinod*, the date of the conference was July 13, 1734.

[57]Letter from Abhay Singh to Maharana Jagat Singh, dated *Jeyshtha vadi* 1, 1733.

[58]*Jodhpur-Khyat*, ii, 229. It was reported at the court that Abhay Singh was in a mood of rebellion.

[59]At the Mughal court a decision was taken according to which two huge armies under the command of *wazir* Qumar-ud-din Khan and Khan-i-Dauran were sent against the Marathas. Dighe, 118-19; For details, see, *Parties and Politics*, 220-1.

[60]*Jodhpur-Khyat*, ii, 130-1; *Parties and Politics*, 221.

[61]*S.P.D.*, xiv, 21, 33; *Vamsha Bhaskar*, iv, 3227.

[62]*Hingane Daftar*, i, 2; S.P.D., xiv, 23, 27.

[63]*Hingane Daftar*, i, 2; S.P.D., xiv, 23, 27; *Parties and Politics*, 221.

[64]Letter from Kanhi Ram to Abhay Singh dated 25 May 1735 (*Jyeshtha sudi* 15). Cit. *The Researcher*, Ed. Dr. Satya Prakash, Vol. III-IV, 1963-64.

[65]*Jodhpur-Khyat*, ii, 232.

[66]*Ibid.*

[67]In Februaıy 1735, Jai Singh and Khan-i-Dauran had agreed to pay 22 lacs of rupees annually to the Marathas as a *chauth* for Malwa (S.P.D., xiv 23, 27). Abhay Singh was not in favour of making such a concession to the Marathas. *Jodhpur-Khyat*, ii, 144; *Basta* No. 11/49, 10-12 (R.S.A.B.) For details, see *Parties and Politics*, 222-3.

[68]*S.P.D.*, XV, 89, 91; Siyar, i, 286; *Jodhpur-Khyat*, ii, 244.

[69]*Basta* No. 11/49, R.S.A.B.; 13; *Jodhpur-Khyat*, ii, 145-6; *S.P.D.*, xiv, 14; *Mirat*, ii, 192-3.

[70]For details, see, *Parties and Politics*, 226-38.

[71]Mirat, ii, 194-236; *Jodhpur Rajya*, ii, 642-6.

[72]S.P.D., xv pp. 30; The dates of Abhay Singh's departure and his arrival at Jodhpur have been given differently.

[73]Letter from Durjansal to Abhay Singh dated *Ashadh sudi* 6, 1795. *Kharita Bahi*, 3/186, R.S.A.B.

[74]Letter from Maharana Jagat Singh to Abhay Singh dated *Ashadh vadi* 3, 1795. *Kharita Bahi* No. 3, R S.A.B.

[75]*Jodhpur-Khyat*, ii, 237.

[76]*Ibid.*, 237-8.

[77]According to the treaty of 1734, the ruler of Bikaner had surrendered some areas of his territory where Abhay Singh had established his *thanas*. As Zorawar Singh, after his succession, had removed these

thanas, Abhay Singh felt offended. *Dayaldas Khyat*, ii, f. 63; *Arya Khyan Kalp*, 265; *Bikaner Rajya*, i, 307.

[78]When the Rathor army laid siege to Bikaner, Bakht Singh sent Bareth Dalpat for preparing his plan of action against Abhay Singh. But as Zorawar Singh wanted a proof of Bakht Singh's sincerity towards him, the latter attacked Merta. *Dayaldas Khyat*, ii, f. 63-4; *Jodhpur Rajya* ii, 648-9.

[79]*Jodhpur-Khyat*, ii, 239; *Rathora-ri-Vamshavali* (*Bahi*).

[80]*Jodhpur-Khyat*, ii, 241; *Basta* No. 40, Reg. 38, R.S.A.B. *Mundiara-ri-Khyat* (ORIJ), 309.

[81]*Jodhpur-Khyat*, ii, 241.

[82]*Jodhpur Rajya*, ii, 653.

[83]*Jai Singh-ri-Jodhpur par Chadhai* (ORIJ-*MS*), 1.

[84]*Mundiara-ri-Khyat* (ORIJ), 310; *Jodhpur-Khyat*, ii, 241.

[85]*Mundiara-ri-Khyat* (ORIJ), 315-16; *Jodhpur-Khyat*, ii, 241.

[86]*Sawai Jai Singh-ri-Jodhpur par Chadhai* (MS), 127-8 (ORIJ); *Jodhpur-Khyat*, 241.

[87]*Ibid.*

[88]*Jodhpur-Khyat*, ii, 243.

[89]It is said that some of the payment was made through delivering the ornaments of Rani Kachhawahi and for the balance five *sardars* were sent as hostages to Jaipur who were returned after the recovery. *Jodhpur-Khyat*, ii, 243.

[90]Letter from Bakht Singh to Durjansal dated 2 April 1734 (*Baishakh vadi* 13 1797). *Jaipur Records*, iii, 67 (Sitamau).

[91]Ojha, *Bikaner Rajya*, i, 318.

[92]*S.P.D.*, xi, 2.

[93]*Jodhpur-Khyat*, ii, 152-3.

[94]Letter of Abhay Singh to Maharaja Jai Singh, dated August 31, 1741 (*Bhadrapada vadi* 7, 1798). (*Kapatdwara Records*, Reg. No. 913, R.S.A.B.). Letter from Abhay Singh to Jai Singh, dated 30 January 1741 (*Margsir vadi* 2, 1798). *Kharita Bahi*, 3, R.S.A.B.

[95]*Vir Vinod* ii, 774-5; *Udaipur Rajya*, i, 914-15.

[96]Ojha, *Udaipur Rajya*, i, 944; *Kota Rajya*, ii, 382-3.

[97]Ojha, *Udaipur Rajya*, i, 944; *Kota Rajya*, ii, 382-3.

[98]*Vamsha Bhaskar*, 3324-8 and 3333-6.

[99]*Ibid.*

[100]*Jodhpur-Khyat*, ii, 157-8; *Marwar Rajya*, ii, 509.

[101]Letter from Raj Singh to Ishwari Singh dated January 4, 1744 (*Bhadrapada sudi* 1, 1800). *Jaipur Records*, (Hindi), ii (Sitamau).

[102]*Kharita Bahi*, 4/18, *Jodhpur Section*, R.S.A.B. It is said that Durjansal received the help from Fakhruddaullah, *subadar* of Ajmer. Ojha, *Jodhpur Rajya*, ii, 661.

[103]*Vamsha Bhaskar*.

[104]Ojha, *Udaipur Rajya*, i, 945. This event took place in A.D. 1744.

[105]*Vamsha Bhaskar*, 3376-80; *Vir Vinod*, 1232.

[106]*Dayaldas-ri-Khyat*, ii, f. 69; Ojha, *Bikaner Rajya*, i, 323.

[107]*Bikaner-Rajya* i, 323.

[108]*Jodhpur-Khyat*, ii, 160; *Rathora-ri-Vamshavali* (ORIJ).

[109]*Mirat*, ii, 376-7; *Hingne Daftar*, i, 32; *Jodhpur-Khyat*, ii, 160-1. At the time of Ahmad Shah's succession, Bakht Singh was at the Mughal court.

[110]*Jodhpur-Khyat*, ii, 160-1.

[111]*Dayaldas-ri-Khyat*, ii, f. 70-2; *Jodhpur-Khyat*, ii, 160; *Vir Vinod*, 504.

[112]*Jodhpur-Khyat*, ii, 160(9); *Vir Vinod*, 504.

[113]*Vamsha Bhaskar*, 3583-4.

CONCLUSION

The state of Marwar denoted the territory over which the Rathor clan or its branches (*khamps*) claimed domination by right of occupation or conquest. This was the territory over which the Rathor rulers could claim their *watan* rights. Initially acquiring the rights to a few perquisites, the Rathor rulers gradually established *thakurai* over a number of villages. With the extension of the Rathor rule, the Rathor rulers adopted the system of *bhai-bant*, according to which all the territories conquered by them were parcelled out among the Rathor *sardars* mainly among the leaders of sub-clans (*khamps*) and their offshoots. Under this system the supreme authority was the ruler who was supposed to be the nearest legitimate descendant in the direct male line from the founder of the state. However, there was a rider attached to the rule of primogeniture: a minimum level of competence on the part of the ruler was required, in the absence of which, the *sardars* could assert their right of choosing another member of the same family. The land was, for the most part, divided among the *sardars* (leaders of the Rathor *khamps*) of the ruling clan and their right was hereditary. While they were politically and morally obliged to support the Raja in times of war, such political support could, in practice, be secured only when the Raja was strong enough to assert his authority. In such a decentralized political structure, the *sardars* often assumed independence as soon as there was a crisis at the centre, or when the Raja became so weak as to be unable to keep any check over them. Thus, in the beginning, the problems of power in Marwar state had a remarkable similarity with analogous problems of the early Turkish rulers of Delhi. When Rao Maldeo (A.D. 1532) ascended the throne, he could assert his claim only over two *parganas*—Jodhpur and Sojat. He challenged the concept of *bhai-bandh*, and put forward the alternative concept of *bhai-bandh-chakar*. Basically the latter concept implied the subordination of the Rathor *sardars* to the ruler. And, in order to enforce this concept, he began to dislodge those *sardars* who were reluctant to accept it. However, he could not bring about any fundamental change in the basic framework of the system of *bhai-bant* (distribution of land among the members of ruling clan). The new assignees enjoyed the same rights as were enjoyed by the dislodged *sardars*. By adopting this practice Maldeo in fact created a number of enemies within the Rathor nobility. This practice could not guarantee the loyalty of the new *sardars* as these newly created *sardars* belonged to the same ruling clan as Maldeo and thought of him as a brother clansman rather than a sovereign. The situation gave rise to strong internal rivalries and stresses which weakened the position of Maldeo and provided opportune moments to Sher Shah and later to Akbar in their struggle against Marwar. Under the system of *bhai-bant*, the Rathor *sardars* adopted the same administrative pattern, as adopted by the Raja, within their territories. Thus Maldeo was only partially successful in changing the early pattern of decentralised government.

Only after the Rathor rulers had accepted the suzerainty of the Mughal Emperor and enrolled themselves as imperial *mansabdars*, did the politico-administrative organization based on the concept of *bhai-bandh* change. Under the changed political equilibrium, the ruler, like other imperial *mansabdars*, had to fulfil definite obligations to the Mughal state. He had to maintain a fixed contingent according to the *mansab* he held. This required a drastic change in the system of *bhai-bant*, for it was extremely difficult for the Raja to maintain peace in his territory as well as the required quota of troops under the old system. Thus, during the time of Raja Sur Singh (A.D. 1595-1619) the old relationship based on the concept of *bhai-bandh* was replaced by a new relationship which was based upon a definite hierarchy. The Rathor *sardars* had to accept certain *pattas* (land revenue assignments). Since a *patta* (*chakari-ka-patta*) was granted in lieu of salary, the state had to determine in each case an area which would yield the revenue equivalent to the sanctioned salary. This made it necessary for the Rathor rulers to assess the land revenue of the entire area under their control. An assessment of the land revenue demand from each village was made separately and was known as *rekh.* The Rathor rulers did not make revenue assignments to the Rathor *sardars* on the basis of the *jama* of the Mughal court.

It has been shown that *rekh* represented an independent practice of assessment. The *rekh* assessment was made by the local chief (Raja) for the purpose of internal administration while the *jama* represented an assessment on the basis of which the Mughal court assigned *jagirs* such as that to the Rathor rulers in Marwar. Moreover, since *rekh* figures represented only the assessed land revenue demand (and did not include the revenue from agricultural and non-agricultural cesses), they were analogous to the *mal*, of the Mughal court rather than the *jama*. From the present study it emerges that there were considerable differences between *jama* and *rekh.* The proportion between *jama* and *rekh* was 3:7 in *pargana* Jodhpur, 2:2.7 in *pargana* Jaitaran, 3:6 in *pargana* Merta and 2:3 in *pargana* Sojat. A study of these figures and their comparison to the *hasil* figures reveal that the *rekh* figures were assessed on the high side and were different from the *jama* of the Mughal court. Although *rekh* was calculated separately for every village by the Raja or an autonomous chief of the area, we do not know if the calculation was made directly with the help of the peasants. Perhaps it may have been calculated through the agency of the local *zamindars* or the clan dominating the area or with their combined assistance.

The *pattadars* were obliged to render military service, and the number of the *sawar* and *paidal* to be maintained, was determined in relation to the amount of *rekh.* The military service was computed at the rate of one *sawar* for each thousand rupees of *rekh* and, one camel *sawar* and a *paidal* for each Rs. 700/- and Rs. 500/- of *rekh*, respectively. This rule was in the most part, strictly observed but could also be flexible. Sometimes for example, a grantee could be exempted from maintaining an animal contingent after payment of a particular amount as *peshkash*. This system of land revenue assignment was to some extent similar to the system prevailing in the Mughal State. Though the practice of granting *pattas* existed even prior to the Mughal intervention, the introduction of well defined obligations on the part of the *pattadars* was the result of the influence of the Mughal administration.

The above-mentioned *pattadari* system was followed during the reign of Maharaja Ajit Singh also. Although this system worked on the same pattern as earlier, a definite change in the system took place during the last decade of Maharaja Abhay Singh's reign. With the decline of the central power and the increasing inroads of the Marathas, the *jagirs* granted to him by the Mughal government outside Marwar were hardly of any significance, as the collection of revenue from such *jagirs* became uncertain. Therefore, the Rathor ruler started realizing a lump-sum amount from the *pattadars*. Although the rate of the amount to be realized during Abhay Singh's reign is not available, it seems that the amount was charged at the rate of Rs. 300/- for every Rs. 1000/- *rekh*, the rate which was regularized in 1755, six years after Abhay Singh's death. On account of the adoption of this practice, the character of the Marwar nobility changed completely. Under the changed situation, the *pattadars* started paying a fixed amount to the *durbar*, and thus assumed the status of *pesh-kashi zamindars*: their holdings or *pattas* became hereditary. Thus the *rekh* figures also changed in time basic characteristics. These changes in the basic character of the *pattadari* system took place in Marwar at a time when the *jagirdari* crisis reached its climax in the Mughal Empire. To some extent both the issues were related to the decline of power and position of the Mughal Emperors. Significantly, almost the same changes in the organization of the nobility have been observed in Mewar in the beginning of the 18th century. These changes in the character of the nobility later on confused the British historians who equated the system with European feudalism.

A study of the holdings of the Rathor sub-clans reveals that the Kumpawat Rathors in *pargana* Jodhpur, Udawat Rathors in *pargana* Jaitaran, Jaitawat Rathors in *pargana* Sojat, Patawat Rathors in *pargana* Phalodi, Mertia Rathors in *pargana* Merta, Narawat Rathors in *pargana* Pokaran, Balawat Rathors in *pargana* Siwana and Jodha Rathors in *pargana* Jalor had very large holdings. Apparently the Rathor *sardars* of one *khamp* could not possess the largest *pattas* simultaneouly in two *parganas* at a time. It was also in the interest of the state that a balance was maintained among the various clans of the Rathor nobility.

The Marwar nobility comprised both the Rathor and non-Rathor *sardars*. The ratio between the two was 50:1 during the time of Maharaja Jaswant Singh. Among the Rathor *sardars* the Jodhas, Mertias, Kumpawats and Udawats held the largest number of *pattas*. But these Rathor families (sub-clans) could not maintain the same position during the time of Maharaja Ajit Singh and Abhay Singh. The Champawat Rathors who constituted numerically the eighth largest group in the Marwar nobility during the time of Maharaja Jaswant Singh, held the largest number of *pattas* during Ajit Singh's reign. The situation further changed during the time of Maharaja Abhay Singh when the Mertia Rathors acquired the largest *pattas*. Thus, the Champawat Rathors, who had raised their status considerably during the period of instability, which they had managed to maintain during Ajit Singh's reign were reduced considerably in number and status during Maharaja Abhay Singh's reign. On the other hand the Mertia Rathors regained their former position during Maharaja Abhay Singh's reign. These changes in the composition of the Rathor nobility were the result of the politico-administrative problems that cropped up after the death of Maharaja Jaswant Singh. During the period of instability, the Champawats rose to the highest position due to the fact that after 1681, when Durgadas left Marwar for Deccan, they remained as the leaders of the Marwar *sardars*. And while the Champawats were active, the Jodhas, the

Mertias and the Kumpawats remained comparatively inactive, and most of them either agreed to pay a lump-sum amount to the imperial officers or remained neutral. Since the beginning of Maharaja Ajit Singh's occupation of Jodhpur, there was a constant opposition to the Champawats from the *sardars* of other Rathor sub-clans but their position remained unaffected due to the support given to them by the Maharaja. The opposition of the Marwar *sardars* to the Champawats provided the Mertia Rathors an opportunity to acquire the highest position of power in the Rathor nobility.

Although the *pattas* held by the non-Rathor *sardars* were comparatively few, they held a commanding position in the administration of the state. Among the non-Rathor *sardars*, the Bhatis, Chauhans and Kachhawahs held the largest number of the *pattas*. The Bhatis and the Chauhans maintained their position in state administration even during the reign of Ajit Singh and Abhay Singh. The number of *pattas* held by the Gahlots, Parihars, Muhtas, Musalman, etc., was negligible.

Beside the *pattas* assigned in lieu of services, the state also granted *thikanas* or *bhoms* to the nobles. Such grants were given as *mund katai*, i.e., compensation for the losses sustained in war or as a reward for meritorious services. These were revenue-free holdings but the grantees paid a quit-rent known as *bhugat-bhog* or *bhom-bab*. There is no doubt that these grants in general were enjoyed by those who held the *chakari-ka-patta*. This practice also served the purpose of extending the area under cultivation, as in most of the cases, the grantee had to live in the area under him and invite cultivators for farming the waste land.

The present study further reveals that even after their accepting the suzerainty of the Mughal Emperor, the Rathor rulers continued to recognize the tradition of the *Bhomi-chara-ra-gaon*, i.e., the villages which had been inhabited and held by the dislodged ruling families or those which had been established by the Rathor princes and continued to be in possession of their descendants. It has been observed that a *bhom* or *thikana* generally included a village (sometimes a part of a village in case of *bhom* grant) or villages. Thus, the *bhom* or *thikana* signified a right which belonged to a rural class other than, and standing above, the peasantry. In villages where the peasants belonged to the family of the same clan which held these rights, they enjoyed the *khud-kasht* rights. In those areas where the peasants had been engaged in cultivation before the establishment of a *bhom* or *thikana*, they rarely interfered with peasants' holdings. Under these circumstances the proprietary rights of the *bhomias* or *thikanadars* and peasants were inter-related.

A study of the *thikanas* held during Maharaja Jaswant Singh's reign shows that the number of such grants was quite negligible in comparison to that of the *chakari-ka-pattas*, the latter being eleven times more than the former. Although within the Marwar nobility, the number of the Rathor *Sardars* was comparatively larger, the administration was dominated by the non-Rathor *sardars*. Significantly, while the office of the *pradhan* of the state and the *hakim* of the *parganas* remained in the hands of the Rathors and non-Rathor *sardars*, the office of the *diwans* always remained with the non-Rathor *sardars*, particularly those who belonged to the *vaishya* community. This was a part of the state policy according to which both the offices of the *pradhan* and the *diwan* were not kept in the hands of Rathor *sardars*. It has been noted that the offices of *desh-diwan*, *tan-diwan* and the *hakim* of the *parganas* remained mostly with Bhandaris during Maharaja Ajit Singh's reign. The significant feature of the offices of *des-diwan* and *tan-diwan* was that the appointees used to pay a lump-sum amount to the state as *peshkash*. In most cases they were fined and were imprisoned if they failed to deposit the money demanded by the state. This shows that as the departments of the *desh-diwan* and *tan-diwan* managed the finances of the state, the officers in charge of these offices were held personally responsible if the realization was low; they thus were held guilty for corruption or mismanagement. The overwhelming power enjoyed by these officers created dissatisfaction among the Rathor *sardars*. During Maharaja Abhay Singh's reign the Rathor *sardars* showed their dissatisfaction by supporting the rebellion of Rai Singh and Anand Singh, the brothers of Abhay Singh. Although Abhay Singh removed the Bhandaris from their offices to satisfy the Rathor *sardars*, he did not keep them out of the administration for a long time.

He did not throw the Bhandaris out of administration because unlike the Rathor *sardars* they were completely dependent upon the good-will of the Maharaja.

It has been noticed that at the time of Maharaja Jaswant Singh's succession, a definite administrative pattern had already been evolved. This was the result of the administrative reforms introduced during the time of Maharaja Sur Singh who followed the Mughal pattern of administration. Significantly, the *pargana* administration was put under the charge of a *hakim*, who combined the function of the *faujdar* and the *amil* of the imperial territory. Under Maharaja Jaswant Singh, the functions of the various state officials remained the same, but the office of the *diwan* was divided into two, viz., *desh-diwan* and *tan-diwan*. No change was observed in the functions of the various officials during the reign of Maharaja Ajit Singh and Abhay Singh, although a constant attempt was made to check the various irregularities in the field of revenue administration.

A study of the nature and the magnitude of the state's land revenue demand shows that the rates of *bhog* (*mal*) and *kharach-bhog* (*mal-o-jihat*) varied from *pargana* to *pargana*. Different rates were fixed for *kharif* and *rabi* crops which varied from 50 per cent to 33 per cent of the produce. This was slightly different from the general formula according to which the land revenue demand varied from 40 per cent to 33 per cent. As the *zabt* was adopted mostly in the case of cash crops and in some areas for wheat also, the *batai* system was the widely accepted mode of assessment for the cereal crops. In the areas where the state share was 50 per cent of the produce, the rate of *kharach-bhog* was reduced from 18.75 per cent to 4 per cent of the *bhog*; but in the areas where the state demand was 25 per cent, the rate of *kharach-bhog* remained at 18.75 per cent of the *bhog*. These rates were revised during the time of Maharaja Jaswant Singh and later on continued during the reigns of Ajit Singh and Abhay Singh. During this period (the period of Jaswant Singh and his two successors) attempts were made to check the irregular practices of the officials engaged in the collection of land revenue.

During the occupation of Marwar by Akbar, especially after the grant of Jodhpur to Mota Raja Udai Singh in A.D. 1583, the Rathor rulers of Marwar entered a new phase. Being imperial *mansabdars*, they were assigned *jagirs* in Marwar in lieu of the salary they claimed against their *mansabs*. Thus the *jagirs* granted to them was treated as *tankhwah-jagir*. Since the revenue of their *watan jagir* was not sufficient to meet the claim of their salary, they were granted *jagirs* outside Marwar. This provided extra financial resources to the rulers.

By virtue of being the *tikayat* to the *gaddi*, the Rathor rulers always held Jodhpur in their *jagir*, but in practice the ruler was never granted all the *tappas* or the *parganas* of Jodhpur. Although it was not obligatory on the part of the Mughal Emperor to assign all the *parganas* of Marwar to the ruler of Jodhpur, a favourable attitude was adopted towards him by granting to him his ancestral territory. In fact, the assignment of the *jagirs* in Marwar to the rulers of Jodhpur was for the benefit of both the parties, though the Emperor used to keep some territory under *khalisa* with a view to maintaining a check on the Rathor ruler. The Mughal Emperor could grant the Rathor ruler *jagirs* outside Marwar even before he had granted him all the *parganas* within Marwar.

By adopting such a practice, the Mughal Emperor wanted to keep the rulers of Marwar aware of their subordinate position. It is worth noting that the *jagirs* granted outside Marwar were purely of a temporary nature. But the *jagirs* granted within Marwar remained with Rathor ruler till his death and the resumption of any of them was treated as a punishment. At the same time continuous efforts were made by the Raja to regain his control over all the *parganas* of Marwar.

The Mughal Emperor assigned *jagirs* in Marwar on the basis of *jama* figures recorded at the court. The *jama* figures when studied in relation to the *hasil* show that Jaswant Singh enjoyed the *jagirs* for almost twelve months in his territories. In some of the cases the *hasil* was even higher than the *jama* figures. The advantageous position enjoyed by Maharaja Jaswant Singh was on account of the fact that the *jama* figures (on the basis of which the *jagir* in Marwar was assigned) had remained static since the time of Akbar. But the *jama* figures had increased considerably in the imperial territory since the time of Akbar.

In this situation, although the Rathor rulers enjoyed the *jagir* according to the old *jama* figures, they adopted a separate arrangement for internal administration. The ruler did not assign the *pattas* to the *sardars* on the basis of the *jama* figures. He made his own assessment which was considerably higher than the *jama* figures of the Mughal court. The assignment of the *pattas* on the basis of *rekh* figures implied that the *pattadars* were given the *jagir* for six to seven months. The practice adopted by the Rathor ruler was similar to that adopted by the Mughal Emperor in the imperial territory.

Besides enjoying the right of internal assessment, the Rathor rulers fixed the rates of the agricultural and non-agricultural cesses also. Thus they enjoyed internal autonomy in their *watan-jagir*, although in case of any irregular demand made by the Raja, the cultivators could invite imperial interference.

The important feature of the Mughal-Marwar relations was the political stability which prevailed in Marwar till the time of Jaswant Singh. The *mansab* and the *jagir* held by Jaswant Singh make it clear that after the death of Mirza Raja Jai Singh, he enjoyed the highest position at the court among the Rajput Rajas during Aurangzeb's reign. His control over the territory of Marwar was also extended during this period. The revenue of the *jagir* which he was assigned at Shahjahan's reign was 6.30 crores of *dams* which rose to 7.17 crores of *dams* during Aurangzeb's reign. This was apparently the result of the favours shown to Jawant Singh by Aurangzeb.

As the Mughal Emperor determined the territory enjoyed by each Rajput ruler, inter-state disputes were considerably reduced. This situation could be maintained so long as the Mughal Emperor was powerful enough to punish a Rajput ruler in case of any impertinence on his part. After the death of Aurangzeb the political weakness of the court created instability among the Rajput states. The period of Ajit Singh and Abhay Singh witnessed some important changes in the external politics of Marwar. Repeated violations of imperial orders became a general practice. The co-operation among the Rajput Rajas was mainly motivated by their personal interests. As soon as one achieved his target, he withdrew his support to the cause of the other Rajput ruler. This created suspicion among the Rajput rulers against each other and pushed them into internal feuds. The Mughal Emperor failed to maintain any check over the activities of these Rajput rulers due to the intrigues at the Mughal court.

GLOSSARY

Abwab	*Abwab* is plural of *bab*: the casses imposed by the Government in addition to the regular assessment of the land. Miscellaneous cesses, imports and charges levied by *zamindars* and the government officers.
Amal-dastur	Rules and regulations which came into effect with the accession of a ruler.
Amil	Under Akbar *amil* was the head of the entire *pargana's* revenue administration.
Amin	Revenue Officer appointed to take charge of *pargana* to exercise some supervisory authority over the *pargana* officers. He was also entrusted with the work of assessing the *Jama*.
Asami	In the Rajasthani literature of the 17th and 18th centuries the term *asami* implied the revenue payers as

	well as, in general, subordinates to the officer or officers. It also used to indicate the name of places and persons.
Bakhshi	A military officer-in-charge for payments of salaries or an officer who kept an account of all disbursements connected with military tenures.
Bandobast	Settlement of revenue to be paid by the *zamindars* to the government.
Barawurdi	In the present work, the term *barawurdi* has been used for the *sawars* or a *sawar*, i.e., *yak-aspa*. Muhnot Nainsi has used it in this sense.
Batai	Crop-sharing (in Persian *ghalla-bakhshi*). In Marwar two types of crop-sharing were in prevalence. (a) *Lata*—The crop was guarded till it was carried to and thrashed out in the barn. Division of actual produce on the thrashing floor, is known as *lata*. (b) *Kunta*—It is a probable estimate of the standing crop. From this estimated gross yield, the state share is worked out and converted into cash by applying current price.
Basi	Residence of the *thikanadar* or the place where he kept his family.
Bigha	Measure of land varying in extent in different parts of India. A standard *bigha* is equal to 3025 sq. yds. or 5/8th of an acre.
Biswa	Twentieth part of a *bigha*.
Dam	A copper coin. In the days of Akbar a rupee could be divided into 40 *dams*. During the period of Aurangzeb, the theoretical value of *dam* was put at 1/60 of a rupee. However, the market rate of the *dam* was the basis for

	making payments in the market by the treasury officials.
Darobast	Assignment of the entire *pargana* in *patta* or *jagir*.
Dastur-ul-amal	Compilation of the old rules and regulations which were approved by the ruler. These were the guidelines for the state officials according to which the work was done.
Diwan	Under the Rathor rule (during the Mughal period) the title was especially applied to the incharge of the finance department of the state.
Dogani	A copper coin. 40 *dogani* was equivalent to a rupee during the 17th century Marwar.
Faujdar	He was an officer under the Mughals who was invested with the charge of the police and had jurisdiction on all criminal matters.
Gaddi	Throne.
Pirozi	A small coin prevalent during the Mughal period in Rajasthan.
Gughari	A tax collected to meet the expenses of the army.
Hakim	In-charge of the *pargana* who looked after the military and civil administration of the area under his control.
Hasbul-Hukm	A document issued on behalf of the royal authority by the *wazir*, *diwan* or other high officers of the government.
Hasil	Actual realization: the amount derived by the government or on its behalf as a share of the produce of the soil and from any other source of taxation or import.
Haweli	The tract of country adjacent to a capital town which was held in *khalisa*.

Ijara — A farm or lease of revenue of a village or *pargana* or *mahal*: also used for customs or collection of any other description.

Izafa — Any increase in the amount of revenue received from the court or increase in *mansab* or *patta*.

Jagir — A tenure common under the Mughal government in which the public revenue of a given tract of land were made over to a servant (*mansabdar*) of the state together with the powers required to enable him to collect and appropriate such revenue, and administer the general government of the assigned territory. The assignment could be conditional or unconditional.

Jihat — Cesses collected to meet the expenses incurred on the assessment of *mal*.

Jama — The state land revenue demand. It includes the assessment made under the three heads, namely *mal*, *jihat* and *sair-jihat*.

Jital — 1/25 of a *dam*.

Karori — Official designation of a collector of the revenue to the extent of a *karor* of *dams* (Rs. 2,50,000). He also at various times invested with the general superintendence of the lands in his *pargana*, and the charge of the police.

Khalisa — The term applied to lands of which the revenue remained the property of the state; land or villages controlled directly by the state.

Khyat — Compilation of the accounts of the glorious deeds of the rulers and other historical events.

Kurab — An honour showed by the ruler according to the rank and status of the nobles in his court (*diwan-i-am*).

Lag — Customary cesses paid by the cultivators to the revenue officials.

Mal — The revenue claimed by the Government from the produce of cultivated lands.

Mansab — Office, a military title and rank conferred by the Mughal Government. Also, the supposed number of *sawars*, which the holder of the title could, if so demanded by the imperial officers bring into battlefield or during peace time for inspection and verification. The holder was also paid for the maintenance of *zat*. The *zat* rank, besides indicating the salary according to the pay scale in force, determined the personal status of the holder in the official hierarchy.

Mapa-dan — The tax levied on goods imported and exported. The term *mapa* was often employed as a generic term for various taxes imposed on sales. The *dam* was in fact the same as *mapa* but was calculated *ad valorem*.

Pargana — Sub-division of a *sarkar*: a tract of country consisting of many *tappas* or villages.

Patta — A deed or lease. A document issued by the ruler to the *sardar* or *zamindar* specifying the terms and conditions on which the lands were held and the value or the proportion of the produce which they were entitled to realize from the cultivators. Villages which were thus granted were called *Patta* villages. The assignment was either conditional or unconditional. In the former case some public services and maintenance of troops or other specified duty was called for: in the latter it was left entirely at the disposal of the grantee. The assignment was either for a fixed term, or more usually for the lifetime of the holder lapsing on his death to the *khalisa.* A *Patta* was also liable to forfeiture on failure of performance of the conditions on which it was granted, or on the holder's incurring the displeasure of the ruler.

Patti — A land revenue unit of the village.

Peshkash — Offering or tribute paid to a superior or the government. The payment of the *peshkash* was a mark of subordination to the superior.

Piyal — Land under irrigation.

Rahdari — (*Margvahin*); a levy on the goods passing from one political jurisdiction to another. It was essentially a sovereign tax. No *thikanadar* or *pattadar* could enjoy *rahdari* rights unless such rights have been conferred on him by the state.

Rekh — Assessed land revenue of a particular tract of land.

Sair-jihat — Cesses which were collected over and above *mal-o-jihat*. *Sair Jihat* included both agricultural and non-agricultural cesses.

Sardar — A Chief of the territory or one who held *patta* in lieu of military service to the ruler.

Sasan — Revenue grant given for religious purposes.

Sewej — Land flooded with water during rainy season and later used for cultivating *rabi* crops.

Siropao — A special honour showed by the ruler by presenting robe of honour.

Talab — Demand or claim: the salary claim: the salary claim of the *mansabdar* against one's *mansab*. In the *vigat* the term *talab* has been used for the *baqaya*, the balance to be paid to the *mansabdar* after assigning the *jagir*.

Tappa — Sub-division of a *pargana*: a small tract or a sub-division of a country, smaller than a *pargana* but comprising one or more villages.

Thakurai — *Thakurai* is an *abstract* noun of *Thakur*. In Medieval Rajasthan this term has been used for sovereign as well as for intermediaries. The latter enjoyed the hereditary rights over the area held by them.

Tika — Anointing ceremony.

Tikayat — The person entitled for the *tika*, the successor.

Umara — Plural of *amir*: the collective name of the top-most officers at a Muslim court, especially that of the great Mughals.

Vamshavali — Chronology of rulers. Some *vamshavalis* also discuss the deeds, in detail or in brief, of the rulers.

Varta — (Perhaps related to sanskrit *vritta*). Compilation of happenings during the reign of any individual ruler.

Vigat — Description of political and other aspects pertaining to the past.

Watan — Hereditary land or area held by the

	ruling clan families: also place of residence.
Zabt	Method of assessing state land revenue demand in cash on the basis of measurement of land.

BIBLIOGRAPHY

I—Contemporary Archival Records (in Rajasthan)

The contemporary Rajasthani records of the erstwhile states of Jaipur and Jodhpur available at the Rajasthan State Archives, Bikaner are valuable sources of information on the polity of Marwar during the period of the present study.

(*a*) *Jaipur Records*

It contains letters and copies of letters written in Rajasthanī and are in manuscript form. The informations available in the *Vakil Reports, Khutut-i-Maharajgan, Khutut-i-Ahalkaran, Kharitas*, draft *Kharitas and Parwanas, Waqai, Amber records* have been used. Although these records are mainly related with the erstwhile state of Amber, they are very useful for studying the various political aspects of other states also. *Vakil Reports Maharajgan* (A.D. 1656-1723) are an important source of information for the period of Maharaja Jaswant Singh and Ajit Singh of Jodhpur. These are the reports sent by the *Vakils* of the rulers of Amber (Jaipur) posted at the Mughal court. They inform us about the political atmosphere at the Mughal court, attempts of the Rajput Rajas to obtain honour, increments in *mansab* and *jagir*, the attitude of the Emperor, *wazir* and other imperial officials towards the rulers of the Amber and other Rujput states. These reports also provide additional information useful for understanding the inter-state relations and the attitude of the Rajput Rajas towards the Mughal Emperors during the period A.D. 1708-1720.

Khutut-i-Maharajgan (A.D. 1644-1737) are the letters written by the various officials to the rulers of Amber (Jaipur). The letters written between A.D. 1707 to 1737 have been very useful as they throw light on the inter-state disputes and the policy of the Rajput rulers towards each other.

Khutut-i-Ahalkaran (A.D. 1633-1768) are the letters exchanged between various officials. These letters contain detailed information about the political condition of the place where they were posted. The information given in these letters enable us to examine the political atmosphere of Rajasthan prevailing during the period covered by the present study.

Draft Kharitas aud Parwanas (A.D. 1662 onwards)—These are the copies of the letters sent to the various Rajput rulers by the rulers of Amber (Jaipur). The information available in these *Kharitas* has been used to understand and evaluate the inter-state relations and the nature of internal crisis in Marwar during the reign of Maharajas Ajit Singh and Abhay Singh.

Waqai Reports (A.D. 1733-1918)—It is a record of the personal and official activities of the rulers and contains information about the movements of the rulers of Amber, their meetings with other Rajas and dignitaries, the places of encampment and brief account of the battles and conquests. The *Waqai* reports have been very useful in informing us about the policy of Jai Singh and Ajit Singh towards the Saiyid brothers and other Mughal nobles.

Amber Records (A.D. 1660 onwards)—It is a collection of miscellaneous letters containing *Kharitas, draft Kharitas, Arzdasht*, etc. The information available in these letters has been very useful in understanding the politics of Rathor Durgadas during A.D. 1692-1947 and Ajit Singh's activities after the battle of Sambhar. Further, these letters throw a flood of light on the attitude of the various Kachhawah *sardars* towards the political activities in Rajasthan and their relations with the Rathor *sardars* and the Rathor rulers.

(*b*) *Jodhpur Records*

Although the documents available in the section of *Jodhpur Records* are less in number in comparison with the *Jaipur Records*, they are very useful for understanding the polity of Marwar during the period under study. The most important for the present study are *Patta-bahis* (A.D. 1707-1939), *Kharita bahis* (1730-1940 A.D.), *Khas Ruqqa-Parwana Bahi* (A.D. 1665-1888), *Pardhangiri files* (A.D. 1708-1912), *Files of Dholia ka Kothar* (A.D. 1708-1912), *Byav-bahis* (A.D. 1729-1865) and *Oadha-Bahis* (A.D. 1709-1919).

The documents available in these records though are not many in number related with the period under study, yet the information gathered through these documents helps us in examining the nature of the relationship between the Rathor rulers and the *sardars*, policy of the Rathor rulers towards the Mughal court, and the administrative arrangements in the state.

Bastas (*Jodhpur Records*)

There are 104 *bastas* contained original and copies of the *bahis*, *Khyats*, documents, letters and registers. The collection of this material was made by the enquiry commissions appointed to make enquiries about the rights and obligations of the *sardars*, *thikanadars* and *bhomias*, boundary disputes, nature of state dues, etc. A significant feature of this collection is that it possesses the copies of the *Chakari-ka-pattas*, *Gair-chakari-ka-pattas* and also the letters which throw light on the interests of the *pattadars* of the state. These provide valuable information about various aspects of state administration and Marwar nobility of the period under study.

Among the *Khyats*, which are available in the *Bastas* the *Mundiara thikana ri Khyat* (Basta No. 5), *Khamp Mertia ri Khyat* (Basta No. 101), *Ajit Singhji ri Khayt* (Basta No. 40), *Sindhi Priyagdas ri Khyat* (Basta No. 5), *Maharaja Jaswant Singh ri Khyat* (Basta No. 10), *Champawata ri Khyat* (Basta No. 101), *Kumpawata ri Khyat* (Basta No. 101), are worth-mentioning. Although most of these *Khyats* were written during the latter half of the 19th century, they provide useful information about the various *Khamps* (sub-clans) of the Rathors and evolution of the various *thikanas* held by the Rathor and non-Rathor *sardars*. The transcript copies of some of these *Khyats* are available in the personal library of Dr. Satish Chandra, Professor of History, Jawahar Lal Nehru University, New Delhi.

Jodhpur Administration

1. *Lag-bag enquiry Reports* (A.D. 1813).
2. *Lag-bag* file No. 202.

(*c*) *Kavi Shyamaldas Collection*

(Rajasthan State Archives, *Bikaner*).

It contains the copies of the letters which were under the possession of Shyamaldas, the author of the *Vir Vinod*. Apart from the copies of the letters given in *Vir Vinod* there are many others which provide additional information regarding the political developments of the period under study. For example, the copies of the letters that were exchanged between Durgadas Rathor and the *diwan* of Marwar are very significant.

(*d*) *Private Collections*

Apart from the documents available in the State Archives, Bikaner, the records available in the personal collections of the *thakur* of Diggi (Diggi House Collection) and the *diwan* of Bilada (Bilada Archives) have been used in this study.

The *thakur* of Diggi belonged to the Kangarot family of the Kachhawah clan. Some of the letters procured from this collection are of great historical significance as they provide important information on the role of Durgadas Rathor in the politics of Marwar during A.D. 1690-97.

The *Bilada Archives* contain the letters (original copies in MS form) written by the Rulers of Jodhpur to the *thikanadars* of Bilada. As the *thikanadars* of Bilada were in the confidence of the Rathor rulers and held the office of the *qanungo* and enjoyed some other political appointment also, the letters available in this collection furnish important information about the administrative arrangements in the Marwar state. The copies of some of the letters are also available in the State Archives, Bikaner.

II—Rajasthani and Samskrit Chronicles (MSS) (*Khyats, Bats, Bahis, Vamshavalis*, **etc.**)

(*a*) *Oriental Research Institute, Jodhpur* (ORIJ)

1. *Maharaja Jaswant Singhji-ri-Varta* (S. No. 3546) contains 10 ancedotes of the time of Maharaja Jaswant Singh.
2. *Achaldas Khichi-ri-Varta* (S. No. 3362); written during the latter half of the 17th century provides valuable informations on the socio-political aspects of the period.
3. *Maharaja Ajit Singh-ri-Khyat* (S. No. 15663, 15664, 15665). It is in three volumes. This was written about the middle of the 18th century and contains a detailed account of the time of Maharaja Ajit Singh. Apart from the political accounts, it also containts information about various aspects of the soico-administrative institutions of Marwar.
4. *Sawai Jai Singh-ri-Jodhpur-per-Chadhai* (S. No. 4287) is a very important manuscript containing the details of the campaign of Jai Singh against Maharaja Abhay Singh in A.D. 1740.
5. *Merta-adi-ki-Aitihasik Haqiqat* (S. No. 3550). It contains the geographical account of the *pargana* of Merta.
6. *Rathora-ri-Vamshavali* (S. No. 20130) was written about the middle of the 19th century. It has 500 pages in the form of *Bahi*. It begins with the origin of the Rathor dynasty and ends with the account of Maharaja Man Singh of Jodhpur. A study of this *Vamshavali* suggests that this might have served as the basis of the *Jodhpur Rajya-ki-Khyat*. Apart from the account of the political events, we also get detailed lists of the *mansabs* and *jagirs* held by the Rathor rulers and the account of the administrative arrangements made by the Rathor rulers from Udai Singh to Abhay Singh. This furnishes some of the important aspects of the politico-administrative organization of the period under review. A transcript copy of this *Vamshavali* is available in Professor Satish Chandra's library.
7. *Mundiyara-Thikana-ri-Khyat* (S. No. 34547) was written at

the end of the 18th century. It contains a detailed description of the political events till the end of the 18th century of Marwar.

8. *Rajkia hisab-ri-Khyat* (S. No. 2832) records a detailed account of the income and expenditure of the reign of Maharaja Man Singh (1803-1843 A.D.). It is useful in forming an idea of the various items of income and expenditure of the state.

(b) *Shodha Samsthan, Chaupasani, Jodhpur* (JSS)

1. *Kumpawata-ri-Khyat* (MS No. 182) gives an account of the history of the Kumpawat Rathors. It was written at the end of the 19th century.
2. *Rathora-ri-Khampha-ri-Vigat* (MS No. 988) is a useful work written towards the end of the 19th century. It gives a detailed account of the origin and evolution of the various Rathor sub-clans.
3. *Jodhpur-Vamshavali* (MS No. 500) contains a brief but systematic account of the Rathor rulers till the time of Maharaja Man Singh.
4. *Khyat Maharaja Abhay Singh-ri* (MS No. 213) was written in 1858 A.D. It is a short political history of the reign of Maharaja Abhay Singh.
5. *Rathora-ka-Itihas* (MS No. 1005) is a short history of the Rathors of Jodhpur written about the middle of the 19th century.
6. *Vividh-Rajya-Vamsha-ri-Khyat* (MS No. 1125) contains the account of the Rajput ruling families of Rajasthan. It furnishes information regarding the role of the nobility in the politics of Marwar.
7. *Reet Bahi* (MS No. 1725) record information on marriages and other social customs and traditions of the ruling family of Jodhpur. This was compiled about the middle of the 19th century.

(c) *Pustak Prakash, Ummed Palace Library, Jodhpur*

1. *Nainsi Maheta-ri-Hundi* (MS No. 1143) by Ratandas is an

account of the life of Muhnot Nainsi, the *das-diwan* of Maharaja Jaswant Singh.

2. *Ajitodaya* (Samskrit MS No. 1122) written by Jag Jiwan Bhatt, the priest of Maharaja Ajit Singh furnishes valuable information on the role of the Marwar nobility during the period of instability (1678-1707) and the period of Ajit Singh's reign (1708-24), internal politics of Marwar and Marwar's relations with Marwar, Jaipur, Kota, Sirohi and other states. A transcript of the work is in the personal collection of Professor Satish Chandra.
3. *Ajit-granth* (Samskrit MS No. 15). It traces the history of Marwar ruler upto the year A.D. 1969. It is an important source of information about the activities of the Rathor *sardars* between A.D. 1680 to 1700.
4. *Adhyodaya* (Samskrit MS No. 51) by Bhatt Jagjiwan. The work is on the same pattern as *Ajitodaya.* It gives a detailed account of the political activities of Abhay Singh period.
5. *Pali Hukumat-ri-Bahi* (MS No. 1506) contains an account of the administration of *pargana* Pali during the first half of the 19th century.

(*d*) *Anup Sanskrit Library, Bikaner*

1. *Arya-khyankalpdrum* (MS No. 180) by Sindaicha Dayaldas is a valuable account of the first half of the 19th century of Marwar. The account can be divided into three parts: (a) a short historical description of the Rathor rulers of Jodhpur, (b) a description of the *pattas* of the *sardars* of Marwar, according to their *Khafs*, (c) a description of the various *thikanas* of Marwar. Although it is not a contemporary account, it gives a clear picture of the holdings of the various Rathor *sardars* which enables us to determine the nature of the *pattas* held at the time of Maharaja Abhay Singh's death.
2. *Bikaner-ke-Rathoro-ki-Khyat* (MS No. 188) by Dayaldas contains a detailed history of the rulers of Bikaner. Part second of this work has been edited by Dr. Dasharatha Sharma.
3. *Marwar-ki-Khyat* or *Jodhpur Rajya-ki-Khyat* (MS No. 199)

is a detailed political history of the rulers of Marwar from Rao Siha to the end of the 19th century. Its different parts were written at different time by different persons and were later on compiled at one place at the end of the 19th century. The transcribed copies of this *Khyat* are available at the Rajasthani Shodha Samsthan, Chaupasani and the Raghubir Library, Sitamau.

(*e*) *Raghubir Library, Sitamau*

Kaviraj Khyat (MS in two volumes) was written during the last decade of Jaswant Singh's reign. This is in the form of a transcribed copy and contains the account from the early settlements of the Rathors in Marwar to the reign of Jaswant Sidgh.

(*f*) *Private Collection of the Thakur of Khivsar*

Hukumat Bahi (transcript in the possession of Thakur Kesri Singh of Khivsar) is the most valuable manuscript compiled in the beginning of the Marwar war (1678). Apart from the description of some of the political events of the time of Jaswant Singh and the period following his death, it contains a list of the *sardars* who held *pattas.* This is the only account available which provides significant information on the events of the Marwar war. This work is equally important for an understanding of the *pattadari* system.

(*g*) *Shri Bhupal Library, Udaipur*

Raj Vilas by Man Kavi (MS) was composed during the reign of Maharana Raj Singh. It gives information about the Rathor-Sisodia alliance in the beginning of the Marwar war.

III—Contemporary and Non-Contemporary Published Rajasthani Khyat Literature

1. *Achaldas Khichi-ri-Varta*, Bikaner, 1966.

2. *Bankidas-ri-Khyat*, Jaipur, 1956.
3. *Dalpat Vilas*, Ed. Dr. Dasharatha Sharma, Bikaner, 1965.
4. *Dayaldas-ri-Khyat* by Dayaldas, Ed. Dr. Dasharatha Sharma, Bikaner, 1952.
5. *Gajgunrupakgranth*, Jodhpur.
6. *Hukumat-ri-Bahi*, Meerut, 1976
7. *Marwar-ra-Pargana-ri-Vigat* by Muhnot Nainsi, Ed. by Narain Singh Bhàti, Vols. I-II, III, Jodhpur, 1968-69, 1974.
8. *Nainsi-ri-Khyat*, I-III, Jodhpur, 1962.
9. *Rajrupak*, Ed. Ramkaran Asopa, Banaras, V.S. 1968.
10. *Vachanika, Ratan Singhji-ri*, Delhi, V.S. 2017.

IV—Contemporary Marathi Sources

Selections from Peshwa Daftar, Ed. by G.S. Sardesai, Vol. ii, x, xii, xiii, xv, xxi, xxii (1930-35).

Expansion of the Maratha Power, (Selection from Peshwa Daftar, New Series), Ed. by V.V. Joshi, Vol. I.

Marathi Itihasanche Sadhane, Ed. by Rajwade, Vols. II, III, IV and VI only.

Aitihasik Patra Vyavahar, Ed. by G.S. Sardesai.

Brahmendra Swamichan Charitra, Ed. by Parasnis.

Hingane Dafter (Vol. I), Ed. by G.S. Sardesai,

V—Contemporary Persian Work

A—Chronicles

Abul Fazl, *Akbarnama*, Bib. Ind. Vols. I-III, Calcutta, 1873-87.

———, *Ain-i-Akbari*, Nawal Kishore Ed. 1882. Also tr. of Blochmann (i) and Jarrett (ii and iii); revised, Sarkar, Vols. II and III, Calcutta, 1949.

Abdul Qadir Badayuni, *Muntakhab-ut-Tawarikh*, Ed. Ahmad Ali and Lees; Bib. Ind., Calcutta, 1865, 68.

Jahangir, *Tuzuk-i-Jahangiri*, Ed. Saiyid Ahmad Khan, Ghazipur, and Aligarh, 1863, 64.

Abdul Hamid Lahori, *Badshahnama*, Ed. Maulvi Kabiruddin and Maulvi Abdur Rahim, Bib. Ind. Calcutta, 1867-68.

Amin Qazwini, *Padshahnama*, Transcript copy, Raghubir Library, Sitamau.

Muhammad Salih Kambu, *Amal-i-Salih*, Ed. G. Yazdani, Bib. Ind. Calcutta, 1923, 1946.

Muhammad Kazim, *Alamgir Nama*, Bib. Ind. Calcutta, 1865, 73.

Isar Das Nagar, *Futuhat-i-Alamgiri*, MS, Transcript Copy, Raghubir Library, Sitamau.

Bhimsen, *Nuskha-i-Dilkusha*, MS. Transcript Copy. Raghubir Library, Sitamau.

Saqi Mustaid Khan, *Massir-i-Alamgiri*, Bib. Ind. Calcutta, 1871.

Muhammad Hashim titled as Khafi Khan *Muntakhab-ul-Lubab*, Vol II, Bib. Ind. Calcutta, 1874.

Ali Muhammad Khan, *Mirat-i-Ahmadi*, Ed. Saiyid Nawab Ali, Baroda, 1927-28.

Shah Nawaz Khan, *Maasir-ul-Umara*, Ed. Molvi Abdur Rahim, Bib. Ind. Vols. I-III, 1888.

Nimat Khan-i-Ali, *Bahadur Shah Nama* (MS), Raza library, Rampur.

Qasim Lahori, *Ibrat Nama* (MS), Transcript Copy, Raghubir Library, Sitamau.

Kamraj, *Ibrat Nama* (MS), Transcript Copy, Raghubir Library, Sitamau.

Khush-hal Rai, *Nadir-uz-Zamani* (MS), Khalsa College, Amritsar.

Yahya Khan, *Tazkirat-ul-Muluk* (MS), Transcript Copy, Raghubir Library, Sitamau.

Muhammad Bakhsh 'Ashub', *Tarikh-i-Shahadat-i-Farrukh Siyar wa Julus-i-Muhammad Shahi*, Sarkar's Collection, Calcutta.

Mahta Balmukund, *Balmukund Nama*, Ed. Dr. Satish Chandra, English translation with Introduction and notes, Bombay, 1972.

VI--Contemporary Official Records of the Mughal Court

1. The *Akhbarat* or news latters or (Court Bulletins): They are the minutes of the proceedings of the court transmitted to the Maharaja of Jaipur through messengers by their agents residing at Aurangzeb's court. They are at present well preserved state in the Rajasthan State Archives

office, in a Bikaner. They are in the form of sheets bearing news of each day on a separate sheet with the heading *Akhbarat-i-Darbar-i-Muala*.

2. Official correspondence: it includes letters, diaries and *farmans*. We have several such collections—mostly in MSS preserved at various places in India :

   (a) The *Kalimat-i-Aurangzeb* (MS, in the Raza Library, Rampur) completed by Inayatullah and contains notes of Aurangzeb written to 31 persons mostly about public affairs. It contains a letter of Aurangzeb to Prince Akbar blaming him for trusting the Rajputs.
   (b) The *Ahkam-i-Alamgiri* of Inayatullah; course 610 MS pages (Sitamau).
   (c) The *Abad-i-Alamgiri* edited by Sadiq Mutallib (MS). It contains letters of Aurangzeb and his son Prince Akbar compiled during the reign of Aurangzeb.
   (d) *Waqai-Sarkar Ajmer wa Ranthambor* (MS). Transcribed copy in Asifiya Library, Hyderabad, Sitamau Collection and also in the Department of History Library, Aligarh Muslim University, Aligrah.

3. *Vakil Reports* (Jaipur Records, MS. Sarkar) of the former Jaipur State; records are available for the latter half of Maharaja Ajit Singh's reign.
4. *Farmans* and *Nishans* (MSS. R.S.A,B.) *Farmans* of the Mughal Experors, mainly Shahjahan and Aurangzeb addressed to Mirza Raja Jai Singh during the war of succession and after *nishans* of Mughal princes addressed to Mirza Raja Jai Singh after 1656 onwards.

VII—Secondary Sources (English)

Ali, Athar, *The Mughal Nobility under Aurangzeb*, Bombay, 1966.

Ashraf, K.M., *Life and Conditions of the people of Hindostan*, 2nd ed., Delhi, 1959.

A descriptive list of the Farmans, Manshurs and Nishans, Rajasthan State Archives, Bikaner, 1962.

Aziz, Abdul, *Mansabdari System and the Mughal Army*, Reprint, Delhi, 1972

Bernier, F., *Travels in India*, tr. into English, 2nd ed. revised by V.A. Smith, London, 1916.

Baden Powell, B.H., *The Land System of British India*, Vols, I-III, Oxford, 1892.

———, *The Indian Village Community*, London, 1896.

Banerjee, A.C., *Lectures on Rajput History*, Calcutta, 1962.

———, *Medieval Studies*, Calcutta, 1958.

———, *Rajputs Studies*, 1944.

Banerjee, S.K., *Humayun Badshah*, Vol. I-II, Oxford University Press, 1938, 1941.

Beni Prasad, *Jahangir*, Allahabad, 1940.

Bhargava, V.S., *Marwar and the Mughal Emperors, Delhi.*

Chandra, Satish, *Parties and Politics at the Mughal Court*, Aligarh, 1959. 2nd ed., New Delhi, 1973.

Chaudhary, R., *Some Historical Aspects of Feudalism in Ancient India*. Trivandrum, 1959.

Commissariat, M.S.. *A History of Gujarat*, Bombay, 1938.

Day, U.N., *Medieval Malwa*, Delhi, 1965.

Dighe, V.G., *Peshwa Baji Rao I and Maratha Expansion*, Bombay, 1944.

Ghoshal, U.N., *Agrarian System in Ancient India*, Calcutta, 1930.

Ghose, L.N., *The Modern History of the Indian Chiefs, Rajas, Zamindars, etc.*, Calcutta, 1873.

Gopal, L., *Economic Life of North India*, Delhi, 1965.

Grant-Duff, J., *A History of the Mahrattas*, Vols. I-III. London, 1826.

Habib, Irfan., *Agrarian System of Mughal India*, Bombay, 1963.

Hasan, Ibn., *Central Structure of the Mughal Empire*, London, 1936.

Irvine, W., *Later Mughals*, Vols. I-II. Calcutta, 1921.

———, *Army of the Indian Mughals*, London, 1903.

Kane, P.V., *History of the Dharmashastras*, Vols. II-IV, Poona, 1941, 1946, 1953.

Khan, Yusuf Husain, *Selected Documents of Aurangzeb's Reign, 1659-1706*, Hyderabad, 1963.

Khosla, R.P., *Mughal Kingship and Nobility*, Allahabad, 1934.

Manucchi, N., *Storia do Mogor, 1656-1712*, tr. W. Irvine, 4 vols. London, 1907-8.

Marc, Bloch, *Feudal Society*, London, 1967.

Misra, S.C., *The Rise of the Muslim Power in Gujarat*, London. 1962.

Moreland, W.H., *The Agrarian System of Muslim India*, Allahabad, 1929.

———, *Indian at the death of Akbar*, London, 1920.

———, *From Akbar to Aurangzeb*, London, 1923.

Nurul Hasan, Saiyid,

Qanungo, K.R., *Studies in Rajput History*, Delhi, 1952.

———, *Shershah*, Calcutta, 1921.

———, *Dara Shikoh*, Calcutta, 1934.

Qureshi, I.H., *The Administration of the Sultanate of Delhi*, London, 1944.

Relation de l'Indostan. Lovell's tr. of 1687 reprinted with corrections, notes and introduction by S.N. Sen in the *Indian Travels of Thevenot and Careri*, New Delhi, 1949.

Reu, V.N., *Glories of Marwar and Glorious Rathors*, Jodhpur, 1943.

———, *Rathor Durgadas*.

———, *History of Rastrakutas*.

Saksena, B.P., *History of Shahjahan of Delhi*, Allahabad, 1932.

Saran, P., *Studies in Medieval Indian History*, Delhi, 1952.

———, *Provincial Government of the Mughals*, Allahabad, 1941.

Sarkar, J.N., *The India of Aurangzeb*, Calcutta, 1941.

———, *History of Aurangzeb*, Vols. I-IV, Calcutta, 1924.

———, *Studies of Mughal India*, Calcutta, 1919.

———, *Fall of the Mughal Empire*, Vol. I, Calcutta, 1938.

———, *House of Shivaji*, Calcutta, 1948.

———, *Mughal Administration*, Calcutta, 1952.

Sardesai, G.S , *New History of the Marathas*. Vols. I-III, Bombay, 1948-1957.

Sen, S.N., *The Military System of the Marathas*, Bombay, 1958.

Sharma, Dasharatha, *Early Chauhan Dynasties*, Delhi, 1956.

———, (Ed.), *Rajasthan Through the Ages*, Vol. I, Rajasthan State Archives, Bikaner, 1966.

Sharma, G.N., *Mewar and the Mughal Emperors*, Agra, 1951.

———, *Social Life in Medieval Rajasthan*, Agra, 1965.

Sharma, R.S., *Indian Feudalism*, C. 300-1200. Calcutta, 1965.

———, *Land Revenue in India*.

Sharma, S.R., *Mughal Government and Administration*, Bombay, 1951.
Siddiqi, I.H., *Some Aspects of Afghan Despotism in India*, Aligarh, 1969.
Siddiqi, N.A., *Land Revenue Administration under the Mughal*, (1700-1750), Bombay, 1971.
Singh, Raghubir, *Malwa in Transition*, 1936.
S. Nurul Hasan, *Thoughts on Agrarian Relations in Mughal India*, New Delhi, 1971.
Srivastava, A.L., *Akbar the Great*, Vols. I-II, Agra, 1962.
The Ruling Princes, Chief and Leading personages of Rajasthan and Ajmer, Government Publication, Calcutta, 1924.
Thompson, Edward, *Making of the Indian Princes*, 1943.
Tod, J., *Annals and Antiquities of Rajasthan*, Vols. I-II. Calcutta, 1916.
Tripathi, R.P., *Some Aspects of Muslim Administration*, Allahabad, 1936.
———, *Rise and Fall of the Mughal Empire*, Allahabad, 1956.

VIII—Published Works in Rajasthani and Hindi

Asopa, R.K., *Marwar ka Mool Itihas*, Jodhpur, 1932.
———, *Marwar ka Sankshipt Itihas*, Jodhpur, 1934.
Bhagwat Singh, *Champawat Rathors*, Jodhpur, 1972.
Bhatnagar, V.S., *Sawai Jai Singh*, Jaipur, 1972.
Chandra, Satish, *Uttar Mughal Kalin Bharat*, Meerut, 1974.
Haldar, R.R., *Rathor Durgadas*, Ajmer, 1938.
Hardayal, Munshi, *Tawarikh-Jagirdaran*, Jodhpur Government Publication, 1911.
Ojha, G.H., *Rajputana ka Itihas*, Ajmer, 1937.
———, *Udaipur Rajya ka Itihas*, Vols. I-II, Ajmer, 1925.
———, *Dungarpur Rajya ka Itihas*, Ajmer, 1936.
———, *Banswara Rajya ka Itihas*, Ajmer, 1937.
———, *Bikaner Rajya ka Itihas*, Ajmer, 1939-40.
———, *Jodhpur Rajya ka Itihas*, Vols. I-II, Ajmer, 1938, 1941.
———, *Sirohi Rajya ka Itihas*, Ajmer, 1911.
———, *Ojha Nibandha Saugraha*, Vols. I-IV, Udaipur, 1954.
Reu, V.N., *Marwar ka Itihas*, Vols. I-II, Jodhpur, 1938.
Sharma, M.L., *Kotah Rajya ka Itihas*, Vols. I, 1939.
Shyamal Das, *Vir Vinod*, Vols. I-IV, Udaipur, 1886.

Surajmal, *Vamsha Bhaskar*, Jodhpur, V.S. 1956.

IX—Journals

Annals of the Bhandarkar Oriental Research Institute, Poona.
Bengal, Past and Present, Calcutta.
Epigraphica Indica.
Indian Historical Review, New Delhi.
Journal of Indian History, Trivendrum.
Journal of Pakistan Historical Society.
Journal of the Rajasthan Institute of Historical Research, Jaipur.
Journal of Royal Asiatic Societies of London, Bengal and Bombay.
Maru Bharti (Hindi), Pilani.
Medieval India Quarterly, Aligarh.
Nagari Pracharini Patrika (Hindi), Varanasi.
Parampara (Hindi), Jodhpur.
Proceedings of Indian History Congress.
Proceedings of Rajasthan History Congress.
Proceeding Volumes of Indian Historical Records Commission.
Shodha Patrika (Hindi), Udaipur.
The Calcutta Review, July, 1949.
The Indian Economic and Social History Review, Delhi.
The Journal of Social and Economic History of the Orient, Holland.
The Researcher, Jaipur.

X—Gazetteers and Reports

Archaeological Survey Reports, 1935-36.
Census Report of Marwar, 1891.
Marwar Gazetteer, 1885.
Gazetteer of Marwar, Mallani and Jaysulmere, Walter, 1877.
Imperial Gazetteer of India, Provincial Series, 1908.
Mazmum-i-Halat-o-Intizam-i-Marwar, 1883-84.
Rajputana Gazetteer, 1879.
Reports on the Adminisitration of Jodhpur State, 1885-86.

INDEX